CW00544948

Advanced MPLS Design and Implementation

Vivek Alwayn, CCIE #2995

Cisco Press

Cisco Press
201 West 103rd Street
Indianapolis, IN 46290 USA

Advanced MPLS Design and Implementation

Vivek Alwayn, CCIE #2995

Copyright © 2002 Cisco Press

Published by:
Cisco Press
201 West 103rd Street
Indianapolis, IN 46290 USA

All rights reserved. No part of this book may be reproduced or transmitted in any form or by any means, electronic or mechanical, including photocopying, recording, or by any information storage and retrieval system, without written permission from the publisher, except for the inclusion of brief quotations in a review.

Printed in the United States of America 1 2 3 4 5 6 7 8 9 0

First Printing September 2001

Library of Congress Cataloging-in-Publication Number: 2001086617

ISBN: 1-58705-020-x

Warning and Disclaimer

This book is designed to provide information about MPLS. Every effort has been made to make this book as complete and as accurate as possible, but no warranty or fitness is implied.

The information is provided on an "as is" basis. The author, Cisco Press, and Cisco Systems, Inc. shall have neither liability nor responsibility to any person or entity with respect to any loss or damages arising from the information contained in this book or from the use of the discs or programs that may accompany it.

The opinions expressed in this book belong to the author and are not necessarily those of Cisco Systems, Inc.

Trademark Acknowledgments

All terms mentioned in this book that are known to be trademarks or service marks have been appropriately capitalized. Cisco Press or Cisco Systems, Inc. cannot attest to the accuracy of this information. Use of a term in this book should not be regarded as affecting the validity of any trademark or service mark.

Feedback Information

At Cisco Press, our goal is to create in-depth technical books of the highest quality and value. Each book is crafted with care and precision, undergoing rigorous development that involves the unique expertise of members from the professional technical community.

Readers' feedback is a natural continuation of this process. If you have any comments regarding how we could improve the quality of this book, or otherwise alter it to better suit your needs, you can contact us through e-mail at feedback@ciscopress.com. Please make sure to include the book title and ISBN in your message.

We greatly appreciate your assistance.

Publisher	John Wait
Editor-in-Chief	John Kane
Cisco Systems Management	Michael Hakkert, Tom Geitner, William Warren
Managing Editor	Patrick Kanouse
Development Editor	Andrew Cupp
Project Editor	Marc Fowler
Copy Editor	Gayle Johnson
Technical Editors	Ibrahim Bac
	Brian Beck
	Matthew J. "Cat" Castelli
	Mark Gallo
	Brian Melzer
	David Rosedale
Team Coordinator	Tammi Ross
Book Designer	Gina Rexrode
Cover Designer	Louisa Klucznik
Production Team	Octal Publishing, Inc.
Indexer	Tim Wright
	Ginny Bess

CISCO SYSTEMS

Corporate Headquarters
Cisco Systems, Inc.
170 West Tasman Drive
San Jose, CA 95134-1706
USA
http://www.cisco.com
Tel: 408 526-4000
  800 553-NETS (6387)
Fax: 408 526-4100

European Headquarters
Cisco Systems Europe
11 Rue Camille Desmoulins
92782 Issy-les-Moulineaux
Cedex 9
France
http://www-europe.cisco.com
Tel: 33 1 58 04 60 00
Fax: 33 1 58 04 61 00

Americas Headquarters
Cisco Systems, Inc.
170 West Tasman Drive
San Jose, CA 95134-1706
USA
http://www.cisco.com
Tel: 408 526-7660
Fax: 408 527-0883

Asia Pacific Headquarters
Cisco Systems Australia,
Pty., Ltd
Level 17, 99 Walker Street
North Sydney
NSW 2059 Australia
http://www.cisco.com
Tel: +61 2 8448 7100
Fax: +61 2 9957 4350

Cisco Systems has more than 200 offices in the following countries.
Addresses, phone numbers, and fax numbers are listed on the
Cisco Web site at www.cisco.com/go/offices

Argentina • Australia • Austria • Belgium • Brazil • Bulgaria • Canada • Chile • China • Colombia • Costa
Rica • Croatia • Czech Republic • Denmark • Dubai, UAE • Finland • France • Germany • Greece • Hong
Kong • Hungary • India • Indonesia • Ireland • Israel • Italy • Japan • Korea • Luxembourg • Malaysia
Mexico • The Netherlands • New Zealand • Norway • Peru • Philippines • Poland • Portugal • Puerto Rico
Romania • Russia • Saudi Arabia • Scotland • Singapore • Slovakia • Slovenia • South Africa • Spain
Sweden • Switzerland • Taiwan • Thailand • Turkey • Ukraine • United Kingdom • United States • Venezuela
Vietnam • Zimbabwe

Copyright © 2000, Cisco Systems, Inc. All rights reserved. Access Registrar, AccessPath, Are You Ready, ATM Director, Browse with Me, CCDA, CCDE, CCDP, CCIE, CCNA, CCNP, CCSI, CD-PAC, CiscoLink, the Cisco NetWorks logo, the Cisco Powered Network logo, Cisco Systems Networking Academy, Fast Step, FireRunner, Follow Me Browsing, FormShare, GigaStack, IGX, Intelligence in the Optical Core, Internet Quotient, IP/VC, iQ Breakthrough, iQ Expertise, iQ FastTrack, iQuick Study, iQ Readiness Scorecard, The iQ Logo, Kernel Proxy, MGX, Natural Network Viewer, Network Registrar, the Networkers logo, Packet, PIX, Point and Click Internetworking, Policy Builder, RateMUX, ReyMaster, ReyView, ScriptShare, Secure Script, Shop with Me, SlideCast, SMARTnet, SVX, TrafficDirector, TransPath, VlanDirector, Voice LAN, Wavelength Router, Workgroup Director, and Workgroup Stack are trademarks of Cisco Systems, Inc.; Changing the Way We Work, Live, Play, and Learn, Empowering the Internet Generation, are service marks of Cisco Systems, Inc.; and Aironet, ASIST, BPX, Catalyst, Cisco, the Cisco Certified Internetwork Expert Logo, Cisco IOS, the Cisco IOS logo, Cisco Press, Cisco Systems, Cisco Systems Capital, the Cisco Systems logo, Collision Free, Enterprise/Solver, EtherChannel, EtherSwitch, FastHub, FastLink, FastPAD, IOS, IP/TV, IPX, LightStream, LightSwitch, MICA, NetRanger, Post-Routing, Pre-Routing, Registrar, StrataView Plus, Stratm, SwitchProbe, TeleRouter, are registered trademarks of Cisco Systems, Inc. or its affiliates in the U.S. and certain other countries.

All other brands, names, or trademarks mentioned in this document or Web site are the property of their respective owners. The use of the word partner does not imply a partnership relationship between Cisco and any other company. (0010R)

Printed in the USA on recycled paper containing 10% postconsumer waste.

About the Author

Vivek Alwayn, CCIE # 2995, is the Chief Technology Officer of BNETSYS, Inc. (www.bnetsys.net), an internet-working company focused on service provider MPLS. He has over 14 years of experience with data communications technologies and protocols. He has designed and implemented numerous large-scale WAN-switched, LAN-switched, and routed networks for service provider and enterprise customers worldwide. Recently, he participated in the architecture and led the implementation of AT&T's MPLS backbone network in South America. This is one of the first successful implementations of BPX WAN switches and LSRs in a production MPLS environment. He holds a B.S. in Electronics Engineering and is working on his Masters in Telecommunications. He is also an active member of the IEEE and IETF. He can be reached at valwayn@bnetsys.net.

About the Technical Reviewers

Ibrahim Bac, CCIE #4452, is a Senior Consulting Engineer with Salomon Smith Barney. Previously he has worked with several Cisco Gold partners in the United States and Canada. He has extensive experience with designing, migrating, and deploying large-scale IP networks and services. Ibrahim has been involved with advanced BGP deployments with large enterprise/service provider customers.

Brian Beck has been in the networking/telecommunications industry for 16 years. He currently holds a CCNP Routing and Switching certification as well as a CCNP in WAN switching. Brian enjoys reading and constantly trying to expand his knowledge of this rapidly changing industry.

Matthew J. "Cat" Castelli has over thirteen years of experience in the telecommunications networking industry, starting as a Cryptologic Technician in the United States Navy. Cat has since been working as a Principal Consultant for a Cisco Professional Services Partner and as a Senior Technical Consultant/Enterprise Network Design Engineer for a global telecommunications integrator. He has broad exposure to LAN/WAN, Internet, and alternative (such as VoX) technologies for service provider and enterprise networks of all sizes including implementation, application configuration and integration, network management, and security solutions. Cat holds CCNA, CCDA, CCNP, and CCDP certifications and is currently authoring another Cisco Press title, *"Network Consultants Handbook."* When not involved with network design or engineering, Cat may be found, among several things, pursuing his degree, reading, cheering for the Los Angeles Dodgers, shooting a game of pool, or enjoying a cigar with a glass of scotch. Cat currently is a Network Architect Engineer for Global Crossing. Cat may be contacted at mjcastelli@earthlink.net.

Mark Gallo is a technical manager with America Online. His network certifications include Cisco CCNP and Cisco CCDP. He has led several engineering groups responsible for designing and implementing enterprise LANs and international IP networks. While working for a major international telecommunications company, his group was instrumental in developing an industry-leading service based on Cisco's MPLS solution. He has a B.S. in electrical engineering from the University of Pittsburgh. Mark resides in northern Virginia with his wife, Betsy, and son, Paul.

Brian Melzer, CCIE #3981, is an Internetwork Solutions Engineer for ThruPoint, Inc. out of its Raleigh, NC office. He has worked as a consultant for ThruPoint since September of 2000. ThruPoint is a global networking services firm and one of the few companies selected as a Cisco System Strategic Partner. Before working for ThruPoint, he spent five years working for AT&T Solutions on design and management of outsourcing deals involving Fortune 500 clients. As a member of the Wolfpack, Brian received his undergraduate degree in Electrical Engineering and his Masters in Management at North Carolina State University.

David Rosedale has had direct involvement in telecommunication operations and field service engineering working in a LAN/WAN environment for 14 years, specializing in routers, switches, and LAN-to-WAN connections utilizing multiplexer and broadband access devices. David has experience in a technical, data communication, field service, system engineering, and management environment with increasing responsibility and achievements successfully managing, developing, implementing, testing, maintaining, and field servicing network operations with a variety of network architectures and in a multivendor, multiprotocol environment.

Dedications

This book is dedicated to my wife Sarita C. Alwayn for her continuous support, without which this book would not have been possible. I thank you.

In memory of my father, Urban Alwayn, whose words of encouragement are still with me, and continue to be my inspiration.

To my mother, Belinda Alwayn, whose support and prayers have made this endeavor possible.

I thank you all.

"These fundamentals have got to be simple."

—Lord Ernest Rutherford, Circa 1908

Acknowledgments

This book is a result of various inputs and is essentially a combined effort. There are several people I would like to thank for helping me with this book.

The Cisco Press Team—John Kane, the Cisco Press Editor-in-Chief, who was responsible for the planning and development of the book from proposal stage to publication. Andrew Cupp, Development Editor at Cisco Press, for his meticulous development editing, which has helped create a high-quality, error-free manuscript. I would also like to acknowledge the efforts and thank the editorial and production team at Cisco Press.

The Technical Reviewers—Thank you to all of the technical editors, Cat Castelli, Ibrahim Bac, Brian Beck, Mark Gallo, Brian Melzer, and David Rosedale, for their valuable technical feedback and comments which helped the manuscript evolve into a comprehensive document covering all relevant aspects of the technology.

The BNETSYS Engineers—Mohit Chauhan, CCNP, and the BNETSYS consultants for helping with the proto-typing and testing of the MPLS configurations in the lab, without whose help this project would not have been possible.

Contents at a Glance

Contents

Introduction

Ever since its inception and the introduction of commercial traffic in 1992, the Internet has grown rapidly from a research network to a worldwide commercial data network. The Internet has become a convenient and cost-effective medium for user collaboration, learning, electronic commerce, and entertainment. A common consensus is that the Internet will metamorphose into a medium for the convergence of voice, video, and data communications. The Internet has seen growth in terms of bandwidth, number of hosts, geographic size, and traffic volume. At the same time, it is evolving from best-effort service toward an integrated or differentiated services framework with quality of service (QoS) assurances, which are necessary for many new applications such as Managed VPNs, Voice over IP, videoconferencing, and broadband multimedia services.

Service Provider backbone infrastructures are currently used to provide multiple services such as TDM leased lines, ATM, Frame Relay, Voice, video, and Internet services. ATM backbones are extremely popular due to their reliability and versatility in offering multiple service types. However, ATM does not integrate very well with IP and there are massive scalability issues that need to be dealt with, when running IP over ATM.

The industry has been searching for an approach to combine the best features of IP and Asynchronous Transfer Mode (ATM), for example, IP routing with the performance and throughput of ATM switching. This has led to the recent development of Multiprotocol Label Switching (MPLS) which is a convergence of various implementations of "IP switching" that use ATM-like Label Swapping to speed up IP packet forwarding without changes to existing IP routing protocols. Various vendor implementation approaches to IP switching led to the formation of the IETF's MPLS working group in 1997 to establish common agreements on the base technology for label-switched IP routing. The major motivations behind MPLS are higher scalability, faster packet forwarding performance, IP + ATM integration, Traffic Engineering, MPLS Virtual Private Networks, fast rerouting, and hard Quality of Service.

The deployment of MPLS in service provider Internet backbones is possible since it is transparent to the end user. This has had some profound consequences at the architectural level. It has changed the basic longest match destination-based unicast-forwarding model, which has remained essentially unchanged since the inception of the Internet. In turn, it also impacts the routing architecture, requiring that routing protocols perform new and more complex routing tasks.

Who Should Read This Book

This book is intended for Internetwork Engineers and Administrators who are responsible for designing, implementing, and supporting service provider or enterprise MPLS backbone networks. It contains a broad range of technical details on MPLS and its associated protocols, Packet-based MPLS, ATM-based MPLS, MPLS traffic engineering, MPLS QoS, MPLS design, and advanced MPLS architectures. As an advanced title, this book can be used as a reference and guide for anyone designing, implementing, or supporting an MPLS network.

Even if you're not using Cisco gear, this book can increase your awareness and understanding of MPLS technology as well as provide you with detailed design concepts and rules for building scalable MPLS networks.

Scope and Definition

This section defines the scope of this book and synopsizes content by chapter. It provides an outline of the book and gives you a high-level overview of what to expect.

Chapter 1 "Introduction to MPLS"

MPLS is introduced as a technology that is driving future IP networks including the Internet. It describes MPLS as providing a new forwarding paradigm for the Internet, which has affected its traffic engineering, quality of service as well as the implementation of Virtual Private Networks. It also details the various other benefits obtained by implementing MPLS in core backbone networks.

Chapter 2 "WAN Technologies and MPLS"

Various cloud technologies such as TDM, Frame Relay, and ATM are discussed in this chapter. It has presented the fundamentals of Layer 3 routing and Label switching as well as made an extensive comparison of MPLS versus Layer 3 routing. It also discusses various expanded service offerings available to service providers such as Virtual Private Networks and Traffic Engineered IP networks which can be easily achieved by implementing MPLS technology.

Chapter 3 "MPLS Architecture"

The architecture and operation of MPLS networks is covered in this chapter. It also discusses the advantages of MPLS over conventional Layer 3 forwarding. It describes the architecture and operation of MPLS nodes in detail, which includes MPLS enabled Routers and ATM switches. The various elements, which constitute an MPLS network, are also described in this chapter. The MPLS Label-Switched Router (LSR), Label-Switched Path (LSP) mechanisms, and the working of the Label Distribution Protocol (LDP) are explained in detail.

Chapter 4 "Virtual Private Networks"

This chapter provides a look at Virtual Private Networks (VPNs) and discusses VPN technologies such as GRE, IPSec, L2TP, PPTP, and MPLS. This chapter discusses Connection-oriented VPNs built on Layer 2 or Layer 3 infrastructures. It also discusses connectionless VPNs such as conventional IP VPNs or MPLS VPNs, which do not require a predefined logical or virtual circuit, provisioned between two end-points to establish a connection between the two end-points.

Chapter 5 "Packet-Based MPLS VPNs"

The Virtual Private Network (VPN) feature for Multiprotocol Label Switching (MPLS), which allows a Service Provider network to deploy scalable IPv4 Layer 3 VPN backbone services is discussed in this chapter. These services can be deployed over a Layer 3 routed backbone or over an ATM backbone. This chapter covers MPLS deployment over Packet-based LSRs. It provides detailed configuration information accompanied with case studies.

Chapter 6 "ATM-Based MPLS VPNs"

ATM MPLS and its implementation by Service Providers who currently operate ATM backbone networks are discussed in this chapter. These Service Providers can leverage the benefits provided by MPLS and utilize their existing infrastructure to provide VPN services using MPLS. This is possible if the ATM switches are MPLS-aware. For non-MPLS ATM switches, MPLS can be configured on MPLS-aware routers and the underlying ATM virtual circuits will be considered ATM links.

Chapter 7 "MPLS Traffic Engineering"

MPLS Traffic Engineering is discussed this chapter. For a service provider to truly and successfully implement commercial IP services, a *hard* quality of service with guaranteed delivery of packets is required. This can be accomplished by deploying MPLS traffic engineering across the core backbone. Traffic engineering encompasses many aspects of network performance. These include the provisioning of a guaranteed hard quality of service (QoS), improving the utilization of network resources by distributing traffic evenly across network links, and providing for quick recovery when a node or link fails.

Chapter 8 "MPLS Quality of Service"

IP quality of service with respect to MPLS networks is covered in this chapter. Service Providers who offer IP services over an MPLS backbone must support IP QoS over their MPLS infrastructure. This means supporting IP QoS over MPLS VPNs or MPLS Traffic Engineered paths. MPLS can help Service Providers to offer IP QoS services more efficiently over a wider range of platforms such as ATM LSRs. There are also certain useful QoS capabilities such as guaranteed bandwidth LSPs that can be supported over MPLS networks.

Chapter 9 "MPLS Design and Migration"

MPLS design with an emphasis on ATM-based MPLS is discussed in great detail. The various design approaches to practical MPLS VPN deployment are described in this chapter. MPLS VPNs can be implemented in a variety of ways, using a combination of packet-based and ATM MPLS Label-Switched Routers. This chapter also describes how MPLS can be deployed into a traditional ATM network gradually, starting with just a single pair of ATM-LSRs in an otherwise purely ATM network.

Chapter 10 "Advanced MPLS Architectures"

This chapter discusses advanced MPLS architectures. It begins with a primer on dense wavelength division multiplexing (DWDM) which is the process of multiplexing signals of different wavelengths onto a single fiber. It then discusses Multiprotocol Lambda Switching (MPλS), which is the optical analogy of MPLS. The MPLS control plane performs all crucial control functions for MPLS data networks. MPLS RSVP-TE extensions or CR-LSDP extensions can be applied to optical networks to unify the control plane for optical Network Elements.

Appendixes

The appendixes contain useful reference information related to MPLS, which can be used in either an engineering or operations environment. They are organized as follows:

- Appendix A "MPLS Command Reference"

- Appendix B "MPLS Equipment Design Specifications"

- Appendix C "MPLS Glossary"

- Appendix D "References"

Command Conventions

The conventions used to present commands in this book are the same conventions used in the IOS Command Reference. The Command Reference describes these conventions as follows:

- **Boldface** indicates commands and keywords that are entered literally as shown.

- *Italics* indicate arguments for which you supply values.

- Optional keywords and/or arguments (or a choice of optional keywords and/or arguments) are in brackets [ ]

- Choice of mandatory keywords and/or arguments are in braces { }

- Vertical bars (l) separate alternative, mutually exclusive elements.

- Braces within square brackets [{ }] indicate a required choice within an optional element.

- Commands that are too long and do not fit on one line are displayed with an indented second line.

Note that these conventions are for syntax only. Actual configurations and examples do not follow these conventions.

Illustration Iconography

The icons displayed in Figure I-1 are used in the figures presented in this book. Some of these icons are MPLS specific, while the rest are Cisco or industry standard.

Figure I-1   *Iconography*

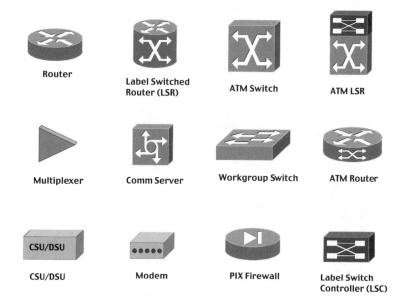

Router

Label Switched
Router (LSR)

ATM Switch

ATM LSR

Multiplexer

Comm Server

Workgroup Switch

ATM Router

CSU/DSU

Modem

PIX Firewall

Label Switch
Controller (LSC)

This chapter covers the following topics:

- **A New Forwarding Paradigm**—This section discusses conventional technologies versus Multiprotocol Label Switching (MPLS) techniques that are being implemented in carrier and service provider networks. MPLS is the technology that is driving future IP networks, including the Internet. MPLS gives the Internet a new forwarding paradigm that affects its traffic engineering and the implementation of VPNs.

- **What Is MPLS?**—This section discusses MPLS as an improved method for forwarding packets through a network using information contained in labels attached to IP packets. It also discusses the evolution and the various benefits of MPLS, such as Layer 3 VPNs, traffic engineering, quality of service (QoS), and the integration of IP and ATM.

CHAPTER 1

Introduction to MPLS

A New Forwarding Paradigm

From a technology perspective, the Internet has impacted our lives more than anything in the last century. Today, we see wireless handheld devices, Internet appliances, Voice over IP (VoIP) phones, webcast video, PCs, hosts, and even mainframe traffic over the Internet. The sheer growth due to the emergence of the World Wide Web has propelled IP to the forefront of data communications.

Carriers and service providers are in a constant state of backbone capacity expansion. More recently, with the introduction of Dense Wavelength Division Multiplexing (DWDM) in the core, multiple wavelengths injected into the fiber-optic cable have essentially multiplied the throughput using the existing fiber pair. Such enormous bandwidth in the Internet core has led to a newer archetype of sharing public Internet infrastructure with enterprise Virtual Private Networks (VPNs). This infrastructure can also be used to service voice and ultimately replace parallel time-division multiplexing (TDM) voice networks.

Traditional enterprise Layer 2 VPNs were (and, in most cases, still are) partially meshed Frame Relay or Asynchronous Transfer Mode (ATM) private virtual circuits.

Economics always plays a major role in the selection and implementation of next-generation networks. Carriers and service providers that run an existing ATM backbone are not ready for a forklift upgrade of their entire infrastructure in order to implement a new technology, no matter how promising it might seem. Many service providers will continue to maintain ATM in their existing backbone networks for the foreseeable future. Consequently, any implementation of a next-generation technology should leverage existing equipment and technologies such as ATM and IP.

Over the past few years, various efforts and activities on Multiprotocol Label Switching (MPLS) have been initiated, many of which have already impacted IP networks considerably. MPLS techniques are being implemented in carrier and service provider networks. This has resulted in the reshaping of service provider backbone architectures day by day. MPLS is the technology that is driving future IP networks, including the Internet. MPLS provides for the Internet a new forwarding paradigm that affects its traffic engineering and the implementation of VPNs.

Any technology that has the ability to influence the rearchitecture and reengineering of the Internet must be thoroughly understood and appreciated.

What Is MPLS?

MPLS is an improved method for forwarding packets through a network using information contained in labels attached to IP packets. The labels are inserted between the Layer 3 header and the Layer 2 header in the case of frame-based Layer 2 technologies, and they are contained in the virtual path identifier (VPI) and virtual channel identifier (VCI) fields in the case of cell-based technologies such as ATM.

MPLS combines Layer 2 switching technologies with Layer 3 routing technologies. The primary objective of MPLS is to create a flexible networking fabric that provides increased performance and stability. This includes traffic engineering and VPN capabilities, which offer quality of service (QoS) with multiple classes of service (CoS).

In an MPLS network (see Figure 1-1), incoming packets are assigned a label by an Edge Label-Switched Router. Packets are forwarded along a Label-Switched Path (LSP) where each Label-Switched Router (LSR) makes forwarding decisions based solely on the label's contents. At each hop, the LSR strips off the existing label and applies a new label, which tells the next hop how to forward the packet. The label is stripped at the egress Edge LSR, and the packet is forwarded to its destination.

Figure 1-1   *MPLS Network Topology*

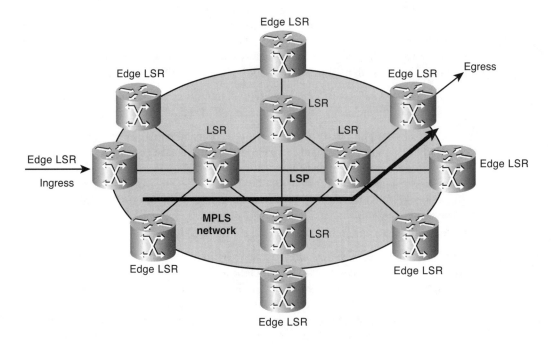

NOTE   The term *multiprotocol* indicates that MPLS techniques are applicable to any network layer protocol. However, in this book, I focus on the use of IPv4 as the network layer protocol.

Evolution of MPLS

The initial goal of label-based switching was to bring the speed of Layer 2 switching to Layer 3. This initial justification for technologies such as MPLS is no longer perceived as the main benefit, because newer Layer 3 switches using application-specific integrated circuit (ASIC)-based technology can perform route lookups at sufficient speeds to support most interface types.

The widespread interest in label switching initiated the formation of the IETF MPLS working group in 1997.

MPLS has evolved from numerous prior technologies, including proprietary versions of label-switching implementations such as Cisco's Tag Switching, IBM's Aggregate Route-Based IP Switching (ARIS), Toshiba's Cell-Switched Router (CSR), Ipsilon's IP Switching, and Lucent's IP Navigator.

Tag Switching, invented by Cisco, was first shipped to users in March 1998. Since the inception of Tag Switching, Cisco has been working within the IETF to develop and ratify the MPLS standard, which has incorporated most of the features and benefits of Tag Switching. Cisco currently offers MPLS support in its version 12.x releases of IOS.

Cisco supports MPLS on its carrier class line of BPX and MGX ATM switches as well as router-based MPLS.

Benefits of MPLS

Label-based switching methods allow routers and MPLS-enabled ATM switches to make forwarding decisions based on the contents of a simple label, rather than by performing a complex route lookup based on destination IP address. This technique brings many benefits to IP-based networks:

- **VPNs**—Using MPLS, service providers can create Layer 3 VPNs across their backbone network for multiple customers, using a common infrastructure, without the need for encryption or end-user applications.

- **Traffic engineering**—Provides the ability to explicitly set single or multiple paths that the traffic will take through the network. Also provides the ability to set performance characteristics for a class of traffic. This feature optimizes bandwidth utilization of underutilized paths.

- **Quality of service**—Using MPLS quality of service (QoS), service providers can provide multiple classes of service with hard QoS guarantees to their VPN customers.

- **Integration of IP and ATM**—Most carrier networks employ an overlay model in which ATM is used at Layer 2 and IP is used at Layer 3. Such implementations have major scalability issues. Using MPLS, carriers can migrate many of the functions of the ATM control plane to Layer 3, thereby simplifying network provisioning, management, and network complexity. This technique provides immense scalability and eliminates ATM's inherent *cell tax* (overhead) in carrying IP traffic.

Service providers and carriers have realized the advantages of MPLS as compared to conventional IP over ATM overlay networks. Large enterprise networks currently using public ATM as a Layer 2 infrastructure for IP will be among the first to benefit from this technology.

MPLS combines the performance and capabilities of Layer 2 (data link layer) switching with the proven scalability of Layer 3 (network layer) routing. This allows service providers to meet the challenges of explosive growth in network utilization while providing the opportunity to differentiate services without sacrificing the existing network infrastructure. The MPLS architecture is flexible and can be employed in any combination of Layer 2 technologies.

MPLS support is offered for all Layer 3 protocols, and scaling is possible well beyond that typically offered in today's networks. MPLS efficiently enables the delivery of IP services over an ATM switched network. MPLS supports the creation of different routes between a source and a destination on a purely router-based Internet backbone. By incorporating MPLS into their network architecture, many service providers reduced costs, increased revenue and productivity, provided differentiated services, and gained a competitive advantage over carriers who don't offer MPLS services such as Layer 3 VPNs or traffic engineering.

MPLS and the Internet Architecture

Ever since the deployment of ARPANET, the forerunner of the present-day Internet, the architecture of the Internet has been constantly changing. It has evolved in response to advances in technology, growth, and offerings of new services. The most recent change to the Internet architecture is the addition of MPLS.

It must be noted that the forwarding mechanism of the Internet, which is based on destination-based routing, has not changed since the days of ARPANET. The major changes have been the migration to Border Gateway Protocol Version 4 (BGP4) from Exterior Gateway Protocol (EGP), the implementation of classless interdomain routing (CIDR), and the constant upgrade of bandwidth and termination equipment such as more powerful routers.

MPLS has impacted both the forwarding mechanism of IP packets and path determination (the path the packets should take while transiting the Internet). This has resulted in a fundamental rearchitecture of the Internet.

MPLS can simplify the deployment of IPv6 because the forwarding algorithms used by MPLS for IPv4 can be applied to IPv6 with the use of routing protocols that support IPv6 addresses.

MPLS is being deployed because it has an immediate and direct benefit to the Internet. The most immediate benefit of MPLS with respect to an Internet service provider's backbone network is the ability to perform traffic engineering. Traffic engineering allows the service provider to offload congested links and engineer the load sharing over underutilized links. This results in a much higher degree of resource utilization that translates into efficiency and cost savings.

Internet VPNs are currently implemented as IP Security (IPSec) tunnels over the public Internet. Such VPNs, although they do work, have a very high overhead and are slow. MPLS VPNs over the Internet let service providers offer customers Internet-based VPNs with bandwidth and service levels comparable to traditional ATM and Frame Relay services.

Another disadvantage of GRE and IPSec tunnels is that they are not scalable. MPLS VPNs can be implemented over private IP networks.

IP VPN services over MPLS backbone networks can be offered at a lower cost to customers than traditional Frame Relay or ATM VPN services due to the lower cost of provisioning, operating, and maintaining MPLS VPN services. MPLS traffic engineering can optimize the bandwidth usage of underutilized paths. This can also result in cost savings that can be passed on to the customer. MPLS QoS gives the service provider the ability to offer multiple classes of service to customers, which can be priced according to bandwidth and other parameters.

This book reviews existing WAN technologies such as TDM, ATM, and Frame Relay and describes their interaction with MPLS. It describes all the relevant details about MPLS and discusses practical applications of MPLS in the design and implementation of MPLS VPNs, traffic engineering, and QoS from an ATM WAN-switched and router-based approach.

Summary

MPLS is the technology that is driving future IP networks, including the Internet. MPLS provides a new forwarding paradigm for the Internet, which affects traffic engineering and the implementation of Virtual Private Networks.

MPLS is an improved method for forwarding packets through a network using information contained in labels attached to each IP packet, ATM cell, or Layer 2 frame.

Label-based switching methods allow routers and MPLS-enabled ATM switches to make forwarding decisions based on the contents of a simple label, rather than by performing a complex route lookup based on destination IP address.

MPLS allows carriers and service providers to offer customers services such as Layer 3 VPNs and traffic-engineered networks across their backbone network, using a common infrastructure, without the need for encryption or end-user applications.

MPLS has impacted both the forwarding mechanism of IP packets and path determination. This has resulted in a fundamental rearchitecture of the Internet.

This chapter covers the following topics:

- **Inside the Cloud**—This section describes circuit, packet, and cell switching technologies. A fundamental understanding of existing WAN switching technologies will enhance your understanding of MPLS technology as applied to wide-area technology.

- **Layer 3 Routing**—This section describes the forwarding and control components of the routing function and Forwarding Equivalence Classes (FECs).

- **Label Switching**—An introduction to label switching and MPLS is presented in this section. MPLS is compared with conventional Layer 3 routing.

- **Integration of IP and ATM**—This section presents conventional methods of overlaying IP over ATM. It also compares MPLS versus traditional methods of carrying IP over ATM.

- **Challenges Faced by Service Providers**—This section examines the service provider marketplace and identifies ways by which service providers may differentiate themselves from their competition by providing their customers with expanded service offerings such as VPNs, traffic engineering, and QoS over the WAN at a lower cost.

CHAPTER 2

WAN Technologies and MPLS

Inside the Cloud

This section gives you an overview of carrier and service provider backbone network technologies. The technologies discussed are time-division multiplexing (TDM), Frame Relay, and Asynchronous Transfer Mode (ATM). It is important to understand the architecture of Layer 2 WAN switched networks, protocols, and their interaction with Layer 3 protocols such as IP before delving into MPLS.

Circuit Switching and TDM

Time-division multiplexing combines data streams by assigning each stream a different time slot in a set. TDM repeatedly transmits a fixed sequence of time slots over a single transmission channel. Within T-carrier systems, such as T1/E1 and T3/E3, TDM combines pulse code modulated (PCM) streams created for each conversation or data stream. TDM circuits such as T1/E1 or T3/E3 lines can be used for voice as well as data.

PCM is used to encode analog signals into digital format. Voice calls need 4 kHz of bandwidth. This 4-kHz channel is sampled 8000 times per second. The amplitude of each sample is quantified into an 8-bit binary number (one of 256 levels), resulting in a 64-kbps rate (8000 samples per second × 8 bits per sample). This 64-kbps channel is called a DS0, which forms the fundamental building block of the Digital Signal level (DS level) hierarchy.

The signal is referred to as DS1, and the transmission channel (over a copper-based facility) is called a T1 circuit. Leased lines such as DS3/T3, DS1/T1, and subrate fractional T1 are TDM circuits. TDM circuits typically use multiplexers such as channel service units/digital service units (CSUs/DSUs) or channel banks at the customer premises equipment (CPE) side and use larger programmable multiplexers such as Digital Access and Crossconnect System (DACS) and channel banks at the carrier end.

The TDM hierarchy used in North America is shown in Table 2-1.

NOTE	The DS2 and DS4 levels are not used commercially. The SONET OC levels have largely replaced the DS levels above DS3.

Table 2-1   *DS-Level Hierarchy*

Digital Signal Level	Number of 64-kbps Channels	Equivalent	Bandwidth
DS0	1	$1 \times DS0$	64 kbps
DS1	24	$24 \times DS0$	1.544 Mbps
DS2	96	$4 \times DS1$	6.312 Mbps
DS3	672	$28 \times DS1$	44.736 Mbps

NOTE   Some TDM systems use 8 kbps for in-band signaling. This results in a net bandwidth of only 56 kbps per channel.

The E1/E3 TDM hierarchy used in Europe, Latin America, and Asia Pacific is shown in Table 2-1a.

Table 2-1a   *DS-Level Hierarchy*

Digital Signal Level	Number of 64-kbps User Channels	Equivalent	Bandwidth
E1	30	$30 \times DS0$	2.048 Mbps
E3	480	$480 \times DS0$	34 Mbps

An example of a circuit-switched network from a customer's perspective is shown in Figure 2-1. This topology is also referred to as a point-to-point line or nailed circuit. Typically, such lines are leased from a local exchange carrier (LEC) or interexchange carrier (IXC) and are also referred to as *leased* or *private lines*. One leased line is required for each of the remote sites to connect to the headquarters at the central site.

The private nature of the leased-line networks provides inherent privacy and control benefits. Leased lines are dedicated, so there are no statistical availability issues, as there are in public packet-switched networks. This is both a strength and a weakness. The strength is that the circuit is available on a permanent basis and does not require that a connection be set up before traffic is passed. The weakness is that the bandwidth is being paid for even if it is not being used, which is typically about 40 to 70 percent of the time. In addition to the inefficient use of bandwidth, a major disadvantage of leased lines is their mileage-sensitive nature, which makes it a very expensive alternative for networks spanning long distances or requiring extensive connectivity between sites.

Leased lines also lack flexibility in terms of changes to the network when compared to alternatives such as Frame Relay. For example, adding a new site to the network requires a new circuit to be provisioned end-to-end for every site with which the new location must communicate. If there are a number of sites, the costs can mount quickly. Leased lines are priced on a mileage basis by a carrier, which results in customers incurring large monthly costs for long-haul leased circuits.

Figure 2-1   *Leased Lines from a Customer Perspective*

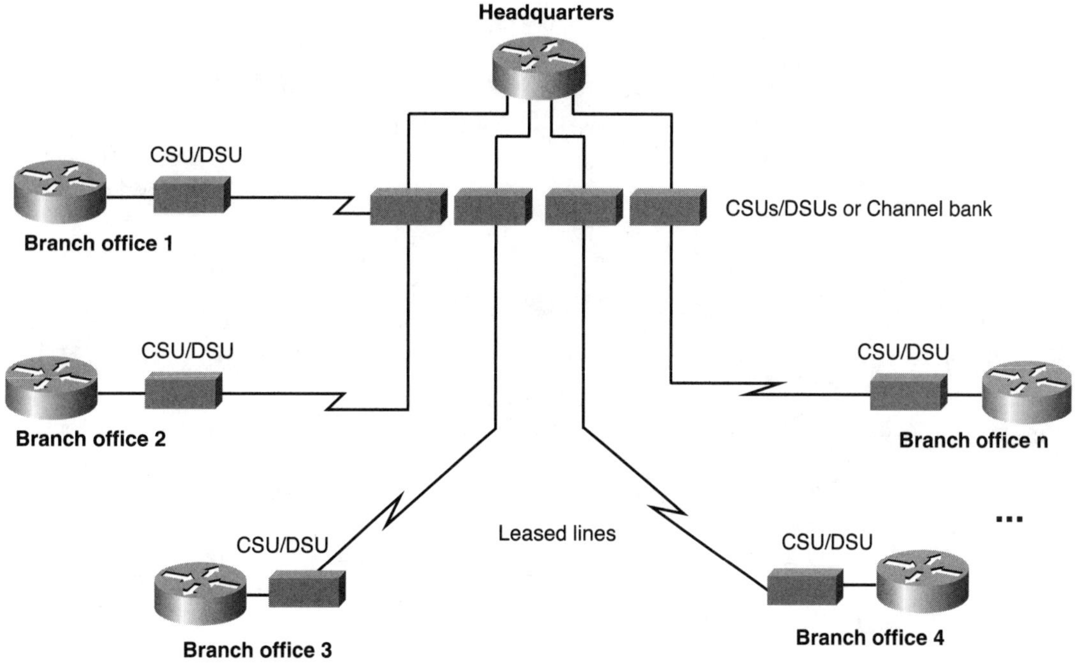

In comparison, public networks such as Frame Relay simply require an access line to the nearest central office and the provisioning of virtual circuits (VCs) for each new site with which it needs to communicate. In many cases, existing sites simply require the addition of a new virtual circuit definition for the new site.

From the carrier perspective, the circuit assigned to the customer (also known as the local loop) is provisioned on the DACS or channel bank. The individual T1 circuits are multiplexed onto a T3 and trunked over a terrestrial, microwave, or satellite link to the destination, where it is demultiplexed and fanned out into individual T1 lines. In Figure 2-2, FT1 means Fractional T-1. Fractional T-1 or E-1 is provided in multiples of 64 kbps and is representative of a fraction of the T1/E1 or T3/E3 bandwidth.

DS Framing

Two kinds of framing techniques are used for DS-level transmissions:

- D4 or Super Frame (SF)
- Extended Super Frame (ESF)

The frame formats are shown in Figure 2-3 and Figure 2-4. D4 typically uses alternate mark inversion (AMI) encoding, and ESF uses binary 8-zero substitution (B8ZS) encoding.

Figure 2-2 *Leased Lines from a Carrier Perspective*

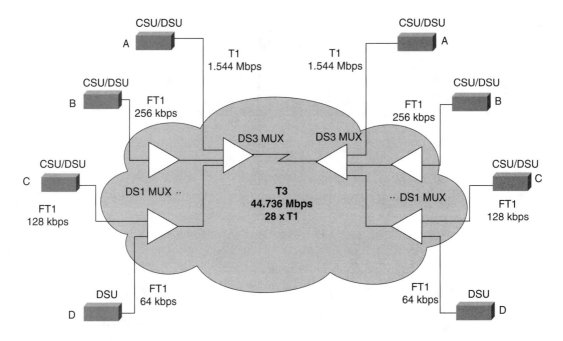

Figure 2-3 *D4 Super Frame (SF) Format*

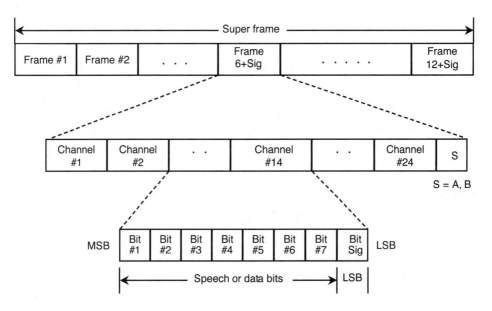

As shown in Figure 2-3, the SF (D4) frame has 12 frames and uses the least-significant bit (LSB) in frames 6 and 12 for signaling (A, B bits). Each frame has 24 channels of 64 kbps.

Figure 2-4   *Extended Super Frame (ESF) Format*

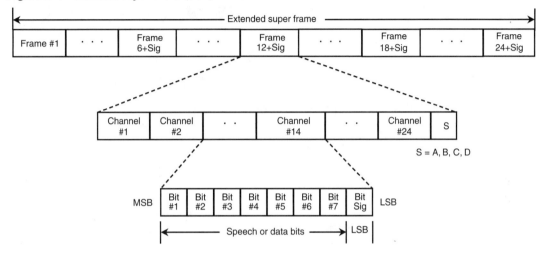

As shown in Figure 2-4, the ESF frame has 24 frames and uses the least-significant bit (LSB) in frames 6, 12, 18, and 24 for signaling (A, B, C, D bits). Each frame has 24 channels of 64 kbps.

NOTE   The E1 carrier uses CRC4 (Cyclic Redundancy Check-4) or Non-CRC4 Framing options with HDB3 (High-Density Bipolar-3) or AMI (Alternate Mark Inversion) encoding options.

Synchronous Optical Network (SONET)

The SONET hierarchy is the optical extension to the TDM hierarchy and uses the optical carrier (OC) levels. SONET is an American National Standards Institute (ANSI) standard for North America, and Synchronous Digital Hierarchy (SDH) is the standard for the rest of the world.

The basic signal is known as Synchronous Transport Signal level 1 (STS-1), which operates at 51.84 Mbps. The SONET signal levels are shown in Table 2-2. SONET systems can aggregate the T-carrier TDM systems using SONET add/drop multiplexers (ADMs). SONET systems implement collector rings, which provide the network interface for all access applications (see Figure 2-5). The collector rings connect to backbone rings using ADMs, which provide a bandwidth-management function. They also route, groom, and consolidate traffic between the collectors and backbone networks.

SONET systems offer network management, protection, and bandwidth management. They can be implemented using various topologies, including ring, point-to-point, full mesh, and partial mesh. SONET backbone networks are normally constructed using the ring topology.

Table 2-2   *SONET Hierarchy*

Signal Level	T-Carrier Equivalent	SDH Equivalent	Bandwidth
OC3	$100 \times T1$	STM-1	155 Mbps
OC12	$401 \times T1$	STM-4	622 Mbps
OC48	$1606 \times T1$	STM-16	2.5 Gbps
OC192	$6424 \times T1$	STM-64	10 Gbps
OC768	$25699 \times T1$	STM-256	40 Gbps

Figure 2-5   *SONET Topology—Logical View*

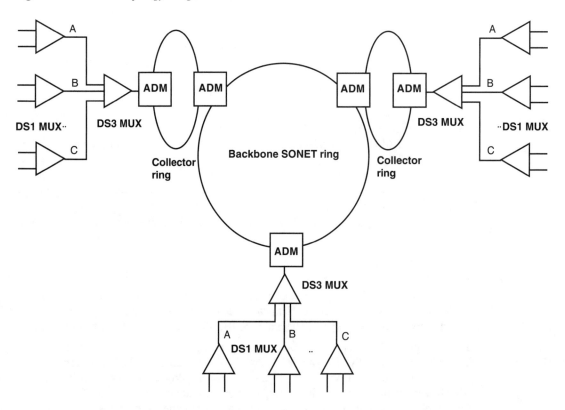

Packet and Cell Switching

Some of the most widely used technologies employed by enterprise networks are Frame
Relay, X.25, SMDS, and ATM. Frame Relay is a packet-switched technology. X.25, a much

older protocol, also uses packet-switching techniques and is similar to Frame Relay in many respects.

ATM and Switched Multimegabit Data Service (SMDS) are cell-switched technologies. Data link layer switching technologies such as ATM and Frame Relay are connection-oriented technologies, meaning that traffic is sent between two endpoints only after a connection (virtual circuit) has been established. Because traffic between any two points in the network flows along a predetermined path, technologies such as ATM make a network more predictable and manageable. Frame Relay and ATM circuits offer a higher level of security because the endpoints are pre-determined and operate over a private underlying infrastructure. This is the main reason that large networks often have an ATM backbone.

Frame Relay

Frame Relay is a protocol and standard derived from narrowband ISDN and developed by ANSI and the International Telecommunication Union Telecommunication Standardization Sector (ITU-T), formerly the Consultative Committee for International Telegraph and Telephone (CCITT).

The Frame Relay Forum (FRF) addresses various implementation issues, ensuring that multivendor networks can operate. The Frame Relay protocol operates at the data link layer only and does not include any network or higher-layer protocol functions. As a result, the protocol overhead is much less than with packet-switching technologies such as X.25, which operates over Layers 2 and 3. The reduction of the protocol overhead is dependent on the assumptions that the underlying physical layer is relatively error-free and that if errors do occur, upper-layer protocols such as TCP on end-user devices will recover from such errors. As such, Frame Relay does not provide any data integrity, nor does it provide any means of flow control. Frame Relay uses an error-checking mechanism based on a 16-bit CRC polynomial. This polynomial provides error detection for frames up to 4096 bytes in length.

Frame Relay was envisioned as an interim technology to bridge the transition from legacy X.25 and leased-line TDM networks to *ATM everywhere*. The ATM everywhere concept meant running ATM as an end-to-end protocol spanning desktop systems, LANs, and WANs. However, this was not the case. Frame Relay has proven its reliability and cost effectiveness as a WAN technology for enterprise WAN backbones operating below the DS3 rate.

In the case of Frame Relay, carriers provision permanent virtual circuits (PVCs) for customers. These circuits are logical channels between the Frame Relay access device (FRAD) and are provisioned across the Frame Relay network. A Frame Relay-capable router is an excellent example of a FRAD. Some carriers also provision switched virtual circuits (SVCs), depending on their respective service offering. SVCs use E.164 addressing versus the data link connection identifier (DLCI) addressing found with PVCs.

Data-Link Connection Identifier (DLCI)

A data-link connection identifier (DLCI) identifies the Frame Relay PVC. Frames are routed through one or more virtual circuits identified by DLCIs. Each DLCI has a permanently configured switching path to a certain destination. Thus, by having a system with several DLCIs configured, you can communicate simultaneously with several different sites. The User-Network Interface (UNI) provides the demarcation between the FRAD and the Frame Relay network. The combination of the UNI and the DLCI specifies the endpoint for a particular virtual circuit. The DLCI has local significance and the numbering is usually decided by the user and assigned by the Frame Relay Service Provider. The customer assigned DLCI numbers are usually in the range of 1 <= DLCI <= 1022.

Frame Relay PVCs are extremely popular. Most enterprise circuit migrations usually take place from leased lines to Frame Relay PVCs. Other forms of Frame Relay virtual circuits provisioned by carriers include SVCs and soft PVCs. Refer to Figure 2-6. The bandwidth of the local loop access line, which connects the FRAD to the Frame Relay network, is also called *port speed*. Frame Relay services can be offered from subrate fractional T1 up to port speeds of $n \times$ DS1. The carrier's choice of Frame Relay point of presence (PoP) equipment usually influences the maximum port speed that can be offered to the customer. The Cisco MGX 8220 concentrator can support Frame Relay up to 16 Mbps using an HSSI-based port.

Figure 2-6 *Frame Relay Virtual Circuits from a Customer Perspective*

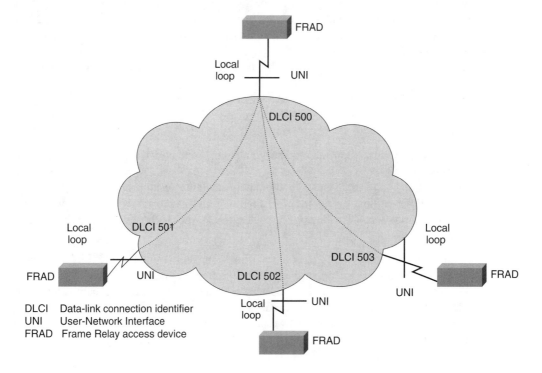

Committed Information Rate (CIR)

Another parameter, called the Committed Information Rate (CIR), defines an agreement between the carrier and the customer regarding the delivery of data on a particular VC. CIR is measured in bits per second. It measures the average amount of data over a specific period of time, such as 1 second, that the network will attempt to deliver with a normal priority. In the event of congestion, data bursts that exceed the CIR are marked as Discard Eligible (DE) and are delivered at lower priority or possibly discarded.

For example, assume that a Frame Relay circuit with an access rate (port speed) of 256 k could have three PVCs. The PVC carrying critical data could have a CIR of 128 k, and the remaining two PVCs, mostly used for FTP and other noncritical functions, could have a CIR of 32 k each. The aggregate CIR on the line is 128 k + 32 k + 32 k (192 k), which is well within the access rate of the local loop.

If the CIR sum total exceeds the port speed access rate, it is known as *oversubscription*. Most carriers do not provision a Frame Relay service with CIR or port oversubscription, because it would affect the Service-Level Agreements (SLAs) with their customers. If a customer requests this type of provisioning, the carrier might ask the customer to sign an SLA waiver.

Frame Relay Frame

The Frame Relay frame, shown in Figure 2-7, is defined by ANSI T1.618 and is derived from the High-Level Data Link Control (HDLC) standard, ISO 7809.

Figure 2-7   *Frame Relay Frame (ANSI T1.618 Format)*

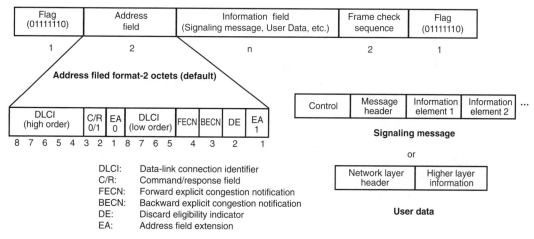

The Frame Relay fields are as follows:

- **Flag**—One-octet fixed sequence containing 01111110 (binary) or 7E (hex).

- **Address field**—This field includes the address and control functions for the frame. The default length is two octets, although longer fields of three or four octets are also defined.

  — DLCI—The data-link connection identifier represents a single logical channel between the FRAD and the network, through which data can pass.

  — C/R—The command/response field is provided for the use of the higher-layer protocols and is not examined by the Frame Relay protocol itself. This single bit may be used by FRADs for signaling and/or control purposes.

  — EA—The address field extension bits are used to extend the addressing structure beyond the two-octet default to either three or four octets. EA=0 indicates that more address octets will follow, and EA=1 indicates the last address octet.

  — FECN—The forward explicit congestion notification bit is set by the network to indicate that congestion has occurred in the same direction as the traffic flow.

  — BECN—The backward explicit congestion notification bit is set by the network to indicate that congestion has occurred in the direction opposite the flow of that traffic.

  — DE—The discard eligibility bit indicates the relative importance of the frame. It also indicates whether it is eligible for discarding, should network congestion indicate. This bit may be set by either the FRAD or the Frame Relay network.

- **Information field**—This field contains the upper-layer protocol information and user data. This field is passed transparently from source to destination and is not examined by any intermediate FRAD or Frame Relay switch. The maximum negotiated length of the information field is 1600 bytes to minimize segmentation and reassembly functions with LAN traffic.

- **FCS**—The frame check sequence implements a two-octet cyclic redundancy check (CRC) sequence using the CRC-16 polynomial. The use of this polynomial provides error detection for frames with a length of up to 4096 bytes.

Local Management Interface (LMI) Status Polling

The operational support protocol for the UNI is called the Local Management Interface (LMI). The LMI standards in use are ANSI T1.617 Annex D, Q.933 Annex A, and the Cisco LMI. The LMI defines a polling protocol between the FRAD and the Frame Relay switch. The FRAD periodically issues a STATUS ENQUIRY message, and the Frame Relay switch should respond with a STATUS message. The polling period is a negotiable parameter, with a default of 10 seconds. The LMI verifies link integrity, status of PVCs, and error conditions, which may exist on the signaling link or may indicate internal network problems. LMI types Annex-A and Annex-D use DLCI 0 for signaling. LMI type LMI (original) uses DLCI 1023.

NOTE	Cisco Routers used as Frame Relay access devices can auto-sense the LMI type used by the Frame Relay service provider switches beginning with IOS version 11.2.

Congestion Control

Frame Relay networks have two methods of congestion control:

- Explicit congestion notification
- Implicit congestion notification

Explicit congestion notification uses the forward (FECN) and backward (BECN) bits that are included in the T1.618 address field. The use of these bits is determined by the direction of traffic flow. The FECN bit is sent to the next-hop Frame Relay switch in the direction of the data flow, and the BECN bit is sent in the opposite direction of the data flow.

Implicit congestion notification relies on the upper-layer protocols in the FRADs or other terminal device, such as a host, to control the amount of data that is entering the network. This function is generally implemented by a transport layer flow control mechanism in both the transmitter and the receiver using acknowledgments to control traffic. Processes within these devices monitor network conditions such as frame loss. The implicit congestion notification process then controls the offered traffic, which in turn controls the congestion.

ATM

Asynchronous Transfer Mode is derived from standards developed by the ITU-T that were based on BISDN (Broadband ISDN) technology.

ATM is a connection-oriented service in which transmitted data is organized into fixed-length cells. Upper-layer protocols and user data such as an IP packet are segmented into 48-byte protocol data units (PDUs). These PDUs are prepended with a 5-byte ATM header, and the resulting 53-byte cells are input into an ATM switch and multiplexed together. These cells then contend for vacant slots in the outgoing ATM cellstream.

Each ATM cell header contains a virtual path identifier (VPI) and a virtual channel identifier (VCI), which together define the ATM virtual circuit the cell needs to follow on its path toward its destination. The arrival rate, or delay, of one particular cell stream is not periodic. Therefore, the cell transfer is referred to as Asynchronous Transfer Mode, in contrast to synchronous transfer, such as TDM transport, which uses fixed time periods for frame transmission and reception.

ATM was envisioned as an end-to-end technology spanning LANs and WANs worldwide. The connection-oriented virtual circuit technology made ATM suitable to multiservice WAN implementations, giving carrier networks the ability to carry data, voice, and video. However, emulating a broadcast environment, as found on most LANs, led to the development of complex LAN emulation protocols such as LANE (LAN Emulation), which have enjoyed limited success, mainly as a collapsed backbone bridge for legacy LAN segments. ATM on the LAN as a high-speed technology of sorts has been overtaken by Fast Ethernet and Gigabit Ethernet. These protocols are simple and easy to implement on the local-area network. More importantly, enterprise users are familiar with the Ethernet protocol and already have large installed bases of Fast Ethernet.

I shall focus the discussion of ATM with respect to the WAN, where it has become the protocol of choice for implementations up to OC-48 (2.5 Gbps).

In the case of ATM, carriers provision PVCs for customers (as they would in the case of Frame Relay). These circuits are identified by virtual path identifier/virtual channel identifier (VPI/VCI) pairs. Similar to Frame Relay DLCIs, other forms of ATM virtual circuits provisioned by carriers include SVCs and soft PVCs.

ATM is based on the Broadband ISDN protocol architecture model. This model varies from the OSI reference model in that it uses three dimensions, as shown in Figure 2-8, instead of the two-dimensional model used with OSI.

Figure 2-8   *Mapping of the OSI Model to the ATM Model*

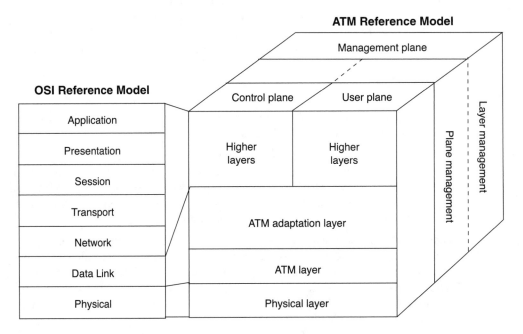

The ATM architecture uses a logical model to describe the functionality it supports. ATM functionality corresponds to the physical layer and part of the data link layer of the OSI reference model.

The ATM Reference Model Planes

There are three ATM reference model planes, which are responsible for signaling, user data transfer, and management:

- **Control plane**—This plane is responsible for generating and managing signaling requests. The Control plane supports call control and connection control functions such as signaling. The signaling establishes, supervises, and releases calls and connections.

- **User plane**—The User plane is responsible for managing the transfer of data. The User plane provides for user-to-user information transfer, plus controls that are required for that information transfer, such as flow control and error recovery.

- **Management plane**—This plane contains two components: layer management and plane management.

NOTE   The Control, User, and Management planes span all layers of the ATM reference model.

Layer Management Layer management manages layer-specific functions, such as the detection of failures and protocol problems. It deals with the resources and parameters residing at each protocol layer. Operation, Administration, and Maintenance (OAM) information flow, which is specific to a particular layer, is an example of a layer management function.

Plane Management Plane management manages and coordinates functions related to the complete system. It deals with the management of the other planes and coordination between the planes.

ATM Layers

The ATM layers explain data flow to and from upper-layer protocols such as TCP/IP. These layers are as follows:

- **Physical layer**—Analogous to the physical layer of the OSI reference model, the ATM physical layer manages the medium-dependent transmission. The physical layer is responsible for sending and receiving bits on the transmission medium, such as SONET, and for sending and receiving cells to and from the ATM layer. ATM operates on various media from clear-channel T1 (1.544 Mbps) upward.

- **ATM layer**—Combined with the ATM adaptation layer (AAL), the ATM layer is roughly analogous to the data link layer of the OSI reference model. The ATM layer is responsible for establishing connections and passing cells through the ATM network. To do this, it uses information in the header of each ATM cell. At the

ATM layer, ATM cells are routed and switched to the appropriate circuit, which connects with an end system and its specific application or process. The ATM layer adds a 5-byte ATM header to the 48-byte PDU received from the AAL. This header contains virtual path identifier (VPI) and virtual channel identifier (VCI) information.

- **ATM adaptation layer (AAL)**—Combined with the ATM layer, the AAL is roughly analogous to the data link layer of the OSI model. The AAL is responsible for isolating higher-layer protocols from the details of the ATM processes. Upper-layer protocols are segmented into 48-byte PDUs at the AAL. The AAL is divided into the convergence sublayer and the segmentation and reassembly (SAR) sublayer.

A brief description of the various ATM adaptation layers follows:

- **AAL1**—A connection-oriented service that is suitable for handling circuit-emulation services and applications, such as voice and videoconferencing.

- **AAL3/4**—Supports both connection-oriented and connectionless data. It was designed for service providers and is closely aligned with SMDS. AAL3/4 is used to transmit SMDS packets over an ATM network.

- **AAL5**—The primary AAL for data. Supports both connection-oriented and connectionless data. It is used to transfer most non-SMDS data, such as classical IP over ATM and LANE.

ATM Cell

An ATM cell is 53 octets in length, as shown in Figure 2-9. It consists of a five-octet header and a 48-octet payload. Two formats for the header are defined: one at the UNI, and a second at the Network Node Interface (NNI). The following two sections examine these formats separately.

ATM Cells at the UNI   The ATM header at the UNI consists of six fields (see Figure 2-9):

- **Generic flow control (GFC)**—A 4-bit field that may be used to provide local functions, such as flow control. This field has local (not end-to-end) significance and is overwritten by intermediate ATM switches. The UNI 3.1 specification states that this field should be filled with all 0s by the transmitting host.

- **Virtual path identifier (VPI)**—An 8-bit field that identifies the virtual path across the interface.

- **Virtual channel identifier (VCI)**—A 16-bit field that identifies the virtual channel across the interface. The UNI 3.1 specification defines some VPI/VCI values for specific functions, such as meta-signaling, used to establish the signaling channel; point-to-point signaling; and OAM cells. Examples of preassigned VPI/VCI values are shown in Table 2-3.

Figure 2-9   *ATM Cells at the UNI and NNI*

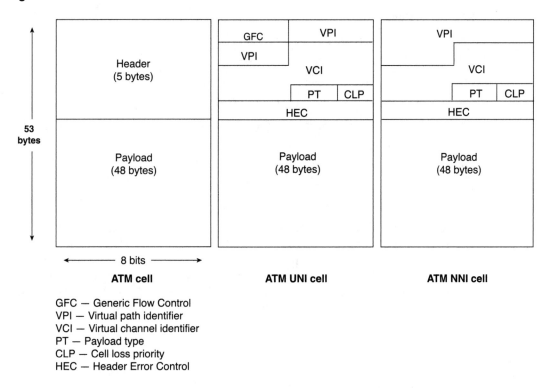

GFC — Generic Flow Control
VPI — Virtual path identifier
VCI — Virtual channel identifier
PT — Payload type
CLP — Cell loss priority
HEC — Header Error Control

Table 2-3   *Well-Known VPI/VCI Values*

Function	VPI	VCI
Meta-signaling	0	1
Signaling	0	2
SMDS	0	15
ILMI	0	16

- **Payload type (PT)**—A 3-bit field that identifies the type of information contained in the payload. The PT field has eight defined values, as shown in Table 2-4.

- **Cell loss priority (CLP)**—A single-bit field that is used by either the user or the network to indicate the cell's explicit loss priority.

- **Header error control (HEC)**—An 8-bit field that is used to detect and/or correct bit errors that occur in the header.

Table 2-4   *Payload Type Values*

PT	Description
000	User data, no congestion, SDU type=0
001	User data, no congestion, SDU type=1
010	User data, congestion, SDU type=0
011	User data, congestion, SDU type=1
100	OAM segment data, F5 flow related
101	Reserved
110	Reserved
111	Reserved

ATM Cells at the NNI   The ATM header at the NNI is also five octets in length and is identical to the UNI format with the exception of the first octet, as shown in Figure 2-9. The 4 bits used for the generic flow control (GFC) field have been replaced by 4 additional bits for the VPI field. The NNI, which provides bundles of VCIs between switches, defines an additional 4 bits for the VPI. In other words, the NNI has 12 bits for the VPI and 16 for the VCI, whereas the UNI header has only 8 bits for the VPI and 16 bits for the VCI. This means that the NNI header allows for 4096 Virtual Path (VP) values and 65,536 Virtual Channel (VC) values, whereas the UNI header allows for 256 VP values and 65,536 VC values.

ATM Cell Generation

User information such as voice, data, and video traffic is passed from the upper layers to the convergence sublayer (CS) portion of the ATM adaptation layer being used. At the CS, header and trailer information is added and subsequently passed to the segmentation and reassembly (SAR) sublayer. The SAR sublayer is responsible for generating the 48-octet payloads, which are then passed to the ATM layer. The ATM layer adds the appropriate header (UNI or NNI), resulting in a 53-octet cell. That cell is then transmitted over the physical medium, such as a SONET connection, to an intermediate or destination switch and is eventually delivered to the end-user device or process.

ATM Interfaces and Signaling

A broadband ATM network may include a number of distinct interfaces. The UNI connects the ATM network to customer premises equipment, such as an ATM switch or router. Two types of UNIs may be present, public and private, as shown in Figure 2-10.

Figure 2-10 *ATM UNI and NNI Interfaces*

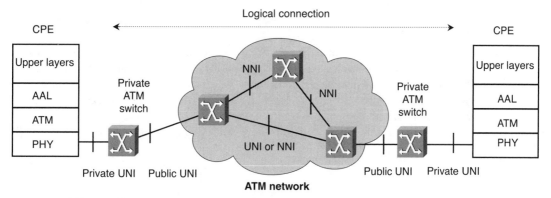

AAL: ATM adaptation layer
ATM: Asynchronous Transfer Mode layer
PHY: Physical layer

A public UNI connects a private ATM switch to a public ATM service provider's network. A private UNI connects ATM users to the ATM switch. The term *trunk* is used to indicate the ATM link between carrier switches, and the term *line* is used to indicate the link between the customer equipment to the carrier's closest point of presence (POP) ATM switch. UNI ATM headers are typically used between the CPE and the carrier's ATM switch. However, ATM trunk lines may use either UNI or NNI ATM headers for operation. NNI headers are used if an extremely large number of virtual circuits are provisioned by the carrier.

In some applications, the ATM protocol functions are divided between the data terminal equipment (DTE), such as a router, and the hardware interface to the UNI, such as an ATM CSU/DSU. The ATM Data Exchange Interface (DXI) defines the protocol operations between these two devices.

The term Network Node Interface (NNI) is used to describe several network interconnection scenarios, either within a single carrier's network or between two distinct carrier networks. The ATM Forum's designation for this is the Broadband Inter-Carrier Interface (BICI), which allows interconnection between public carriers that provide ATM service.

When an end ATM device wants to establish a connection with another end ATM device, it sends a signaling-request packet to its directly connected ATM switch. This request contains the ATM address of the desired ATM endpoint, as well as any quality of service (QoS) parameters required for the connection. ATM signaling protocols vary by the type of ATM link, which can be either UNI signals or NNI signals. UNI is used between an ATM end system and an ATM switch across ATM UNI, and NNI is used across NNI links.

The ATM Forum UNI 3.1 specification is the current standard for ATM UNI signaling. The UNI 3.1 specification is based on the Q.2931 public network signaling protocol developed by the ITU-T. UNI signaling requests are carried in a well-known default connection: VPI = 0, VCI = 5.

Virtual Connections

Each ATM cell, whether sent at the UNI or the NNI, contains information that identifies the virtual connection to which it belongs. That identification has two parts: a virtual channel identifier and a virtual path identifier. Both the VCI and VPI are used at the ATM layer. The virtual channels, with their VCIs, and the virtual paths, with their VPIs, are contained within the physical transmission path, as shown in Figure 2-11. Figure 2-12 shows ATM virtual circuits from a customer perspective. These virtual circuits could be ATM PVCs or SVCs.

Figure 2-11 *ATM Virtual Paths and Virtual Channels*

Figure 2-12 *ATM Virtual Circuits from a Customer Perspective*

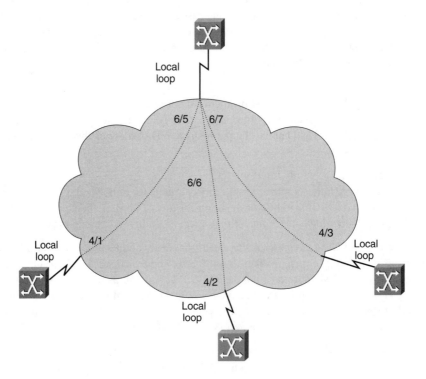

The virtual channel is a unidirectional communication capability for the transport of ATM cells. To originate or terminate a virtual channel link, a VCI is either assigned or removed. Virtual channel links are concatenated to form a virtual channel connection (VCC), which is an end-to-end path at the ATM layer.

A virtual path is a group of virtual channel links, all of which have the same endpoint. To originate or terminate a virtual path link, the VPI is either assigned or removed. Virtual path links are concatenated to form a virtual path connection (VPC).

It is imperative to understand that each end-user service is addressed by two VCI/VPI pairs: one for the transmit function and one for the receive function. VPI/VCI pairs are not end-to-end, but hop-by-hop. They can and almost certainly will change at every switch the cell goes through.

ATM Management

One of the significant elements of the BISDN architecture is the management plane. The ATM Forum developed the Interim Local Management Interface (ILMI) to address those management requirements. The ILMI assumes that each ATM device that is supporting at least one UNI has a UNI Management Entity (UME) associated with each UNI. Network management information is then communicated between UMEs, as shown in Figure 2-13. The protocol chosen for the ILMI communication is the Simple Network Management Protocol (SNMP), which is designated as SNMP/AAL. At the ATM layer, one VCC is provisioned for this ILMI communication, with a default VPI/VCI = 0/16.

Figure 2-13 *ATM Interim Local Management Interface (ILMI)*

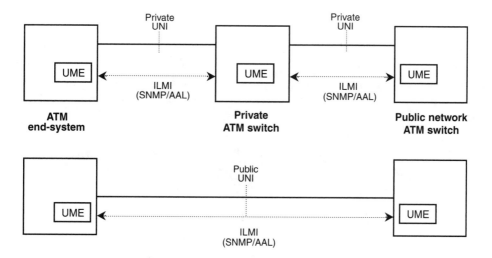

The management information defined by the ILMI provides status and configuration information from the UME regarding the UNI. This information is organized into a Management Information Base (MIB), which contains several groups of managed objects. Examples include physical layer details, such as the transmission media type (SONET, DS3, and so on) and ATM layer statistics, such as the number of ATM cells transmitted or received.

NOTE   Further details on the ILMI are found in the ATM Forum's UNI 3.1 and 4.0 specifications. These specifications are available at http://cell-relay.indiana.edu/cell-relay/docs/atmforum/pdf.html or can be sourced from www.atmforum.com.

ATM-to-Frame Relay Interworking

When an ATM network connects to another network, such as Frame Relay or SMDS, conversions between the two network protocols are required. These conversions are performed by processes called interworking functions (IWFs), which are defined in the ATM Forum's BICI specifications. ATM and Frame Relay networks usually share the same switched infrastructure. This is accomplished via the ATM-to-Frame Relay IWF. This is illustrated in Figure 2-14.

Figure 2-14 *ATM-to-Frame Relay Interworking Function*

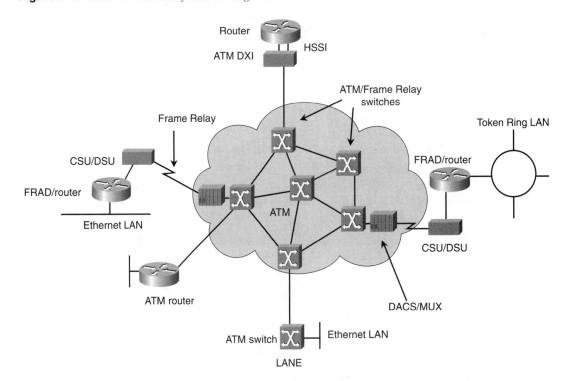

ATM Quality of Service (QoS)

Traffic management is the key feature of ATM that distinguishes it from current networking protocols and makes it suitable for deployment in high-speed networks and for providing performance guarantees in an integrated environment. ATM supports QoS guarantees composed of traffic contract, traffic shaping, and traffic policing.

A traffic contract specifies an envelope that describes the intended data flow. This envelope specifies values for peak bandwidth, average sustained bandwidth, and burst size, among others. When an ATM end system connects to an ATM network, it enters a contract with the network, based on QoS parameters. Traffic shaping is the use of queues to constrain data bursts, limit peak data rate, and smooth jitters so that traffic will fit within the promised envelope. ATM devices are responsible for adhering to the contract by means of traffic shaping.

ATM switches can use traffic policing to enforce the contract. The switch can measure the actual traffic flow and compare it against the agreed-upon traffic envelope. If the switch finds that traffic is outside of the agreed-upon parameters, it can set the cell loss priority (CLP) bit of the offending cells. Setting the CLP bit makes the cell discard-eligible, which means that any switch handling the cell is allowed to drop the cell during periods of congestion. *Cell loss* and *cell delay* are ATM QoS parameters; *peak cell rate* is one of its traffic parameters. QoS and traffic parameters together determine the ATM service category.

The ATM Forum has defined four ATM layer service classes, each with scalable QoS levels:

- **Class A: constant bit rate (CBR)**—CBR traffic is characterized by a continuous stream of bits at a steady rate, such as TDM traffic. Class A traffic is low-bandwidth traffic that is highly sensitive to delay and intolerant of cell loss. Carriers use the CBR class of service to provide Circuit Emulation Services (CESs) that emulate TDM like leased-line circuits.

- **Class B: variable bit rate, real time (VBR-RT)**—VBR-RT traffic has a bursty nature where end-to-end delay is critical. It can be characterized by voice or video applications that use compression, such as interactive videoconferencing.

- **Class C: variable bit rate, non-real time (VBR-NRT)**—VBR-NRT traffic has a bursty nature in which delay is not so critical, such as video playback, training tapes, and video mail messages.

- **Class D: available bit rate (ABR)**—ABR traffic can be characterized as bursty LAN traffic and data that is more tolerant of delays and cell loss. ABR is a best-effort service that is a managed service based on minimum cell rate (MCR) and with low cell loss.

   Class D: unspecified bit rate (UBR)—UBR is a best-effort service that does not specify bit rate or traffic parameters and has no QoS guarantees. Originally devised as a way to make use of excess bandwidth, UBR is subject to increased cell loss and the discard of whole packets.

Layer 3 Routing

Network layer routing is based on the exchange of network reachability information. As a packet traverses the network, each router extracts all the information relevant to forwarding from the Layer 3 header. This information is then used as an index for a routing table lookup to determine the packet's next hop. This is repeated at each router across the network. At each hop in the network, the optimal forwarding of a packet must again be determined.

The information in IP packets, such as information on IP QoS, is usually not considered in order to get maximum forwarding performance. Typically, only the destination address or prefix is considered. However, IP QoS makes other fields, such as the ToS field, in an IPv4 header relevant; therefore, a complex header analysis must be performed at each router the packet encounters on its way to the destination network.

The routing function can be considered two separate components:

- Forwarding component
- Control component

Forwarding Component

The forwarding component uses information held in the forwarding table and in the Layer 3 header. The forwarding component uses a set of algorithms, which define the kind of information extracted from the packet header and the procedure that the router will use to find an associated entry in the forwarding table. The router then forwards the packet based on this information. Forwarding is as follows:

- **Unicast forwarding**—The router uses the destination address from the Layer 3 header and the longest match algorithm on the destination address to find an associated entry in the forwarding table.

- **Unicast forwarding with ToS (type of service)**—The router uses the destination address and ToS field value from the Layer 3 header and the longest match algorithm on the destination address as well as an exact match on the ToS value to find an associated entry in the forwarding table.

- **Multicast forwarding**—The router uses the source and destination addresses from the Layer 3 header as well as the ingress interface the packet arrives on. The router then uses the longest match algorithm on the source and destination addresses as well as an exact match on the ingress interface to find an associated entry in the forwarding table.

Control Component

The control component is responsible for the construction and maintenance of the forwarding table. This is implemented by dynamic routing protocols such as OSPF, EIGRP, IS-IS, BGP, and PIM, which exchange routing information between routers as well as algorithms such as Dijkstra's algorithm or the diffusion algorithm that a router uses to convert topology tables into forwarding tables.

Forwarding Equivalency Class

Forwarding Equivalency Class (FEC) is a set of Layer 3 packets that are forwarded in the same manner over the same path with the same forwarding treatment. While assigning a packet to an FEC, the router might look at the IP header and also some other information, such as the interface on which this packet arrived. FECs might provide a coarse or fine forwarding granularity based on the amount of information considered for setting the equivalence.

Here are some examples of FECs:

- A set of unicast packets whose Layer 3 destination addresses match a certain address prefix

- A set of unicast packets whose destination addresses match a particular IP address prefix with similar type of service (ToS) bits

- A set of unicast packets whose destination addresses match a particular IP address prefix and have the same destination TCP port number

- A set of multicast packets with the same source and destination Layer 3 addresses

- A set of multicast packets with similar source and destination Layer 3 addresses and the same incoming interface

For example, as shown in Figure 2-15, 200.15.45.9 and 200.15.45.126 are in the same FEC with an address prefix of 200.15.45.0/25 and TCP destination port 23.

Figure 2-15 *Forwarding Equivalence Class (FEC)*

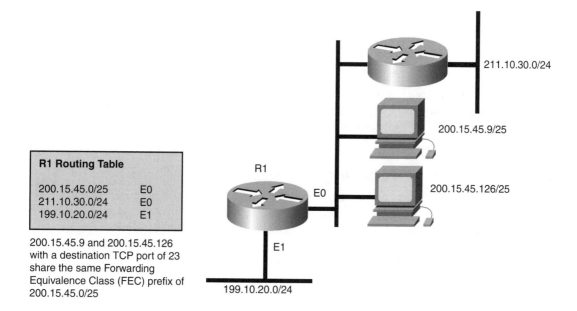

Label Switching

Label-switching devices assign short fixed-length labels to packets or cells. Switching entities perform table lookups based on these simple labels to determine where data should be forwarded.

The label summarizes essential information about forwarding the packet or cell. This information includes the destination, precedence, Virtual Private Network membership, QoS information, and the traffic-engineered route for the packet.

With label switching, the complete analysis of the Layer 3 header is performed only once: at the ingress of the label-switched network. At this location, the Layer 3 header is mapped into a fixed-length label.

At each label-switching entity or router across the network, only the label needs to be examined in the incoming cell or packet in order to send the cell or packet on its way across the network.

At the egress or the other end of the network, an edge label-switching entity or router swaps the label out for the appropriate Layer 3 header linked to that label. MPLS integrates the performance and traffic-management capabilities of Layer 2 with the scalability and flexibility of network Layer 3 routing. This integration is applicable to networks using any Layer 2 switching, but it has particular advantages when applied to ATM networks. MPLS integrates IP routing with ATM switching to offer scalable IP-over-ATM networks. It lets routers at the edge of a network apply simple labels to packets or cells. ATM switches or existing routers in the network core can switch packets according to the labels with minimal lookup overhead.

Forwarding decisions based on some or all of these different sources of information can be made by means of a single table lookup from a fixed-length label. For this reason, label switching makes it feasible for routers and switches to make forwarding decisions based on multiple destination addresses.

Label switching integrates switching and routing functions, combining the reachability information provided by the router function, plus the traffic engineering benefits achieved by the optimizing capabilities of switches.

Conventional Layer 3 Routing Versus MPLS

As Layer 3 packets are forwarded from one router to the next, each router makes an independent forwarding decision for that packet. Each router analyzes the destination Layer 3 address in the packet's header and runs a network layer routing algorithm. Each router independently chooses a next hop for the packet based on its analysis of the packet's header and the results of running the routing algorithm.

Forwarding decisions are the result of two functions:

- Classification of Layer 3 packets into FECs based on longest-match address prefixes
- Mapping of FECs to a next hop

All packets that belong to a particular FEC and that travel from a particular node follow the same path. If multipath routing is in use, the packets all follow one of a set of paths associated with the FEC.

As the packet traverses the network, each hop in turn reexamines the packet and assigns it to an FEC.

In MPLS, the assignment of a particular packet to a particular FEC is done just once, as the packet enters the network. The FEC to which the packet is assigned is encoded as a short fixed-length value known as a label. When a packet is forwarded to its next hop, the label is sent along with it; that is, the packets are labeled before they are forwarded. At subsequent hops, there is no further analysis of the packet's network layer header. Rather, the label is used as an index into a table that specifies the next hop and a new label. The old label is replaced with the new label, and the packet is forwarded to its next hop.

In the MPLS forwarding paradigm, as soon as a packet is assigned to an FEC, no further header analysis is done by subsequent routers. All forwarding is driven by the labels. This has a number of advantages over conventional network layer forwarding.

MPLS forwarding can be done by switches, which can perform a label lookup and replacement even if they cannot analyze the Layer 3 headers or cannot analyze the Layer 3 headers at an adequate speed.

MPLS routers can assign packets arriving on different ports to different FECs. This forms the basis for building MPLS Virtual Private Networks. Conventional forwarding, on the other hand, can consider only information that travels with the packet in the Layer 3 header.

A packet that enters the network at a particular router can be labeled differently than the same packet entering the network at a different router. As a result, forwarding decisions that depend on the ingress router can easily be made. This cannot be done with conventional forwarding, because the identity of a packet's ingress router does not travel with the packet.

Traffic engineering forces packets to follow particular routes in order to optimize and load-balance traffic over underutilized links. In MPLS, a label can be used to represent the route so that the identity of the explicit route need not be carried with the packet. In conventional forwarding, this requires the packet to carry an encoding of its route along with it (source routing).

Conventional routers analyze a packet's network layer header not merely to choose the packet's next hop, but also to determine a packet's precedence or class of service. They may then apply different discard thresholds or scheduling disciplines to different packets.

MPLS allows for QoS in terms of precedence or class of service to be fully or partially inferred from the label. In this case, the label represents the combination of an FEC and a precedence or class of service.

Integration of IP and ATM

The early proponents and developers of ATM envisioned it to be a ubiquitous technology, spanning the desktop, LAN, and WAN. Today, few people still cling to that vision. Instead, IP has proliferated with the explosion of the Internet. The concept of "IP over anything" has taken precedence over the focus on forcing ATM to behave like a legacy LAN protocol. ATM on the LAN, driven by LANE (LAN Emulation), classical IP over ATM, and MPOA (multiprotocol over ATM), has seen limited growth and has been overtaken by Fast Ethernet (100 Mbps) and Gigabit Ethernet (1000 Mbps).

However, ATM has seen massive growth in the WAN arena. QoS and class of service guarantees offered by ATM have led to its widespread deployment in the carrier and service provider arena. QoS has given ATM the multiservice capability to offer separate classes of service for voice, video, and data.

Frame Relay services are also offered over ATM backbones, utilizing the ATM-to-Frame Relay interworking function (IWF). This has led to the extensive deployment of Frame Relay Virtual Private Networks.

The relationship between IP and ATM has been a source of great contention and debate. Both technologies are widely deployed, and each has its strengths. The Internet Engineering Task Force (IETF) via the internetworking over nonbroadcast multiaccess networks (ION) working group, and the ATM Forum via the multiprotocol over ATM (MPOA) group, have provided standards for the integration of IP over ATM. The work of these groups has focused mainly on how the capabilities of ATM and IP can be leveraged to provide a solution, resulting in the proliferation of IP networks overlaid on an ATM infrastructure.

IP and ATM are two completely different technologies. ATM is connection-oriented and establishes circuits (PVCs or SVCs) before sending any traffic over a predetermined path using fixed-length cells with a predetermined QoS. ATM also has its own routing protocol in Private Network-to-Network Interface (PNNI). PNNI is a hierarchical link-state protocol in which each node builds a complete topological view of the network and determines the best path through the network based on this information and QoS parameters inherent in ATM.

IP, on the other hand, is a connectionless technology. Its widespread acceptance is based on its ability to use any Layer 2 and physical transport mechanism. At each node (router) in an IP network, a decision is made about the next destination or hop for each packet arriving at that router.

IP uses Interior Gateway Protocols (IGPs) for routing decisions within private enterprise networks or within an Internet service provider's autonomous system (AS). Open Shortest Path First (OSPF) and Intermediate System-to-Intermediate System (IS-IS) are examples of commonly used IGPs. Both OSPF and IS-IS are dynamic link-state protocols in which each router builds network topology tables and computes the shortest path to every destination in the network, typically using a Dijkstra shortest-path algorithm. These computations are placed in forwarding tables that are used to determine the next hop for a packet based on its destination address. The result is a best-effort mechanism that has no concept of QoS or alternative paths based on network constraints.

Routing between autonomous systems of different service providers is handled via an Exterior Gateway Protocol (EGP), such as the Border Gateway Protocol, version 4 (BGP4). BGP4 is a path-vector protocol as opposed to the link-state operation of IGPs. IP and its associated routing protocols typically run on top of ATM or Frame Relay with little integration. ISPs, for example, build ATM or Frame Relay cores inside their routed networks; these cores are used to build pipes between the routed edges.

IP routed networks are connected using permanent virtual circuits (PVCs) across an ATM or Frame Relay cloud. This creates an overlay model that is neither scalable nor manageable (see Figure 2-16, Topology A), primarily because all routers on the cloud become IP neighbors. This method also uses network resources inefficiently, because the ATM Layer 2 switches are invisible to IP routing. This means, for example, that a PVC using many ATM switch hops will be used by IP routing just as readily as a single-hop PVC, because both PVCs from an IP perspective are each a single IP hop.

The overlay model requires each router to have an adjacency with every other router in the network. Because the adjacencies must be established via ATM virtual circuits, the network now requires a full mesh of VCs to interconnect the routers. As the number of routers grows, the number of fully meshed virtual circuits required grows at the rate of $n (n-1) / 2$, where n is the number of nodes. Anything less would mean that there would be an extra router hop between some pair of routers. As shown in Figure 2-16, Topology A, there are eight routers, which leads to 28 VCs that need to be provisioned. The result is an ATM network with a large number of VCs that has a scalability problem. Over and above that, provisioning and deprovisioning of VCs becomes an arduous task for network administrators.

Another problem with traditional networks results from routing protocols, such as OSPF, that do not perform well on large, fully meshed clouds due to the link state update duplication and the large number of neighbor state machines that have to be maintained. The route oscillation caused by circuit failures can exceed router CPU use and cause an indeterministic route convergence behavior. In Figure 2-16, Topology A, router R2 has seven adjacencies. The amount of routing information that is propagated in such a network during a topology change due to a link or node state change can be as much as the order of n^4, where n is the number of routers in the core. As the value of n increases, the amount of routing traffic can overwhelm the core routers, leading to indeterministic behavior.

Figure 2-16 *Overlay Model Versus Integrated Model*

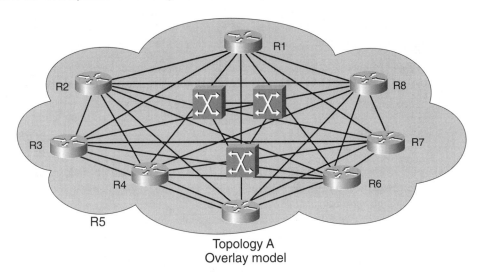

Topology A
Overlay model

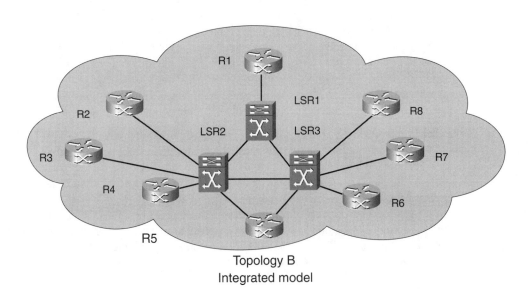

Topology B
Integrated model

NOTE   In order to alleviate the preceding issues, intermediate routers could be placed between edge routers to eliminate the full mesh of VCs and reduce the number of adjacencies seen by the edge routers. However, these routers would need adequate performance capabilities in order to handle the extra traffic. The Next Hop Resolution Protocol (NHRP) could also be used to let routers establish VCs over which they send data, without the need to establish a routing adjacency over the VC. However, NHRP supports only unicast traffic and is not defined for multicast traffic types. Furthermore, NHRP requires the deployment of NHRP servers and could potentially introduce routing loops in the backbone network.

MPLS solves the overlay meshing problem by eliminating the notion of an ATM cloud. With MPLS, ATM switches are made IP-aware, and the ATM links are treated as IP links. This way, each ATM switch can become an IP routing peer, as illustrated in the integrated model shown in Figure 2-16, Topology B. Router R2 forms only three adjacencies—with R3, R4, and LSR2.

The maximum number of adjacencies that any one router has is greatly reduced and no longer grows with the size of the network. This introduces immense scalability in the core network.

In addition, this integration of the layers results in a distributed routing and switching model that takes advantage of the capabilities offered in each layer. The router part is needed to make use of Layer 3 routing algorithms such as OSPF, IS-IS, and BGP4 for exchanging reachability information and calculating paths.

The MPLS part is needed to translate that reachability information into label-switched elements that can be understood by the switches. The switching part uses advanced hardware capabilities of the Layer 2 switches to switch data at wire speed.

MPLS Versus Traditional IP over ATM

When integrated with ATM switches, label switching takes advantage of switch hardware optimized to take advantage of the fixed length of ATM cells and to switch the cells at high speeds. For multiservice networks, label switching allows the BPX/MGX switches to provide ATM, Frame Relay, and IP Internet service all on a single platform in a highly scalable way. Support of all these services on a common platform provides operational cost savings and simplifies provisioning for multiservice providers.

For carriers and ISPs using ATM switches at the core of their networks, label switching allows the Cisco BPX 8600 series, MGX 8800 series, 8540 Multiservice Switch Router, and other Cisco ATM switches to provide a more scalable and manageable networking solution than overlaying IP over an ATM network. Label switching avoids the scalability problem of too many router peers and provides support for a hierarchical structure within an ISP's network.

Integration

When applied to ATM, MPLS integrates IP and ATM functionality rather than overlaying IP on ATM. This makes the ATM infrastructure visible to IP routing and removes the need for approximate mappings between IP and ATM features. MPLS does not need ATM addressing and routing techniques such as PNNI, although these can be used in parallel if required.

Higher Reliability

In wide-area networks with ATM infrastructures, MPLS is an easy solution for integrating routed protocols with ATM. Traditional IP over ATM involves setting up a mesh of PVCs between routers around an ATM cloud. However, there are a number of problems with this approach, all arising from the method by which the PVC links between routers are overlaid on the ATM network. This makes the ATM network structure invisible to the routers. A single ATM link failure could make several router-to-router links fail, creating problems with large amounts of routing update traffic and subsequent processing.

Without extensive tuning of routing weights, all PVCs are seen by IP routing as single-hop paths with the same cost. This might lead to inefficient routing in the ATM network.

Direct Class of Service Implementation

When used with ATM hardware, MPLS makes use of the ATM queuing and buffering capabilities to provide different classes of service. This allows direct support of IP Precedence and CoS on ATM switches without complex translations to the ATM Forum Service Classes.

Efficient Support of Multicast and RSVP

In contrast to MPLS, overlaying IP on ATM has other disadvantages, particularly in support of advanced IP services such as IP multicast and Resource Reservation Protocol (RSVP). Support of these services entails much time and work in the standards bodies and implementation; the resulting mapping between IP features and ATM features is often approximate.

VPN Scalability and Manageability

MPLS can make IP Virtual Private Network services highly scalable and very easy to manage. VPN services are an important service for providing enterprises with private IP networks within their infrastructures. When an ISP offers a VPN service, the carrier supports many individual VPNs on a single infrastructure. With an MPLS backbone, VPN information can be processed only at the ingress and exit points, with MPLS labels carrying packets across a shared backbone to their correct exit point. In addition to MPLS, the

Multiprotocol Border Gateway Protocol (MBGP) is used to deal with information about the VPNs. The combination of MPLS and Multiprotocol BGP makes MPLS-based VPN services easier to manage, with straightforward operations to manage VPN sites and VPN membership. It also makes MPLS-based VPN services extremely scalable, with one network able to support hundreds of thousands of VPNs.

Reduced Load on Network Cores

VPN services demonstrate how MPLS supports a hierarchy of routing knowledge. Additionally, you can isolate Internet routing tables from service provider network cores. Like VPN data, MPLS allows access to the Internet routing table only at the ingress and exit points of a service provider network. With MPLS, transit traffic entering at the edge of the provider's autonomous system can be given labels that are associated with specific exit points. As a result, internal transit routers and switches need only process the connectivity with the provider's edge routers, shielding the core devices from the overwhelming routing volume exchanged in the Internet. This separation of interior routes from full Internet routes also provides better fault isolation, security, and improved stability.

Traffic Engineering Capabilities

MPLS provides traffic engineering capabilities needed for the efficient use of network resources. Traffic engineering allows you to shift the traffic load from overutilized portions to underutilized portions of the network according to traffic destination, traffic type, traffic load, time of day, and so on.

Challenges Faced by Service Providers

Deregulation of the telecommunications industry after the passage of the Telecom Act of 1996 has led to a proliferation of alternative carriers and service providers, such as competitive local exchange carriers (CLECs), who compete with each other and with the incumbent local exchange carriers (ILECs) and interexchange carriers (IXCs).

Due to the extremely competitive nature of the local exchange carrier (LEC), ISP, and application service provider (ASP) marketplace, service providers are seeking ways to differentiate themselves from their competition by providing their customers with expanded service offerings at a lower cost.

Carriers and service providers also need to closely examine their network infrastructure costs and operational costs. Providing a homogenous transport infrastructure is viewed as the most cost-efficient and flexible way to address these issues.

Carriers and service providers are looking for ways to integrate their various offerings, such as managed ATM services, managed Frame Relay services, managed IP services, or unmanaged versions of IP services, as well as Internet, intranet, and extranet access over a single network infrastructure rather than parallel networks.

Voice networks using 5ESS systems have been distinct from multiservice data networks. However, as Voice over IP (VoIP) compression methods, signaling methods, QoS, Mean Opinion Score (MOS), and other standards approach pulse code modulation (PCM) quality, or toll quality, with the implementation of in-band SS7 capabilities, we shall see the migration of voice from traditional PCM/TDM circuits to VoIP over high-speed backbone networks.

Enterprise customers are no longer content to deal with separate networks for voice, data, and videoconferencing. They prefer a single hybrid circuit termination with a uniform access protocol, such as IP. They also want guaranteed levels of service, as promised in the Service-Level Agreement (SLA) and implemented by the service provider in the form of QoS utilizing multiple classes of service for voice, data, and video.

Current IP networks do not meet the challenges faced by service providers today. The capabilities of MPLS are designed to meet these challenges and provide a unified transport for large-scale, multiservice IP networks.

Summary

This chapter covered cloud technologies such as TDM, Frame Relay, and ATM. It presented the fundamentals of Layer 3 routing and label switching and made extensive comparisons between MPLS and Layer 3 routing.

Time-division multiplexing combines data streams by assigning each stream a different time slot in a set. TDM repeatedly transmits a fixed sequence of time slots over a single transmission channel. Frame Relay, X.25, and SMDS are packet-switched technologies, and ATM is a cell-switched technology.

The routing function can be considered two components—a forwarding component and a control component. The forwarding component uses information held in the forwarding table and in the Layer 3 header to make a forwarding decision, and the control component is responsible for the construction and maintenance of the forwarding table.

Label-switching devices assign short fixed-length labels to packets or cells. Switching entities perform table lookups based on these simple labels to determine where data should be forwarded. The label summarizes essential information about forwarding the packet or cell. This information includes the destination, precedence, Virtual Private Network membership, QoS information, and the traffic-engineered route for the packet or cell.

Service providers are seeking ways to differentiate themselves from their competition by providing their customers with expanded service offerings such as Virtual Private Networks and traffic-engineered IP networks. This can be easily achieved by implementing MPLS technology.

This chapter covers the following topics:

- **MPLS Operation**—This section describes the operation of MPLS networks and discusses the advantages of MPLS over conventional Layer 3 forwarding.

- **MPLS Node Architecture**—This section describes the architecture of MPLS nodes. These nodes include MPLS-enabled routers and ATM switches. MPLS nodes consist of a control plane and a forwarding plane.

- **MPLS Elements**—The various elements that constitute an MPLS network are described here. The MPLS Label-Switched Router (LSR), Label-Switched Path (LSP) mechanisms, and the workings of the Label Distribution Protocol (LDP) are explained in detail.

- **Loop Survival, Detection, and Prevention in MPLS**—This section covers the effect of routing loops on MPLS and describes various loop survival, detection, and prevention methods used by MPLS.

CHAPTER 3

MPLS Architecture

MPLS Operation

MPLS networks use labels to forward packets. The ingress MPLS node assigns a packet to a particular Forwarding Equivalence Class (FEC) just once, as the packet enters the network.

NOTE   Please refer to Chapter 2, "WAN Technologies and MPLS," for a full description of the Forwarding Equivalence Class (FEC).

The FEC to which the packet is assigned is encoded as a short fixed-length value known as a *label*. The packets are labeled before they are forwarded. At subsequent hops, there is no further analysis of the packet's network layer header. The label is used as an index into a table, which specifies the next hop, and a new label. The old label is replaced with the new label, and the packet is forwarded to its next hop.

In MPLS networks, labels drive all forwarding. This has a number of advantages over conventional network layer forwarding:

- MPLS forwarding can be performed by switches, which can do label lookup and replacement but can't analyze the network layer headers. ATM switches perform a similar function by switching cells based on VPI/VCI values found in the ATM header. If the VPI/VCI values are replaced with label values, ATM switches can forward cells based on label values. The ATM switches would need to be controlled by an IP-based MPLS control element such as a Label Switch Controller (LSC). This forms the basis of integrating IP with ATM using MPLS.

- A packet is assigned to a FEC when it enters the network. The ingress router may use any information it has about the packet, such as ingress port or interface, even if that information cannot be obtained from the network layer header. A packet that enters the network at a particular router can be labeled differently than the same packet entering the network at a different router. As a result, forwarding decisions that depend on the ingress router can be made easily. This cannot be done with conventional forwarding, because the identity of a packet's ingress router does not travel with the packet. For example, packets arriving on different interfaces connected to CPE routers might be assigned to different FECs. The attached labels would represent the corresponding FECs. This functionality forms the basis for the building of MPLS Virtual Private Networks.

- Traffic-engineered networks force packets to follow a particular path, such as an underutilized path. This path is explicitly selected when or before the packet enters the network, rather than being selected by the normal dynamic routing algorithm as the packet travels through the network. In MPLS, a label can be used to represent the route, so the identity of the explicit route need not be carried with the packet. This functionality forms the basis of MPLS traffic engineering.

- A packet's "class of service" may be determined by the ingress MPLS node. An ingress MPLS node may then apply different discard thresholds or scheduling disciplines to police different packets. Subsequent hops may enforce the service policy using a set of per-hop behaviors (PHBs). MPLS allows (but does not require) the precedence or class of service to be fully or partially inferred from the label. In this case, the label represents the combination of a FEC and a precedence or class of service. This functionality forms the basis of MPLS Quality of Service (QoS).

MPLS Node Architecture

MPLS nodes have two architectural planes: the MPLS forwarding plane and the MPLS control plane. MPLS nodes can perform Layer 3 routing or Layer 2 switching in addition to switching labeled packets. Figure 3-1 shows the basic architecture of an MPLS node.

Figure 3-1   *MPLS Node Architecture*

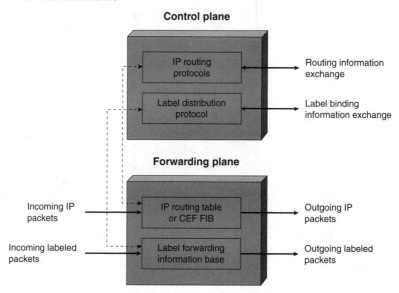

Forwarding Plane

The MPLS forwarding plane is responsible for forwarding packets based on values contained in attached labels. The forwarding plane uses a label forwarding information base (LFIB) maintained by the MPLS node to forward labeled packets. The algorithm used by the label switching forwarding component uses information contained in the LFIB as well as the information contained in the label value. Each MPLS node maintains two tables relevant to MPLS forwarding: the label information base (LIB) and the LFIB. The LIB contains all the labels assigned by the local MPLS node and the mappings of these labels to labels received from its MPLS neighbors. The LFIB uses a subset of the labels contained in the LIB for actual packet forwarding.

MPLS Label

A label is a 32-bit fixed-length identifier that is used to identify a FEC, usually of local significance. The label, which is attached to a particular packet, represents the FEC to which that packet is assigned.

In the case of ATM, the label is placed in either the VCI or VPI field of the ATM header. However, if the frame is a Frame Relay frame, the label occupies the DLCI field of the Frame Relay header.

Layer 2 technologies such as Ethernet, Token Ring, FDDI, and point-to-point links cannot utilize their Layer 2 address fields to carry labels. These technologies carry labels in shim headers. The shim label header is inserted between the link layer and the network layer, as shown in Figure 3-2. The use of the shim label header allows MPLS support over most Layer 2 technologies.

Figure 3-2   *MPLS Label Formats*

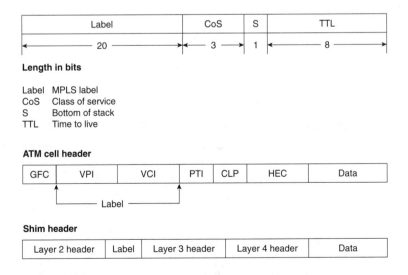

Support for the shim header requires that the sending router have a way to indicate to the receiving router that the frame contains a shim header. This is facilitated differently in various technologies. Ethernet uses ethertype values 0x8847 and 0x8848 to indicate the presence of a shim header. Ethertype value 0x8847 is used to indicate that a frame is carrying an MPLS unicast packet, and ethertype value 0x8848 is used to indicate that a frame is carrying an MPLS multicast packet. Token Ring and FDDI also use the type values as part of the SNAP header.

PPP uses a modified Network Control Program (NCP) known as MPLS control protocol (MPLSCP) and marks all packets containing a shim header with 0x8281 in the PPP protocol field. Frame Relay uses the SNAP Network Layer Protocol ID (NLPID) and SNAP header marked with type value 0x8847 in order to indicate frames carrying shim headers. ATM forum PVCs use a SNAP header with ethertype values 0x8847 and 0x8848. Table 3-1 lists reserved label values.

Table 3-1   *Reserved Label Values*

Label	Description
0	IPv4 explicit null label. This label value is legal only at the bottom of the label stack. It indicates that the label stack must be popped and the forwarding of the packet must then be based on the IPv4 header.
1	Router alert label. This label is analogous to the use of the "router alert" option in IP packets. This label value is legal anywhere in the label stack except at the bottom.
2	IPv6 explicit null label. This label value is legal only at the bottom of the label stack. It indicates that the label stack must be popped and that the forwarding of the packet must then be based on the IPv6 header.
3	Implicit null label. This is a label that an MPLS node may assign and distribute but that never actually appears in the encapsulation. This is used for penultimate hop popping.
4–15	Reserved for future use.

The MPLS label contains the following fields:

- **Label field (20 bits)**—Carries the actual value of the MPLS label.
- **CoS field (3 bits)**—Affects the queuing and discard algorithms applied to the packet as it is transmitted through the network.
- **Stack field (1 bit)**—Supports a hierarchical label stack.
- **TTL (time-to-live) field (8 bits)**—Provides conventional IP TTL functionality.

NOTE   ATM MPLS nodes carry labels in the VCI or VPI/VCI field of the ATM header. The CoS, Stack, and TTL fields are not supported. However, QoS and loop-detection features are still available and can be implemented using ATM mechanisms.

Label Stack

The stack bit implements MPLS label stacking, wherein more than one label header can be attached to a single IP packet. The stack bit is set to 1 in order to indicate the bottom of the stack. All other stack bits are set to 0. In packet-based MPLS, the top of the stack appears right after the link layer header, and the bottom of the label stack appears right before the network layer header. Packet forwarding is accomplished using the label values of the label on the top of the stack. Unicast IP routing does not use stacked labels, but MPLS VPNs and traffic engineering utilize stacked labels for their operation.

TTL

The TTL field is similar to the time-to-live field carried in the IP header. The MPLS node only processes the TTL field in the top entry of the label stack. The IP TTL field contains the value of the IPv4 TTL field or the value of the IPv6 Hop Limit field—whichever is applicable.

NOTE   Refer to RFC 3032, "MPLS Label Stack Encoding," E. Rosen et al, January 2001, for further details on the implementations of the various MPLS label fields.

NOTE   Ethernet supports a maximum transmission unit (MTU) frame size of 1518 bytes. Cisco supports a two-level label stack of 64 bits or eight octets by increasing the Ethernet MTU to 1526 bytes. However, the Layer 2 switches must also be configured to pass *giant* frames in this scenario. Another option is to use Path MTU Discovery, as documented in RFC 1191.

Label Forwarding Information Base

The label forwarding information base (LFIB) maintained by an MPLS node consists of a sequence of entries. As illustrated in Figure 3-3, each entry consists of an incoming label and one or more subentries. The LFIB is indexed by the value contained in the incoming label.

Each subentry consists of an outgoing label, outgoing interface, and next-hop address. Subentries within an individual entry may have the same or different outgoing labels. Multicast forwarding requires subentries with multiple outgoing labels, where an incoming packet arriving at one interface needs to be sent out on multiple outgoing interfaces. In addition to the outgoing label, outgoing interface, and next-hop information, an entry in the forwarding table may include information related to resources the packet may use, such as an outgoing queue that the packet should be placed on.

Figure 3-3   *Label Forwarding Information Base (LFIB)*

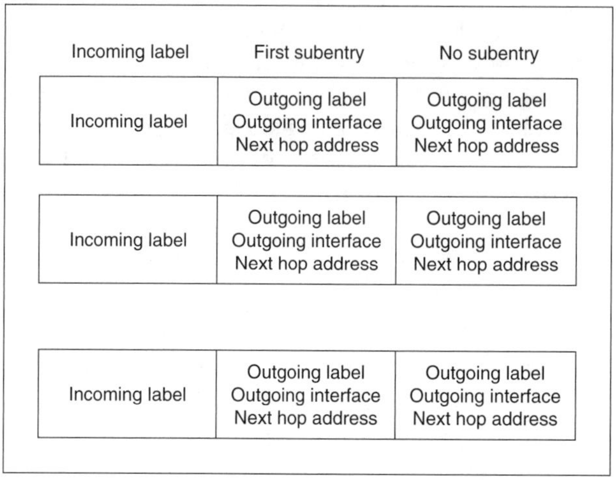

Incoming label	First subentry	No subentry
Incoming label	Outgoing label Outgoing interface Next hop address	Outgoing label Outgoing interface Next hop address
Incoming label	Outgoing label Outgoing interface Next hop address	Outgoing label Outgoing interface Next hop address
Incoming label	Outgoing label Outgoing interface Next hop address	Outgoing label Outgoing interface Next hop address

Label forwarding information base (LFIB) structure

An MPLS node can maintain a single forwarding table, a forwarding table per each of its interfaces, or a combination of both. In the case of multiple forwarding table instances, packet forwarding is handled by the value of the incoming label as well as the ingress interface on which the packet arrives.

Label Forwarding Algorithm

Label switches use a forwarding algorithm based on label swapping. MPLS nodes that maintain a single LFIB extract label values from the label field found in incoming packets and use the value as an index in the LFIB. After an incoming label match is found, the MPLS node replaces the label in the packet with the outgoing label from the subentry and sends the packet over the specified outgoing interface to the next hop specified by the subentry. If the subentry specifies an outgoing queue, the MPLS node places the packet in the specified queue.

If the MPLS node maintains multiple LFIBs for each of its interfaces, it uses the physical interface on which the packet arrived to select a particular LFIB, which is used to forward the packet.

Conventional forwarding algorithms use multiple algorithms to forward unicast, multicast, and unicast packets with ToS bits set. However, MPLS uses just one forwarding algorithm based on label swapping.

An MPLS node can obtain all the information it needs to forward a packet as well as determine resource reservations needed by a packet using a single memory access. This high-speed lookup and forwarding ability makes label switching a high-performance switching technology. MPLS can also be used to transport other Layer 3 protocols such as IPv6, IPX, or AppleTalk apart from IPv4. This property makes MPLS attractive with respect to the migration of networks from IPv4 to IPv6.

Control Plane

The MPLS control plane is responsible for populating and maintaining the LFIB. All MPLS nodes must run an IP routing protocol to exchange IP routing information with all other MPLS nodes in the network. MPLS enabled ATM nodes would use an external Label Switch Controller (LSC) such as a 7200 or 7500 router or use a Built-in Route Processor Module (RPM) in order to participate in the IP routing process.

Link-state routing protocols such as OSPF and IS-IS are the protocols of choice, because they provide each MPLS node with a view of the entire network. In conventional routers, the IP routing table is used to build the Fast Switching cache or the Forwarding Information Base (FIB) used by Cisco Express Forwarding (CEF). However, in MPLS, the IP routing table provides information on destination network and subnet prefixes used for label binding.

Label-binding information can be distributed using the Label Distribution Protocol (LDP) or Cisco's proprietary Tag Distribution Protocol (TDP) or by piggybacking the label-binding information on top of modified routing protocols.

Link-state routing protocols such as OSPF flood routing information among a set of routers that are not necessarily adjacent, whereas label-binding information is distributed only among adjacent routers. This makes link-state routing protocols unsuitable for distributing label-binding information. However, extensions to routing protocols such as PIM and BGP can be used to distribute label-binding information. This makes the distribution of label-binding information consistent with the distribution of routing information and avoids a rare condition wherein an MPLS node might receive label-binding information and not have proper routing information. It also simplifies overall system operation because it obviates the need for a separate protocol such as LDP to distribute label-binding information.

The labels exchanged with adjacent MPLS nodes are used to build the LFIB. MPLS uses a forwarding paradigm based on label swapping that can be combined with a range of different control modules. Each control module is responsible for assigning and distributing a set of labels, as well as for maintaining other relevant control information. IGPs are used to define reachability, binding, and mapping between FEC and next-hop addresses.

MPLS control modules include:

- Unicast routing module
- Multicast routing module
- Traffic engineering module

- Virtual Private Network (VPN) module
- Quality of service (QoS) module

Unicast Routing Module

The unicast routing module builds the FEC table using conventional Interior Gateway Protocols (IGPs) such as OSPF, IS-IS, and so on. The IP routing table is used to exchange label bindings with adjacent MPLS nodes for subnets contained in the IP routing table. The label-binding exchange is performed using LDP or Cisco's proprietary TDP.

Multicast Routing Module

The multicast routing module builds the FEC table using a multicast routing protocol such as Protocol-Independent Multicast (PIM). The multicast routing table is used to exchange label bindings with adjacent MPLS nodes for subnets contained in the multicast routing table. The label-binding exchange is performed using the PIM v2 protocol with MPLS extensions.

Traffic Engineering Module

The traffic-engineering module lets explicitly specified label-switched paths be set up through a network for traffic engineering purposes. It uses MPLS tunnel definitions and extensions to IS-IS or the OSPF routing protocol to build the FEC tables. The label-binding exchange is performed using the Resource Reservation Protocol (RSVP) or Constraint-based Routing LDP (CR-LDP), which is a set of extensions to LDP that enables constraint-based routing in an MPLS network.

Virtual Private Network (VPN) Module

The VPN module uses per-VPN routing tables for the FEC tables, which are built using routing protocols run between the CPE routers and service provider edge MPLS nodes. The label-binding exchange for the VPN-specific routing tables is performed using extended Multiprotocol BGP inside the service provider network.

Quality of Service (QoS) Module

The QoS module builds the FEC table using conventional Interior Gateway Protocols (IGPs) such as OSPF, or ISIS, etc. The IP routing table is used to exchange label bindings with adjacent MPLS nodes for subnets contained within the IP routing table. The label-binding exchange is performed using extensions to LDP or Cisco's proprietary TDP.

MPLS Elements

A detailed understanding of the various MPLS elements will help you understand the interaction between MPLS and the various Layer 2 and 3 protocols and devices.

The following MPLS elements are discussed in this chapter:

- Label-Switched Router (LSR)
- Label-Switched Path (LSP)
- Label Distribution Protocol (LDP)

Label-Switched Router (LSR)

The LSR is a device that implements the MPLS control and forwarding components. The LSR forwards a packet based on the value of a label encapsulated in the packet. The LSR can also forward native Layer 3 packets.

LSRs are MPLS-enabled routers or MPLS-enabled ATM switches that use labels to forward traffic. Packet-based LSRs can easily be built by loading an IOS image with the MPLS feature set on a conventional router. ATM MPLS LSRs are built using an ATM switch with integrated MPLS software or by adding MPLS functionality using an external LSC. A fundamental step in label switching is that LSRs agree on the labels they should use to forward traffic. They come to this common understanding by using the Label Distribution Protocol or extensions to PIM, BGP, RSVP, or CR-LDP.

Edge LSRs are located at the point of presence (POP) boundaries of an MPLS network and apply labels (or a stack of labels) to packets. Label imposition or prepending of labels to packets is also called a label *push* action. The edge LSRs also perform a label disposition or label removal function at the egress point of the MPLS domain, which is also called a label *pop* action. Edge LSRs can also perform a conventional IP forwarding function.

The various actions that can be performed on labeled packets by an LSR are enumerated in Table 3-2.

Table 3-2   *Label Actions*

Action	Description
Aggregate	Removes the top label in the stack and performs a Layer 3 lookup.
Pop	Removes the top label in the stack and transmits the remaining payload as either a labeled packet or unlabeled IP packet.
Push	Replaces the top label in the stack with a set of labels.
Swap	Replaces the top label in the stack with another value.
Untag	Removes the top label and forwards the IP packet to the specified IP next hop.

Packet-Based LSR Operation

Packet-based MPLS uses the label-based forwarding paradigm to transport Layer 3 packets over a router-based network. Packet-based MPLS is also called frame mode MPLS.

The basic operation of packet-based MPLS in support of unicast routing with a single level label stack is illustrated in Figure 3-4. LSR1 performs the edge LSR function. It applies the initial label to the packet after performing a conventional longest-match lookup on the IP header and determining a FEC for the packet. Parameters such as the ingress interface, in case of a VPN or a predetermined traffic-engineered path, could also determine the selection of the FEC. This determination is performed just once, at the ingress.

Figure 3-4   *Packet-Based LSR Operation with a Single Level Stack*

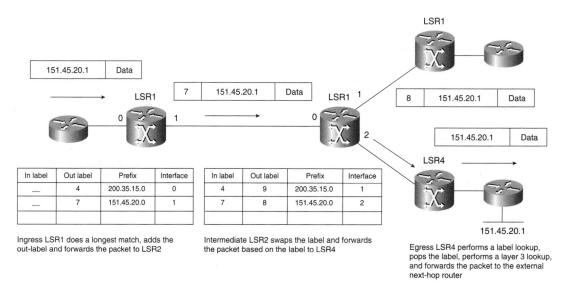

Ingress LSR1 does a longest match, adds the out-label and forwards the packet to LSR2

Intermediate LSR2 swaps the label and forwards the packet based on the label to LSR4

Egress LSR4 performs a label lookup, pops the label, performs a layer 3 lookup, and forwards the packet to the external next-hop router

Each FEC maps to a corresponding label. After the packet is labeled, subsequent LSRs forward the packet using only the label. LSRs usually replace the label on an incoming packet with a new value as they forward it. At the egress, LSR4 performs a label lookup, pops the label, performs a Layer 3 lookup, and forwards the packet to the external next-hop router.

Figure 3-5 illustrates packet-based LSR operation with multiple levels of labels in the stack. LSR1 performs the edge LSR function. It applies the initial set of labels to the packet after performing a conventional longest-match lookup on the IP header and determining a FEC for the packet. Intermediate LSR2 swaps out the top-label 7 and replaces its value with 8. At the egress, LSR4 performs a label lookup, pops the label, performs a Layer 3 lookup, and forwards the packet to the external next-hop router.

Figure 3-5 *Packet-Based LSR Operation with a Multi-Level Stack*

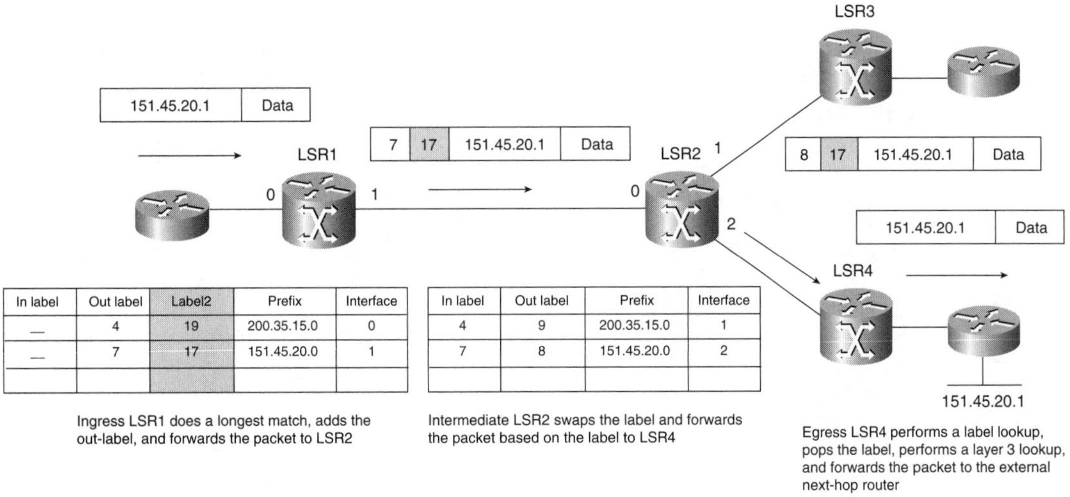

In label	Out label	Label2	Prefix	Interface
—	4	19	200.35.15.0	0
—	7	17	151.45.20.0	1

In label	Out label	Prefix	Interface
4	9	200.35.15.0	1
7	8	151.45.20.0	2

Ingress LSR1 does a longest match, adds the
out-label, and forwards the packet to LSR2

Intermediate LSR2 swaps the label and forwards
the packet based on the label to LSR4

Egress LSR4 performs a label lookup,
pops the label, performs a layer 3 lookup,
and forwards the packet to the external
next-hop router

Penultimate Hop Popping

The packet-based LSR operation described in the preceding section has certain drawbacks associated with the double lookup performed at the egress LSR4. LSR4 would need to examine the label stack and look up the label in its LFIB, only to realize that it needs to be popped. It then would need to perform a Layer 3 lookup in its global or VPN-specific routing table in order to correctly forward the packet to the external next-hop router. The double lookup at LSR4 can result in a performance degradation as well as complexity in the hardware implementation of MPLS in certain ASICs used in high-end multilayer switches.

In order to implement penultimate hop popping, the edge LSR, LSR4 (as shown in Figure 3-6), requests a label pop operation from its upstream neighbor, LSR2, via LDP or TDP using a special *implicit-null* label. This label has a value of 3 for LDP and 1 for TDP.

LSR2 pops the label before forwarding the IP-only packet to LSR4. LSR4 then performs a Layer 3 lookup based on the destination address contained in the packet and forwards the packet accordingly to a local subnet or an external next-hop router.

NOTE   Penultimate hop popping is necessary only for directly connected subnets or aggregated routes, because the Layer 2 outgoing interface can be deducted from the label entry looked up in the LFIB.

Figure 3-6   *Penultimate Hop Popping*

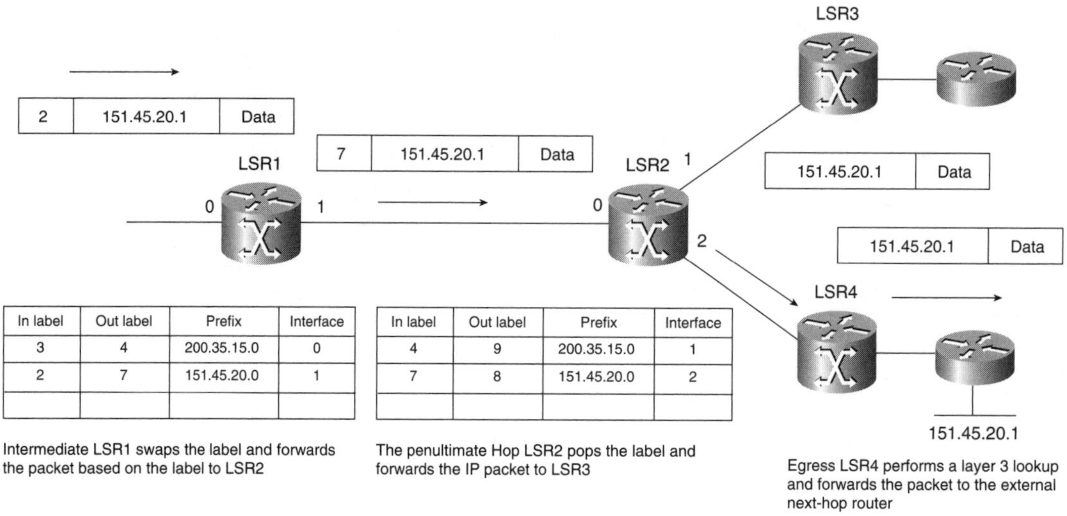

LSR3

| 2 | 151.45.20.1 | Data |

LSR1

| 7 | 151.45.20.1 | Data |

LSR2

| 151.45.20.1 | Data |

| 151.45.20.1 | Data |

LSR4

| 151.45.20.1 | Data |

151.45.20.1

In label	Out label	Prefix	Interface
3	4	200.35.15.0	0
2	7	151.45.20.0	1

In label	Out label	Prefix	Interface
4	9	200.35.15.0	1
7	8	151.45.20.0	2

Intermediate LSR1 swaps the label and forwards the packet based on the label to LSR2

The penultimate Hop LSR2 pops the label and forwards the IP packet to LSR3

Egress LSR4 performs a layer 3 lookup and forwards the packet to the external next-hop router

ATM LSR Operation

ATM MPLS uses the label-based forwarding paradigm to transport Layer 3 packets as ATM cells over an ATM-based network. ATM MPLS is also called cell mode MPLS.

An ATM-LSR is an MPLS-enabled ATM switch that can act as an LSR. ATM-LSRs normally have an LSC, which performs an IP routing function with other LSRs in the MPLS network. A label-switching-controlled ATM (LC-ATM) interface is an ATM interface controlled by the label-switching control component. When a packet traversing such an interface is received, it is treated as a labeled packet. The packet's top label is inferred either from the contents of the VCI field or the combined contents of the VPI and VCI fields. An ATM-LSR is an LSR with a number of LC-ATM interfaces that forwards cells between these interfaces, using labels carried in the VCI or VPI/VCI field, without reassembling the cells into frames before forwarding.

The ATM-LSR runs MPLS control protocols in the control plane and sets up Label Virtual Circuits (LVCs), which are the MPLS analogy of conventional ATM PVCs. Labeled packets are forwarded as ATM cells. The ATM switching matrix of the ATM switch is used as the Label Forwarding Information Base. ATM switches such as the LS1010 or 8500 series switches implement MPLS control in software run on the switch processor. The BPX 8650 is an example of an ATM-LSR that needs an external LSC. The LSC is physically implemented as a 7200 or 7500 router connected to the BPX over an OC3 ATM interface. The Virtual Switch Interface (VSI) protocol runs between the LSC, and the ATM switch supports the MPLS control plane, which uses the control virtual circuit (VC) 0/32. The

MPLS control VC uses LLC/SNAP encapsulation of IP packets as defined in RFC 1483. The 0/32 control PVC is also used to carry IP routing protocol traffic between the LSC and other ATM LSRs.

NOTE   Support of MPLS on an ATM switch does not require the switch to support the ATM control component or ATM routing protocols defined by the ITU and ATM Forum, such as PNNI.

If the LSR has any ATM interfaces that connect through MPLS to an ATM-LSR, it is called an ATM edge LSR. The ATM edge LSR receives labeled or unlabeled packets, segments them into ATM cells, and forwards these cells to next-hop ATM-LSRs. An ATM edge LSR is normally a packet-based LSR that has at least one LC-ATM interface.

As illustrated in Figure 3-7, the ATM LSRs use the *ordered control* method of LSP establishment in order to build the label-switched path, because the label assignment is controlled in an orderly manner from the egress to the ingress of the LSP. The label distribution method used by LDP is called *downstream on demand* because the ATM LSRs assign labels on demand (or, rather, a request) from an upstream neighbor. If a downstream ATM LSR does not have a label it could use to reply to a label request from an upstream neighbor, the ATM LSR would in turn request a label from its own downstream neighbor. It would reply to the upstream neighbor only after receiving a label from its downstream LSR.

Figure 3-7   *ATM LSR Operation*

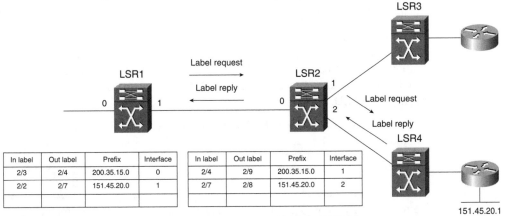

1. ATM LSR1 requests a label for the 151.45.20.0 FEC from its neighbor ATM LSR2

2. ATM LSR2 requests a label for the 151.45.20.0 FEC from its neighbor ATM LSR4

3. Egress ATM LSR4 allocates a label for the 151.45.20.0 FEC which corresponds to its inbound VPI/VCI value and sends this VPI/VCI value to ATM LSR2

5. ATM LSR1 uses the VPI/VCI value received from ATM LSR2 as its outbound VPI/VCI value

4. ATM LSR2 uses the VPI/VCI value received from ATM LSR4 as its outbound VPI/VCI value, maps it to a local inbound VPI/VCI pair, and sends this VPI/VCI value to ATM LSR1

The ATM LSRs are ATM switches that have limited ATM VCs that can be supported across the physical ATM interfaces. These limits vary between platforms and are detailed in Chapter 9, "MPLS Design and Migration." The scarcity of VC resources requires that the allocation and distribution of ATM VCs must be performed in a conservative manner, typically using Conservative Label Retention Mode LDP, which requires that the LSR only maintain label-to-FEC mappings, which it requires for packet forwarding.

NOTE   The forwarding mechanism used by ATM MPLS LSRs is conventional ATM cell switching based on VPI/VCI values in the cell headers. These VPI/VCI values actually contain the label values. The MPLS stack header is not used by ATM LSRs, and the top-of-stack label is set to 0 by the ingress ATM edge LSR.

The step-by-step label allocation procedure of the ATM MPLS network shown in Figure 3-7 is as follows:

Step 1   ATM LSR1 requests a label for the 151.45.20.0 FEC using LDP or TDP label mapping request from its downstream neighbor ATM LSR2.

Step 2   ATM LSR2 in turn requests a label for the 151.45.20.0 FEC using an LDP or TDP label mapping request from its downstream neighbor ATM LSR4.

Step 3   Egress ATM LSR4 allocates a label for the 151.45.20.0 FEC, which corresponds to its inbound VPI/VCI value, modifies the entry in its LFIB corresponding to the FEC, and sends this VPI/VCI value to ATM LSR2 using a TDP/LDP reply.

Step 4   ATM LSR2 uses the VPI/VCI value received from ATM LSR4 as its outbound VPI/VCI value, allocates a free VC, which it maps to a local inbound VPI/VCI pair, and modifies the entry in its LFIB corresponding to the FEC. ATM LSR2 then sends this VPI/VCI value to ATM LSR1 using a TDP/LDP reply.

Step 5   ATM LSR1 uses the VPI/VCI value received from ATM LSR2 as its outbound VPI/VCI value and modifies the entry in its LFIB corresponding to the FEC.

NOTE   VC merge functionality allows ATM LSRs to transmit cells coming from different VCIs over the same outgoing VCI toward the same destination. This greatly reduces the number of label virtual circuits and the number of labels required in the MPLS network. Implementation of VC merge functionality requires ATM switch firmware and software upgrades because traditional ATM switches do not provide VC merge capability.

Label-Switched Path (LSP)

The LSP is a configured connection between two LSRs in which label-switching techniques are used for packet forwarding.

An LSP is a specific traffic path through an MPLS network. LSPs are provisioned using LDP or Cisco's prestandard TDP, Resource Reservation Protocol with Traffic Engineering extensions (RSVP-TE), Constraint-based Routed LDP (CR-LDP), or extensions to routing protocols such as Multiprotocol BGP.

NOTE	RSVP-TE or CR-LDP can be used to establish a path through an MPLS network. RSVP-TE runs over UDP, and CR-LDP runs over TCP. Although there is no significant difference between RSVP-TE and CR-LDP with regard to scalability, reliability, and operational impact, RSVP-TE has an advantage over CR-LDP: It is better suited for interoperability with IP networks. It supports integrated end-to-end signaling and QoS and real-world multivendor interoperability.

The LSP can be considered the path over a set of LSRs that packets belonging to a certain FEC travel in order to reach their destination.

MPLS allows a hierarchy of labels known as the label stack. It is therefore possible to have different LSPs at different levels of labels for a packet to reach its destination. LSPs are unidirectional. This means that a packet could take a different return path on its way back.

In Figure 3-8, LSR1 and LSR6 are edge LSRs, and LSR2, LSR3, LSR4, and LSR5 are core LSRs. For the purpose of label forwarding, LSR1 and LSR6 are peers at the border gateway level, and LSR2, LSR3, LSR4, and LSR5 are peers at the interior gateway level. This illustration shows two LSPs: an end-to-end Level 1 LSP from LSR1 to LSR6 and a Level 2 LSP through LSR4 and LSR5.

In order to build an LSP, the LSRs make use of the routing protocols and the routes learned from these protocols. They may use other protocols such as RSVP, but they are not required to.

LSP Establishment

LSP establishment can be performed in one of two ways:

- Independent control
- Ordered control

Figure 3-8   *Label-Switched Path (LSP) Levels*

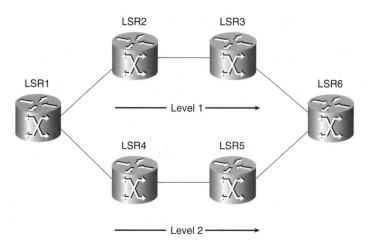

Independent and ordered control for LSP establishment may coexist on the same network without any architecture or interoperability issues. The independent method provides faster convergence and establishment of LSPs, because the LSR can establish and advertise label bindings at any time, without the delay of waiting for messages to propagate in order from one side of the network to the other. LSP establishment immediately follows the convergence of the routing protocols. In the ordered control method, bindings are propagated across the network before the LSP is established. However, the ordered control method provides better loop prevention capabilities.

Independent Control LSP Establishment

In the independent control method of LSP establishment, each LSR partitions its destination prefixes into FECs. Labels are assigned to each FEC, and the label bindings are advertised to the LSRs' neighbors. The LSRs create an LFIB using mappings between the FECs and their next hops. The LSR typically runs a unicast routing protocol such as OSPF or IS-IS and uses information provided by the unicast routing protocol to create the FEC-to-next-hop mapping.

As shown in Figure 3-3, the LFIB stores information about the following fields: incoming label, outgoing label, next hop, and outgoing interface. The LSR creates a local binding for a particular FEC by arbitrarily selecting a label from a pool of free labels in the label information base (LIB) and updates its LFIB. The LFIB *incoming* label is set to the label selected from the label pool. The next hop is set to the Layer 3 address of the next hop associated with the FEC, and the *outgoing interface* is set to the egress interface used to reach the next hop.

After creating the local binding, the LSR distributes information about the local bindings to its neighboring LSRs using LDP or extensions to a modified routing protocol. The binding information distributed consists of a set of tuples of the form *address prefix*, *label*, where *address prefix* identifies the FEC (in the case of simple unicast routing) and label identifies the *label* value that the LSR uses for its local bindings associating the label with that particular FEC.

When an adjacent LSR receives label-binding information from a neighbor, it checks for the presence of a local binding in its LFIB. If the local binding is present, it updates the *outgoing label* for that entry with the newly received label value. The LSR now has a fully populated LFIB entry and is ready for packet forwarding.

If the LSR receives label-binding information from a neighbor and does not have a local binding for the FEC in its LFIB, it has the option of retaining the information (in case the local binding is created later) or discarding it. If the information is discarded, LDP facilitates the neighbor to retransmit binding information. The label-binding information is distributed only among adjacent routers. An LSR will share label-binding information with only a neighboring LSR that shares a common subnet with at least one interface of the local LSR.

As mentioned earlier, link-state routing protocols such as OSPF and IS-IS are unsuitable for the distribution of label-binding information, because these protocols flood their protocol information over a set of routers running the link-state process that might not necessarily be neighboring routers. Distance-vector protocols such as IGRP, RIP, and RIP v2, although suited to distribute label information between adjacent routers, would need extensive modifications to distribute label-binding information.

However, in the case of MPLS traffic engineering, the distribution of constraint-based information must be performed in order to find appropriate paths through the network. LSP traffic-engineered tunnels must be routed with an understanding of the traffic load they need to carry. The constraint information must be distributed across the MPLS network in a consistent way. The flooding mechanism used by link-state routing protocols such as OSPF and IS-IS can help in this regard to create an integrated constraint and forwarding database.

BGP, on the other hand, can be suitably modified to carry label-binding information as a separate BGP attribute. This is due to the fact that BGP can distribute information about address prefixes (FECs) and can also carry the associated label mappings as extended BGP attributes. MPLS uses Extended Multiprotocol BGP to facilitate the distribution of label-binding information—especially for the implementation of MPLS VPNs.

As shown in Figure 3-9, the address prefix 172.16.0.0/16 is directly connected to LSR6. LSR3 and LSR5 use LSR6 as the next hop for the 172.16.0.0/16 FEC.

LSR1 determines that LSR2 is the next hop for the FEC associated with the 172.16.0.0/16 FEC via a unicast routing protocol such as OSPF. LSR1 then arbitrarily selects a label from its label pool using its LIB. Suppose that the value of this label is 50. LSR1 uses this label as an index in its LFIB to find a matching entry to update. After it finds a match, the *incoming label* of the entry is set to 50. The *next hop* is set to LSR2, and the *outgoing interface* is set to S0. At this point, the *outgoing label* has not been assigned a value.

Figure 3-9 *Independent Control LSP Establishment*

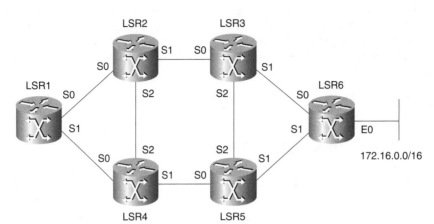

LSR1 then sends its local binding information to LSR2 and LSR4. Now, neither LSR2 nor LSR4 uses LSR1 as a next hop to get to 172.16.0.0/16, so they cannot update their outgoing labels in their LFIB entries for 172.16.0.0/16. However, when LSR2 sends its local bindings to LSR1, it recognizes that this information came from its next hop for 172.16.0.0/16 and uses this information as a remote binding for 172.16.0.0/16. Let's assume that the value of the label arbitrarily selected by LSR3 is 25. LSR1 then uses the label provided by LSR2 to update the *outgoing label* in its LFIB entry associated with the 172.16.0.0/16 FEC. If LSR1 performs an ingress function for the LSP, it does not assign a value for the incoming label.

LSR2 determines that LSR3 is the next hop for the FEC associated with 172.16.0.0/16 FEC. LSR2 then arbitrarily selects a label from its label pool using its LIB. Suppose that the value of this label is 25. LSR2 uses this label as an index in its LFIB to find a matching entry to update. After it finds a match, the *incoming label* of the entry is set to 25. The *next hop* is set to LSR3, and the *outgoing interface* is set to S1. At this point, the *outgoing label* has not been assigned a value.

LSR2 then sends its local binding information to LSR1, LSR3, and LSR4. Now, neither LSR1, LSR3, nor LSR4 uses LSR2 as a next hop to get to 172.16.0.0/16, so they cannot update their outgoing labels in their LFIB entries for 172.16.0.0/16.

However, when LSR3 sends its local bindings to LSR2, LSR5, and LSR6, LSR2 recognizes that this information came from its next hop for 172.16.0.0/16 and uses this information as a remote binding for 172.16.0.0/16. Assume that the value of the label arbitrarily selected by LSR3 is 45. LSR2 then uses the label provided by LSR3 to update the *outgoing label* in its LFIB entry associated with the 172.16.0.0/16 FEC.

Similarly, LSR4 determines that LSR5 is the next hop for the FEC associated with 172.16.0.0/16. LSR4 then arbitrarily selects a label from its label pool using its LIB. Suppose that the value of this label is 65. LSR4 then uses this label as an index in its LFIB to find a matching entry to update. After it finds a match, the *incoming label* of the entry is set to 65. The *next hop* is set to LSR5, and the *outgoing interface* is set to S1. LSR4 then sends its local binding information to LSR1, LSR2, and LSR5. Now, neither LSR1, LSR2, nor LSR5 uses LSR2 as a next hop to get to 172.16.0.0/16 and thus cannot update their outgoing labels in their LFIB entries for 172.16.0.0/16.

However, when LSR5 sends its local bindings to LSR4, LSR3, and LSR6, LSR4 recognizes that this information came from its next hop for 172.16.0.0/16 and uses this information as a remote binding for 172.16.0.0/16. Assume that the value of the label arbitrarily selected by LSR5 is 95. LSR4 then uses the label provided by LSR5 to update the *outgoing label* in its LFIB entry associated with the 172.16.0.0/16 FEC.

When LSR6 sends its local bindings to LSR3 and LSR5, LSR3 and LSR5 recognize that the information came from their next hop for 172.16.0.0/16, and they both use this information as a remote binding for 172.16.0.0/16. Assume that the value of the label arbitrarily selected by LSR6 is 33. LSR3 and LSR5 both use the label provided by LSR6 to update the *outgoing label* in their LFIB entries associated with the 172.16.0.0/16 FEC. LSR6 does not have an outgoing label in the label entry for 172.16.0.0/16 in its LFIB because it is directly connected to the 172.16.0.0/16 network. LSR6 is the edge LSR in this network and pops the label from the packet before forwarding it to the 172.16.0.0/16 network.

At this point, as shown in Table 3-3, all the LSRs have their LFIBs fully populated for the 172.16.0.0/16 FEC and are ready for packet forwarding. When LSR1 receives a packet with a label value of 50, it uses this label as an index in its LFIB to locate the entry it would use for forwarding. After it finds the entry, it swaps the label with the outgoing label value of 25 and forwards the packet over interface S0 to LSR2. LSR2 performs a similar lookup, swaps the label with a label value of 45, and forwards the packet to LSR3 over interface S1. LSR3 performs another LFIB lookup, swaps the label with a label value of 33, and forwards the packet to LSR6 over interface S1. Finally, LSR6 strips the label from the packet and forwards it to its destination over E0. LSR6 could perform either an LFIB lookup or a Layer 3 routing table lookup in the case of a penultimate hop popping of the label at LSR3.

Table 3-3   *LFIB Entries After Label Distribution*

	Incoming Label	Outgoing Label	Next Hop	Outgoing Interface
LSR1	50	25	LSR2	S0
LSR2	25	45	LSR3	S1
LSR3	45	33	LSR6	S1
LSR4	65	95	LSR5	S1
LSR5	95	33	LSR6	S1
LSR6	33	—	LSR6	E0

Ordered Control LSP Establishment

In the ordered control method of LSP establishment, the ingress or egress LSR initiates the LSP setup. Label assignment is controlled in an orderly manner from the egress to the ingress of the LSP. LSP setup may be initiated from either end, the ingress or the egress. The initiator of the LSP makes the selection of FECs, and all LSRs along the LSP use the same FECs. The ordered control of LSP establishment requires that the label bindings propagate over all LSRs before an LSP can be established. This results in slower convergence times than would be provided by independent control. However, the ordered control method has better LSP loop prevention capabilities than the independent control method.

An example of this process is shown in Figure 3-10. In this example, LSR7 is the egress LSR, which initiates LSP establishment. LSR7 knows this because it has a directly connected route to 192.168.0.0/16. Suppose that LSR7 assigns a label with a value of 66 for the 192.168.0.0/16 FEC. It then advertises the local binding to its neighbor LSR6. Upon receipt of the advertisement, LSR6 assigns a new label with a value of 33 for the FEC and advertises the binding to its neighbors, LSR3 and LSR5. The orderly LSP establishment continues in this manner all the way to the ingress or the other end of the LSP at LSR1.

Figure 3-10 *Ordered Control LSP Establishment*

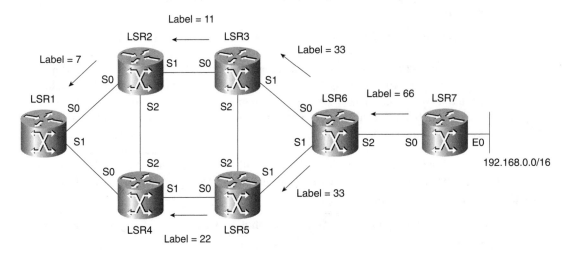

NOTE	Cisco IOS uses the *independent control* mode of LSP establishment for packet-based MPLS and the *ordered control* mode of LSP establishment for ATM MPLS.

Label Distribution Protocol (LDP)

The Label Distribution Protocol (LDP) is used in conjunction with standard network layer routing protocols to distribute label-binding information between LSR devices in a label-switched network. LDP lets an LSR distribute labels to its LDP peers using TCP port 646, whereas TDP uses TCP port 711. The use of TCP as the transport layer protocol results in reliable delivery of LDP information with robust flow control and congestion-handling mechanisms.

NOTE	Cisco's Tag Distribution Protocol (TDP) and the MPLS standards based LDP (Label Distribution Protocol) are nearly identical in function, but use incompatible message formats and some different procedures. Cisco is changing from TDP to a fully compliant LDP. This section focuses on LDP.

When an LSR assigns a label to an FEC, it needs to let its relevant peers know of this label and its meaning. LDP is used for this purpose. A set of labels from the ingress LSR to the egress LSR in an MPLS domain defines an LSP. Labels are maps of network layer routing to the data link layer switched paths. LDP helps in establishing an LSP by using a set of procedures to distribute the labels among the LSR peers.

LDP provides an LSR discovery mechanism to let LSR peers locate each other and establish communication. It defines four classes of messages:

- DISCOVERY messages run over UDP and use multicast HELLO messages to learn about other LSRs to which LDP has a direct connection. It then establishes a TCP connection and an eventual LDP session with its peers. The LDP sessions are bidirectional. The LSR at either end can advertise or request bindings to or from the LSR at the other end of the connection.

- ADJACENCY messages run over TCP and provide session initialization using the INITIALIZATION message at the start of LDP session negotiation. This information includes the label allocation mode, keepalive timer values, and the label range to be used between the two LSRs. LDP keepalives are sent periodically using KEEPALIVE messages. Teardown of LDP sessions between peer LSRs results if the KEEPALIVE messages are not received within the timer interval.

- LABEL ADVERTISEMENT messages provide label-binding advertisements using LABEL MAPPING messages that advertise the bindings between FECs and labels. LABEL WITHDRAWAL messages are used to reverse the binding process. LABEL RELEASE messages are used by LSRs that have received label mapping information and want to release the label because they no longer have a need for it.

- NOTIFICATION messages provide advisory information and also signal error information between peer LSRs that have an LDP session established between them.

LDP runs over TCP to provide reliable messages, with the exception of LDP DISCOVERY messages, which run over UDP. The LDP messages are specified as a set of TLV (type, length, value) objects. LDP label distribution and assignment may be performed in several different modes. They are discussed in the following sections.

Downstream-on-Demand Mode LDP

The MPLS architecture allows an LSR to explicitly request, from its next hop for a particular FEC, a label binding for that FEC. This is known as *downstream-on-demand* label distribution. This mode uses LABEL REQUEST messages to request label mappings from downstream LSRs. The LABEL REQUEST ABORT message is used to abort the LABEL REQUEST message during or prior to the completion of the request.

Unsolicited Downstream Mode LDP

The MPLS architecture also allows an LSR to distribute bindings to LSRs that have not explicitly requested them. This is known as *unsolicited downstream* label distribution. Both of these label distribution techniques may be used in the same network at the same time. On any given label distribution adjacency, the upstream LSR and the downstream LSR must agree on which technique is to be used. This is negotiated between the LSRs during LDP session negotiation using the INITIALIZATION message exchange.

NOTE   Cisco IOS uses the *unsolicited downstream* distribution mode LDP for packet-based MPLS and *downstream-on-demand* mode LDP for ATM MPLS.

Liberal Label Retention Mode LDP

If an LSR supports liberal label retention mode, it maintains the bindings between a label and a FEC that are received from LSRs and that are not its next hop for that FEC.

An LSR may receive a label binding for a particular FEC from a peer LSR even though the LSR peer is not the next hop for that FEC. It then has the choice of whether to keep track of such bindings or discard them. If the LSR keeps track of such bindings, it may immediately begin using the binding again if the peer LSR eventually becomes its next hop for the FEC in question. If the LSR discards such bindings, and if the peer becomes the next hop later, the binding will have to be reacquired using LDP.

Conservative Label Retention Mode LDP

If an LSR supports conservative label retention mode, it discards the bindings between a label and a FEC that are received from LSRs and that are not its next hop for that FEC. The LSR only maintains label-to-FEC mappings, which it requires for packet forwarding. Conservative mode does not waste labels and is widely used on ATM-LSRs.

NOTE   Liberal label retention mode allows for quicker adaptation to routing changes, and conservative label retention mode requires an LSR to maintain fewer labels. Cisco IOS uses liberal label retention mode for packet-based MPLS and conservative label retention mode for ATM MPLS. LDP is available from IOS release 12.2T onward.

NOTE   Combining liberal retention mode with independent control LSP establishment results in faster TDP or LDP convergence. Convergence occurs upon link failure. However, link-state IGP routing convergence must complete before LSPs can be reestablished. This might result in temporary packet loss due to the inability of the LSRs to forward labeled packets.

Loop Survival, Detection, and Prevention in MPLS

LSPs are built using LDP, TDP, or extensions to routing protocols such as BGP, PIM, or RSVP. The LDP makes use of information gathered by the Layer 3 routing protocols and therefore is susceptible to routing loops unless the Layer 3 protocol itself can avoid loop prevention. In spite of attempts by routing protocols to establish loop-free routes, almost all protocols can lead to looping during transient conditions.

In distance-vector routing protocols such as RIP, nodes do not have a complete topological view of the network. In such networks, *counting to infinity* could occur, where the metric for a looping route is incremented and advertised among the nodes until it reaches its maximum value.

In link-state routing protocols such as OSPF, each node maintains the entire topological database of its routing area in the network. In such networks, there is a possibility of transient routing loops if synchronization of the database update is not achieved upon topological change—especially during the period immediately following the failure of a link.

The Effect of Routing Loops on MPLS

If routing loops are not prevented, MPLS-level traffic is affected in the following ways:

- **LSP control packet looping**—The packets used for LSP establishment are forwarded in an endless routing loop, and the LSP is never properly established end-to-end. This continues until the routing loop breaks.

- **MPLS data packet looping**—Data packets injected into an established looping LSP continue to be label-switched in the LSP until the routing loop breaks.

Loop Control in MPLS

There are three basic ways to control loops in MPLS:

- Loop survival
- Loop detection
- Loop prevention

Loop Survival

In this method of loop control, the LSPs are allowed to form loops. However, looping packets are not allowed to impact the transmission of nonlooping packets. MPLS nodes that have the ability to perform time-to-live (TTL) decrement for LSPs have this capability. Non-TTL segments such as ATM links use per-VC buffer space allocation on ATM switches as a loop-control mechanism.

Loop Survival in TTL Segments

IP forwarding uses the TTL field in a packet, which is decremented at every IP hop. If it reaches 0, the packet is assumed to be looping and is discarded. This lets routers conserve resources and focus on forwarding nonlooping packets and updating routing tables. As soon as the routing tables have converged and are stable, the loop is normally broken, unless there is a configuration error on one of the routers.

MPLS uses a similar approach to handle loops that IP uses. MPLS labeled packets using a shim header placed between the data link and network layer headers carry a TTL field that operates just like the IP TTL to let packets caught in transient loops be discarded. Figure 3-11 shows a looped LSP. However, as shown in Figure 3-12, the TTL decrements to a value of 0, and the loop is eventually broken.

Loop Survival in Non-TTL Segments

The TTL field is unavailable on ATM links. Such links are referred to as non-TTL segments by the MPLS architecture. ATM LSRs are ATM switches with Layer 3 routing capability. The buffer space consumed by a single virtual circuit can be limited via configuration. This method of controlled buffer allocation is used to control loops. This way, packets stuck in a loop can consume only a limited amount of switch buffer space and will not overwhelm the ATM LSR. The switch should still be able to forward routing update packets, which ensures that routing eventually converges and that transient loops are broken. Nontransient loops created due to misconfiguration can also be suppressed, because the ATM LSR can still forward control packets and nonlooping packets. Only looping packets are starved of resources in terms of buffer space.

Figure 3-11 *Looped Label-Switched Path*

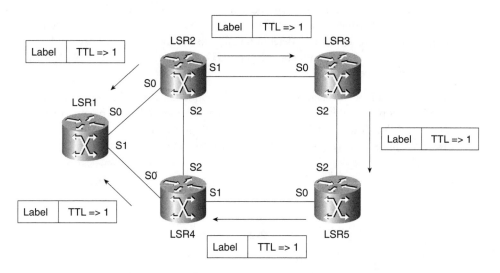

LSRs receive labels with TTL => 1 and forward
the packets in the looped LSP

Figure 3-12 *LSP Loop Detection Using TTL*

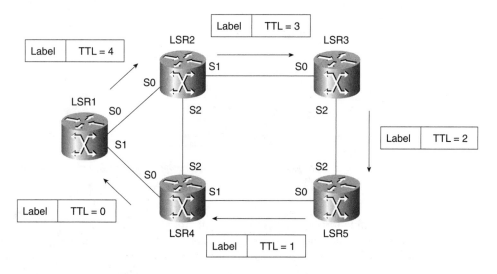

Loop Detection

This method of loop control allows an LSP to form a loop, but it can detect and disconnect the loop in a short period of time. LDP and Cisco's TDP are examples of protocols that support loop detection. Loop detection makes use of the techniques used in loop survival methods such as TTL decrement and per-VC buffer space allocation on ATM switches as a loop-control mechanism.

In addition to loop survival techniques, a technique known as the *hop count* approach is used for loop control in Cisco's Tag switching technology. The hop count method works just like TTL. However, the hop count information is carried in LDP or TDP request and response messages. The hop count mechanism is shown in Figure 3-13.

Figure 3-13 *Hop Count Method of Loop Detection*

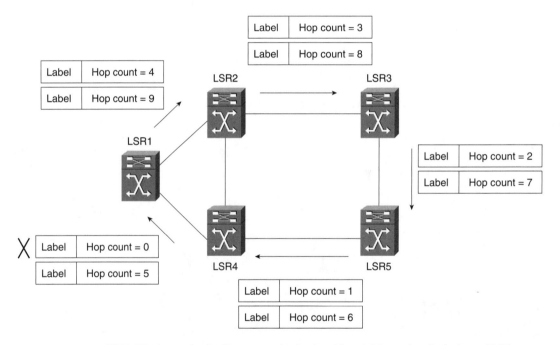

ATM LSRs decrement the *Hop count* value by 1 and forward the packets in the looped LSP.
The LSP loop is broken when *Hop count* = 0

On-demand binding forces requests to propagate from the point of topology change to the egress of the MPLS network. Assume that the hop count variable starts with a value of 7. This value is decremented at each and every ATM LSR hop participating in the loop and eventually reaches 0. When the value reaches 0, the label binding fails, and the LSP is torn down. After the routing converges and stabilizes, a new binding request is issued, resulting in the formation of a new LSP.

Loop Prevention

The loop prevention method of loop control prevents the formation of a looping path before any packets are sent on it. With this method, LSPs are categorized as follows:

- Nonstate merging LSPs
- State merging LSPs

Nonstate Merging LSPs

A single incoming link state exists for each outgoing link state. LSPs built using CR-LDP or RSVP belong to this type. Each control message used to request a label contains a list of LSR node addresses, in which each address is added by an LSR when the LSR forwards the message. If an LSR finds its own address in the receiving message, it detects a loop and prevents the looping LSP from being built.

State Merging LSPs

Multiple incoming link states exist for each outgoing link state. LSPs built using LDP belong to this type. State merging LSPs have two methods of loop prevention:

- Path vector diffusion
- Colored thread method

Path Vector Diffusion (PD) Algorithm   In the PD algorithm, an LSP loop can be prevented from forming by using a list of LSR addresses, referred to as the path vector. The path vector is a list of LSRs that a LABEL REQUEST or a LABEL MAPPING message has passed through. The LABEL REQUEST message sent by an LSR to its neighbor contains a path vector with just the address of the requesting LSR. The receiving LSR adds its own address to the vector before issuing a label request for this FEC to its next hop. If a routing loop causes a REQUEST or MAPPING message to travel in a loop, eventually the LSR will see its own address in the REQUEST or MAPPING message and thus will detect the loop. In this case, it prevents the looping LSP from being built.

NOTE   Another form of the PD algorithm does not allow the LSR node to store the path vector. The LSRs for this variant of the PD create, for each incoming label mapping, a query with a path vector containing the creator's address only. This query is sent to the upstream node, which acknowledges each query.

For more details on the PD algorithm variants, refer to "Loop-Free Routing Using Diffusion Computations," IEEE/ACM Trans. Net Vol. 1, No. 1., J. Garcia-Lune-Aceves.

Colored Thread (CT) Algorithm   The Colored Thread method of loop prevention requires the use of the ordered control method of LSP establishment. The colored thread method can be modeled by considering a colored thread extended from the ingress to the egress of the LSP. Any intermediate LSR would sense a loop if the thread loops back on itself. This would trigger the LSR to prevent the looping LSP from being built. The LSRs would then wait for the routing tables to converge and stabilize before attempting to extend another thread from ingress to egress. The Colored Thread algorithm lends itself well to LSP loop prevention in ATM LSRs.

Figure 3-14 *Colored Thread Algorithm Method of Loop Prevention*

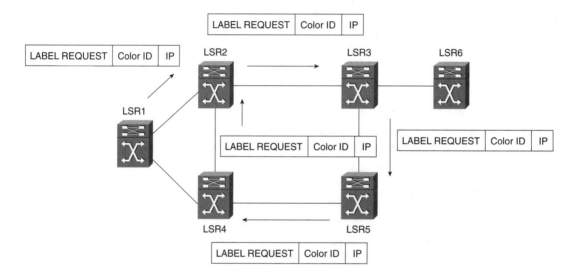

Extending the Thread   Consider the network shown in Figure 3-14. Assume that LSR1 tries to establish an LSP using downstream-on-demand label allocation. LSR1 extends a thread by issuing a LABEL REQUEST message. This thread includes a *color* that is LSR1's IP address along with a unique identifier. As the LSP gets built and the LABEL REQUEST message proceeds over nodes LSR2, LSR3, LSR4, and LSR5, each node stores the color of the incoming thread and passes on the same color in the outgoing label request. Eventually, a label request from LSR4 arrives at LSR2. Because this label request contains the same color that was stored at LSR2 when the LABEL REQUEST from LSR1 was received, LSR2 detects that a loop is present. At this point, LSR2 stops forwarding the LABEL REQUEST message and does not provide a response to the label request. This breaks down the LSP and the potential loop.

Rewinding the Thread   After the routing tables converge and the routes stabilize, the loop is broken. This might happen, for example, if LSR3 decides that its next hop for this LSP is not LSR5 but LSR6. LSR3 withdraws the label request it issued to LSR5 and requests a label from LSR6. Because LSR6 is the egress of the MPLS domain (its next hop for this FEC is not an LSR), it can now return a label binding to LSR3, which can return a binding to LSR2, and so on, back to LSR1, causing a loop-free LSP to be established.

Summary

MPLS networks use labels to forward packets. The ingress MPLS node assigns a packet to a particular FEC just once, as the packet enters the network. The FEC to which the packet is assigned is encoded as a short fixed-length value known as a *label*. The packets are labeled before they are forwarded. At subsequent hops, there is no further analysis of the packet's network layer header. The label is used as an index into a table, which specifies the next hop, and a new label. The old label is replaced with the new label, and the packet is forwarded to its next hop.

MPLS nodes have two architectural planes: the MPLS forwarding plane and the MPLS control plane. MPLS nodes can perform Layer 3 routing or Layer 2 switching in addition to switching labeled packets. The MPLS forwarding plane is responsible for forwarding packets based on values contained in attached labels. The forwarding plane uses an LFIB maintained by the MPLS node to forward labeled packets. The MPLS control plane is responsible for populating and maintaining the LFIB.

The LSR is a device that implements the MPLS control and forwarding components. The LSR forwards a packet based on the value of a label encapsulated in the packet. The LSR can also forward native Layer 3 packets. LSRs are MPLS-enabled routers or MPLS-enabled ATM switches that use labels to forward traffic.

The LSP is a configured connection between two LSRs in which label-switching techniques are used for packet forwarding. An LSP is a specific traffic path through an MPLS network. LSPs are provisioned using LDP, TDP, RSVP-TE, CR-LDP, or extensions to routing protocols.

LSP establishment can be performed in one of two ways: with independent control or ordered control. Independent and ordered control for LSP establishment may coexist on the same network without any architecture or interoperability issues. The independent method provides faster convergence and establishment of LSPs, because the LSR can establish and advertise label bindings at any time without the delay of waiting for messages to propagate in order from one side of the network to the other. LSP establishment immediately follows the convergence of the routing protocols. In the ordered control method, bindings are propagated across the network before the LSP is established. However, the ordered control method provides better loop-prevention capabilities.

LDP is used in conjunction with standard network layer routing protocols to distribute label-binding information between LSR devices in a label-switched network. LDP lets an LSR distribute labels to its LDP peers using TCP. The use of TCP as the transport layer protocol results in reliable delivery of LDP information with robust flow control and congestion-handling mechanisms.

The MPLS architecture allows an LSR to explicitly request, from its next hop for a particular FEC, a label binding for that FEC. This is known as downstream-on-demand label distribution. The MPLS architecture also allows an LSR to distribute bindings to LSRs that have not explicitly requested them. This is known as unsolicited downstream label distribution. Both of these label distribution techniques may be used in the same network at the same time.

There are three basic ways to control loops in MPLS: loop survival, loop detection, and loop prevention. In the loop survival mechanism, looping packets are not allowed to impact the transmission of nonlooping packets. MPLS nodes that have the ability to perform TTL decrement for LSPs have this capability. Non-TTL segments such as ATM links use per-VC buffer space allocation on ATM switches as a loop-control mechanism. In addition to loop-survival techniques, a technique known as the hop count approach is used for loop control in loop detection mechanisms. The hop count method works just like TTL. However, the hop count information is carried in LDP or TDP request and response messages. The loop prevention method of loop control prevents the formation of a looping path before any packets are sent on it.

This chapter covers the following topics:

- **Overview of VPNs**—Virtual Private Networks identify closed user groups over a common network infrastructure. This section examines and compares TDM, X.25, Frame Relay, SMDS, and ATM services. It also discusses private IP VPNs.

- **Connection-oriented VPNs**—Connection-oriented VPNs can be built on Layer 2 or Layer 3 infrastructures. This section discusses Layer 2 VPNs built using connection-oriented point-to-point overlays such as Frame Relay and ATM virtual connections. It also discusses Layer 3 connection-oriented VPNs such as Generic Route Encapsulation and IP Security.

- **Connectionless VPNs**—Connectionless VPNs do not require a predefined logical or virtual circuit provisioned between two endpoints to establish a connection between the two endpoints. This section discusses connectionless VPNs such as conventional IP and MPLS.

- **Comparison of VPN technologies**—This section compares the various VPN technologies and provides recommendations for the choice of a VPN technology based on application, security, scalability, cost, and other factors.

- **Advantages of MPLS VPNs**—This section discusses the advantages of deploying MPLS VPNs from a service provider perspective. Topics such as scalability, security, addressing, traffic engineering, and quality of service are discussed.

CHAPTER 4

Virtual Private Networks

Overview of VPNs

Service providers have been offering VPN (Virtual Private Network) services to enterprise customers since the inception of TDM-based networks and X.25 packet-switched data networks. More recently, Frame Relay and ATM-based networks with multiple classes of service have largely replaced X.25 and dedicated leased-line circuits. Service providers charge either a fixed or usage-based rate for VPN services.

The term VPN has been in use with carriers and service providers to identify closed user group virtual circuits since the creation and deployment of X.25, Frame Relay, SMDS, and ATM services. More recently, the term has been used by Enterprise Network Management to identify private IP closed user groups.

Enterprise customers have long realized the advantages of outsourcing their IP network services and consolidation of data, voice, and video services. They want Managed IP services with end-to-end service-level agreements (SLAs) and a guaranteed quality of service (QoS).

The IP-based VPN is rapidly becoming the foundation of the delivery of consolidated data and voice and video services. Many service providers are offering value-added applications on top of their VPN transport networks.

Emerging services such as e-commerce, application hosting, and multimedia applications will allow service providers to generate new incremental revenue and maintain a long-term competitive advantage. Two unique and complementary VPN architectures based on IP Security (IPSec) and Multiprotocol Label Switching (MPLS) technologies are emerging to form the predominant foundations for the delivery of consolidated services. This chapter discusses the various VPN topologies and architectures available today.

The IP VPN feature for MPLS allows a Cisco IOS network to deploy scalable IPv4 Layer 3 VPN backbone services. An IP VPN is the foundation that companies use to deploy or administer value-added services, including applications and data hosting network commerce and telephony services to business customers.

In Enterprise networks, IP-based intranets have fundamentally changed the way companies conduct their business. Companies are moving their business applications to their intranets to extend over a wide-area network (WAN). Companies are also embracing the needs of their customers, suppliers, and partners by using extranets (an intranet that encompasses multiple businesses). With extranets, companies reduce business process costs by facilitating supply-chain automation, electronic data interchange (EDI), and other forms of network commerce. To take advantage of this business opportunity, service providers must have an IP VPN infrastructure that delivers private network services to businesses over a shared infrastructure.

Because most interexchange carriers (IXCs), incumbent local exchange carriers (ILECs), and competitive local exchange carriers (CLECs) own an existing ATM and Frame Relay infrastructure, MPLS tends to be the technology of choice for building stable, secure, scalable VPNs.

Connection-Oriented VPNs

Connection-oriented VPNs can be built on Layer 2 or Layer 3 infrastructures. VPNs built using connection-oriented, point-to-point overlays such as Frame Relay and ATM virtual connections are examples of Layer 2 connection-oriented VPN networks.

VPNs built using a full or partial mesh of tunnels utilizing IPSec (with encryption for privacy) or Generic Routing Encapsulation (GRE) are examples of Layer 3 connection-oriented VPN networks.

Access VPNs are circuit-switched, connection-oriented VPNs that provide a temporary secure connection for remote access between individuals (mobile users or telecommuters) and a corporate intranet or extranet over a shared service provider network with the same policies as a private network. Access VPNs that use dial access into an ISP point of presence (PoP) with transport over the public Internet and ultimate access into a corporate intranet.

The key deficiency of connection-oriented VPNs is scalability. Specifically, connection-oriented VPNs without meshed connections between customer sites are not optimal. Furthermore, in the case of Layer 3 IP VPNs, you cannot truly guarantee a firm QoS (Quality of Service) over the public Internet. From the perspective of telecom management, the complexity associated with provisioning ATM or Frame Relay Virtual Circuits is comparable to the complexity of provisioning private lines.

Virtual circuit-based VPNs require service providers to build and manage separate virtual circuits or logical paths between each pair of communicating sites within each user group. This requirement equates to building a mesh of virtual circuits for each customer.

Layer 2 Connection-Oriented VPNs

Layer 2 connection-oriented networks form the basis of the overlay VPN model. In the overlay VPN model, the service provider provides the virtual circuits, and the routing information is exchanged directly between the CPE routers.

TDM-Based Networks

Most service providers offer private-line networks to enterprise customers. This involves digital multiplexing, in which two or more apparently simultaneous channels are derived from a bit stream by interleaving bits from successive channels. Typically, service providers or carriers offer DS1 and DS3 circuits in North America. E1 and E3 circuits are commonly found in Europe and Asia Pacific.

As shown in Figure 4-1, Customers A and B share the physical infrastructure of the carrier, but they are logically separated from each other by port mappings and electronic cross-connections provisioned by the carrier. The cross-connections are typically provisioned on a DACS (Digital Automatic and Crossconnect System). However, physical crossconnects are also used extensively.

Figure 4-1   *Leased Line VPN—Logical View*

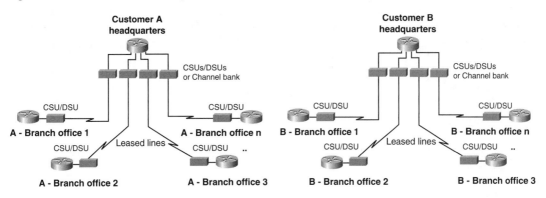

Figure 4-2 shows the physical connectivity among Customer A, Customer B, and the service provider network.

The TDM network is the simplest form of a Virtual Private Network that assures high-quality fixed bandwidth to customers. Most carriers offer bandwidth as multiples of 64 kbps, which is the bandwidth of a single DS0 channel. For more information on TDM, refer to the section "Circuit Switching and TDM" in Chapter 2, "WAN Technologies and MPLS."

Frame-Based VPNs

Frame-based VPNs such as Frame Relay and X.25 use logical paths as defined by switched and permanent virtual circuits. As shown in Figure 4-3, multiple closed user groups or customers share the service provider's switched infrastructure. Customers perceive virtual circuits that have been exclusively provisioned for their private use. These PVCs or SVCs can be provisioned with a fixed CIR and port speed (local loop access line bandwidth).

Figure 4-2   *Leased Line VPN—Physical View*

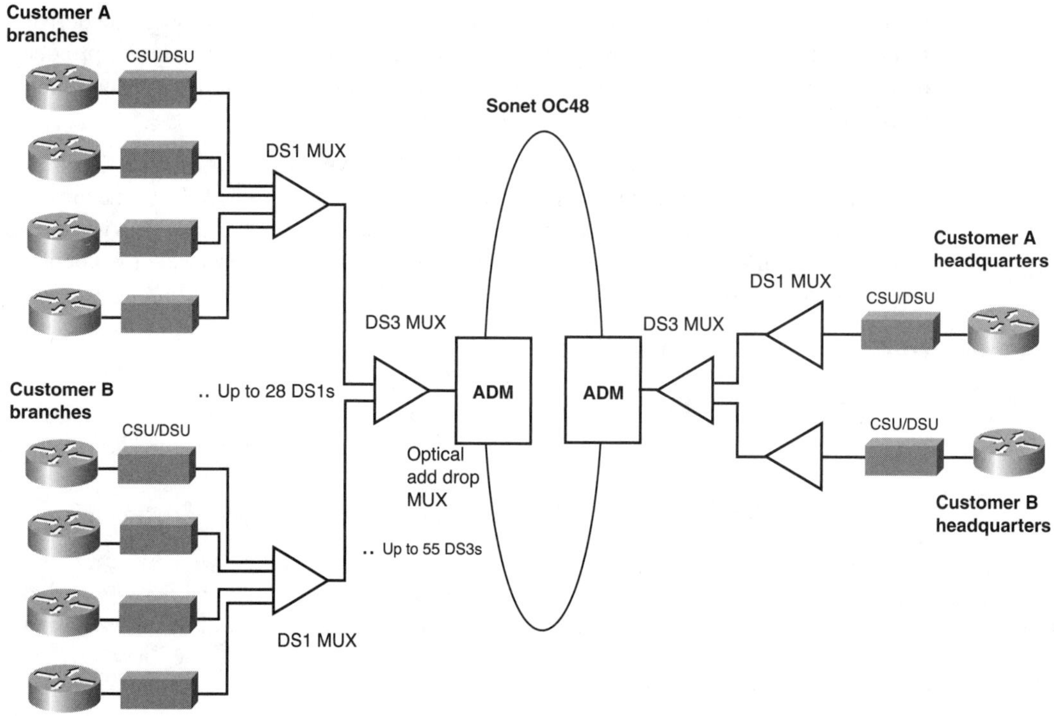

Figure 4-4 shows the physical Frame Relay network. Customers A and B both connect to various Frame Relay points of presence (POPs) using TDM local loops. The Frame Relay protocol is run between the local CPE FRAD (router) and the Frame Relay switch. The Frame Relay interworking function converts Frame Relay frames into ATM cells for transport across the ATM backbone.

For more details on Frame Relay technology, refer to the section "Packet and Cell Switching" in Chapter 2.

NOTE   X.25 uses X.25 frames at Layer 2 and X.25 packets at Layer 3, unlike Frame Relay, which uses only Layer 2 framing. X.25 service providers normally provision X.25 on-demand SVCs or fixed PVCs identified by a Logical Channel Identifier (LCI). The LCI includes a 4-bit Logical Group Number (LGN) and an 8-bit Logical Channel Number (LCN). X.25 uses Link Access Procedure Balanced (LAPB) as its Layer 2 framing protocol.

For more information on the X.25 protocol, refer to the International Telecommunications Union—Telecommunication Standardization sector, Recommendation X.25, 1996. This document can be downloaded from www.itu.int/itudoc/itu-t/rec/x/x1-199/s_x25.html.

Figure 4-3   *Logical Frame Relay VPN Architecture*

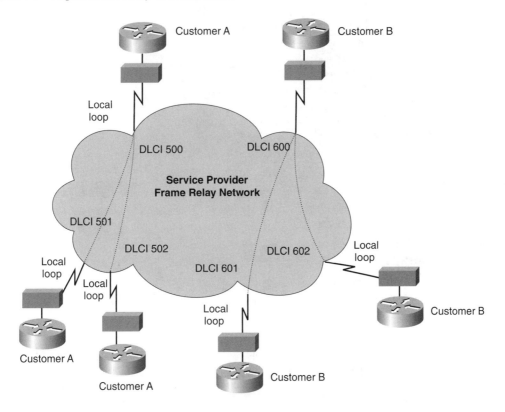

Cell-Based VPNs

Cell-based VPNs such as ATM and SMDS use logical paths as defined by switched and permanent virtual circuits. As shown in Figure 4-5, multiple closed user groups or customers share the Service Providers Switched infrastructure. Customers perceive virtual circuits that have been exclusively provisioned for their private use. These PVCs or SVCs can be provisioned with a class of service such as CBR, VBR-RT, VBR-NRT, ABR, or UBR. ATM also enables the provisioning of soft PVCs, which are a hybrid of SVCs and PVCs.

Figure 4-4   *Physical Frame Relay VPN Architecture*

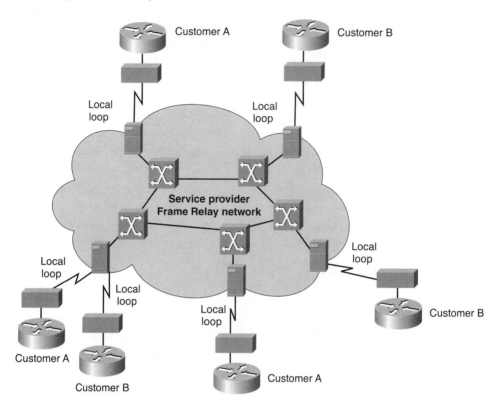

Figure 4-6 shows the physical ATM network. Customers A and B both connect to various
ATM points of presence (POPs) using clear-channel TDM local loops or SONET/SDH. The
ATM routers at the CPE use ATM virtual circuits as a Layer 2 transport mechanism to carry
IP or any other Layer 3 protocol.

Layer 3 Connection-Oriented VPNs

Layer 3 connection-oriented networks form the basis of the tunneled VPN model. The GRE
and IP Security (IPSec) models provide a point-to-point tunneled model over an IP intranet
or the public Internet, whereas virtual private dialup networks (VPDNs) provide a hybrid
combination of dialup along with a secure tunnel connection over the Internet to an
enterprise aggregation point such as a *home gateway.*

Figure 4-5   *Logical ATM VPN Architecture*

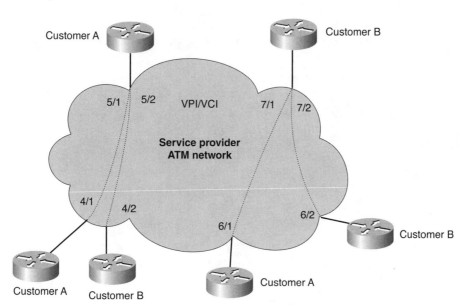

GRE Tunneled VPNs

Generic Route Encapsulation (GRE) tunnels can be used to create point-to-point IP connections. A combination of these GRE tunnels can be used to build a VPN. However, the lack of inherent security by virtue of the lack of encryption makes GRE tunnels susceptible to security violations.

As shown in Figure 4-7, GRE tunnels are useful for building VPNs within a service provider's private IP backbone network. They are also useful for tunneling non-IP Layer 3 traffic across a private IP network.

Figure 4-6   *Physical ATM VPN Architecture*

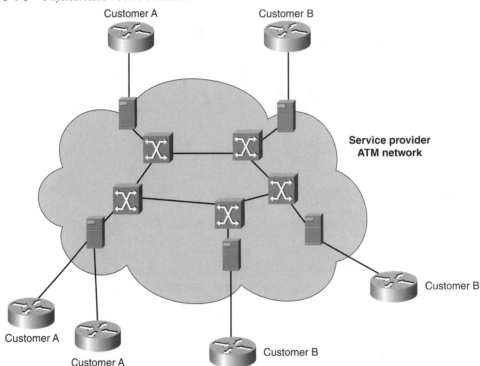

IPSec Tunneled VPNs

IPSec is a highly secure technology that uses a combination of encryption and a tunneling mechanism, which protects packet payloads as they traverse an IP network. IPSec is normally implemented over untrusted public IP networks such as the Internet. A combination of point-to-point IPSec tunnels can be used to construct a VPN over a public IP network. Most IPSec architectures are implemented on the CPE, and service providers would normally provide Managed IPSec VPN services. An example of an IPSec network topology is shown in Figure 4-7. For mobile users and telecommuters who require secure remote access, IPSec is the only practical option at present to enable secure remote access VPNs.

NOTE   VPDNs using L2F and L2TP also provide secure remote access although not nearly as secure as IPSec. The strength of IPSec resides in it strong payload encryption using variations of DES (Data Encryption Standard) such as 168 bit 3DES and header authentication.

Virtual Private Dialup Network

Telecommuters and mobile users remotely access corporate networks over the Public Switched Telephone Network (PSTN) or ISDN. As shown in Figure 4-8, Virtual Private

Dialup Network (VPDN) services are mostly implemented over a service provider's private IP backbone. The protocols used to implement VPDN service over an IP network include Layer 2 Forwarding (L2F) and Layer 2 Tunneling Protocol (L2TP).

Figure 4-7   *GRE and IPSec Tunneled VPNs*

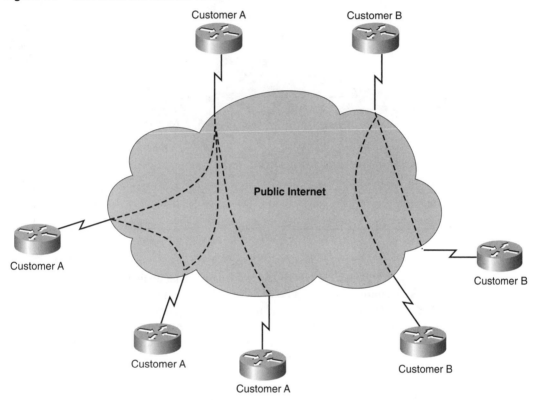

The remote users initiate a dial-up connection to the Network Access Server (NAS) using PPP. The NAS authenticates the call and forwards the call via L2F or L2TP to the customer's home gateway. The home gateway accepts the call forwarded by the NAS, performs additional authentication, authorization, and terminates the user PPP session. The AAA (Authentication, Authorization and Accounting) function can also be performed by an AAA server such as a TACACS+ server. All PPP session parameters are negotiated between the dial-up user and the home gateway. Access VPNs such as VPDNs suffer from certain limitations in the sense that they are not scalable and do not provide any-to-any connectivity.

The Point-to-Point Tunneling Protocol (PPTP) along with Microsoft Point-to-Point Encryption (MPPE) allow Cisco VPNs to use PPTP as the tunneling protocol. PPTP is a network protocol that enables the secure transfer of data from a remote client to a private enterprise server by creating a VPN across an IP-based network. PPTP utilizes voluntary tunneling (also referred to as client-initiated tunneling), which allows clients to configure and establish encrypted tunnels to tunnel servers without an intermediate NAS participating in tunnel negotiation and establishment.

Figure 4-8   *Virtual Private Dialup Network (VPDN)*

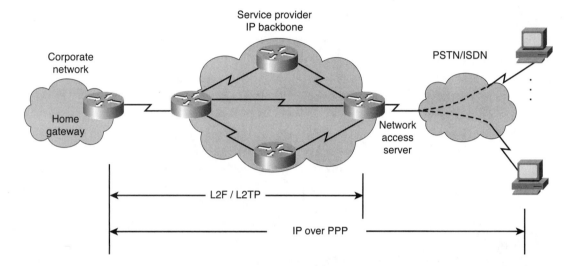

PPTP utilizes MPPE as its encryption technology over a dialup line or a VPN tunnel. MPPE works as a subfeature of Microsoft Point-to-Point Compression (MPPC). MPPE uses either 40- or 128-bit keys. All keys are derived from the user's clear-text authentication password. The MPPE algorithm is stream cipher; therefore, the encrypted and decrypted frames are the same size as the original frame. The Cisco implementation of MPPE is fully interoperable with that of Microsoft and uses all available options, including historyless mode.

Connectionless VPNs

Connectionless VPNs do not require a predefined logical or virtual circuit provisioned between two endpoints to establish a connection between the two endpoints.

Layer 3 Connectionless VPNs

Layer 3 connectionless networks form the basis of the peer-to-peer model. In the peer-to-peer model, the customer routing information is exchanged between the CPE and the service provider's routers.

Conventional IP VPNs

Many carriers provide a *managed IP service*s offering that basically lets customers hook up their CPE IP routers to a service provider's private IP backbone. Most IP service providers run an IP network over a Layer 2 infrastructure such as an ATM or Frame Relay network. An example of a conventional IP VPN is shown in Figure 4-9.

Figure 4-9   *Conventional IP Router-Based VPN Network*

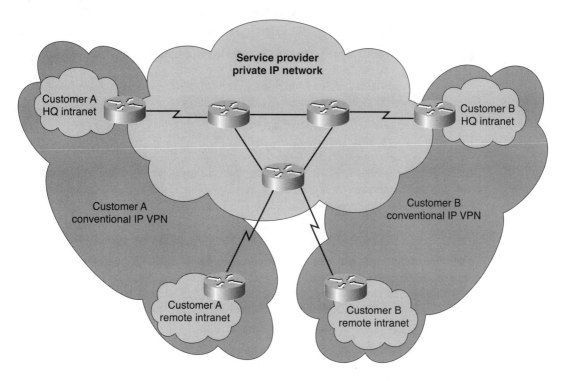

The service provider typically configures multiple routing protocols or runs multiple routing processes on its backbone routers for various customers. Typically, the Cisco Routing engine supports the operation of multiple routing protocols in a single router in order to connect networks that use different routing protocols. The routing protocols available are inherently designed to operate independently of each other. Each protocol collects different types of information and reacts to topology changes in its own way. For example, RIP uses a hop count metric and EIGRP uses a five-element vector of metric information.

More importantly, a Cisco router can typically handle simultaneous operation of up to 30 dynamic IP routing processes. The combination of routing processes on a router can consist of the following protocols (with the limits noted):

- Up to 30 IGRP routing processes
- Up to 30 OSPF routing processes
- One IS-IS process

- One RIP routing process
- One BGP routing process
- Up to 30 EGP routing processes

Customers perceive a private IP VPN by virtue of a combination of access lists, routing protocols, and processes.

The biggest issue facing managed IP service providers is scalability and complexity of implementation. The number of available routing protocols and routing processes supported per router platform sometimes forces service providers to deploy separate routers for each customer VPN at the service provider's point of presence.

MPLS VPNs

MPLS VPNs are connectionless. MPLS separates traffic and provides privacy without the need for Layer 2 tunneling protocols and encryption. This eliminates significant complexity during the provisioning process.

MPLS solves the scalability issues encountered by Frame Relay and ATM deployments by allowing service providers to provision multiple VPNs for multiple customers without the chore of provisioning tens to hundreds of virtual circuits for each and every closed user group or customer. An example of an MPLS VPN is shown in Figure 4-10. Customers A and B share the service provider infrastructure while having the ability to form their own closed user groups with utmost security. They also can run their own routing protocols.

The MPLS model requires the CPE routers to directly exchange routing information with provider edge routers, as opposed to exchanging routing information with all other CPE routers that are members of the VPN. Members of the VPN are identified as belonging to the closed user group by means of labels. These labels carry next-hop information, service attributes, and a VPN identifier, which keeps communications within a VPN private.

At the ingress into the provider network, incoming packets from the CPE router are processed, and labels are assigned based on the physical interface these packets were received from. Labels are applied using VRF (VPN Routing and Forwarding) tables. The forwarding tables are predetermined, and incoming packets are examined only at the ingress LSR. The core devices or Provider (P) LSRs merely forward these packets based on labels.

MPLS makes service provider-routed backbones VPN-capable and provides Layer 3 visibility even across Layer 2 infrastructures. This makes it possible to create closed user groups and associate services with them. MPLS VPN design and configuration are discussed in detail in Chapter 5, "Packet-Based MPLS VPNs."

Figure 4-10 *MPLS Virtual Private Network*

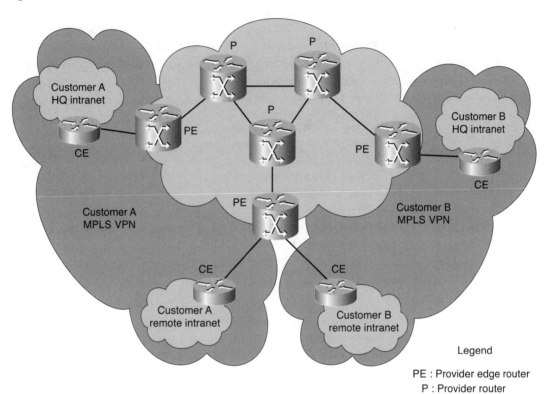

Comparison of VPN Technologies

To address the unique needs and requirements of varied enterprise customers, service providers should consider using both MPLS and IPSec in their VPN deployment mix. Each of these technologies has its relative strengths and complements the other in an end-to-end secure VPN environment extending over the service provider's secure infrastructure as well as circuits over the public Internet.

The decision matrix in Table 4-1 provides a comparison of the various VPN technologies and recommendations for the choice of a VPN technology based on application, security, scalability, cost, and other factors.

Table 4-1   *VPN Provisioning Platform Decision Matrix*

	Comment	Layer 2 Virtual Circuits	Layer 3 Tunnels	MPLS VPNs
Ease of setup and management	Must have advanced monitoring and automated flow-through systems to quickly roll out new services, enforce security and QoS policies, and support Service-Level Agreements (SLAs).	Low	Medium	High
Security	Must offer different levels of security, including tunneling, encryption, traffic separation, authentication, and access control.	High	High	High
Scalability	Must be able to scale the provisioning of VPN services from small and medium-sized businesses to large enterprise customers.	Medium	Medium	High
QoS	Must be able to assign priority to mission-critical or delay-sensitive traffic and manage congestion across varying bandwidth rates.	High	Must be implemented using other technologies	High
Provisioning costs	Direct and indirect costs of provisioning the VPNs.	High	Medium	Low

Advantages of MPLS VPNs

This section covers the following advantages of MPLS VPNs:

- Scalability
- Security
- Ease of VPN creation
- Flexible addressing
- Standards-based
- Flexible architecture
- End-to-end priority services
- Consolidation
- Traffic engineering
- Centralized service

- Integrated class of service (CoS) support
- Migration
- Centralized management and provisioning via Cisco Service Management (CSM)

Scalability

MPLS was designed specifically for highly scalable solutions, enabling tens of thousands of VPNs over the same network. MPLS-based VPNs use the peer model and Layer 3 connectionless architecture to leverage a highly scalable VPN solution. The peer model requires a customer site to peer with only one provider edge (PE) router as opposed to all other CPE or customer edge (CE) routers that are members of the VPN. The connectionless architecture allows the creation of VPNs in Layer 3, eliminating the need for tunnels or VCs.

Security

MPLS VPNs offer the same level of security as connection-oriented VPNs (such as Frame Relay and ATM). Packets from one VPN do not cross into another VPN involuntarily. Security is provided at the edge of the provider network, ensuring that packets received from a customer are placed on the correct VPN. At the backbone, VPN traffic is kept separate. Spoofing (an attempt to gain access to a PE router) is nearly impossible, because the packets received from customers are IP packets that must be received on a particular interface or subinterface to be uniquely identified with a VPN label.

Ease of VPN Creation

Specific point-to-point connection maps or topologies are not required. Sites can be added to VPN intranets and extranets to form closed user groups. When VPNs are managed in this manner, it enables membership of any given site in multiple VPNs, maximizing flexibility in building intranets and extranets. MPLS functionality resides in the provider network, requiring little or no configuration on the customer premises. MPLS is transparent to the CPE router and customer CPE devices and do not need to run MPLS.

Flexible Addressing

To make a VPN service more accessible, customers of a service provider can design their own addressing plan, independent of addressing plans for other service provider customers. Many customers use private address spaces, as defined in RFC 1918, and do not want to invest the time and expense of converting to public IP addresses to enable intranet connectivity. MPLS VPNs allow customers to continue using their present address spaces without network address translation (NAT) by providing a public and private view of the address. A NAT is required only if two VPNs with overlapping address spaces want to communicate. This allows customers to use their own unregistered private addresses and communicate freely across a public IP network.

Standards-Based

MPLS is available to all industry vendors to ensure interoperability in multivendor networks.

Flexible Architecture

Cisco IOS software and Cisco routers and switches make it easy for providers to negotiate interconnections with other provider networks for global IP coverage.

End-to-End Priority Services

QoS mechanisms present the industry with a true end-to-end QoS solution, allowing providers to guarantee SLA compliance. MPLS makes QoS services more scalable and extends their reach end-to-end across multiple technologies.

Consolidation

Data, voice, and video consolidation capabilities give providers an opportunity to lower capital expenditures and reduce operations costs.

Traffic Engineering

Routing with Resource Reservation (RRR) using extensions to the RSVP protocol lets providers maximize the utilization of network resources and operate their IP networks as efficiently as possible. RRR allows the network operator to apply and enforce explicit routing, which overrides the traditional IP forwarding techniques and provides fast restoration and protection mechanisms. Underutilized links can be forced to carry traffic, thereby resulting in an optimum routing scenario.

Centralized Service

Building VPNs in Layer 3 allows delivery of targeted services to a group of users represented by a VPN. A VPN must give service providers more than a mechanism for privately connecting users to intranet services. It must also provide a way to flexibly deliver value-added services to targeted customers. Scalability is critical, because customers want to use services privately in their intranets and extranets. Because MPLS VPNs are seen as private intranets, you may use new IP services such as:

- Multicast
- Quality of service (QoS)
- Telephony support within a VPN
- Centralized services, including content and Web hosting to a VPN
- Any to Any connectivity

You can customize several combinations of specialized services for individual customers. For example, a service that combines IP multicast with a low-latency service class enables videoconferencing within an intranet.

Integrated Class of Service (CoS) Support

CoS is an important requirement for many IP VPN customers. It provides the ability to address two fundamental VPN requirements:

- Predictable performance and policy implementation
- Support for multiple levels of service in an MPLS VPN

Network traffic is classified and labeled at the edge of the network before traffic is aggregated according to policies defined by subscribers and implemented by the provider and transported across the provider core. Traffic at the edge and core of the network can then be differentiated into different classes by drop probability or delay.

Migration

VPN service deployment requires a straightforward migration path. MPLS VPNs are unique because you can build them over multiple network architectures, including IP, ATM, Frame Relay, and hybrid networks. Migration for the end customer is simplified, because there is no requirement to support MPLS on the customer edge (CE) router, and no modifications are required to a customer's intranet.

Centralized Management and Provisioning via Cisco Service Management (CSM)

This feature greatly simplifies and speeds service creation, provisioning, operation, and billing of intranet and extranet VPN services without complex, per-VC configurations.

Summary

The term Virtual Private Network (VPN) is used to identify a closed user group within a network. The IP-based VPN is rapidly becoming the foundation for the delivery of consolidated data, voice, and video services. IPSec and MPLS technologies are emerging to form the predominant foundations for delivery of consolidated services.

Connection-oriented VPNs can be built on Layer 2 or Layer 3 infrastructures. Frame Relay and ATM virtual connections are examples of Layer 2 connection-oriented VPN networks. IPSec Layer 2 tunneling protocol (L2TP), Layer 2 forwarding (L2F) protocol, and Generic Routing Encapsulation (GRE) are examples of Layer 3 connection-oriented VPN networks. Access VPDNs are also examples of connection-oriented VPNs.

Connectionless VPNs do not require a predefined logical or virtual circuit provisioned between two endpoints to establish a connection between the two endpoints. Layer 3 connectionless networks form the basis of the peer-to-peer model. In the peer-to-peer model, the customer routing information is exchanged between the CPE and the service provider routers. Conventional IP VPNs and MPLS VPNs are examples of connectionless VPNs.

Two distinct technologies have emerged as the preeminent building blocks from which to create VPNs: MPLS and IPSec. Service providers should deploy one of these VPN architectures primarily based on the customers and market segments they serve, the value-added services they want to offer, and their own network priorities.

This chapter covers the following topics:

- **MPLS VPN Operation**—MPLS Virtual Private Networks can be built over existing Layer 2 infrastructures. This section details the various MPLS VPN building blocks and the interaction between the various MPLS elements. This section also explains VPN route target communities, distribution of VPN routing information, and MPLS forwarding. The various packet-based MPLS LSR commands used to build VPN networks are explained. These commands are later exemplified in the case study section.

- **Verifying VPN Operation**—Packet-based MPLS VPN operation can be verified using various IOS commands on the LSRs. This section illustrates the use of these commands in order to verify proper VPN operation. These commands can also be applied in an operations environment on production MPLS VPN networks.

- **Case Study of an MPLS VPN Design and Implementation**—This section presents a case study of a service provider with points of presence in Chicago, Seattle, San Diego, Miami, and Washington. The service provider offers MPLS VPN services to three customers across its backbone MPLS network. The customers operate a single VPN each. This case study reinforces concepts explained earlier in this chapter.

- The remainder of the chapter covers BGP route reflectors, inter-autonomous system MPLS VPNs, carrier-over-carrier MPLS VPNs, Internet access over MPLS VPNs, MPLS redundancy using HSRP, trace route enhancements, and MPLS VPN management using the Cisco VPN Solution Center.

CHAPTER 5

Packet-Based MPLS VPNs

A Virtual Private Network (VPN) is for all intents and purposes a set of sites sharing common Layer 3 routing information. Although MPLS VPNs are connectionless, they combine the benefits of Layer 2 switching with the connection-oriented Layer 3 routing paradigm to build VPNs. MPLS VPNs also offer secure communications by allowing only sites that belong to a VPN to exchange routing information.

This allows a service provider to build intranets and extranets and provide public Internet connectivity to these various VPNs over a common infrastructure that can also be used to provision ISP, ATM, and Frame Relay services.

The VPN feature for Multiprotocol Label Switching (MPLS) allows a service provider network to deploy scalable IPv4 Layer 3 VPN backbone services. These services can be deployed over a Layer 3 routed backbone or over an ATM backbone. This chapter explains deployment over a routed backbone. Deploying MPLS over an IP+ATM backbone is an extrapolation of the technology explained in this chapter and is covered in Chapter 6, "ATM-Based MPLS VPNs." Either approach allows a service provider to deliver VPN services in an integrated manner on the same infrastructure it uses to provide Internet services or other Layer 2 services such as connection-oriented Frame Relay or ATM VPNs. Currently, IP is the only Layer 3 protocol supported by Cisco's MPLS/VPN implementations.

MPLS VPN Operation

Figure 5-1 illustrates an example of a VPN deployed by a service provider. It is in the service provider's best interests to have the capability to provision scalable VPNs for its customers. Enterprise networks that own or lease private Layer 2 infrastructures can also deploy this technology.

Figure 5-1   *MPLS Virtual Private Network*

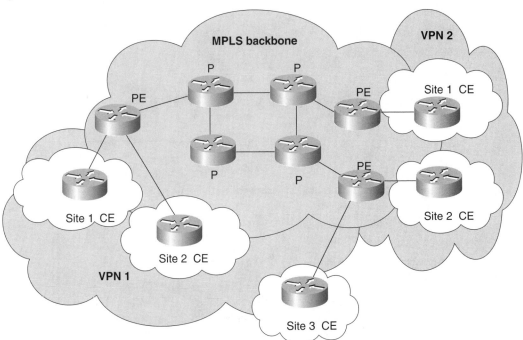

The various MPLS components that are used to build a VPN include the following:

- **MPLS core routers (P)**—The core routers, also known as provider routers (P routers), do not maintain any VPN routes. They typically reside in a full- or partial-mesh configuration with other P LSRs and interface with provider edge (PE) routers. P routers are never directly connected to customer routers.

- **MPLS edge routers (PE)**—Point-of-presence routers, also known as provider edge routers (PE routers), maintain VPN routes for VPNs that are members. They peer with the customer edge (CE) routers and interface to the core provider routers. PE routers peer with P routers or may be directly connected to other PE routers.

- **Customer edge routers (CE)**—The customer edge routers (CE routers) do not have to support MPLS and can use conventional routing methods to achieve connectivity. The peer model requires a customer site to peer with only one PE router as opposed to all other CPE or CE routers that are members of the VPN. CE routers are never directly connected to P routers.

- **Customer routers (C)**—The customer-owned internal routers, also known as C routers, do not have to support MPLS and can use conventional routing methods to achieve connectivity with the CE router and each other.

The VPN contains customer devices attached to the CE routers. The CE routers in either VPN can be connected to any of the service provider's PE routers. The PE routers connect to each other through a core network of P routers.

VPN Routing and Forwarding

Each VPN is associated with one or more VPN routing and forwarding instances (VRFs). A VRF defines the VPN membership of a customer site attached to a PE router. A VRF consists of an IP routing table, a derived Cisco Express Forwarding (CEF) table, a set of interfaces that use the forwarding table, and a set of rules and routing protocol parameters that control the information that is included in the routing table.

A one-to-one relationship does not necessarily exist between customer sites and VPNs. A given site can be a member of multiple VPNs, as shown in Figure 5-2. However, a VRF can only define a single VPN. A customer site's VRF contains all the routes available to the site from the VPNs of which it is a member.

Figure 5-2   *Multiple VPN Membership*

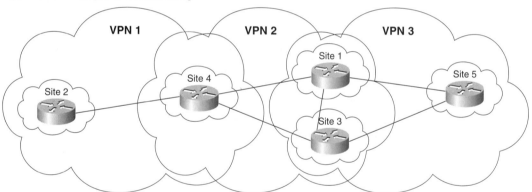

Packet forwarding information is stored in the IP routing table and the CEF table for each VRF. A separate set of routing and CEF tables is maintained for each VRF. These tables prevent information from being forwarded outside a VPN and also prevent packets that are outside a VPN from being forwarded to a router within the VPN.

Each customer VPN must preserve the uniqueness of its IP addressing space. However, if two customer VPNs decide to combine to form an extranet by the controlled import of routes, they must preserve the uniqueness of their IP addressing by avoiding an IP address overlap.

The PE routers use the global IP table to forward IPv4 packets between each other. The VRF IP routing and forwarding tables are used to forward information within the VPN. Because a PE router can have multiple VRF instances, each VRF IP routing and CEF forwarding table combination can be perceived as a virtual router within the physical PE router.

Each VRF IP routing and forwarding table combination contains routes that belong to one or more customer VPNs.

Limiting the routing protocol used within the VPN to a single VRF table supports overlapping VPNs (such as extranet VPN support). Interfaces on PE routers are associated with individual VRFs. Routing information learned through these interfaces is associated with the configured VRFs and is known as the routing context. Some routing protocols such as RIP support several instances or contexts of the same protocol, whereas other protocols such as OSPF require a separate copy of the routing protocol process for each VRF.

VPN Route Target Communities

The distribution of VPN routing information is controlled through the use of VPN route target communities, implemented by border gateway protocol (BGP) extended communities. The distribution of VPN routing information works as follows:

When a VPN route learned from a CE router is injected into Multiprotocol IBGP (MP-IBGP), a list of VPN route target extended community attributes is associated with it when it is exported from the local VRF to be presented to other VRFs. Typically, the list of route target community values is set from an export list of route targets associated with the VRF from which the route was learned.

An import list of route target extended communities is associated with each VRF. The import list defines route target extended community attributes that a route must have in order for it to be imported into the VRF. For example, if the import list for a particular VRF includes route target communities A, B, and C, any VPN route that carries any of the route target extended communities A, B, or C is imported into the VRF.

Distribution of VPN Routing Information

A service provider edge (PE) router can learn an IP prefix from a customer edge (CE) router by static configuration, through a BGP session with the CE router, or through RIPv2 or OSPF sessions with the CE router. The IP prefix is a member of the IPv4 address family. After it learns the IP prefix, the PE converts it into a VPN-IPv4 prefix by combining it with a 64-bit route distinguisher (RD). The generated 96-bit prefix is a member of the VPN-IPv4 address family. It serves to uniquely identify the customer address, even if the customer site is using unregistered private IP addresses.

The route distinguisher used to generate the VPN-IPv4 prefix is specified by a configuration command associated with the VRF on the PE router.

NOTE	BGP is an extremely scalable protocol that can support the provisioning of a large number of VPNs. BGP also supports the exchange of routing information between routers not directly connected to each other. This is possible as long as there is an underlying IGP such

as OSPF or IS-IS that provides Layer 3 connectivity between the BGP peers. BGP also has the flexibility to carry optional parameters (attributes), which makes it the protocol of choice for use with the MPLS/VPN architecture.

BGP distributes reachability information for VPN-IPv4 prefixes for each VPN. BGP communication takes place at two levels: within autonomous systems (internal BGP or IBGP) and between autonomous systems (external BGP or EBGP). PE-PE or PE-RR (route reflector) sessions are IBGP sessions, and PE-CE sessions are EBGP sessions. A separate E-BGP session between the PE and CE router is required for each customer VPN.

NOTE   RFC 2283, Multiprotocol Extensions for BGP4, permits BGP to carry extended attributes. This technology forms the basis of current implementations of MPLS, wherein the PE routers communicate with other PE routers using IBGP across a core of provider P routers that do not participate in the BGP process. The PE routers form a full IBGP mesh.

BGP propagates reachability information for VPN-IPv4 prefixes among PE routers by means of multiprotocol BGP extensions, which define support for address families other than IPv4. It does this in a way that ensures that the routes for a given VPN are learned only by other members of that VPN, allowing members of the VPN to communicate with each other. The address family is created to allow the Multiprotocol Border Gateway Protocol (MP-BGP) to carry protocols other than IPv4. The BGP extended communities draft specifies two new communities defined as the route target and the route origin. The route target defines import and export policies for VRFs. The route origin is referred to as Site of Origin (SOO) in the Cisco implementation and prevents routing loops between sites. MP-BGP propagates the extended community along with other BGP attributes between PE routers.

NOTE   PE routers maintain and store routes for directly connected VPNs. This feature improves scalability by importing only VPN IPv4 routes that are associated with VRFs configured on the PE router. However, BGP stores all BGP routes in its table, regardless of whether they are used by the VRFs or not. This consumes resources in terms of DRAM and overhead in terms of bandwidth consumed for the advertisement of these messages to other PE routers. The Route Refresh and Automatic Route Filtering features provide methods to reduce the amount of BGP routing information that the PE router needs to hold. However, none of these mechanisms prevents the arrival of unnecessary routing information to a PE router.

The Route Refresh feature ensures that a change in a PE router policy, such as an addition, deletion, or modification of a VRF, triggers the request for a retransmission of routing updates from its neighbors.

The Automatic Route Filtering feature automatically filters VPNv4 routes that contain a route target extended community that does not match any of the PE's VRFs.

Outbound Route Filters (ORFs) are locally configured outbound filters that prevent the unwanted routes from leaving the source.

MPLS Forwarding

Based on routing information stored in the VRF IP routing table and the VRF CEF table, packets are forwarded to their destination using MPLS.

A PE router binds a label to each customer prefix learned from a CE router and includes the label in the network reachability information for the prefix that it advertises to other PE routers. When a PE router forwards a packet received from a CE router across the provider network, it labels the packet with the label learned from the destination PE router. When the destination PE router receives the labeled packet, it pops the label and uses it to direct the packet to the correct CE router.

NOTE   The provider P routers do not take part in the MP-BGP process and don't carry VPN routes. They are not required to make any routing decisions based on VPN addresses. The P routers forward packets based on label values of labels attached to IP packets. The P routers participate in MPLS label swapping, however do not teminate MPLS VPNs.

Unique identifiers such as loopback IP addresses with 32-bit masks (host routes) typically identify the PE routers. The loopback addresses are used with the BGP next-hop attribute for VPN routes advertised by PE routers. Labels are assigned by P routers for the host routes and are transmitted to all neighbors. MPLS LDP ensures that all PE routers receive a label associated with the PE router. The MPLS network is ready to perform VPN packet exchange when the ingress PE router receives a label for the egress PE router.

Label forwarding across the provider backbone is based on either dynamic label switching or traffic-engineered paths. A customer data packet carries two levels of labels when traversing the backbone. The first label forwards the packet to the correct next-hop PE router, and the second label indicates the VRF associated with the egress interface on the destination CE router. The two level mechanism is commonly called hierarchical tag or label switching.

When an IP packet is received through a particular interface from the CE, the PE associates it with a VRF, and a label associated with the egress PE router (which identifies the target VRF and the outgoing interface of the egress PE router) is obtained (bottom label). The PE router also obtains another label from the global forwarding table that points to the next-hop PE router (top label) and combines the two labels in an MPLS label stack. The label stack is attached to the VPN packet and is forwarded to the next hop. The P routers in the

MPLS network examine the top label and forward the packet correctly to the next hop across the network.

At the egress PE router, the top label is stripped, and the bottom label is examined, which identifies the target VRF and egress interface. The bottom label is then stripped, and the IP packet is sent toward the correct CE router.

NOTE   An additional Layer 3 lookup is performed in the target VRF for summary VPN routes to determine a more specific route.

NOTE   The second-to-last router to the egress PE router might remove the top label in the label stack. This method of label stripping in MPLS is called penultimate hop popping. This method is used only for directly connected subnets or aggregate routes.

Configuring Router-Based MPLS VPNs

Your network must be running the following Cisco IOS services before you configure VPN operation:

- MPLS in provider backbone routers, or GRE tunnel connectivity among all PE routers
- MPLS with VPN code in provider routers with VPN PE routers
- BGP in all routers providing a VPN service
- CEF switching in every MPLS-enabled router
- Class of Service (CoS) feature (optional)

NOTE   Cisco Express Forwarding (CEF) is a topology-driven switching architecture that isolates processing tasks to avoid contention for system resources. This approach stabilizes CPU processing, speeds up packet processing, and renders network performance consistent and predictable.

CEF builds two main data structures: the FIB (Forwarding Information Base), which contains the best paths to all known destinations, and an adjacency table, which defines the next-hop forwarding information.

In order to enable CEF on the router, simply enter the command **ip cef** in global configuration mode.

The following tasks must be performed on the PE router to configure and verify MPLS VPN operation:

Step 1   Configure your interfaces and IGP.

Step 2   Define your VPNs.

Step 3   Configure your PE-to-PE routing sessions.

Step 4   Configure your PE-to-CE routing sessions.

Step 5   Configure your P routers.

Step 6   Configure your CE routers.

Step 1: Configuring Your Interfaces and IGP

To configure your interfaces and IGP, do the following:

Step 1   Enable CEF on the PE router in global configuration mode. CEF switching is essential for running MPLS.

```
Router(config)#ip cef
```

Step 2   Configure the IP address of the loopback interface for use as an identifier in your IGP routing process:

```
Router(config)#interface loopback n
Router(config-interface)#ip address IP-address mask
```

Step 3   Configure your IGP. For this example, I have enabled OSPF routing, which places you in router configuration mode.

```
Router(config)# router ospf ospf-process-id
```

Step 4   Define an interface on which OSPF runs, and define the area ID for that interface:

```
Router(config-router)# network address wildcard-mask area area-id
```

Step 5   Configure the interfaces that connect to PE routers with an IP address. For this example, I have configured a serial DS3 interface.

```
Router(config)#interface Serial slot/adapter/port
Router(config-interface)#ip address IP-address mask
```

Step 6   Enable Tag Switching for the interface:

```
Router(config-interface)#tag-switching IP
```

Step 2: Defining Your VPNs

As discussed, MPLS supports multiple VPNs for various customers and is extremely scalable. Each customer VPN is associated with a routing instance. In order to define VPN routing instances, follow these steps on the PE router:

Step 1   Define the various VPN routing and forwarding instances by assigning VRF names and entering VRF configuration mode:

```
Router(config)#ip vrf vrf-name
```

vrf-name is the name assigned to the VRF. This must be a unique name used to identify the customer VPN. The *vrf-name* is case-sensitive. All customer CE routers, which are connected to the PE router, should have their VRFs defined.

Step 2   Create routing and forwarding tables for the customer VPN by identifying the VPN using a Route Distinguisher (RD). The RD is added in VRF submode. There is no default value for the RD. The RD must be configured in order for a VRF to be functional.

The RD adds a 64-bit value to the 32-bit IPv4 prefix to create a 96-bit VPN IPv4 prefix. The RD creates routing and forwarding tables and specifies the default RD for a VPN. The RD is added to the beginning of the customer's IPv4 prefixes to change them into globally unique VPN-IPv4 prefixes. This permits VPN customers to use the same private IP addressing scheme.

```
Router(config-vrf)#rd route-distinguisher
```

The RD is either ASN-relative, in which case it is composed of an autonomous system number and an arbitrary number, or it is IP address-relative, in which case it is composed of an IP address and an arbitrary number:

— ASN-relative format—16-bit AS number : 32-bit arbitrary user number (*ASN:nn*). For example, 100:1.

— IP address-relative format—32-bit IP address : 16-bit arbitrary user number (*IP-address:nn*). For example, 192.168.10.1:1.

NOTE   The RD does not have any semantics in either format *ASN:nn* or *IP-address:nn* and is interpreted by BGP as a sequence of bits.

Step 3 Import or export routing information from or to the target VPN extended community. Create a route target extended community for the VRF using the **route-target** command in VRF submode. The route target specifies a target VPN extended community. Like a route distinguisher, an extended community is composed of either an autonomous system number and an arbitrary number or an IP address and an arbitrary number.

```
Router(config-vrf)#route-target {import | export | both}
route-target-ext-community
```

Step 4 (Optional) Associate the specified route map with the VRF. Route maps can be created to apply policies for the VRFs. The route maps are configured in VRF submode. Use an import route map when an application requires finer control over the routes imported into a VRF than that provided by the import and export extended communities configured for the importing and exporting VRF.

The **import map** command associates a route map with the specified VRF. You can filter routes that are eligible for import into a VRF, based on the route target extended community attributes of the route, through the use of a route map. The route map might deny access to selected routes from a community that is on the import list.

```
Router(config-vrf)#import map route-map
```

Step 5 Associate a VRF with an interface or subinterface. This is an extremely important step, because MPLS associates the physical interface with the VRF instance.

```
Router(config-if)#ip vrf forwarding vrf-name
```

NOTE Associating an interface with a VRF removes the IP address from that interface. The IP address should be reconfigured after an interface is assigned to a VRF.

Step 3: Configuring PE-to-PE Routing

To configure PE-to-PE multiprotocol IBGP routing sessions in a provider network, follow these steps on the PE routers:

Step 1 Configure the IBGP routing process with the autonomous system number passed along to other IBGP PE routers:

```
Router(config)#router bgp autonomous-system
```

Step 2 Deactivate the advertisement of the IPv4 unicast prefixes:

```
Router(config-router)#no bgp default ipv4-unicast
```

NOTE   The preceding command lets MP-BGP carry VPN-IPv4 sessions only.

Step 3   Specify the neighboring PE's IP address or IBGP peer group identifying
             it to the local autonomous system:

```
Router(config-router)#neighbor {ip-address | peer-group-name} remote-as
    number
```

Step 4   Activate the advertisement of the IPv4 address family to your IBGP
             neighbors:

```
Router(config-router)#neighbor ip-address activate
```

Step 4: Configuring PE-to-CE Routing

The PE router needs to be configured so that any routing information learned from the
customer interface can be associated with a particular VRF. This can be performed through
standard routing protocol processes known as routing contexts.

There are four ways of configuring PE-to-CE routing:

- Static PE-to-CE routing configuration
- RIPv2 PE-to-CE routing configuration
- BGP4 PE-to-CE routing configuration
- OSPF PE-to-CE routing configuration

Customer VPN routes are placed in the VRF that is associated with the interface to which
the CE router is attached. This is achieved either as a separate routing process or as a
separate routing context within a process per VRF. After the VRF is populated with routes,
these routes are advertised using MP-IBGP to other PE routers as VPN-IPv4 (VPNv4)
prefixes. Address families are used to tell BGP which VRF routes to advertise.

NOTE   The redistribution of CE routes into MP-IBGP is required for non-BGP PE-to-CE routing
             sessions. CE routes learned through PE-to-CE EBGP sessions are automatically redistrib-
             uted into MP-IBGP. In comparison to conventional BGP, wherein IBGP routes are not per-
             mitted to be redistributed into the IGP, the VPN routes received through an MP-IBGP
             session can be redistributed into the VRF.

Configuring Static PE-to-CE Routing Sessions

A static route for every destination IP subnet must be configured into the VRF on the PE
router connected to the CE router. The syntax is similar to static route configuration.

The static routing information is advertised between PE routers by redistributing it into IBGP. This is achieved by using the **redistribute** command within the BGP address family configuration. The **route-map** command can be used to control the distribution of routes into IBGP during redistribution. This is useful to prevent specific static routes from reaching other CE routers of the same VPN.

To configure static route PE-to-CE routing sessions, follow these steps on the PE router:

Step 1   Define static route parameters for every PE-to-CE session:

    Router(config)#**ip route vrf** *vrf-name*

Step 2   Define static route parameters for every BGP PE-to-CE routing session:

    Router(config-router)#**address-family ipv4** [**unicast**] **vrf** *vrf-name*

NOTE   The default is Off for auto-summary and synchronization in the VRF address-family submode.

Step 3   Redistribute VRF static routes into the VRF BGP table. This passes the static routing information pertaining to the VRF to all other PEs.

    Router(config-router-af)#**redistribute static**

Step 4   Redistribute directly connected networks into the VRF BGP table:

    Router(config-router-af)#**redistribute connected**

Configuring RIPv2 PE-to-CE Routing Sessions

RIP version 2 can be run as a routing protocol between the PE and CE. The routing information received by the PE via RIPv2 from the CE is placed into the VRF associated with the physical interface connected to the CE. The VRF information is then propagated via IBGP to the peering PE routers.

In normal RIPv1 or RIPv2 routing, the **network** statements that define the RIP-enabled interfaces are placed under the router **rip** routing protocol configuration submode. This would lead to the propagation of RIP routes in the global routing tables of the PE routers. However, the intent is to maintain RIP routes within the closed user group VRF of the customer VPN. This is accomplished by defining network statements in the **address-family** submode. Likewise, the redistribution of IBGP routes must be configured within the **address-family** submode as well so that VPN routes learned from IBGP are advertised to the CE router via the RIP process.

NOTE	Classful RIP version 1 (conventional RIP) does not support VLSM and is not recommended for MPLS PE-to-CE routing.

NOTE	RIP metrics can be transparently carried across the MPLS/VPN backbone by using the **redistribute bgp metric transparent** command, which causes RIP to use the routing table metric for redistributed routes as the RIP metric, with the original metric being carried across the MPLS/VPN backbone in the BGP MED field.

To configure RIP PE-to-CE routing sessions, follow these steps on the PE router:

Step 1   Enable RIP version 2:

```
Router(config)#router rip
Router(config-router)#version 2
```

Step 2   Define RIP parameters for PE-to-CE routing sessions in the address-family submode within the main RIP process configuration:

```
Router(config-router)#address-family ipv4 [unicast] vrf vrf-name
```

NOTE	The default is Off for auto-summary and synchronization in the VRF address-family submode.

Step 3   Associate a network with the RIP routing process under the address-family submode:

```
Router(config-router-af)#network prefix
```

Step 4   Redistribute the IBGP routes into the RIP address family in order to advertise these routes toward the CE:

```
Router(config-router-af)#redistribute bgp asn metric metric
```

Configuring BGP4 PE-to-CE Routing Sessions

Some MPLS/VPN customers might prefer BGP4 connectivity to the PE and prefer to exchange BGP4 routes with the service provider. All routes learned from the CE router are advertised across the MPLS/VPN backbone using MP-IBGP sessions between the service provider's PE routers. The redistribution between the customer EBGP sessions and the MP-IBGP sessions is performed automatically.

NOTE	EBGP multihop is not currently supported on BGP sessions between PE and CE routers.

To configure BGP PE-to-CE routing sessions, follow these steps on the PE router:

Step 1 Configure an IBGP routing process with the autonomous system number passed along to other PE routers:

```
Router(config)#router bgp autonomous-system
```

Step 2 Define EBGP parameters for PE-to-CE routing sessions by entering the address-family submode within the main IBGP process configuration:

```
Router(config-router)#address-family ipv4 [unicast] vrf vrf-name
```

Step 3 Specify a neighboring CE's IP address or EBGP peer group identifying it to the local autonomous system:

```
Router(config-router-af)#neighbor {ip-address | peer-group-name}
  remote-as number
```

Step 4 Activate the advertisement of the IPv4 address family:

```
Router(config-router-af)#neighbor ip-address activate
```

Configuring OSPF PE-to-CE Routing Sessions

Many customers currently run OSPF as their intranet routing protocol. The routing information learned from customer intranets via OSPF is placed in the VRF associated with the interface connected to the CE router. These routes are advertised over IBGP between PE routers and are imported into the VRFs of other PE routers belonging to the same VPN.

The physical topology of most PE-to-CE links is point-to-point links without a designated router (DR). This precludes the need for configuring OSPF network types. However, if multiple CEs connect to the PE over an NBMA network such as Frame Relay, manipulation of OSPF priority and the network type could be a requirement.

It is possible for a VPN customer to run an OSPF Area 0 between PE and CE router links for more than one site in the same VPN. In this case, the CE router becomes the Area Border Router (ABR) for all other OSPF areas in the customer's intranet. The PE router acts as an ABR from the CE router's perspective, and vice versa. The PE router also acts as an ASBR for the OSPF-MPLS backbone. The PE and CE routers form an adjacency and exchange Link-State Advertisements (LSAs) across the adjacency. The CE router inserts summary LSAs from the customer to the PE router, and the PE router inserts summary or external LSAs for customer routes coming across the OSPF-MPLS backbone.

Adjacencies are not formed between PE routers in the MPLS backbone. IBGP is run between the PE routers, and OSPF routes are translated into VPN-IPv4 routes. The redistribution of VRF OSPF routes into IBGP does not convert the OSPF routes into external OSPF routes when advertised to the other CEs.

NOTE   The down-bit is an extension of the OSPF protocol and is a part of the options field of the LSA header. Summary LSAs generated by the PE routers have the down-bit set.

In order to prevent routing loops from occurring when two or more CE sites are connected to the same Area 0, the PE routers propagate summary LSAs into the OSPF-MPLS backbone only if the down-bit is not set. This ensures that the summary LSAs being propagated are generated by the CE routers.

It is also possible to configure the PE-to-CE link as a nonbackbone area. In this case, the PE router acts as an ABR and ASBR for the CE and forms an adjacency with the CE for exchanging LSAs. The LSAs are placed into the customer VRF, which is then redistributed into IBGP and advertised across the MPLS backbone as an intra-area route. When this route is received at the egress PE, it is imported into the customer VRF and is advertised as a summary LSA to the CE router at the far end.

NOTE   A separate OSPF process is required for each VRF that will receive VPN routes via OSPF. This is implemented using the VRF extension to the **router ospf** command in IOS.

To configure OSPF PE-to-CE routing sessions, follow these steps on the PE router:

Step 1   Enable OSPF with VRF extensions:

```
Router(config)#router ospf ospf-process-id vrf vrf-name
```

Step 2   Define an interface on which OSPF runs, and define the area ID for that interface:

```
Router(config)#network address wildcard-mask area area-id
```

Step 3   Redistribute IBGP routes into the OSPF VRF process:

```
Router(config-router-af)#redistribute protocol [process-id]
{level-1 | level-1-2 | level-2} [metric metric-value]
[metric-type type-value] [match internal | external 1 | external 2]
[tag tag-value] [route-map map-tag] [weight weight] [subnets]
```

NOTE   The **redistribute** command might need several options so that all IBGP routes are properly distributed into the VRF.

Step 4   Access the address-family submode within the main IBGP process configuration:

```
Router(config-router)#address-family ipv4 [unicast] vrf vrf-name
```

Step 5   Redistribute VRF OSPF routes into IBGP through the address-family submode configuration:

```
Router(config-router-af)#redistribute protocol [process-id]
{level-1 | level-1-2 | level-2} [metric metric-value]
[metric-type type-value] [match internal | external 1 | external 2]
[tag tag-value] [route-map map-tag] [weight weight] [subnets]
```

NOTE   The **redistribute** command might need several options so that all VRF OSPF routes are properly distributed into IBGP.

Step 5: Configuring P Routers

The provider core routers (P routers) are LSRs that participate in the IGP routing protocol, such as OSPF or IS-IS. However, they do not take part in the multiprotocol IBGP process like the PEs would, so they have a simpler configuration. The P routers do not terminate customer links from CE routers. The following shows the step-by-step configuration of a P router running OSPF:

Step 1   Enable CEF on the PE router in global configuration mode. CEF switching is essential to run MPLS.

```
Router(config)#ip cef
```

Step 2   Configure the IP address of the loopback interface for use as an identifier in your IGP routing process:

```
Router(config)#interface loopback n
Router(config-interface)#ip address IP-address mask
```

Step 3   Configure your IGP. In this example, I have enabled OSPF routing, which places you in router configuration mode.

```
Router(config)#router ospf ospf-process-id
```

Step 4   Define an interface on which OSPF runs, and define the area ID for that interface:

```
Router(config-router)#network address wildcard-mask area area-id
```

Step 5   Configure the interfaces that connect to PE routers with an IP address. In this example, I have configured a DS3 interface.

```
Router(config)#interface Serial slot/adapter/port
Router(config-interface)#ip address IP-address mask
```

Step 6   Enable Tag Switching for the interface:

```
Router(config-interface)#tag-switching IP
```

Step 6: Configuring CE Routers

CE routers can be configured using one of four options:

- Static routing
- RIPv2 routing
- BGP4 routing
- OSPF routing

The PE router must be configured using the same routing protocol as the CE router. CE routers can be customer-owned or service provider-owned. Typically, if the service provider offers Managed IP VPN services, the CE router is owned and maintained by the service provider. The customers are provided detailed IP architecture information and documentation to assist them with IP device numbering and internal intranet routing. Most service providers prefer to manage the CE router(s), especially if their MPLS VPN solution is quite sophisticated. Troubleshooting this type of service is difficult if the Service Provider engineers don't have full access to the CE router.

CE Routers with Static Routing

To configure static routing for CE-to-PE routing sessions, follow these steps on the CE router:

Step 1   Configure the interface that connects to PE routers with an IP address. For this example, I have configured a serial DS1 interface.

```
Router(config)#interface Serial slot/adapter/port
Router(config-interface)#ip address IP-address mask
```

Step 2   Configure a default route to point toward the PE router as the next hop:

```
Router(config)#ip route 0.0.0.0 0.0.0.0 [PE-ip-address |
   CE-egress-interface]
```

CE Routers with RIPv2 Routing

To configure RIPv2 for CE-to-PE routing sessions, follow these steps on the CE router:

Step 1   Enable RIP version 2:

```
Router(config)#router rip
Router(config-router)#version 2
```

Step 2   Associate a network with the RIP routing process under router configuration mode:

```
Router(config-router)#network prefix
```

CE Routers with BGP4 Routing

To configure BGP4 for CE-to-PE routing sessions, follow these steps on the CE router:

NOTE   As mentioned before, EBGP multihop is not currently supported on BGP sessions between PE and CE routers.

Step 1   Configure an IBGP routing process with the autonomous system number passed along to the PE router:

```
Router(config)#router bgp autonomous-system
```

Step 2   Specify the neighboring PE's IP address or EBGP peer group identifying it to an autonomous system:

```
Router(config-router)#neighbor {ip-address | peer-group-name} remote-as
number
```

Step 3   Specify the networks or subnets that are to be announced to the EBGP session:

```
Router(config-router)#network network-number [mask network-mask]
```

CE Routers with OSPF Routing

To configure OSPF for CE-to-PE routing sessions, follow these steps on the CE router:

Step 1   Enable OSPF:

```
Router(config)#router ospf ospf-process-id
```

Step 2   Define an interface on which OSPF runs, and define the area ID for that interface:

```
Router(config)#network address wildcard-mask area area-id
```

Verifying VPN Operation

To verify VPN operation, follow these steps:

Step 1 Display the set of defined VRFs and interfaces:

    Router#**show ip vrf**

Step 2 Display information about defined VRFs and associated interfaces:

    Router#**show ip vrf** [{**brief** | **detail** | **interfaces**}] *vrf-name*

Step 3 Display the IP routing table for a VRF:

    Router#**show ip route vrf** *vrf-name*

Step 4 Display the routing protocol information for a VRF:

    Router#**show ip protocols vrf** *vrf-name*

Step 5 Display the CEF forwarding table associated with a VRF:

    Router#**show ip cef vrf** *vrf-name*

Step 6 Display the VRF table associated with an interface:

    Router#**show ip interface** *interface-number* **vrf** *vrf-name*

Step 7 Display information about BGP VPN:

    Router#**show ip bgp vpnv4 all** [**tags**]

Step 8 Display label forwarding entries that correspond to VRF routes
advertised by the router:

    Router#**show tag-switching forwarding vrf** *vrf-name* [*prefix
        mask/length*][**detail**]

Case Study of an MPLS VPN Design and Implementation

Consider a service provider with points of presence in Chicago, Seattle, San Diego, Miami, and Washington. The service provider offers layered IP VPN services across its MPLS backbone. The service provider offers MPLS VPN services to three customers—A, B, and C. The detailed architecture is shown in Figure 5-3. The customers are operating a single VPN each.

Figure 5-3   *Case Study Service Provider Network*

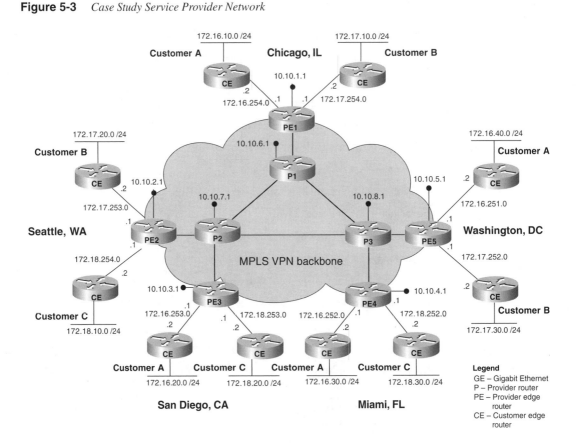

The service provider has provisioned the VPNs as shown in Table 5-1.

Table 5-1   *Case Study Customer VPN Deployment (Point of Presence)*

	Customer A	Customer B	Customer C
Chicago, IL	VPN A	VPN B	
Seattle, WA		VPN B	VPN C
San Diego, CA	VPN A		VPN C
Miami, FL	VPN A		VPN C
Washington, DC	VPN A	VPN B	

The CE routers connect to the PE routers as shown in Table 5-2.

Table 5-2   *Case Study PE Deployment*

	Customer A	Customer B	Customer C
Chicago, IL	PE1	PE1	
Seattle, WA		PE2	PE2
San Diego, CA	PE3		PE3
Miami, FL	PE4		PE4
Washington, DC	PE5	PE5	

The core routers P1, P2, and P3 are fully meshed in this example. However, it is not necessary to have them fully meshed. Layer 3 Interior Gateway Routing Protocol (IGRP) running across the backbone normally provides any-to-any connectivity for IBGP peers to communicate with each other, even though the IBGP peers (PE routers) are not directly connected to each other.

The IP addressing scheme used in this case study is explained in Table 5-3.

Table 5-3   *Case Study VPN IP Address Architecture*

	PE Router	CE WAN Subnet	CE LAN Subnet
Customer A			
Chicago	10.10.1.1/32	172.16.254.0/30	172.16.10.0/24
Seattle	No presence	No presence	No presence
San Diego	10.10.3.1/32	172.16.253.0/30	172.16.20.0/24
Miami	10.10.4.1/32	172.16.252.0/30	172.16.30.0/24
Washington	10.10.5.1/32	172.16.251.0/30	172/16.40.0/24
Customer B			
Chicago	10.10.1.1/32	172.17.254.0/30	172.17.10.0/24
Seattle	10.10.2.1/32	172.17.253.0/30	172.17.20.0/24
San Diego	No presence	No presence	No presence
Miami	No presence	No presence	No presence
Washington	10.10.5.1/32	172.17.252.0/30	172/17.30.0/24
Customer C			
Chicago	No presence	No presence	No presence
Seattle	10.10.2.1/32	172.18.254.0/30	172.18.10.0/24
San Diego	10.10.3.1/32	172.18.253.0/30	172.18.20.0/24
Miami	10.10.4.1/32	172.18.252.0/30	172.18.30.0/24
Washington	No presence	No presence	No presence

The customer MPLS VPNs could have overlapping IP addresses. However, in a conventional peer-to-peer IP overlay model, wherein the service provider runs IP over an ATM or Frame Relay backbone, strict addressing measures must be implemented. In the MPLS VPN model, each PE router maintains multiple VRF routing tables and a single global routing table. Each VRF routing table corresponds to the VPN routes for each customer.

NOTE   Conventional methods used to resolve the issue of overlapping IP address space include tunneling and NAT schemes. However, these methods require operations control and maintenance of address schemes and are an administrative nightmare with respect to customer moves, additions, and changes.

Provider Router Configurations

The P routers are configured for label switching. They do not run multiprotocol IBGP. The P routers shown in the following sections are configured using OSPF as the IGP.

P1 Router Configuration

```
!
hostname P1
!
ip cef
! CEF switching is a prerequisite for label switching
!
interface loopback0
 ip address 10.10.6.1 255.255.255.255
! Configure the P loopback IP address
!
interface Serial2/0/0
! Configure the DS3 for label switching
 ip unnumbered loopback0
 encapsulation ppp
 framing c-bit
 cablelength 3
 dsu bandwidth 44210
 clock source internal
 tag-switching ip
!
interface Serial2/0/1
! Configure the DS3 for label switching
 ip unnumbered loopback0
 encapsulation ppp
 framing c-bit
 cablelength 3
```

```
 dsu bandwidth 44210
 clock source internal
 tag-switching ip
!
interface Serial3/0/0
! Configure the DS3 for label switching
 ip unnumbered loopback0
 encapsulation ppp
 framing c-bit
 cablelength 3
 dsu bandwidth 44210
 clock source internal
 tag-switching ip
!
router ospf 100
 network 10.10.6.1 0.0.0.0 area 0
!
```

P2 Router Configuration

```
!
hostname P2
!
ip ce
! CEF switching is a prerequisite for label switching
!
interface loopback0
 ip address 10.10.7.1 255.255.255.255
! Configure the P loopback IP address
!
interface Serial2/0/0
! Configure the DS3 for label switching
 ip unnumbered loopback0
 encapsulation ppp
 framing c-bit
 cablelength 3
 dsu bandwidth 44210
 clock source internal
 tag-switching ip
!
interface Serial2/0/1
! Configure the DS3 for label switching
 ip unnumbered loopback0
 encapsulation ppp
 framing c-bit
```

continues

```
 cablelength 3
 dsu bandwidth 44210
 clock source internal
 tag-switching ip
!
interface Serial3/0/0
! Configure the DS3 for label switching
 ip unnumbered loopback0
 encapsulation ppp
 framing c-bit
 cablelength 3
 dsu bandwidth 44210
 clock source internal
 tag-switching ip
!
interface Serial3/0/1
! Configure the DS3 for label switching
 ip unnumbered loopback0
 encapsulation ppp
 framing c-bit
 cablelength 3
 dsu bandwidth 44210
 clock source internal
 tag-switching ip
!
router ospf 100
 network 10.10.7.1 0.0.0.0 area 0
 !
```

P3 Router Configuration

```
!
hostname P3
!
ip ce
! CEF switching is a prerequisite for label switching
!
interface loopback0
 ip address 10.10.8.1 255.255.255.255
! Configure the P loopback IP address
!
interface Serial2/0/0
! Configure the DS3 for label switching
 ip unnumbered loopback0
 encapsulation ppp
 framing c-bit
 cablelength 3
 dsu bandwidth 44210
 clock source internal
 tag-switching ip
!
interface Serial2/0/1
```

```
! Configure the DS3 for label switching
 ip unnumbered loopback0
 encapsulation ppp
 framing c-bit
 cablelength 3
 dsu bandwidth 44210
 clock source internal
 tag-switching ip
!
interface Serial3/0/0
 ! Configure the DS3 for label switching
 ip unnumbered loopback0
 encapsulation ppp
 framing c-bit
 cablelength 3
 dsu bandwidth 44210
 clock source internal
 tag-switching ip
!
interface Serial3/0/1
 ! Configure the DS3 for label switching
 ip unnumbered loopback0
 encapsulation ppp
 framing c-bit
 cablelength 3
 dsu bandwidth 44210
 clock source internal
 tag-switching ip
!
router ospf 100
 network 10.10.8.1 0.0.0.0 area 0
!
```

Provider and Customer Router Configurations

The detailed PE router configurations are shown in the following sections. The different sites show examples of various PE-to-CE connectivity options. Typically, a service provider selects only one routing protocol option for PE-to-CE connectivity and maintains a consistent IP and routing architecture for its various customers.

Chicago Configuration

PE1 in Chicago connects to the Chicago customers using static routing sessions. Refer to Figure 5-4 for a partial view of the Chicago area connectivity and addressing information.

Figure 5-4 *Case Study—Chicago Configuration*

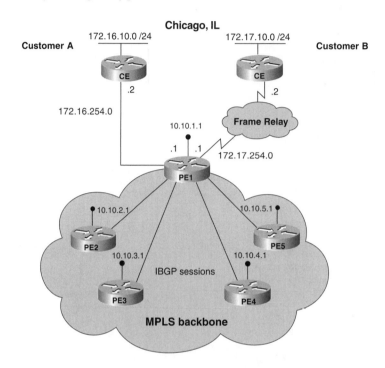

Chicago PE Configuration

```
!
hostname Chicago_PE1
!
ip cef
! CEF switching is a prerequisite for label switching
!
ip vrf vrf1
! Define VPN Routing instance vrf1 (customer A)
 rd 100:1
! Configure the Route Distinguisher for vrf1
 route-target both 100:1
! Configure import and export route-targets for vrf1
!
ip vrf vrf2
! Define VPN Routing instance vrf2 (customer B)
 rd 100:2
! Configure the Route Distinguisher for vrf2
 route-target both 100:2
```

```
! Configure import and export route-targets for vrf2
 route-target import 100:1
! Configure an additional import route-target for vrf2
! This optional command creates a full axtranet between customer A and B
!
interface loopback 0
 ip address 10.10.1.1 255.255.255.255
! Configure the PE loopback IP address
!
interface Serial9/0/0
! Configure the DS3 for label switching to the core
 ip unnumbered loopback0
 encapsulation ppp
 framing c-bit
 cablelength 3
 dsu bandwidth 44210
 clock source internal
 tag-switching ip
!
interface Ethernet4/0/0
! Set up Ethernet interface as VRF link to CE-A router
 ip vrf forwarding vrf1
 ip address 172.16.254.1 255.255.255.252
!
interface Serial 5/0/0
!Set up a Frame Relay PVC as a VRF link to CE-B router
 encapsulation frame-relay
 frame-relay lmi-type ansi
!
interface Serial 5/0/0.1 point-to-point
 ip vrf forwarding vrf2
 ip address 172.17.254.1 255.255.255.252
 frame-relay interface-dlci 101
!
router ospf 100
 network 10.10.1.1 0.0.0.0 area 0
!
router bgp 64512
! Configure BGP sessions
 no synchronization
 no bgp default ipv4-activate
! Deactivate default IPv4 advertisements
 neighbor 10.10.2.1 remote-as 64512
! Define IBGP session with PE2
 neighbor 10.10.2.1 update-source loopback0
 neighbor 10.10.3.1 remote-as 64512
! Define IBGP session with PE3
 neighbor 10.10.3.1 update-source loopback0
 neighbor 10.10.4.1 remote-as 64512
! Define IBGP session with PE4
 neighbor 10.10.4.1 update-source loopback0
 neighbor 10.10.5.1 remote-as 64512
```

continues

```
! Define IBGP session with PE5
 neighbor 10.10.5.1 update-source loopback0
 !
address-family vpnv4 unicast
! Activate PE exchange of VPNv4 NLRI
 neighbor 10.10.2.1 activate
 neighbor 10.10.2.1 send-community extended
 neighbor 10.10.3.1 activate
 neighbor 10.10.3.1 send-community extended
 neighbor 10.10.4.1 activate
 neighbor 10.10.4.1 send-community extended
 neighbor 10.10.5.1 activate
 neighbor 10.10.5.1 send-community extended
 exit-address-family
 !
 address-family ipv4 unicast vrf vrf1
   redistribute static
!Advertise VRF static routes via IBGP to PE routers
   no auto-summary
   exit-address-family
 !
 address-family ipv4 unicast vrf vrf2
   redistribute static
!Advertise VRF static routes via IBGP to PE routers
   no auto-summary
   exit-address-family
 !
! Define a VRF static route for VRF1
ip route vrf vrf1 172.16.10.0 255.255.255.0 e4/0/0
 !
! Define a VRF static route for VRF2
ip route vrf vrf2 172.17.10.0 255.255.255.0 S5/0/0
 !
```

Chicago CE Configuration (Customer A)

```
!
hostname Chicago_CE1
!
interface ethernet0/0
 ip address 172.16.10.254 255.255.255.0
!
interface ethernet0/1
 ip address 172.16.254.2 255.255.255.252
!
ip route 0.0.0.0 0.0.0.0 172.16.254.1
!
```

Chicago CE Configuration (Customer B)

```
!
hostname Chicago_CE2
!
interface ethernet0/0
 ip address 172.17.10.254 255.255.255.0
!
interface Serial 5/0/0
!Set up a Frame Relay PVC as a link to the PE router
 encapsulation frame-relay
 frame-relay lmi-type ansi
!
interface Serial 5/0/0.1 point-to-point
 ip address 172.17.254.2 255.255.255.252
 frame-relay interface-dlci 100
!
ip route 0.0.0.0 0.0.0.0 172.17.254.1
!
```

Seattle Configuration

PE2 in Seattle connects to the Seattle customers using RIPv2 routing sessions. Refer to Figure 5-5 for a partial view of the Seattle area connectivity and addressing information.

Figure 5-5   *Case Study—Seattle Configuration*

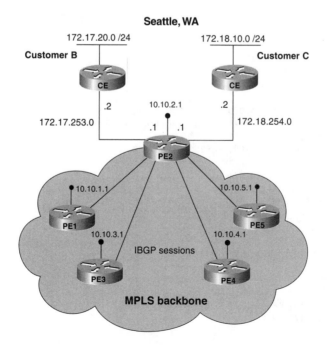

Seattle PE Configuration

```
!
hostname Seattle_PE2
!
ip cef
! CEF switching is a prerequisite for label switching
!
ip vrf vrf2
! Define VPN Routing instance vrf2 (customer A)
 rd 100:2
! Configure the Route Distinguisher for vrf2
 route-target both 100:2
! Configure import and export route-targets for vrf2
 !
ip vrf vrf3
! Define VPN Routing instance vrf3 (customer C)
 rd 100:3
! Configure the Route Distinguisher for vrf3
 route-target both 100:3
! Configure import and export route-targets for vrf3
!
interface loopback 0
 ip address 10.10.2.1 255.255.255.255
! Configure the PE loopback IP address
 !
interface Serial9/0/0
! Configure the DS3 for label switching to the P routers
 ip unnumbered loopback0
 encapsulation ppp
 framing c-bit
 cablelength 3
 dsu bandwidth 44210
 clock source internal
 tag-switching ip
 !
interface Ethernet4/0/0
! Set up Ethernet interface as VRF link to CE-B router
 ip vrf forwarding vrf2
 ip address 172.17.253.1 255.255.255.252
 !
interface Ethernet4/0/1
! Set up Ethernet interface as VRF link to CE-C router
 ip vrf forwarding vrf3
 ip address 172.18.254.1 255.255.255.252
 !
router ospf 100
 network 10.10.2.1 0.0.0.0 area 0
 !
router rip
 version 2
 network 172.18.0.0
 network 172.18.0.0
```

```
address-family ipv4 vrf vrf2
  version 2
  network 172.17.0.0
  redistribute bgp 64512 metric 1
  no auto-summary
  exit-address-family
!
 address-family ipv4 vrf vrf3
  version 2
  network 172.18.0.0
  redistribute bgp 64512 metric 1
  no auto-summary
  exit-address-family


!
router bgp 64512
! Configure BGP sessions
 no synchronization
 no bgp default ipv4-activate
! Deactivate default IPv4 advertisements
 neighbor 10.10.1.1 remote-as 64512
! Define IBGP session with PE1
 neighbor 10.10.1.1 update-source loopback0
 neighbor 10.10.3.1 remote-as 64512
! Define IBGP session with PE3
 neighbor 10.10.3.1 update-source loopback0
 neighbor 10.10.4.1 remote-as 64512
! Define IBGP session with PE4
 neighbor 10.10.4.1 update-source loopback0
 neighbor 10.10.5.1 remote-as 64512
! Define IBGP session with PE5
 neighbor 10.10.5.1 update-source loopback0
!
address-family vpnv4 unicast
! Activate PE exchange of VPNv4 NLRI
 neighbor 10.10.1.1 activate
 neighbor 10.10.1.1 send-community extended
 neighbor 10.10.3.1 activate
 neighbor 10.10.3.1 send-community extended
 neighbor 10.10.4.1 activate
 neighbor 10.10.4.1 send-community extended
 neighbor 10.10.5.1 activate
 neighbor 10.10.5.1 send-community extended
 exit-address-family

address-family ipv4 unicast vrf vrf2
redistribute rip
no auto-summary
no synchronization
exit-address-family
!
```

continues

```
address-family ipv4 unicast vrf vrf3
redistribute rip
no auto-summary
no synchronization
exit-address-family
```

Seattle CE Configuration (Customer B)

```
!
hostname Seattle_CE2
!
interface ethernet0/0
 ip address 172.17.20.254 255.255.255.0
!
interface ethernet0/1
 ip address 172.17.253.2 255.255.255.252
!
router rip
 version 2
 network 172.17.0.0
!
```

Seattle CE Configuration (Customer C)

```
!
hostname Seattle_CE3
!
interface ethernet0/0
 ip address 172.18.10.254 255.255.255.0
!
interface ethernet0/1
 ip address 172.18.254.2 255.255.255.252
!
router rip
 version 2
 network 172.18.0.0
!
```

San Diego Configuration

PE3 in San Diego connects to the San Diego customers using BGP4 routing sessions. Refer to Figure 5-6 for a partial view of the San Diego area connectivity and addressing information.

Figure 5-6   *Case Study—San Diego Configuration*

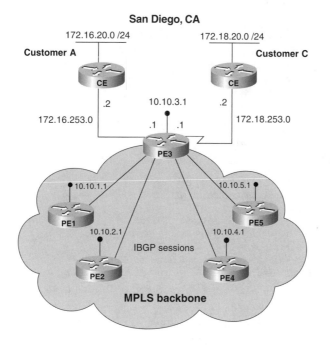

San Diego PE Configuration

```
!
hostname San_Diego_PE3
!
ip cef
! CEF switching is a prerequisite for label switching
!
ip vrf vrf1
! Define VPN Routing instance vrf1 (customer A)
 rd 100:1
! Configure the Route Distinguisher for vrf1
 route-target both 100:1
! Configure import and export route-targets for vrf1
!
ip vrf vrf3
! Define VPN Routing instance vrf3 (customer C)
 rd 100:3
! Configure the Route Distinguisher for vrf3
 route-target both 100:3
! Configure import and export route-targets for vrf3
```

continues

```
!
interface loopback 0
 ip address 10.10.3.1 255.255.255.255
 ! Configure the PE loopback IP address
!
interface Serial9/0/0
 ! Configure the DS3 for label switching to the P routers
 ip unnumbered loopback0
 encapsulation ppp
 framing c-bit
 cablelength 3
 dsu bandwidth 44210
 clock source internal
 tag-switching ip
!
interface Ethernet4/0/0
 ! Set up Ethernet interface as VRF link to CE-A router
 ip vrf forwarding vrf1
 ip address 172.16.253.1 255.255.255.252
!
interface Serial5/0/0
 ! Set up Serial interface as VRF link to CE-C router
 ip vrf forwarding vrf3
 ip address 172.18.253.1 255.255.255.252
!
router ospf 100
 network 10.10.3.1 0.0.0.0 area 0
!
router bgp 64512
 ! Configure BGP sessions
 no synchronization
 no bgp default ipv4-activate
 ! Deactivate default IPv4 advertisements
 neighbor 10.10.1.1 remote-as 64512
 ! Define IBGP session with PE1
 neighbor 10.10.1.1 update-source loopback0
 neighbor 10.10.2.1 remote-as 64512
 ! Define IBGP session with PE2
 neighbor 10.10.2.1 update-source loopback0
 neighbor 10.10.4.1 remote-as 64512
 ! Define IBGP session with PE4
 neighbor 10.10.4.1 update-source loopback0
 neighbor 10.10.5.1 remote-as 64512
 ! Define IBGP session with PE5
 neighbor 10.10.5.1 update-source loopback0
!
address-family vpnv4 unicast
 ! Activate PE exchange of VPNv4 NLRI
 neighbor 10.10.1.1 activate
 neighbor 10.10.1.1 send-community extended
 neighbor 10.10.2.1 activate
 neighbor 10.10.2.1 send-community extended
 neighbor 10.10.4.1 activate
```

```
   neighbor 10.10.4.1 send-community extended
   neighbor 10.10.5.1 activate
   neighbor 10.10.5.1 send-community extended
   exit-address-family
 !
  address-family ipv4 unicast vrf vrf1
   neighbor 172.16.253.2 remote-as 65535
   neighbor 172.16.253.2 activate
   no synchronization
   no auto-summary
   exit-address-family
 !
  address-family ipv4 unicast vrf vrf3
   neighbor 172.18.253.2 remote-as 65534
   neighbor 172.18.253.2 activate
   no synchronization
   no auto-summary
   exit-address-family
 !
```

San Diego CE Configuration (Customer A)

```
 !
hostname San_Diego_CE1
 !
interface ethernet0/0
 ip address 172.16.20.254 255.255.255.0
 !
interface ethernet0/1
 ip address 172.16.253.2 255.255.255.252
 !
router bgp 65535
 neighbor 172.16.253.1 remote-as 64512
 network 172.16.20.0 mask 255.255.255.0
 !
```

San Diego CE Configuration (Customer C)

```
 !
hostname San_Diego_CE3
 !
interface ethernet0/0
 ip address 172.18.20.254 255.255.255.0
 !
interface Serial0/0
 ip address 172.18.253.2 255.255.255.252
```

continues

```
 !
 router bgp 65534
  neighbor 172.16.253.1 remote-as 64512
  network 172.18.20.0 mask 255.255.255.0
 !
```

Miami Configuration

PE4 in Miami connects to the Miami customers using OSPF routing sessions. Refer to Figure 5-7 for a partial view of the Miami area connectivity and addressing information.

Figure 5-7   *Case Study—Miami Configuration*

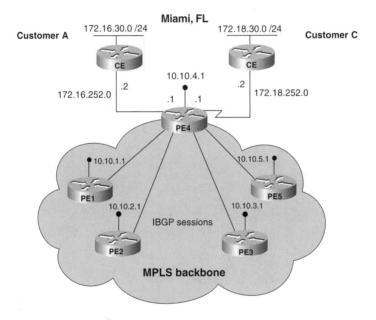

Miami PE Configuration

```
 !
 hostname Miami_PE4
 !
 ip cef
 ! CEF switching is a prerequisite for label switching
 !
 ip vrf vrf1
 ! Define VPN Routing instance vrf1 (customer A)
  rd 100:1
```

```
! Configure the Route Distinguisher for vrf1
 route-target both 100:1
! Configure import and export route-targets for vrf1
!
ip vrf vrf3
! Define VPN Routing instance vrf3 (customer C)
 rd 100:3
! Configure the Route Distinguisher for vrf3
 route-target both 100:3
! Configure import and export route-targets for vrf3
!
interface loopback 0
 ip address 10.10.4.1 255.255.255.255
! Configure the PE loopback IP address
!
interface Serial9/0/0
! Configure the DS3 for label switching to the P routers
 ip unnumbered loopback0
 encapsulation ppp
 framing c-bit
 cablelength 3
 dsu bandwidth 44210
 clock source internal
 tag-switching ip
!
interface Ethernet4/0/0
! Set up Ethernet interface as VRF link to CE-A router
 ip vrf forwarding vrf1
 ip address 172.16.252.1 255.255.255.252
!
interface Serial5/0/0
! Set up Serial interface as VRF link to CE-C router
 ip vrf forwarding vrf3
 ip address 172.18.252.1 255.255.255.252
!
router ospf 100
 network 10.10.4.1 0.0.0.0 area 0
!
router ospf 111 vrf vrf1
 redistribute bgp 64512 subnets metric 10
 network 172.16.0.0 0.0.255.255 area 0
!
router ospf 333 vrf vrf3
 redistribute bgp 64512 subnets metric 10
 network 172.18.0.0 0.0.255.255 area 0
!
router bgp 64512
! Configure BGP sessions
 no synchronization
 no bgp default ipv4-activate
! Deactivate default IPv4 advertisements
 neighbor 10.10.1.1 remote-as 64512
```

continues

```
! Define IBGP session with PE1
 neighbor 10.10.1.1 update-source loopback0
 neighbor 10.10.2.1 remote-as 64512
! Define IBGP session with PE2
 neighbor 10.10.2.1 update-source loopback0
 neighbor 10.10.3.1 remote-as 64512
! Define IBGP session with PE3
 neighbor 10.10.3.1 update-source loopback0
 neighbor 10.10.5.1 remote-as 64512
! Define IBGP session with PE5
 neighbor 10.10.5.1 update-source loopback0
!
address-family vpnv4 unicast
! Activate PE exchange of VPNv4 NLRI
 neighbor 10.10.1.1 activate
 neighbor 10.10.1.1 send-community extended
 neighbor 10.10.2.1 activate
 neighbor 10.10.2.1 send-community extended
 neighbor 10.10.3.1 activate
 neighbor 10.10.3.1 send-community extended
 neighbor 10.10.5.1 activate
 neighbor 10.10.5.1 send-community extended
 exit-address-family
!
 address-family ipv4 unicast vrf vrf1
  redistribute ospf 111 subnets
  no auto-summary
  no synchronization
  exit-address-family
!
 address-family ipv4 unicast vrf vrf3
  redistribute ospf 333 subnets
  no synchronization
  no auto-summary
  exit-address-family
!
```

Miami CE Configuration (Customer A)

```
!
hostname Miami_CE1
!
interface ethernet0/0
 ip address 172.16.30.254 255.255.255.0
!
interface ethernet0/1
 ip address 172.16.253.2 255.255.255.252
!
router ospf 111
 network 172.16.0.0 0.0.255.255 area 0
!
```

Miami CE Configuration (Customer C)

```
!
hostname Miami_CE3
!
interface ethernet0/0
 ip address 172.18.30.254 255.255.255.0
!


interface Serial0/0
 ip address 172.18.252.2 255.255.255.252
!
router ospf 333
 network 172.18.0.0 0.0.255.255 area 0
!
```

Washington Configuration

PE5 in Washington connects to the Washington customers using a mix of static and OSPF routing sessions over Frame Relay. Refer to Figure 5-8 for a partial view of the Washington area connectivity and addressing information.

Figure 5-8   *Case Study—Washington Configuration*

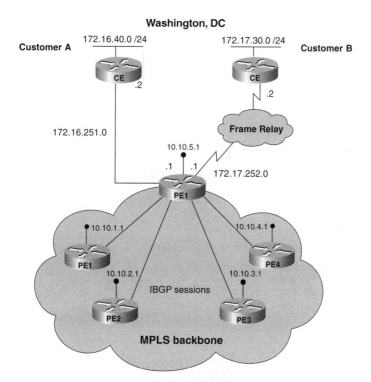

Washington PE Configuration

```
!
hostname Washington_PE5
!
ip cef
! CEF switching is a prerequisite for label switching
!
ip vrf vrf1
! Define VPN Routing instance vrf1
 rd 100:1
! Configure the Route Distinguisher for vrf1 (customer A)
 route-target both 100:1
! Configure import and export route-targets for vrf1
!
ip vrf vrf2
! Define VPN Routing instance vrf2 (customer B)
 rd 100:2
! Configure the Route Distinguisher for vrf2
 route-target both 100:2
! Configure import and export route-targets for vrf2
!
interface loopback 0
 ip address 10.10.5.1 255.255.255.255
! Configure the PE loopback IP address
!
interface Serial9/0/0
! Configure the DS3 for label switching to the P routers
 ip unnumbered loopback0
 encapsulation ppp
 framing c-bit
 cablelength 3
 dsu bandwidth 44210
 clock source internal
 tag-switching ip
!
interface Ethernet4/0/0
! Set up Ethernet interface as VRF link to CE-A router
 ip vrf forwarding vrf1
 ip address 172.16.251.1 255.255.255.252
!
interface Serial 5/0/0
!Set up a Frame Relay PVC as a VRF link to CE-B router
 encapsulation frame-relay
 frame-relay lmi-type ansi
!
interface Serial 5/0/0.1 point-to-point
 ip vrf forwarding vrf2
 ip ospf network point-to-point
 ip address 172.17.252.1 255.255.255.252
 frame-relay interface-dlci 201
!
router ospf 100
```

```
 network 10.10.5.1 0.0.0.0 area 0
 !
router ospf 222 vrf vrf2
 redistribute bgp 64512 subnets metric 10
 network 172.17.0.0 0.0.255.255 area 0
 !
router bgp 64512
! Configure BGP sessions
 no synchronization
 no bgp default ipv4-activate
! Deactivate default IPv4 advertisements
 neighbor 10.10.1.1 remote-as 64512
! Define IBGP session with PE1
 neighbor 10.10.1.1 update-source loopback0
 neighbor 10.10.2.1 remote-as 64512
! Define IBGP session with PE2
 neighbor 10.10.2.1 update-source loopback0
 neighbor 10.10.3.1 remote-as 64512
! Define IBGP session with PE3
 neighbor 10.10.3.1 update-source loopback0
 neighbor 10.10.4.1 remote-as 64512
! Define IBGP session with PE4
 neighbor 10.10.4.1 update-source loopback0
 !
address-family vpnv4 unicast
! Activate PE exchange of VPNv4 NLRI
 neighbor 10.10.1.1 activate
 neighbor 10.10.1.1 send-community extended
 neighbor 10.10.2.1 activate
 neighbor 10.10.2.1 send-community extended
 neighbor 10.10.3.1 activate
 neighbor 10.10.3.1 send-community extended
 neighbor 10.10.4.1 activate
 neighbor 10.10.4.1 send-community extended
 exit-address-family
 !
 address-family ipv4 unicast vrf vrf1
  redistribute static
!Advertise VRF static routes via IBGP to PE routers
  no auto-summary
  exit-address-family
 !
 address-family ipv4 unicast vrf vrf2
  redistribute ospf 222 match internal external 1 external 2
  no auto-summary
  exit-address-family
 !
! Define a VRF static route for VRF1
ip route vrf vrf1 172.16.40.0 255.255.255.0 e4/0/0
 !
```

Washington CE Configuration (Customer A)

```
!
hostname Washington_CE1
!
interface ethernet0/0
 ip address 172.16.40.254 255.255.255.0
!
interface ethernet0/1
 ip address 172.16.251.2 255.255.255.252
!
ip route 0.0.0.0 0.0.0.0 172.16.251.1
!
```

Washington CE Configuration (Customer B)

```
!
hostname Washington_CE2
!
interface ethernet0/0
 ip address 172.17.30.254 255.255.255.0
!
interface Serial0/0
!Set up a Frame Relay PVC as a link to the PE router
 encapsulation frame-relay
 frame-relay lmi-type ansi
!
interface Serial0/0.1 point-to-point
 ip ospf network point-to-point
 ip address 172.17.252.2 255.255.255.252
 frame-relay interface-dlci 200
!
router ospf 222
 network 172.17.0.0 0.0.255.255 area 0
!
```

BGP Route Reflectors

BGP requires that all of the IBGP speakers be fully meshed. However, this requirement does not scale when there are many IBGP speakers. A BGP speaker does not advertise a route learned from another IBGP speaker to a third IBGP speaker. Route reflectors ease this limitation and allow a router to advertise or reflect IBGP-learned routes to other IBGP speakers, thereby reducing the number of IBGP peers within an Autonomous System (AS). BGP confederations can be used to reduce the IBGP full mesh as well by dividing an Autonomous System into Subautonomous Systems. As shown in Figure 5-9, the PE routers form a full BGP mesh. Each PE router peers with four other PE routers, which are IBGP speakers.

Figure 5-9   *BGP Full Mesh*

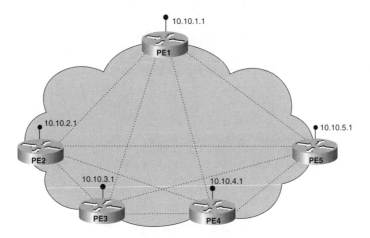

MPLS VPN backbone

The full mesh can be replaced with a proper route reflector design, as shown in Figure 5-10. In this design, PE2 and PE3 are route reflector clients of PE1, which acts as their route reflector. PE4 is a client of PE5. PE1 and PE5 peer with each other to form the backbone IBGP mesh.

Figure 5-10   *Route Reflector Design*

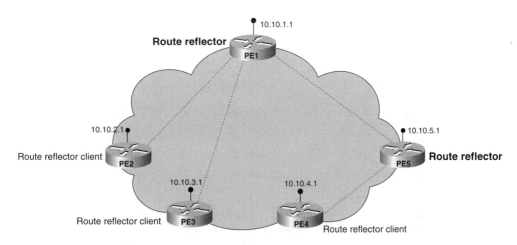

MPLS VPN backbone

When considered as a whole, the route reflector and its clients are called a cluster. Other IBGP peers of the route reflector that are not clients are called nonclients. An AS can have more than one route reflector. When an AS has more than one route reflector, each route reflector treats other route reflectors as normal IBGP speakers. There can be more than one route reflector in a cluster, and there can be more than one cluster in an AS. The BGP configuration for the PE routers in Figure 5-10 is as follows:

```
PE1
!
router bgp 64512
neighbor 10.10.2.1 remote-as 64512
neighbor 10.10.2.1 route-reflector-client
neighbor 10.10.2.1 update-source loopback0
neighbor 10.10.3.1 remote-as 64512
neighbor 10.10.3.1 route-reflector-client
neighbor 10.10.3.1 update-source loopback0
neighbor 10.10.5.1 remote-as 64512
neighbor 10.10.5.1 update-source loopback0
!

PE2
!
neighbor 10.10.1.1 remote-as 64512
neighbor 10.10.1.1 update-source loopback0
!

PE3
!
router bgp 64512
neighbor 10.10.1.1 remote-as 64512
neighbor 10.10.1.1 update-source loopback0
!

PE4
!
router bgp 64512
neighbor 10.10.5.1 remote-as 64512
neighbor 10.10.5.1 update-source loopback0
!

PE5
!
router bgp 64512
neighbor 10.10.4.1 remote-as 64512
neighbor 10.10.4.1 route-reflector-client
neighbor 10.10.4.1 update-source loopback0
neighbor 10.10.1.1 remote-as 64512
neighbor 10.10.1.1 update-source loopback0
!
```

In order to increase redundancy and avoid single points of failure, clusters can be configured. A cluster might have more than one route reflector. When a cluster has more than one route reflector, all the route reflectors in the cluster need to be configured with a 4-byte cluster ID. The cluster ID allows route reflectors to recognize updates from other route reflectors in the same cluster. It is good design practice to fully mesh the clients within a cluster with the route reflectors. This way, if one of the route reflectors fails, the remaining route reflector can pick up the BGP routes and continue forwarding traffic.

Inter-Autonomous System MPLS VPNs

An autonomous system is a single network or group of networks that is controlled by a common system administration group and that uses a single routing protocol. As VPNs increase in size, their geographical scope and requirements expand. In some cases, VPNs need to reside on different autonomous systems in different geographic areas controlled by separate service providers. As VPNs extend across multiple service providers over various locations, the connection between autonomous systems must be seamless to the customer. The Inter-AS feature for MPLS VPNs provides connectivity and integration between service providers and results in seamless customer VPNs.

Separate autonomous systems from different service providers can communicate by exchanging IPv4 network layer reachability information (NLRI) in the form of VPN-IPv4 addresses. The autonomous systems' border routers use the Exterior Border Gateway Protocol (EBGP) to exchange that information. An Interior Gateway Protocol (IGP) then distributes the network layer information for VPN-IPv4 prefixes throughout each VPN and each autonomous system.

The primary function of EBGP is to exchange network reachability information between autonomous systems, including information about the list of autonomous system routes. The autonomous systems use EGBP border edge routers to distribute the routes, which include label switching information. Each border edge router rewrites the next-hop and MPLS labels.

Inter-Autonomous System MPLS VPN Architectures

The following are inter-autonomous system MPLS VPN architectures:

- **Inter-Provider VPN**—MPLS VPNs that include two or more autonomous systems connected by separate border edge routers. The autonomous systems exchange routes using EBGP. No IGP or routing information is exchanged between the autonomous systems.

- **BGP confederations**—MPLS VPNs that divide a single autonomous system into multiple subautonomous systems and classify them as a single, designated confederation. The network recognizes the confederation as a single autonomous system. The peers in the different autonomous systems communicate over EBGP sessions; however, they can exchange route information as if they were IBGP peers.

Inter-Provider MPLS VPN Configuration

Figure 5-11 illustrates two autonomous systems, AS1 and AS2, under separate administrative management. CE1 and CE2 are CE routers that belong to the same VPN (VPN1). Autonomous system 1 (AS1) includes PE1, P1, and EBGP1. The IGP is OSPF.

Figure 5-11 *Inter-Provider MPLS VPN*

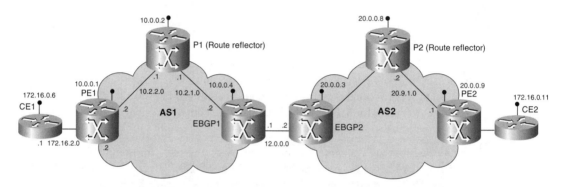

Autonomous system 2 (AS2) includes PE2, P2, and EBGP2. The IGP is IS-IS. The P routers are route reflectors. EBGP1 is configured with the **redistribute connected subnets** command, and EBGP2 is configured with the **neighbor next-hop-self** command. The configurations for the various CE routers and LSRs used for the Inter-Provider MPLS VPN illustrated in Figure 5-11 are shown in the following sections.

Configuration for AS1, CE1

The following is the configuration used for the Customer Edge (CE) router CE1. CE1 and CE2 are both members of Virtual Private Network VPN1.

```
!
interface Loopback0
 ip address 172.16.0.1 255.255.255.255
!
interface Serial0/1
 description CE1 to PE1
 ip address 172.16.2.1 255.255.255.252
!
router ospf 1
 network 172.16.0.0 0.0.255.255 area 0
!
```

Configuration for AS1, PE1

The following is the configuration used for the Provider Edge (PE) router PE1.

```
!
ip cef
!
ip vrf V1
 rd 1:105
 route-target export 1:100
 route-target import 1:100
!
interface Loopback0
 ip address 10.0.0.1 255.255.255.255
!
interface Serial0/0
 description PE1 to CE1
 ip vrf forwarding VPN1
 ip address 172.16.2.2 255.255.255.252
 !
interface Ethernet0/0
 description PE1 to P1
 ip address 10.2.2.2 255.255.255.0
 tag-switching ip
!
router ospf 1
 log-adjacency-changes
 network 10.0.0.0 0.255.255.255 area 0
!
router ospf 10 vrf VPN1
 log-adjacency-changes
 redistribute bgp 1 metric 100 subnets
 network 172.16.0.0 0.0.255.255 area 0
!
router bgp 1
 no synchronization
 neighbor R peer-group
 neighbor R remote-as 1
 neighbor R update-source Loopback0
 neighbor 10.0.0.2 peer-group R
 no auto-summary
 !
 address-family ipv4 vrf VPN1
 redistribute ospf 10
 no auto-summary
 no synchronization
 exit-address-family
 !
 address-family vpnv4
 neighbor R activate
 neighbor R send-community extended
 neighbor 10.0.0.2 peer-group R
```

continues

```
  no auto-summary
  exit-address-family
  !
```

Configuration for AS1, P1

The following is the configuration used for the provider (P) router P1. P1 acts as a route
reflector for all IBGP devices within AS1.

```
!
ip cef
!
interface Loopback0
 ip address 10.0.0.2 255.255.255.255
!
interface Ethernet0/0
 description P1 to EBGP1
 ip address 10.2.1.1 255.255.255.0
 tag-switching ip
!
interface Ethernet0/1
 description P1 to PE1
 ip address 10.2.2.1 255.255.255.0
 tag-switching ip
!
router ospf 1
 log-adjacency-changes
 network 10.0.0.0 0.255.255.255 area 0
!
router bgp 1
 no synchronization
 bgp log-neighbor-changes
 neighbor R peer-group
 neighbor R remote-as 1
 neighbor R update-source Loopback0
 neighbor R route-reflector-client
 neighbor 10.0.0.4 peer-group R
 neighbor 10.0.0.5 peer-group R
 !
 address-family vpnv4
 neighbor R activate
 neighbor R route-reflector-client
 neighbor R send-community extended
 neighbor 10.0.0.4 peer-group R
 neighbor 10.0.0.5 peer-group R
 exit-address-family
 !
```

Configuration for AS1, EBGP1

The following is the configuration used for Exterior Border Gateway Protocol router 1 (EBGP1). EBGP1 is configured with the **redistribute connected subnets** command and interfaces with AS2.

```
!
ip cef
!
interface Loopback0
 ip address 10.0.0.4 255.255.255.255
!
interface Ethernet0/0
 description EBGP1 to P1
 ip address 10.2.1.2 255.255.255.0
 tag-switching ip
!
interface Serial0/0
 description EBGP1 to EBGP2
 ip address 12.0.0.1 255.255.255.252
!
router ospf 1
 log-adjacency-changes
 redistribute connected subnets
 network 10.0.0.0 0.255.255.255 area 0
!
router bgp 1
 no synchronization
 no bgp default route-target filter
 bgp log-neighbor-changes
 neighbor R peer-group
 neighbor R remote-as 1
 neighbor R update-source Loopback0
 neighbor 12.0.0.2 remote-as 2
 neighbor 10.0.0.2 peer-group R
 no auto-summary
 !
 address-family vpnv4
 neighbor R activate
 neighbor R send-community extended
 neighbor 12.0.0.2 activate
 neighbor 12.0.0.2 send-community extended
 neighbor 10.0.0.2 peer-group R
 no auto-summary
 exit-address-family
!
```

Configuration for AS2, EBGP2

The following is the configuration used for Exterior Border Gateway Protocol router 2 (EBGP2). EBGP2 is configured with the **neighbor next-hop-self** command and interfaces with AS1.

```
!
ip cef
!
ip vrf VPN1
 rd 2:103
 route-target export 1:100
 route-target import 1:100
!
interface Loopback0
 ip address 20.0.0.3 255.255.255.255
 ip router isis
!
interface Loopback1
 ip vrf forwarding VPN1
 ip address 172.16.0.3 255.255.255.255
!
interface Serial0/0
 description EBGP2 to P2
 ip unnumbered Loopback0
 ip router isis
 tag-switching ip
!
interface Serial0/1
 description EBGP2 to EBGP1
 ip address 12.0.0.2 255.255.255.252
!
router isis
 net 49.0002.0000.0000.0003.00
!
router bgp 2
 no synchronization
 no bgp default route-target filter
 bgp log-neighbor-changes
 neighbor 12.0.0.1 remote-as 1
 neighbor 20.0.0.8 remote-as 2
 neighbor 20.0.0.8 update-source Loopback0
 neighbor 20.0.0.8 next-hop-self
!
address-family ipv4 vrf V1
 redistribute connected
 no auto-summary
 no synchronization
 exit-address-family
!
address-family vpnv4
 neighbor 12.0.0.1 activate
 neighbor 12.0.0.1 send-community extended
 neighbor 20.0.0.8 activate
 neighbor 20.0.0.8 next-hop-self
 neighbor 20.0.0.8 send-community extended
 exit-address-family
!
```

Configuration for AS2, P2

The following is the configuration used for the provider (P) router P2. P2 acts as a route reflector for all IBGP devices within AS2.

```
!
ip cef
!
ip vrf VPN1
 rd 2:108
 route-target export 1:100
 route-target import 1:100
!
interface Loopback0
 ip address 20.0.0.8 255.255.255.255
 ip router isis
!
interface Loopback1
 ip vrf forwarding VPN1
 ip address 172.16.0.8 255.255.255.255
!
interface Ethernet0/0
 description P2 to PE2
 ip address 20.9.1.2 255.255.255.0
 ip router isis
 tag-switching ip
!
interface Serial0/0
 description P2 to EBGP2
 ip unnumbered Loopback0
 ip router isis
 tag-switching ip
!
router isis
 net 49.0002.0000.0000.0008.00
!
router bgp 2
 no synchronization
 bgp log-neighbor-changes
 neighbor R peer-group
 neighbor R remote-as 2
 neighbor R update-source Loopback0
 neighbor R route-reflector-client
 neighbor 20.0.0.3 peer-group R
 neighbor 20.0.0.9 peer-group R
!
 address-family ipv4 vrf VPN1
  redistribute connected
  no auto-summary
  no synchronization
  exit-address-family
```

continues

```
!
address-family vpnv4
 neighbor R activate
 neighbor R route-reflector-client
 neighbor R send-community extended
 neighbor 20.0.0.3 peer-group R
 neighbor 20.0.0.9 peer-group R
 exit-address-family
!
```

Configuration for AS2, PE2

The following is the configuration used for the provider edge (PE) router PE2.

```
!
ip cef
!
ip vrf VPN1
 rd 2:109
 route-target export 1:100
 route-target import 1:100
!
interface Loopback0
 ip address 20.0.0.9 255.255.255.255
 ip router isis
!
interface Loopback1
 ip vrf forwarding VPN1
 ip address 172.16.0.9 255.255.255.255
!
interface Serial0/0
 description PE2 to CE2
 no ip address
 ip vrf forwarding VPN1
 ip unnumbered Loopback1
!
interface Ethernet0/0
 description PE2 to P2
 ip address 20.9.1.1 255.255.255.0
 ip router isis
 tag-switching ip
!
router ospf 10 vrf V1
 log-adjacency-changes
 redistribute bgp 2 subnets
 network 172.16.0.0 0.0.255.255 area 0
!
router isis
 net 49.0002.0000.0000.0009.00
!
router bgp 2
```

```
no synchronization
bgp log-neighbor-changes
neighbor 20.0.0.8 remote-as 2
neighbor 20.0.0.8 update-source Loopback0
!
address-family ipv4 vrf V1
 redistribute connected
 redistribute ospf 10
 no auto-summary
 no synchronization
 exit-address-family
!
address-family vpnv4
 neighbor 20.0.0.8 activate
 neighbor 20.0.0.8 send-community extended
 exit-address-family
!
```

Configuration for AS2, CE2

The following is the configuration used for the customer edge (CE) router CE2. CE1 and CE2 are both members of Virtual Private Network VPN1.

```
!
interface Loopback0
 ip address 172.16.0.2 255.255.255.255
!
interface Serial0/0
 description CE2 to PE2
 ip unnumbered Loopback0
!
router ospf 1
 network 172.16.0.0 0.0.255.255 area 0
!
```

BGP Confederation Inter-Provider MPLS VPN Configuration

The network topology in Figure 5-12 shows a single Internet service provider (ISP) that is partitioning the backbone with confederations.

The provider's AS number is 100. The two ASs run their own IGPs and are configured with AS1, which includes PE1, P1, and EBGP1. The IGP used for AS1 is OSPF. AS2 includes PE2, P2, and EBGP2. The IGP used for AS2 is IS-IS. CE1 and CE2 belong to the same VPN, which is called VPN1. The P routers are route reflectors. EBGP1 is configured with the **redistribute connected subnets** command. EBGP2 is configured with the **neighbor next-hop-self** command. The configurations for the various CE routers and LSRs used for the BGP Confederation Inter-Provider MPLS VPN illustrated in Figure 5-12 are shown in the following sections.

Figure 5-12 *BGP Confederation Inter-Provider MPLS VPN*

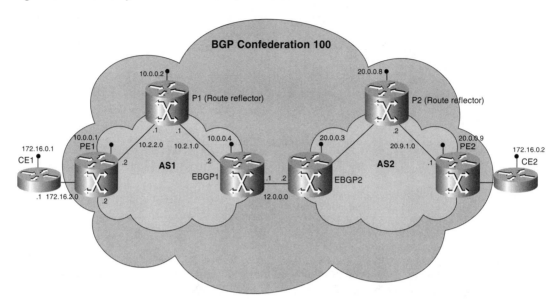

Configuration for AS1, CE1

The following is the configuration used for the customer edge (CE) router CE1. CE1 and CE2 are both members of Virtual Private Network VPN1.

```
!
interface Loopback0
 ip address 172.16.0.1 255.255.255.255
!
interface Serial0/1
 description CE1 to PE1
 ip address 172.16.2.1 255.255.255.252
!
router ospf 1
 network 172.16.0.0 0.0.255.255 area 0
!
```

Configuration for AS1, PE1

The following is the configuration used for the provider edge (PE) router PE1.

```
!
ip cef
!
ip vrf V1
 rd 1:105
 route-target export 1:100
 route-target import 1:100
!
interface Loopback0
 ip address 10.0.0.1 255.255.255.255
!
interface Serial0/0
 description PE1 to CE1
 ip vrf forwarding VPN1
 ip address 172.16.2.2 255.255.255.252
 !
interface Ethernet0/0
 description PE1 to P1
 ip address 10.2.2.2 255.255.255.0
 tag-switching ip
!
router ospf 1
 log-adjacency-changes
 network 10.0.0.0 0.255.255.255 area 0
!
router ospf 10 vrf VPN1
 log-adjacency-changes
 redistribute bgp 1 metric 100 subnets
 network 172.16.0.0 0.0.255.255 area 0
!
router bgp 1
no synchronization
bgp confederation identifier 100
neighbor R peer-group
neighbor R remote-as 1
neighbor R update-source Loopback0
neighbor 10.0.0.2 peer-group R
no auto-summary

!
 address-family ipv4 vrf VPN1
 redistribute ospf 10
 no auto-summary
 no synchronization
 exit-address-family
 !
 address-family vpnv4
 neighbor R activate
 neighbor R send-community extended
 neighbor 10.0.0.2 peer-group R
 no auto-summary
 exit-address-family
!
```

Configuration for AS1, P1

The following is the configuration used for the provider (P) router P1. P1 acts as a route reflector for all IBGP devices within AS1.

```
!
ip cef
!
interface Loopback0
 ip address 10.0.0.2 255.255.255.255
!
interface Ethernet0/0
 description P1 to EBGP1
 ip address 10.2.1.1 255.255.255.0
 tag-switching ip
!
interface Ethernet0/1
 description P1 to PE1
 ip address 10.2.2.1 255.255.255.0
 tag-switching ip
!
router ospf 1
 log-adjacency-changes
 network 10.0.0.0 0.255.255.255 area 0
!
router bgp 1
no synchronization
bgp log-neighbor-changes
bgp confederation identifier 100
neighbor R peer-group
neighbor R remote-as 1
neighbor R update-source Loopback0
neighbor R route-reflector-client
neighbor 10.0.0.4 peer-group R
neighbor 10.0.0.5 peer-group R
!
address-family vpnv4
 neighbor R activate
 neighbor R route-reflector-client
 neighbor R send-community extended
 neighbor 10.0.0.4 peer-group R
 neighbor 10.0.0.5 peer-group R
 exit-address-family
!
```

Configuration for AS1, EBGP1

The following is the configuration used for Exterior Border Gateway Protocol router 1 (EBGP1). EBGP1 is configured with the **redistribute connected subnets** command and interfaces with AS2.

```
!
ip cef
!
interface Loopback0
 ip address 10.0.0.4 255.255.255.255
!
interface Ethernet0/0
 description EBGP1 to P1
 ip address 10.2.1.2 255.255.255.0
 tag-switching ip
!
interface Serial0/0
 description EBGP1 to EBGP2
 ip address 12.0.0.1 255.255.255.252
!
router ospf 1
 log-adjacency-changes
 redistribute connected subnets
 network 10.0.0.0 0.255.255.255 area 0
!
router bgp 1
 no synchronization
 no bgp default route-target filter
 bgp log-neighbor-changes
 bgp confederation identifier 100
 bgp confederation peers 1
 neighbor R peer-group
 neighbor R remote-as 1
 neighbor R update-source Loopback0
 neighbor 12.0.0.2 remote-as 2
 neighbor 12.0.0.2 next-hop-self
 neighbor 100.0.0.2 peer-group R
 no auto-summary
 !
 address-family vpnv4
 neighbor R activate
 neighbor R send-community extended
 neighbor 12.0.0.2 activate
 neighbor 12.0.0.2 next-hop-self
 neighbor 12.0.0.2 send-community extended
 neighbor 100.0.0.2 peer-group R
 no auto-summary
 exit-address-family
 !
```

Configuration for AS2, EBGP2

The following is the configuration used for Exterior Border Gateway Protocol router 2 (EBGP2). EBGP2 is configured with the **neighbor next-hop-self** command and interfaces with AS1.

```
!
ip cef
!
ip vrf VPN1
 rd 2:103
 route-target export 1:100
 route-target import 1:100
!
interface Loopback0
 ip address 20.0.0.3 255.255.255.255
 ip router isis
!
interface Loopback1
 ip vrf forwarding VPN1
 ip address 172.16.0.3 255.255.255.255
!
interface Serial0/0
 description EBGP2 to P2
 ip unnumbered Loopback0
 ip router isis
 tag-switching ip
!
interface Serial0/1
 description EBGP2 to EBGP1
 ip address 12.0.0.2 255.255.255.252
!
router isis
 net 49.0002.0000.0000.0003.00
!
router bgp 2
no synchronization
no bgp default route-target filter
bgp log-neighbor-changes
bgp confederation identifier 100
bgp confederation peers 1
neighbor 12.0.0.1 remote-as 1
neighbor 12.0.0.1 next-hop-self
neighbor 20.0.0.8 remote-as 2
neighbor 20.0.0.8 update-source Loopback0
neighbor 20.0.0.8 next-hop-self
!
address-family ipv4 vrf VPN1
 redistribute connected
 no auto-summary
 no synchronization
 exit-address-family
!
address-family vpnv4
neighbor 12.0.0.1 activate
neighbor 12.0.0.1 next-hop-self
neighbor 12.0.0.1 send-community extended
neighbor 20.0.0.8 activate
```

```
neighbor 20.0.0.8 next-hop-self
neighbor 20.0.0.8 send-community extended
exit-address-family
!
```

Configuration for AS2, P2

The following is the configuration used for the provider (P) router P2. P2 acts as a route reflector for all IBGP devices within AS2.

```
!
ip cef
!
ip vrf VPN1
 rd 2:108
 route-target export 1:100
 route-target import 1:100
!
interface Loopback0
 ip address 20.0.0.8 255.255.255.255
 ip router isis
!
interface Loopback1
 ip vrf forwarding VPN1
 ip address 172.16.0.8 255.255.255.255
!
interface Ethernet0/0
 description P2 to PE2
 ip address 20.9.1.2 255.255.255.0
 ip router isis
 tag-switching ip
!
interface Serial0/0
 description P2 to EBGP2
 ip unnumbered Loopback0
 ip router isis
 tag-switching ip
!
router isis
 net 49.0002.0000.0000.0008.00
!
router bgp 2
no synchronization
bgp log-neighbor-changes
bgp confederation identifier 100
neighbor R peer-group
neighbor R remote-as 2
neighbor R update-source Loopback0
neighbor R route-reflector-client
neighbor 20.0.0.3 peer-group R
```

continues

```
neighbor 20.0.0.9 peer-group R
!
address-family ipv4 vrf VPN1
 redistribute connected
 no auto-summary
 no synchronization
 exit-address-family
!
address-family vpnv4
 neighbor R activate
 neighbor R route-reflector-client
 neighbor R send-community extended
 neighbor 20.0.0.3 peer-group R
 neighbor 20.0.0.9 peer-group R
 exit-address-family
!
```

Configuration for AS2, PE2

The following is the configuration used for the provider edge (PE) router PE2.

```
!
ip cef
!
ip vrf VPN1
 rd 2:109
 route-target export 1:100
 route-target import 1:100
!
interface Loopback0
 ip address 20.0.0.9 255.255.255.255
 ip router isis
!
interface Loopback1
 ip vrf forwarding VPN1
 ip address 172.16.0.9 255.255.255.255
!
interface Serial0/0
 description PE2 to CE2
 no ip address
 ip vrf forwarding VPN1
 ip unnumbered Loopback1
!
interface Ethernet0/0
 description PE2 to P2
 ip address 20.9.1.1 255.255.255.0
 ip router isis
 tag-switching ip
!
router ospf 10 vrf VPN1
 log-adjacency-changes
```

```
   redistribute bgp 2 subnets
   network 172.16.0.0 0.0.255.255 area 0
 !
 router isis
  net 49.0002.0000.0000.0009.00
 !
 router bgp 2
 no synchronization
 bgp log-neighbor-changes
 bgp confederation identifier 100
 neighbor 20.0.0.8 remote-as 2
 neighbor 20.0.0.8 update-source Loopback0
 !
 address-family ipv4 vrf VPN1
  redistribute connected
  redistribute ospf 10
  no auto-summary
  no synchronization
  exit-address-family
 !
  address-family vpnv4
  neighbor 20.0.0.8 activate
  neighbor 20.0.0.8 send-community extended
  exit-address-family
 !
```

Configuration for AS2, CE2

The following is the configuration used for the customer edge (CE) router CE2. CE1 and
CE2 are both members of Virtual Private Network VPN1.

```
 !
 interface Loopback0
  ip address 172.16.0.2 255.255.255.255
 !
 interface Serial0/0
  description CE2 to PE2
  ip unnumbered Loopback0
 !
 router ospf 1
  network 172.16.0.0 0.0.255.255 area 0
 !
```

Carrier-over-Carrier MPLS VPNs

The carrier-supporting-carrier feature lets one MPLS VPN-based service provider allow
other service providers to use a segment of its backbone network. Carrier-supporting-
carrier is a term used to describe a situation in which one service provider allows another

service provider to use a segment of its backbone network. The service provider that provides the segment of the backbone network to the other provider is called the backbone carrier. The service provider that uses the segment of the backbone network is called the customer carrier. This section focuses on a backbone carrier that offers BGP and MPLS VPN services. The customer carrier can be either an ISP or an MPLS VPN service provider.

Providing a Backbone Network to a Customer Carrier (ISP)

Consider an ISP with two major IP networks, as shown in Figure 5-13. One network is in California, and the other is in Virginia. The ISP wants to connect these sites using a VPN service provided by a national backbone carrier. In this example, only the backbone carrier uses MPLS. The customer carrier (ISP) uses only IP. As a result, the backbone carrier must carry all the Internet routes of the customer carrier, which could be as many as 100,000 routes. This poses a scalability problem for the backbone carrier.

Figure 5-13 *Backbone Carrier Supporting an ISP*

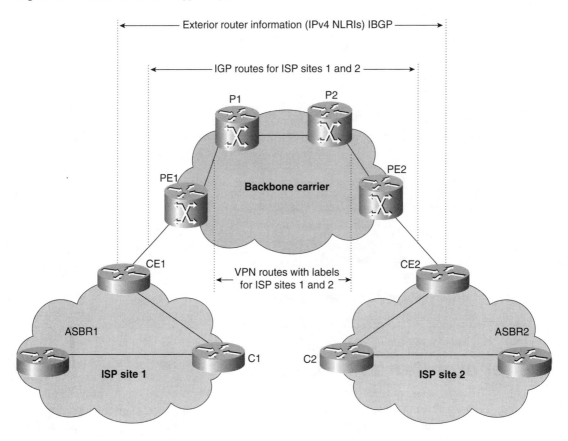

In order to solve the scalability problem, the backbone carrier is configured so that it allows only internal routes of the customer carrier (IGP routes) to be exchanged between the CE routers of the customer carrier and the PE routers of the backbone carrier. MPLS is enabled on the interface between the CE router of the customer carrier and the PE router of the backbone carrier. Internal routes go to any of the routers within the ISP, and external routes go to the Internet. The number of internal routes is much smaller than the number of external routes. Restricting the routes between the CE routers of the customer carrier and the PE routers of the backbone carrier significantly reduces the number of routes that the PE router needs to maintain.

Because the PE routers do not have to carry external routes in the VRF routing table, they can use the incoming label in the packet to forward the customer carrier Internet traffic. Adding MPLS to the routers provides a consistent method of transporting packets from the customer carrier to the backbone carrier. MPLS allows the exchange of an MPLS label between the PE and the CE routers for every internal customer carrier route. The routers in the customer carrier have all the external routes either through IBGP or route redistribution to provide Internet connectivity.

Providing a Backbone Network to a Customer Carrier (MPLS VPN Service Provider)

When a backbone carrier and the customer carrier both provide BGP/MPLS VPN services, the method of transporting data is different from when a customer carrier provides only ISP services. This is illustrated in Figure 5-14.

When a customer carrier provides BGP/MPLS VPN services, its external routes are VPN-IPv4 routes. However, when a customer carrier is an ISP, its external routes are IP routes. Also, when a customer carrier provides BGP/MPLS VPN services, each and every site within the customer carrier network must use MPLS. However, when a customer carrier is an ISP, the sites do not need to use MPLS.

Figure 5-14 *Backbone Carrier Supporting a Customer Carrier Offering MPLS VPN Services*

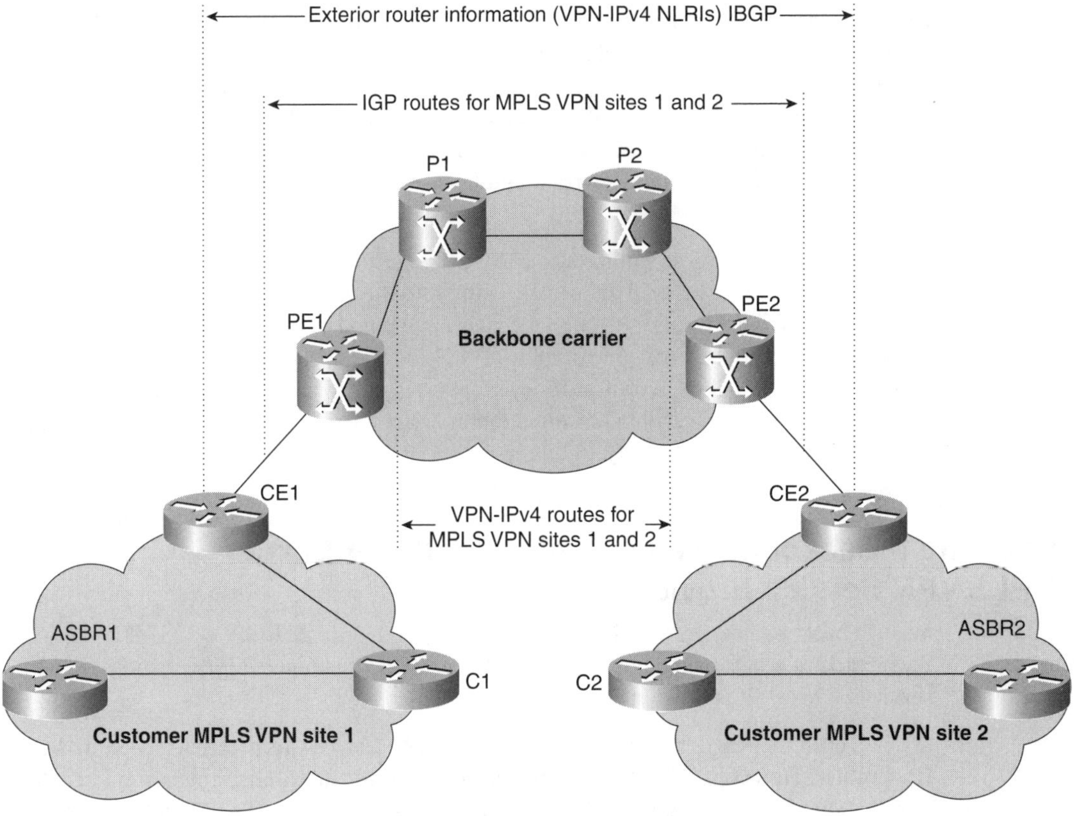

Internet Access over MPLS VPNs

MPLS VPN networks are essentially service provider backbones that provide MPLS Layer 3 VPN services to customers. Customers normally request Internet access from an Internet service provider. In the case of MPLS VPN service provision, it is possible for the MPLS service provider to provide Internet access for its customers as well. Internet access for customer VPNs can be achieved in a variety of ways within the MPLS architecture. The major design constraint while permitting Internet access over your MPLS backbone should be the propagation of full Internet routes. Full-route propagation must be prevented at any cost, because it will overwhelm your MPLS VRF routing tables, increase CPU utilization, and exhaust LSR memory. The design rule of thumb is to propagate default routes wherever possible. Or, as described in the section "Carrier-over-Carrier MPLS VPNs," IGP routes may be propagated over peering CE routers.

Internet Connectivity via an External ISP

This method of connectivity is illustrated in Figure 5-15. VPN1 has a presence in three sites. CE2 and CE3 have full intranet connectivity with CE1. CE1 is connected to an ISP through a PIX firewall and screening router. CE1 has a default route pointing to the PIX, and PE1 has a default route pointing to the next-hop CE1. The default route carried by PE1 for the VPN1 VRF is propagated over MP-BGP to PE2 and PE3, which also have a presence for the VPN1 VRF.

Figure 5-15 *Internet Connectivity via an External ISP*

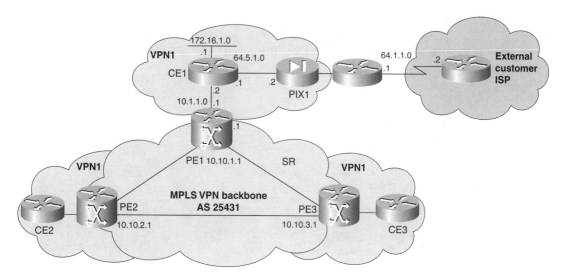

The central site firewall PIX1 provides security and Network Address Translation (NAT) or Port Address Translation (PAT) services for members of VPN1. It is possible for one or more remote sites to have Internet connectivity of their own as well. In this case, multiple default routes could be injected into the VRF instance for VPN1. However, this might result in suboptimal forwarding of packets over multiple default gateways.

CE1 Configuration

The following is a partial configuration for the customer edge router CE1, which acts as the default gateway to the Internet.

```
!
hostname CE1
!
interface ethernet0/0
 ip address 172.16.1.1 255.255.255.0
```

continues

```
!
interface ethernet0/1
 ip address 64.5.1.1 255.255.255.0
!
interface serial0/0
 ip address 10.1.1.2 255.255.255.0
!
ip route 0.0.0.0 0.0.0.0 64.5.1.2
!
```

PE1 Configuration

The following is a partial configuration for the provider edge router PE1, which has an Internet default gateway for the VPN1 VRF pointing to CE1.

```
!
hostname PE1
!
router bgp 64512
 no synchronization
 no bgp default ipv4-activate
 neighbor 10.10.2.1 remote-as 64512
 neighbor 10.10.2.1 update-source loopback0
 neighbor 10.10.3.1 remote-as 64512
 neighbor 10.10.3.1 update-source loopback0
!
address-family vpnv4 unicast
 neighbor 10.10.2.1 activate
 neighbor 10.10.2.1 send-community extended
 neighbor 10.10.3.1 activate
 neighbor 10.10.3.1 send-community extended
 exit-address-family
!
 address-family ipv4 unicast vrf VPN1
  redistribute static
  no auto-summary
  exit-address-family
!
ip route vrf VPN1 0.0.0.0 0.0.0.0 10.1.1.2
ip route vrf VPN1 172.16.1.0 255.255.255.0 10.1.1.2
!
```

Internet Connectivity Using Static Default Routes

As explained earlier in this chapter, PE routers store VPN routes in VRF routing tables and global routes in the global routing table. The global routing table contains routes other than VPN routes, such as management subnets and Internet routes. If the MPLS service provider were to provide Internet connectivity over the MPLS backbone to the various customer

VPNs, default routes could be used to point to an external gateway connected to a central PE router. This means that the default route injected into the VRF table would point to a next-hop address contained in the global routing table. Packets destined for the Internet would leave the VPN space and attempt a next hop that falls within the global address space. This method of connectivity is illustrated in Figure 5-16.

Figure 5-16 *Internet Connectivity Using a Static Default Route*

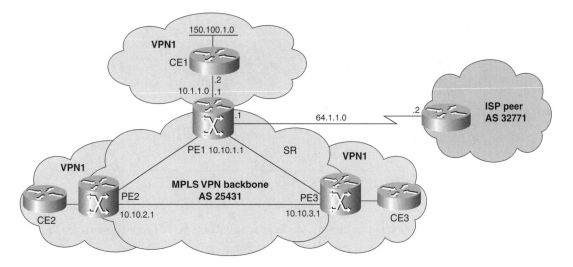

VPN1 has a presence in three sites. CE2 and CE3 have full intranet connectivity with CE1. In this example, static default routes have been configured in the VPN1 VRF on PE2 and PE3 that point to the Internet gateway connected to PE1. The IP address of the Internet gateway (64.1.1.2) must be advertised within the backbone IGP so that it is present in the global routing table. This ensures that packets destined for the Internet can be properly forwarded to the gateway. Because there is no automatic redistribution between IPv4 and VPN-IPv4 routes, routing for Internet packets is achieved through the use of the **global** keyword within the static default route configuration. The **global** keyword indicates that the next-hop address is resolved using the global routing table and not the VRF.

The customer subnets could use registered IP addressing. In this case, static routes need to be configured on the PE routers pointing to next-hop addresses, which belong to the VPN1 VRF. A special feature of MPLS/VPN lets the next-hop address be specified even though the next hop is not present in the global routing table. The presence of the customer static routes in the global routing table enables advertisement of these routes to the Internet via redistribution into BGP4 or via the use of **network** statements. If redistribution is used, route maps must be used to specify which prefixes need to be advertised. PE1 has a choice of using a static default route pointing to the peering ISP router or exchanging full or partial routes with the peering ISP router. If the PE1 router has memory and CPU utilization issues, it is advisable to advertise the registered customer routes using network statements and filter the Internet routes using a route map with a distribute-list filter. Customers can use private IP addresses, in which case NAT or PAT must be performed at the CE routers.

CE1 Configuration

A partial configuration for the customer edge router CE1 is as follows:

```
!
hostname CE1
!
interface ethernet0/0
 ip address 150.100.1.1 255.255.255.0
!
interface serial0/0
 ip address 10.1.1.2 255.255.255.0
!
ip route 0.0.0.0 0.0.0.0 10.1.1.1
!
```

PE1 Configuration

A partial configuration for the provider edge router PE1, which is connected to the Internet, is as follows:

```
!
hostname PE1
!
interface serial0/0
 ip address 64.1.1.1 255.255.255.0
!
router bgp 25431
 no synchronization
 no bgp default ipv4-activate
 neighbor 10.10.2.1 remote-as 24531
 neighbor 10.10.2.1 update-source loopback0
 neighbor 10.10.3.1 remote-as 25431
 neighbor 10.10.3.1 update-source loopback0
 neighbor 64.1.1.2 remote-as 32771
 network 150.100.1.0 mask 255.255.255.0
 network 150.200.1.0 mask 255.255.255.0
 network 150.300.1.0 mask 255.255.255.0
!
address-family vpnv4 unicast
 neighbor 10.10.2.1 activate
 neighbor 10.10.2.1 send-community extended
 neighbor 10.10.3.1 activate
 neighbor 10.10.3.1 send-community extended
 exit-address-family
```

```
 !
  address-family ipv4 unicast vrf VPN1
   redistribute static
   no auto-summary
   exit-address-family
 !
 ip route vrf VPN1 0.0.0.0 0.0.0.0 64.1.1.2 global
 ip route 150.100.1.0 255.255.255.0 ethernet0/0 10.1.1.2
 !
```

Internet Connectivity Using BGP Sessions

Customer CE routers can communicate with PE routers using BGP. These sites can receive Internet routes via BGP. PE routers typically store Internet routes in their global routing tables and VPN routes in the VRF.

If the MPLS service provider has multiple external BGP peering points, the choice of egress points can be determined by customer configuration, such as the setting of BGP next hop or by establishing an EBGP multihop session with the desired egress router.

BGP Next-Hop Configuration

In the case of BGP next-hop configuration, a second interface (physical or logical subinterface) is necessary to distribute routes from the global routing table to the customer site and to recognize routes from the customer site that need to be placed in the global table of the PE rather than the VRF. A BGP session must be established between the PE and CE routers across the second interface, and the CE router must advertise customer routes that will be propagated to the rest of the Internet from the global table. CE routers will learn Internet routes via an interface or subinterface and VPN routes through the other. The traffic flow is asymmetrical in the sense that traffic traveling from a VPN site to the Internet utilizes the VRF interface, and the return traffic uses the global interface. The disadvantage of the BGP next-hop approach is that it requires two physical interfaces or subinterfaces and also does not address the AS_PATH issue. This causes the loss of information if the egress point selected is not the best path selected by the BGP process on the PE router. It is also possible to configure a tunnel for VPN destinations and use the main interface for Internet-destined packets. In this case, the routes learned across the main interface are Internet routes, and the routes learned across the tunnel interface are VPN routes.

NOTE   There are distinct disadvantages associated with the BGP next-hop configuration method for Internet access. There is a requirement to use a second physical interface or subinterface, which leads to scalability issues as well as loss of AS_PATH information. Furthermore, there are security risks associated with the BGP next-hop method in the sense that packets from the Internet can make their way into the customer VPN unless filtering and security policies are enforced on the perimeter. The recommended design method for BGP session connectivity is the EBGP multihop solution, described in the next section.

EBGP Multihop Configuration

The EBGP multihop configuration method requires only one interface and maintains AS_PATH information. Figure 5-17 illustrates Internet connectivity using EBGP multihop configuration. There is no need to reset the routes' BGP next hop. Customer routes can be exchanged directly with the Internet egress point. A default route can be set up within the VRF to forward Internet traffic to the egress point.

Figure 5-17 *Internet Connectivity Using EBGP Multihop Sessions*

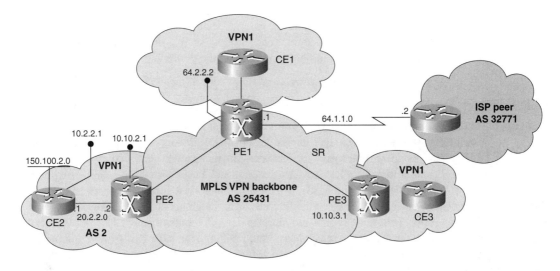

Figure 5-17 illustrates the operation of the EBGP multihop session method of Internet connectivity for MPLS VPNs. CE2 communicates directly with the Internet gateway (64.2.2.2) using an EBGP multihop session. The gateway and BGP next-hop addresses for all routes that will be learned from this peer are injected into the VPN1 VRF via static routes and are advertised across the BGP session between PE2 and CE2.

It is not necessary to run BGP between the PE and CE. Any other supported routing protocol (including static routes) can be configured. The relevant configurations for CE2 and PE2 are illustrated in the following sections.

CE1 Configuration

A partial configuration for the customer edge router CE1 is as follows:

```
!
hostname CE1
!
interface loopback0
 ip address 10.2.2.1 255.255.255.0
!
interface ethernet0/0
 ip address 150.100.2.1 255.255.255.0
!
interface serial0/0
 ip address 20.2.2.1 255.255.255.0
!
router bgp 2
 neighbor 64.2.2.2 remote-as 25431
 neighbor 64.2.2.2 ebgp-multihop 255
 neighbor 64.2.2.2 update-source loopback0
 neighbor 10.10.2.1 remote-as 25431
 neighbor 10.10.2.1 update-source loopback0
 neighbor 10.10.2.1 activate
!
```

PE2 Configuration

A partial configuration for the provider edge router PE2 is as follows:

```
!
hostname PE2
!
interface serial0/0
 ip address 20.2.2.2 255.255.255.0
!
router bgp 25431
 no synchronization
 no bgp default ipv4-activate
 neighbor 64.2.2.2 remote-as 25431
 neighbor 64.2.2.2 update-source loopback0
 neighbor 64.2.2.2 activate
!
address-family vpnv4 unicast
 neighbor 64.2.2.2 activate
 neighbor 64.2.2.2 send-community extended
 exit-address-family
!
 address-family ipv4 unicast vrf VPN1
  redistribute static
  redistribute connected
```

continues

```
   neighbor 10.2.2.1 remote-as 2
   neighbor 10.2.2.1 activate
   no auto-summary
   no synchronization
   exit-address-family
 !
 ip route 10.2.2.1 255.255.255.255 serial0/0
 ip route vrf VPN1 0.0.0.0 0.0.0.0 64.2.2.2 global
 ip route vrf VPN1 64.2.2.2 255.255.255.255 20.2.2.2
 !
```

MPLS Redundancy Using HSRP

HSRP provides network redundancy in a way that ensures that user traffic immediately and transparently recovers from first-hop failures in network edge devices and access circuits. By sharing an IP address and a MAC (Layer 2) address, two or more routers can act as a single virtual router to the hosts on a LAN. The members of the router group continually exchange status messages by detecting when a router goes down. This HSRP group consists of an active router and a standby router to replace the active router should it fail. The address of this HSRP group is called the *virtual IP address*.

Hot Standby Router Protocol (HSRP) support on an MPLS VPN interface is useful when an Ethernet is connected between two PE routers using either a CE with a default route to the HSRP virtual IP address or one or more hosts with the HSRP virtual IP address configured as the default gateway.

HSRP Support Between Two VRF Interfaces

Figure 5-18 illustrates HSRP support between the two VRF interfaces belonging to PE1 and PE2. The CE uses the virtual IP address of 10.10.10.10 as the next-hop address for its default static route. The real IP addresses of 10.10.10.1 and 10.10.10.2 are configured on PE1 and PE2. PE1 can be prioritized to remain active, and PE2 is in standby mode. The serial interfaces to the P router are tracked. This ensures that the links that experience a greater number of flaps will be automatically designated with a lower priority.

Figure 5-18 *HSRP Support Between Two VRF Interfaces*

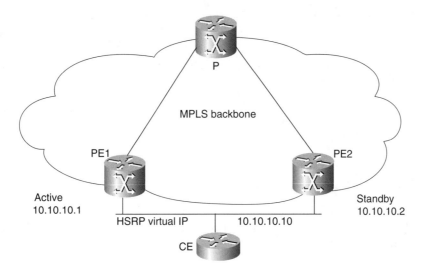

The configuration is as follows:

HSRP configuration of PE1:

```
!
ip cef
!
ip vrf vrf1
 rd 100:1
 route-target export 100:1
 route-target import 100:1
!
interface ethernet0/0
 ip vrf forwarding vrf1
 ip address 10.10.10.1 255.255.255.0
 standby 1 ip 10.10.10.10
 standby 1 priority 110 preempt delay 10
 standby 1 timers 3 1
 standby 1 track serial0/0 10
!
```

HSRP configuration of PE2:

```
!
ip cef
!
ip vrf vrf1
```

continues

```
 rd 100:1
 route-target export 100:1
 route-target import 100:1
 !
interface ethernet0/0
 ip vrf forwarding vrf1
 ip address 10.10.10.2 255.255.255.0
 standby 1 ip 10.10.10.10
 standby 1 priority 100 preempt delay 10
 standby 1 timers 3 1
 standby 1 track serial0/0 10
 !
```

Trace Route Enhancements

Expired TTL packets do not return to a source if there is a break in the Interior Gateway Protocol (IGP) path. Currently, MPLS forwards the expired TTL packets by re-imposing the original label stack and forwarding the packet to the end of a Label-Switch Path (LSP). For provider edge routers forwarding traffic over a virtual private network (VPN), this is the only way to get the packet back to the source.

If there is a break in the IGP path to the end of the LSP, the packet never reaches its source. Packets that have a single label are usually a global address or terminal VPN labels. Those packets can be forwarded using the global IP routing table. Packets that have more than one label can use the original label stack.

With the traceroute enhancements, executing the command on the router, the network manager can display all MPLS hops between PE-PE in a PE-PE trace route, or display MPLS cloud as one hop in CE-CE trace route. This provides better traceroute and debug capabilities and provides reliable traceroute capabilities by providing the support for packets to be forwarded either using the label stack or using the global routing tables depending on the number of labels present.

MPLS VPN Management Using the Cisco VPN Solutions Center

Cisco VPN Solutions Center: MPLS Solution is an MPLS VPN provisioning and auditing tool. The application software focuses on the PE routers, the CE routers, and the links between them. MPLS VPN Solution software integrates with Cisco IP Manager for element management tasks such as downloading configurations to target routers. Additional features include CoS provisioning, VPN-aware NetFlow accounting, and Service-Level Agreement (SLA) monitoring.

Cisco VPNSC lets service providers effectively deploy and manage MPLS VPN services. It comprises a comprehensive and integrated offering of operations management functions

covering the management of MPLS VPN services throughout the service life cycle. The
Collection Architecture of Cisco VPNSC is illustrated in Figure 5-19. Its capabilities
include service provisioning and activation, service auditing, SLA monitoring, and usage
collection and reporting. The Cisco VPNSC provides a set of application programming
interfaces (APIs) and is preintegrated into most Cisco Service Management (CSM)
modules.

Figure 5-19 *Cisco VPNSC Collection Architecture*

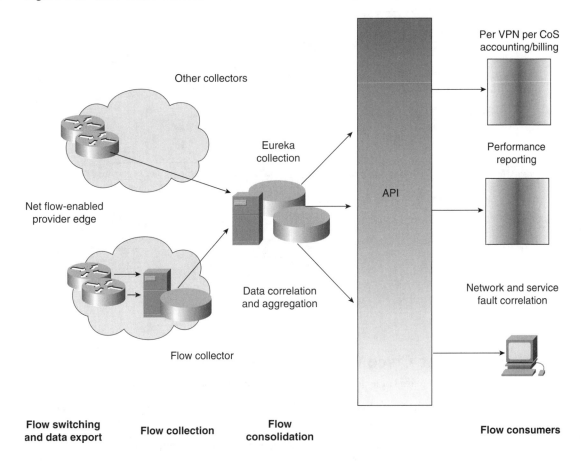

A service provider that opts to deploy other CSM applications extends the value of the
Cisco VPNSC and makes CSM modules VPN-aware. Value-added additions such as Cisco
Provisioning Center and Cisco Info Center extend the VPNSC capability into multivendor
environments. VPNSC can be used by itself to help service providers improve their time to
deploy services, enable error-free deployment, and reduce operational costs associated with
providing VPN services. A schematic of the VPNSC architecture is shown in Figure 5-20.

Figure 5-20 *Cisco VPNSC Architecture*

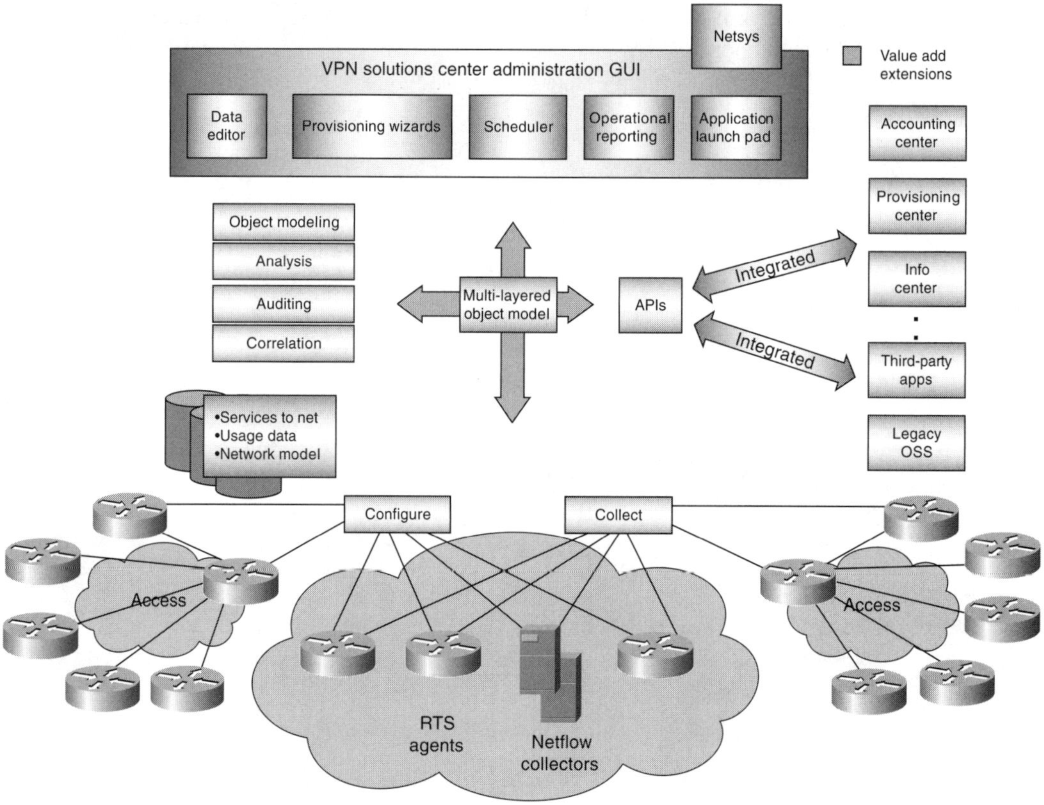

Advantages of the Cisco VPN Solutions Center

The following are some advantages of the Cisco VPN Solutions Center:

- A provisioning subsystem for MPLS VPN service provisioning with a scheduler for time-based provisioning.

- Support for provisioning of quality of service (QoS) parameters for effectively policing and enabling differentiated classes of service.

- A wizard-based service request entry offering ease of use for operators. CVPNSC provides easy-to-use wizard-based setup and administration of VPN memberships. It also checks and reduces errors in service setup and checks for data inconsistencies.

- Comprehensive hub-and-spoke and full-mesh VPN topology views and acts as an auditor for validating IP VPN service configuration and ensuring the integrity of the network.

- An accounting subsystem for VPN and CoS-aware usage collection and reporting.
- An SLA subsystem for VPN-aware SLA monitoring functions.
- Open interfaces via provisioning, accounting, and performance APIs for third-party application and Operations Support System (OSS) integration.
- IOS support for Cisco routers, switches, and gigabit switch routers (GSRs).
- Enables the creation of differentiated VPN service offerings via QoS provisioning.
- Reduces overall operational and management costs and provides reports via Web-based access to near-real-time performance data.
- Promotes confidence in the deployment of VPNs through pre- and post-activation testing and enables rapid delivery of VPN services, thereby increasing overall competitiveness in the market.

Key Functions of Cisco VPNSC

The following are some key functions of Cisco VPNSC:

- **Provisioning**—Cisco VPNSC offers step-by-step information-assisted population of templates. Operators can add, delete, or modify customer VPNs. In addition, they can easily set up extranet relationships. Templates are then converted into the appropriate Cisco IOS software commands, which are then scheduled and downloaded to the network.
- **Scheduling**—When a new service or service change is entered, users can schedule the service activation time, allowing the service provider to make arrangements for hardware delivery or for other steps required prior to activation of the service.
- **Activation**—Service changes are activated in the network through reliable delivery of Cisco IOS software commands to the appropriate network elements. Elements are tested to ensure successful delivery of the commands.
- **Post-activation testing**—When activated, services can be tested to ensure reliable delivery of the service. For instance, a site-to-site ping test ensures correct activation of a new site to an existing VPN service.
- **Service auditing**—VPNSC can generate reports on the status of service requests (pending or deployed). When scheduled, the solution reads the current configuration files for the routers, analyzes the service request history, and generates a report based on the current status of the service deployment.
- **Usage**—Using Cisco NetFlow technology, VPNSC provides per-VPN intranet and extranet performance reporting. NetFlow captures traffic statistics, including information at the application port and customer IP address level. Information provided by VPN reports helps customers evaluate their own internal resource consumption.

- **SLA monitoring and reporting**—VPNSC also monitors SLAs for round-trip time, availability, and usage by taking advantage of agents provided in existing routers. Thresholds can be configured that allow violations to be reported.

- **QoS provisioning and measurement**—VPNSC provides QoS provisioning that allows service providers to offer different CoSs. VPNSC generates the router configuration that allocates bandwidth to different CoSs and measures SLA compliance through the Response Time Reporter (RTR) agent, a feature within Cisco IOS software.

NOTE   Service providers must consider other management solutions, such as Cisco Works 2000 WAN Manager (BPX and MGX support), Cisco View, Resource Manager Essentials, and other applications that will complement Cisco VPNSC for day-to-day operation of the network. A well-managed, organized network with the proper documentation is the key to operational success in the short and long term.

VPNSC provides extensive open APIs and is preintegrated into most CSM modules. In addition, the value of these APIs can be realized by other applications, such as billing (Belle Systems IMS), fault monitoring (Cisco Info Center), and reporting (Concord eHealth). For example, Info Center can use these APIs to query which services were affected because of a certain network outage by querying the VPNSC repository using these open APIs.

NOTE   VPNSC supports the following equipment as PE devices: Cisco MGX 8850; Cisco 75*xx*, 72*xx*, 71*xx*, 47*xx*, 45*xx*, and 36*xx* routers; Cisco DSL 6400; and Cisco uBR7246. The Cisco IOS software versions currently supported are 12.05(T), 12.06(T), 12.07(T), 12.1, 12.1(3)T(uBR 7246), and 12.1.1(DC) (DSL6400) on the PEs.

VPNSC supports the following equipment as CE devices: Cisco 47*xx*, 45*xx*, 3810, 36*xx*, 26*xx*, 25*xx*, 17*xx*, 16*xx*, and 14*xx* routers. The Cisco IOS software version currently supported is 11.1 on the CEs.

Summary

The VPN feature for MPLS allows a service provider network to deploy scalable IPv4 Layer 3 VPN backbone services. These services can be deployed over a Layer 3 routed backbone or over an ATM backbone. This chapter has covered MPLS deployment over packet-based LSRs. MPLS VPNs are built using various MPLS elements such as P routers, PE routers, and CE routers. P routers are found in the service provider core network and do not terminate VPNs. PE routers essentially constitute the service provider's point of presence and terminate VPNs. CE routers are CPE devices that need not be capable of MPLS.

A VRF defines the VPN membership of a customer site attached to a PE router. A VRF consists of an IP routing table, a derived CEF table, a set of interfaces that use the forwarding table, and a set of rules and routing protocol parameters that control the information that is included in the routing table. The list of route target community values is set from an export list of route targets associated with the VRF from which the route was learned.

A PE router can learn an IP prefix from a CE router by static configuration, through a BGP session with the CE router, or through RIPv2 or OSPF sessions with the CE router. The case study presented all aspects of PE-to-CE configuration modes and can be used as an example to build packet-based MPLS VPNs.

BGP requires that all the IBGP speakers be fully meshed. However, this requirement does not scale when there are many IBGP speakers. A BGP speaker does not advertise a route learned from another IBGP speaker to a third IBGP speaker. Route reflectors ease this limitation and allow a router to advertise or reflect IBGP-learned routes to other IBGP speakers, thereby reducing the number of IBGP peers within an AS.

As VPNs extend across multiple service providers over various locations, the connection between autonomous systems must be seamless to the customer. The Inter-AS feature for MPLS VPNs provides connectivity and integration between service providers and results in seamless customer VPNs.

The carrier-supporting-carrier feature lets one MPLS VPN-based service provider allow other service providers to use a segment of its backbone network. Carrier-supporting-carrier describes a situation in which one service provider allows another service provider to use a segment of its backbone network. The service provider that provides the segment of the backbone network to the other provider is called the backbone carrier.

In the case of MPLS VPN service provision, it is possible for the MPLS service provider to provide Internet access for its customers as well. Internet access for customer VPNs can be achieved in a variety of ways within the MPLS architecture. The major design constraint while permitting Internet access over your MPLS backbone should be the propagation of full Internet routes. Full-route propagation must be prevented at any cost, because it will overwhelm your MPLS VRF routing tables, increase CPU utilization, and exhaust LSR memory. Internet connectivity can be configured using static default routes or BGP sessions. BGP sessions can be configured using either the BGP next-hop configuration method or via EBGP multihop configuration.

HSRP support on an MPLS VPN interface is useful when an Ethernet is connected between two PE routers using either a CE with a default route to the HSRP virtual IP address or one or more hosts with the HSRP virtual IP address configured as the default gateway.

Cisco VPN Solutions Center is an MPLS VPN provisioning and auditing tool. The software focuses on the PEs, the CEs, and the link between them. MPLS VPN Solutions software integrates with Cisco IP Manager for element management tasks such as downloading configlets to target routers. Additional features include CoS provisioning, VPN-aware NetFlow accounting, and SLA monitoring.

This chapter covers the following topics:

- **Introduction to ATM-Based MPLS VPNs**—Service providers and carriers that currently provide ATM and Frame Relay services can utilize their existing ATM infrastructure to provide managed VPN services using MPLS. IP transport over ATM networks requires a complex hierarchy of translation protocols to map IP addresses and routing into ATM addressing and routing. MPLS eliminates complexity by mapping IP addressing and routing information directly into ATM switching tables.

- **MPLS and Tag Switching Terminology**—Tag Switching was Cisco's prestandard offering. Cisco has taken the initiative to be fully standards-compliant with respect to MPLS and has migrated many Tag Switching procedures and formats to MPLS standards. IOS supports MPLS commands as well as Tag Switching commands. This section compares MPLS terminology with that used in Tag Switching.

- **Packet-Based MPLS over ATM**—MPLS networks can use conventional ATM switches as a migration step in introducing MPLS to an existing ATM network. They can also be used to backhaul traffic when the access device (CE router) is remote from the Edge LSR, to tunnel through ATM switches between an Edge LSR and an ATM LSR, and to tunnel through ATM switches between ATM LSRs.

- **ATM-Based MPLS**—This section discusses the operation of MPLS over native ATM using ATM LSRs as Provider Edge (PE) routers and WAN switched ATM LSRs as Provider (P) routers. Such an infrastructure offers service providers the QoS levels guaranteed by ATM core networks and completely alleviates the scalability problem posed by the ATM overlay model.

- **Cell Interleaving**—This section discusses the challenges posed by label VC allocation over ATM for multiple sources transmitting data to the same destination. This section also explains how MPLS supports switches that do not have VC merge capability.

- **VC Merge**—This section discusses how VC merge allows ATM LSRs to transmit cells coming from different VCIs over the same outgoing VCI toward the same destination. This helps reduce the number of Label Virtual Circuits required in the MPLS network.

- **Label Virtual Circuits**—ATM Virtual Circuits (VCs) established for MPLS are called Label Virtual Circuits (LVCs). This section discusses how ATM MPLS uses the VCI fields of a few separate VPIs to carry labels. Each label on a link corresponds to a different LVC.

- **Label Switch Controllers**—The Label Switch Controller (LSC) manages the control and forwarding component of the ATM LSR. This section discusses how the ATM LSR differs from an ordinary ATM switch in the way connections are set up.

- **Virtual Switch Interface**—A Virtual Switch Interface (VSI) provides a standard interface so that a resource in the BPX switch can be controlled by an external controller other than the built-in BPX controller card.

- **IP+ATM**—IP+ATM capability of the ATM LSRs can be used to simultaneously provide MPLS service and traditional ATM switching. This is an extremely attractive proposition for service providers that would like to retain their ATM or Frame Relay installed base as well as expand their portfolio to include MPLS-based IP VPN services.

- **Packet-Based MPLS over ATM VPNs**—This section discusses the configuration of packet-based MPLS over ATM virtual circuits.

- **Case Study of a Packet-Based MPLS over ATM VPN**—This section discusses a service provider offering Layer 3 IP VPN services across its MPLS backbone.

- **ATM-Based MPLS VPNs**—This section discusses ATM-based MPLS Virtual Private Networks.

- **Case Study of an ATM-Based MPLS VPN**—This section discusses a service provider offering Layer 3 IP VPN services over its MPLS-enabled ATM backbone.

CHAPTER **6**

ATM-Based MPLS VPNs

Introduction to ATM-Based MPLS VPNs

Service providers that currently operate ATM or Frame Relay networks over an ATM backbone can leverage the benefits provided by Multiprotocol Label Switching (MPLS). From a cost perspective, enormous savings can be realized if you do not have to build an MPLS network from the ground up. Service providers and carriers that currently provide ATM and Frame Relay services can utilize their existing infrastructure to provide managed Virtual Private Network (VPN) services using MPLS. This is possible if the ATM switches are MPLS-aware. For non-MPLS ATM switches, MPLS can be configured on MPLS-aware routers, and the underlying ATM Virtual Circuits (VCs) will be considered ATM links.

Deploying MPLS IP VPNs over an MPLS-aware ATM backbone has huge advantages, in the sense that VPN customers can be provisioned with hard QoS guarantees, similar to those found with ATM. If the ATM backbone is being used as an ISP backbone, MPLS provides immediate value by enabling traffic engineering of traffic flows over underutilized paths, thereby optimizing link usage within the network. MPLS solutions give ATM networks the ability to intelligently see IP application traffic as distinct from ATM or Frame Relay traffic. By harnessing the attributes of both IP and ATM, service providers can provision intranet or extranet VPNs.

Without MPLS, IP transport over ATM networks requires a complex hierarchy of translation protocols to map IP addresses and routing into ATM addressing and routing. MPLS eliminates complexity by mapping IP addressing and routing information directly into ATM switching tables. The MPLS label-swapping paradigm is the same mechanism that ATM switches use to forward ATM cells. This solution has the added benefit of allowing service providers to continue offering their current Frame Relay, leased-line, and ATM services portfolio while allowing them to offer differentiated business-quality IP services.

Service providers or carriers that currently operate a Cisco Stratacom-based BPX or MGX network can benefit greatly from the design principles and case study implementations presented in this chapter. The VPN feature of MPLS allows a service provider network to deploy scalable IPv4 Layer 3 VPN backbone services. These services can be deployed over a Layer 3 routed backbone or over an MPLS-aware ATM backbone. This chapter explains deployment over an ATM backbone.

MPLS and Tag Switching Terminology

Cisco has taken the initiative to be fully standards-compliant with respect to MPLS and has migrated many Tag Switching procedures and formats to MPLS standards. IOS supports **mpls** commands as well as **tag-switching** commands. Table 6-1 compares MPLS terminology with that used in Tag Switching.

Table 6-1   *Tag Switching and MPLS Terminology*

Tag Switching Terminology	MPLS Terminology
Tag Switching	MPLS (Multiprotocol Label Switching)
Tag (item or packet)	Label
TDP (Tag Distribution Protocol)	LDP (Label Distribution Protocol)
Tag-switched	Label-switched
TFIB (Tag Forwarding Information Base)	LFIB (Label Forwarding Information Base)
TSR (Tag-Switched Router)	LSR (Label-Switched Router)
TSC (Tag Switch Controller)	LSC (Label Switch Controller)
ATM TSR (ATM Tag-Switched Router)	ATM LSR (ATM Label-Switched Router)
TVC (Tag Virtual Circuit)	LVC (Label Virtual Circuit)
TSP (Tag Switch Path)	LSP (Label-Switch-Path)
XTag ATM (extended Tag ATM port)	XmplsATM (extended MPLS ATM port)

NOTE   Cisco TDP (Tag Distribution Protocol) and LDP (MPLS Label Distribution Protocol) are nearly identical in function but use incompatible message formats and some different procedures. Cisco is changing from TDP to a fully-compliant LDP.

MPLS Elements

This section defines multiple MPLS elements. Figure 6-1 illustrates the MPLS elements in a network environment.

The MPLS elements are as follows:

- **Label-Switched Router (LSR)**—A device that implements the MPLS control and forwarding components as already described.

- **Label-Controlled ATM interface (LC-ATM interface)**—An ATM interface controlled by the MPLS control component. Cells traversing such an interface carry labels in the VCI field of a user-selected range of VPIs. The control component could be integrated in the switch or on an outside controller.

- **ATM LSR**—An LSR based on an ATM switch. It has LC-ATM interfaces.
- **Packet-based LSR**—An LSR that forwards complete packets between its interfaces. A packet-based LSR can have zero or more LC-ATM interfaces. Packet-based LSRs typically consist of MPLS software running on ordinary router platforms, such as the Cisco 3600, 4700, 7200, or 7500 series. Sometimes there are some hardware features specifically for MPLS, as on the Cisco 12000 series.
- **ATM Edge LSR**—A packet-based LSR that is connected to the ATM-LSR cloud via LC-ATM interfaces. The function of the ATM Edge LSR is to add labels to unlabeled packets and to strip labels from labeled packets.

NOTE   Edge LSRs are part of the same service provider network as ATM-LSRs. Edge LSRs are not intended to be customer premises equipment (CPE) or customer-located equipment.

Figure 6-1   *MPLS Network Elements*

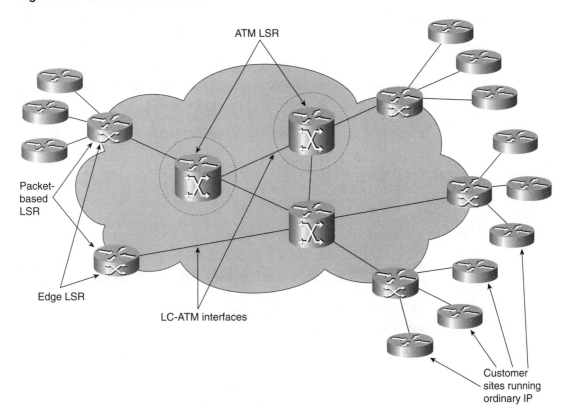

Packet-Based MPLS over ATM

The operation of MPLS over ATM Private Virtual Circuits (PVCs) results in an overlay model. MPLS is configured on ATM routers, which perform Provider (P) and Provider Edge (PE) router functionality. This model does not realize the full advantages of the underlying ATM QoS. However, for service providers that are running core ATM networks with non-MPLS ATM switches, MPLS can still be deployed to create VPNs or leverage the advantages of traffic engineering.

Service providers can run MPLS in an ATM overlay mode during the transition from an IP over ATM overlay model to a full IP+ATM MPLS model.

The ATM overlay model requires $((n)(n-1))/2$ PVCs in order to form a full mesh, where n is the number of routers in the core. Each router peers directly with $(n-1)$ routers and ends up with $(n-1)$ adjacencies. The amount of link-state routing information that is transmitted in the event of a topology change in the core can be as much as n^4.

This leads to scalability issues with respect to adding routers to the core, because routing traffic in itself can overwhelm the core routers.

Other scalability issues are involved with the ATM overlay model. There are limitations on the number of virtual circuits that can be deployed over a physical interface due to limitations on the switch resources required to support the large number of VCs per interface. Also, if a physical links goes down, it takes a large number of VCs down with it.

MPLS networks can use conventional ATM switches as a migration step to introduce MPLS to an existing ATM network. They can also be used to backhaul traffic when the access device (CE router) is remote from the Edge LSR, to tunnel through ATM switches between an Edge LSR and an ATM LSR, and to tunnel through ATM switches between ATM LSRs.

The label allocation scheme uses independent mode. The LDP relationship is established with unsolicited downstream label distribution. MPLS requires ATM adaptation Layer 5 SNAP (AAL5SNAP) encapsulation in order to run over ATM PVCs. The MPLS over ATM encapsulation technique is shown in Figure 6-2.

Figure 6-2 *Packet-Based MPLS over ATM Encapsulation Technique*

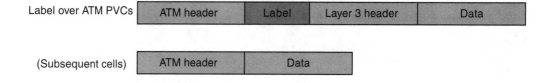

ATM-Based MPLS

The operation of MPLS over native ATM using ATM LSRs as Provider Edge (PE) routers and WAN switched ATM LSRs as Provider (P) routers offers service providers the QoS levels guaranteed by ATM core networks and completely alleviates the scalability problem posed by the ATM overlay model.

Forwarding Component

The VPI/VCI pair identifies the ATM virtual circuit and is local to an interface. The VPI/VCI value of the incoming cell is used to look up the outgoing interface and outgoing VPI/VCI value. In an ATM environment, the label-switching forwarding function is carried out similarly to normal switching. The label information needed for label switching is carried in the VCI field within one or a small number of VPs. The labels are actually the VCIs. 16 bits in the VCI field of the ATM UNI or NNI header permits 65,536 unique label values for a single VPI.

In order to run MPLS, the top label of the label stack is translated into a VCI or VPI/VCI value. The label allocation and distribution procedures are modified so that the ATM LSR looks up the VCI or VPI/VCI label value and determines the outgoing interface and outgoing label. The MPLS ATM encapsulation technique is shown in Figure 6-3.

Figure 6-3   *ATM MPLS Encapsulation Technique*

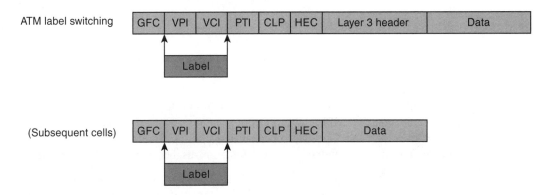

The ATM LSR is controlled by a routing engine such as a 7500 or 7200 in case of a BPX or the RPM in case of the MGX. In Figure 6-4, an unlabeled IP packet with a destination address of 172.16.2.5 arrives at Edge LSR1. LSR1 looks into its label forwarding information base (LFIB) and matches the destination with prefix 172.16.0.0/16 and a label value of 40. LSR1 sends an ATM adaptation Layer 5 (AAL5) frame as a sequence of cells on VCI 40. LSR2, which is an ATM LSR controlled by a Label Switch Controller (LSC), performs a normal switching operation by switching cells coming on interface 2/VCI 40 to interface 0/VCI 50.

Figure 6-4 *LFIB in an ATM MPLS Environment*

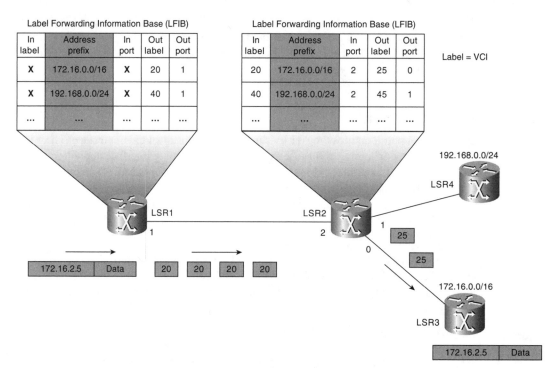

Control Component

The control component of MPLS consists of link-state IP routing protocols such as Open Shortest Path First (OSPF) and Intermediate System-to-Intermediate System (IS-IS) running in conjunction with MPLS label allocation and maintenance procedures. The control component is responsible for setting up label forwarding paths along IP routes. The control component also maintains accuracy for the paths, because network topologies are prone to change.

ATM LSRs use the downstream-on-demand allocating mechanism. Each ATM-LSR maintains an LFIB that contains a list of all IP routes that the ATM LSR uses. This function is handled by the routing engine function, which is either embedded in the switch (RPM in case of the MGX) or run on an outside controller (LSC in case of the BPX). For each route in its Forwarding Information Base (FIB), the edge ATM LSR identifies the next hop for a route. It then issues a request via LDP to the next hop for a label binding for that route.

When the next-hop ATM LSR receives the route, it allocates a label and creates an entry in its LFIB with the incoming label changed to the allocated outgoing label. The next action depends on whether the label allocation is in independent mode or ordered mode. In independent mode, it immediately returns the binding between the incoming label and the route to the LSR that sent the request. However, this might mean that it cannot immediately forward labeled packets that arrive, because the ATM-LSR might not yet have an outgoing label/VCI for the route. In ordered mode, it does not immediately return the binding, but waits until it has an outgoing label.

In ordered mode, the next-hop LSR sends a new binding request to its next hop, and the process repeats until the destination ATM Edge LSR is reached. This returns a label binding to the previous ATM-LSR, causing it to return a label binding, and so on, until the label bindings along the path are established.

Figure 6-5 illustrates ordered behavior. ATM edge LSR1 is an IP routing peer to ATM-LSR2. In turn, ATM-LSR2 is an IP routing peer to ATM-LSR3. LSR1-LSR2 and LSR2-LSR3 exchange IP routing updates over VPI/VCI 0/32.

Figure 6-5   *Ordered Mode Downstream-on-Demand Label Allocation*

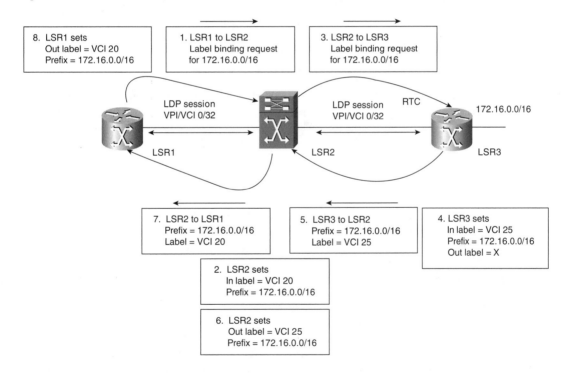

The following are the steps that occur in Figure 6-5:

1 LSR1 sends a label binding request toward LSR2 in order to bind prefix 172.16.0.0/16 to a specific VCI.

2 LSR2 allocates VCI 20 and creates an entry in its LFIB with VCI 20 as the incoming label.

3 LSR2 sends a bind request toward LSR3.

4 LSR3 issues VCI 25 as a label.

5 LSR3 sends a reply to LSR2 with the binding between prefix 172.16.0.0/16 and the VCI 25 label.

6 LSR2 sets the outgoing label to VCI 25. This information is now used by LSR2 to switch cells coming on VCI 20 to VCI 25.

7 LSR2 sends a reply to LSR1 with the binding between prefix 172.16.0.0/16 and VCI 20.

8 LSR1 creates an entry in its LFIB and sets the outgoing label to VCI 20.

Independent mode operation is similar to that shown in Figure 6-5, except that Steps 7 and 8 might occur concurrently with Step 3. In independent mode, the LSR that initiated the request receives the binding information, creates an entry in its LFIB, and sets the outgoing label in the entry to the value received from the next hop. The next-hop ATM LSR repeats the process, sending a binding request to its next hop. The process continues until all label bindings along the path are allocated.

In optimistic mode, the LSR that initiated the request receives the binding information, creates an entry in its LFIB, and sets the outgoing label in the entry to the value received from the next hop. The next-hop ATM LSR then repeats the process, sending a binding request to its next hop. The process continues until all label bindings along the path are allocated.

In conservative mode, the next-hop LSR sends a new binding request to its next hop, and the process repeats until the destination ATM Edge LSR is reached. It then returns a label binding to the previous ATM-LSR, causing it to return a label binding, and so on, until all the label bindings along the path are established.

Cell Interleaving

Label VC allocation over ATM for multiple sources transmitting data to the same destination causes a few challenges. An ATM LSR that receives binding requests from different upstream neighbors toward the same prefix has to request multiple outbound labels from its downstream neighbor. If the ATM LSR allocates only one outgoing VCI, cells from different AAL5 frames are potentially interleaved and dropped at the receiving end. Allocating different outbound VCIs for the same destination ensures that cells are received in order. This setup is illustrated in Figure 6-6.

Figure 6-6   *Cell Interleaving*

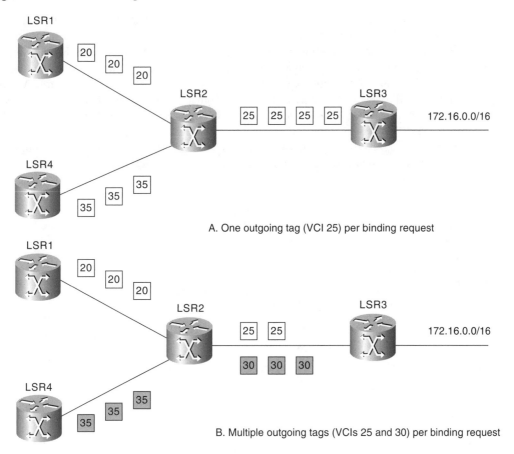

A. One outgoing tag (VCI 25) per binding request

B. Multiple outgoing tags (VCIs 25 and 30) per binding request

Figure 6-6, topology A shows a hypothetical situation. LSR2 has received two different binding requests for prefix 172.16.0.0/16 from LSR1 and LSR4. LSR2 logically creates two entries in its LFIB and assigns incoming labels for each request. In this example, LSR2 has assigned VCI 20 for LSR1 and VCI 35 for LSR4. In case LSR2 does not already have an outbound label for the prefix, LSR2 sends a binding request toward LSR3 and gets VCI 25 assigned as an outbound label. As a result, cells arriving from LSR1 and LSR4 on VCIs 20 and 35 are sent over VCI 50 and potentially get interleaved, causing AAL5 frames to be discarded.

Topology B shows the same scenario, with the difference that LSR2 requests two outgoing labels for prefix 172.16.0.0/16. LSR2 is assigned two VCIs, 20 and 30. Cells from LSR1 are switched using cross-connect (20, 25), and cells from LSR4 are switched using cross-connect (35, 30). As such, complete noninterleaved AAL5 frames are received at the destination. This example explains how MPLS supports switches that do not have VC merge capability.

VC Merge

VC merge, illustrated in Figure 6-7, allows ATM LSRs to transmit cells coming from different VCIs over the same outgoing VCI toward the same destination. This helps reduce the number of Label Virtual Circuits (LVCs) required in the MPLS network. In other words, it allows multipoint-to-point connections to be implemented by queuing complete AAL5 frames in input buffers until the end of frame is received. The cells from the same AAL5 frame are all transmitted before cells from any other frame are sent. This setup requires more buffering capabilities inside the switch, but no more buffering than is required in IP networks. The small additional delay caused by VC merge is of little concern, because VC merge is designed for IP traffic and does not need to be used for delay-sensitive traffic. IP traffic has good delay tolerance compared to other traffic that might be carried on an ATM network.

Figure 6-7   *VC Merge*

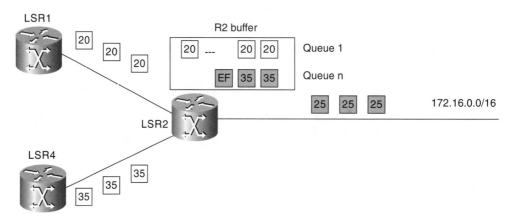

In Figure 6-7, LSR1 and LSR4 are sending traffic toward prefix 172.16.0.0/16. LSR2 has a single outbound VCI 25 bound to that prefix. Cells coming over VCIs 20 and 35 are buffered in separate queues of LSR2 until complete AAL5 frames have been formed. In this example, an end of frame has been detected over VCI 35, and the complete frame has been transmitted over VCI 25. An end of frame has not been detected for cells coming over VCI 20, so these cells are held back in the input buffer, solving the cell interleave problem and minimizing VC usage.

Label Virtual Circuits

ATM Virtual Circuits established for MPLS are called Label Virtual Circuits. A link between two ATM LSRs, or between an ATM Edge LSR and an ATM LSR, is an ordinary

ATM link. Because ATM MPLS uses the VCI fields of a few separate VPIs to carry a label, each label on a link corresponds to a different LVC. LVCs are neither switched virtual circuits (SVCs) nor permanent virtual circuits (PVCs). They are set up using LDP instead of ATM Forum signaling protocols. LVCs, PVCs, and SVCs may all be used on the same link; however, they use different parts of the VPI/VCI space.

As illustrated in Figure 6-8, at least two distinct types of LVCs are used on each link:

- Signaling LVC
- Ordinary LVC

Figure 6-8 *Label Virtual Circuits*

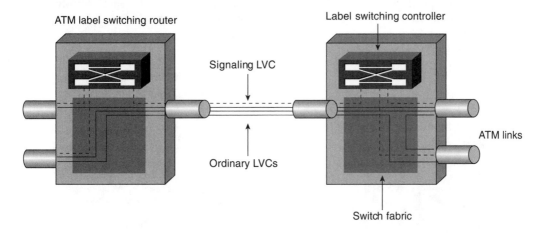

Signaling LVC

This VC carries IP packets that are reassembled and examined at each ATM LSR. It carries routing information such as MP-BGP, OSPF, IS-IS, and LDP. It might also be used to carry management traffic, such as Simple Network Management Protocol (SNMP) traffic or Internet Control Message Protocol (ICMP) traffic. By default, this VC has VPI and VCI 0/32, which can be reconfigured if desired.

Ordinary LVC

This LVC carries label-switched data. Packets on ordinary LVCs are cross-connected by ATM LSRs without being reassembled. On each link, all ordinary LVCs are within the same VP or a small set of VPs.

Label Switch Controllers

The Label Switch Controller (LSC) manages the control and forwarding component of the ATM LSR. The ATM LSR differs from an ordinary ATM switch in the way connections are set up. Normally an ATM connection is set up by control software running a connection routing protocol such as PNNI or automatic routing management. The LSC is a part of an ATM LSR that runs an IP routing protocol such as OSPF or IS-IS.

In addition to MPLS software, the IP routing software of the LSC maintains knowledge of the MPLS network topology. Using this information, LDP establishes labels (such as VCs) on links connected to the ATM LSR. When the LSC has established incoming and outgoing labels for the same route in its LFIB, it then instructs the switch fabric to set up a connection with the parameters (incoming interface, incoming label VCI, outgoing interface, and outgoing label VCI). Figure 6-9 shows possible locations for the LSC.

Figure 6-9 *Label Switch Controller*

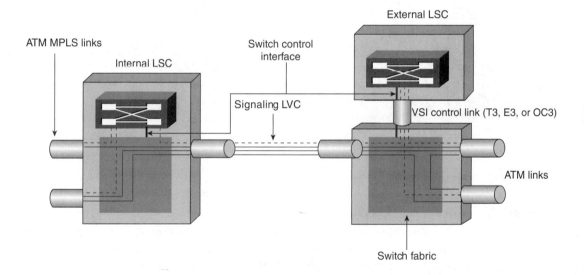

Label Switch Controller Implementation

The LSC can be implemented in a variety of ways. Smaller switches use integrated LSC software, and larger ATM switches use router blades or external router-based LSC architectures.

Integrated LSC software

The LSC could be implemented as integrated software within the ATM switch and might run on the main control card. An example of this kind of implementation is found in the

LightStream 1010, Catalyst 5500, Catalyst 6500, or 8500 ATM-LSR. The LSC software runs on the ATM switch processor, which is the main ATM control card of these units.

Internal LSC

The software runs on an ATM switch shelf card separate from the main switch control card. In the MGX 8800, a route processor module (RPM) card in the switch is used as the LSC. The LSC function is supported on the universal router module (URM) in the IGX 8400 series.

External LSC

The LSC may also be a separate piece of external hardware. The Cisco BPX 8650 ATM LSR switch consists of a BPX 8600 ATM switch shelf and an LSC based on a Cisco 7200 series router. The LSC and switch are interconnected by a switch control link. For the BPX 8650, the switch control link is an ATM link. This link is used in a different way with the other ATM interfaces. On the LSR, it is used to connect the signaling LVCs from all other interfaces on the switch to the LSC, but it does not often carry any data. A similar architecture is also supported in the IGX 8400 series.

An LSC sets up connections in the switch fabric by way of a switch control interface. In the case of the LightStream 1010, Catalyst 5500, Catalyst 6500, or Catalyst 8500, this interface is an internal interface within switch IOS software. In the case of the BPX 8650, IGX 8400 series, and MGX 8850, a switch control interface is used. It is either an external interface or a channel between two cards in the switch.

Figure 6-9 shows how an LSC is connected in a BPX 8650 or IGX 8400 series switch. The physical connection between the LSC and the BPX or IGX series ATM switch shelf is the virtual switch interface (VSI) control link, which is an ATM T3/E3 or OC3 link.

The external LSC model has the advantage of separating the services into logical entities, each having a road map that does not interfere with the other.

If an external router controls a BPX 8650 switch running PNNI and SVC services, an IP MPLS upgrade can be performed without disturbing the operation of the PNNI, PVC, and SVC services. In the WAN space, this is an attractive functionality.

LSC Control of a Switch

The ATM interface on the LSC must be configured as an LSC interface, and a trunk on the ATM switch must be enabled as a control interface. The data connections between the LSC and switch shelf consist of two sets of VCs: signaling LVCs and switch-control VCs.

Signaling LVCs

The signaling LVCs from every interface of the ATM switch must be connected through to the LSC, as shown in Figure 6-9. The signaling LVC on each interface is on VPI and VCI (0, 32) by default but is generally cross-connected to a different VCI on the switch control link. This VCI is selected by the LSC software, which requests the setup of the cross-connects as part of its initialization.

Switch-Control VCs

The LSC uses an interface control protocol to discover the switch's port configuration and make switch connections. This protocol operates using VCs connected to each port card, called the external control VCs, as shown in Figure 6-10. In the BPX 8650, there may be up to 12 of these, one for each BXM port card in the BPX8650. In the IGX 8400 series, there may be up to 30, one per UXM card. The external control VCs are set up automatically if external control is enabled.

Figure 6-10 *LSC Signaling and Control Virtual Circuits*

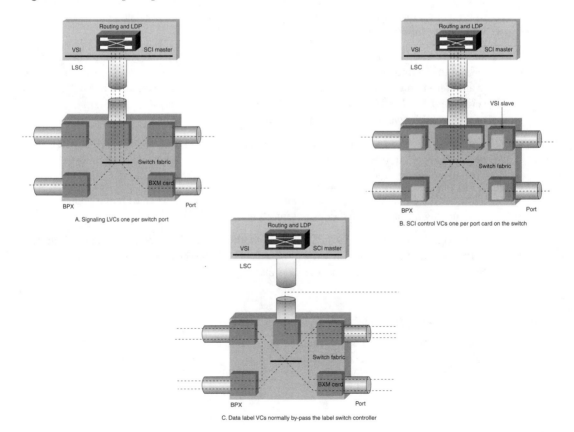

Using the infrastructure of signaling LVCs and external control VCs, the LSC can establish label bindings with the neighboring ATM Edge LSRs and consequently request the setup of LVC cross-connects in the switch. Most data LVCs bypass the LSC.

Virtual Switch Interface

A Virtual Switch Interface (VSI) provides a standard interface so that an external controller other than the built-in BPX controller card can control a resource in the BPX switch. External controllers such as the LSC are usually implemented as an external 7200 or 7500 router. A schematic of such an implementation is shown in Figure 6-11.

Figure 6-11 *Virtual Switch Interface*

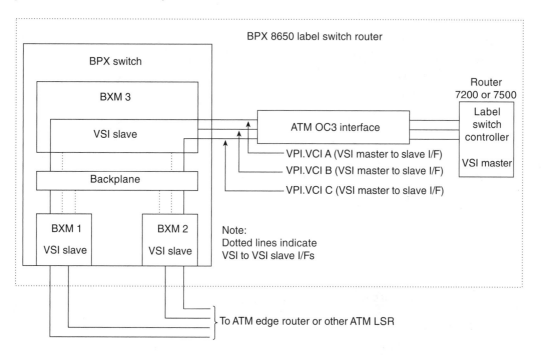

A distributed slave model is used to implement VSI in a BPX. Each BXM in a BPX switch is a VSI slave and communicates with the controller and other slaves if needed when processing VSI commands. The VSI master (LSC) sends a VSI message to one slave. Depending on the command, the slave handles the command entirely by itself or communicates with a remote slave to complete the command. For example, a command to obtain configuration information would be completed by one slave only, as shown in Figure 6-12.

Figure 6-12 *Connection Setup with Endpoints on the Same VSI Slave*

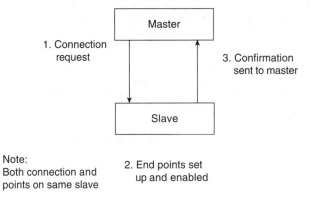

Figure 6-13 *Connection Setup with Endpoints on Different VSI Slaves*

However, a command for connection setup would require the local slave in turn to communicate with a remote slave in order to set up both endpoints of the connection. This is demonstrated in Figure 6-13.

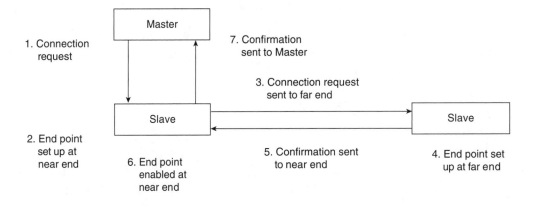

Figure 6-12 shows a simplified example of a connection setup with endpoints on the same VSI slave, and Figure 6-13 shows a connection setup with endpoints on different VSI slaves.

IP+ATM

The LSC can be added to an ATM switch to give it MPLS capability. The IP+ATM capability of the ATM LSRs can be used to simultaneously provide MPLS service and traditional ATM switching. Figure 6-14, Part A shows an ATM switch with an MPLS LSC. Part B of the figure shows a conventional ATM switch under the control of a PNNI controller. As shown in Part C of the figure, IP+ATM switches allow an LSC and a PNNI controller to be simultaneously connected to the same switch. In other words, the same switch can support both optimized IP services using MPLS and conventional ATM services using PNNI.

Figure 6-14 *IP+ATM Capability*

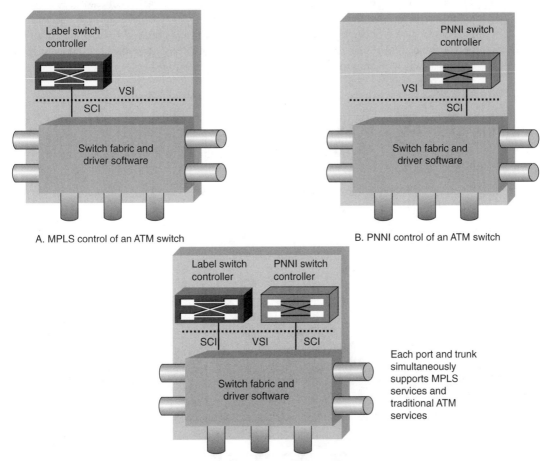

A. MPLS control of an ATM switch

B. PNNI control of an ATM switch

C. IP+ATM switch with both MPLS and PNNI control

Because IP+ATM switches directly support both MPLS and PNNI services, IP+ATM networks offer both native IP services and native ATM services. An IP+ATM network physically consists of ordinary ATM switches and links. As part of the network's initial configuration, the operator assigns resources of the ATM network to PNNI and MPLS. The resources involved include:

- Bandwidth on links
- VPI/VCI space on links
- VC connection table spaces
- Traffic management

The partitioning of resources is quite flexible, with arbitrary divisions of resources between the different control planes. Partitioning can involve giving fixed allocation of resources to the control planes or can involve a pool of link bandwidth or connection table spaces shared between the control planes. Furthermore, the concept of having controllers independently control a switch extends to more than two controllers. Cisco IP+ATM switches can support four or more control planes.

Structure of an IP+ATM Switch

The concept of an IP+ATM switch is shown in Figure 6-15. A single switch contains two logically separate switches:

- An MPLS ATM LSR optimized for IP transport
- A traditional ATM PVC/SVC switch

Figure 6-15 *Logical View of an IP+ATM Switch*

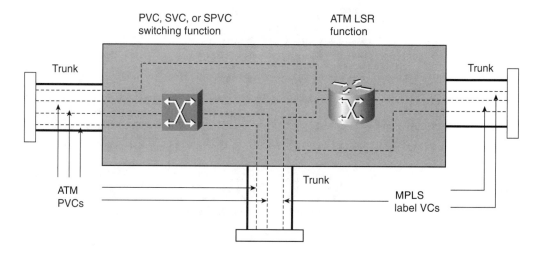

Each trunk can support PVCs, SVCs, soft PVCs, and MPLS LVCs.

Although an IP+ATM switch contains logically separate switches, it is physically one switch. However, it contains two or more separate sets of control software. One set of software controls ATM forum PVCs, SVCs, soft PVCs, and Automatic Routing Management, and the other set controls MPLS. These controllers act independently, allowing the single physical switch to act as two or more virtual switches. In switches such as the BPX 8650 and MGX 8850, this independent control is implemented by using the VSI. The VSI allows two or more separate controllers to independently control a single switch, as shown in Figure 6-16.

Figure 6-16 *VSI Controllers*

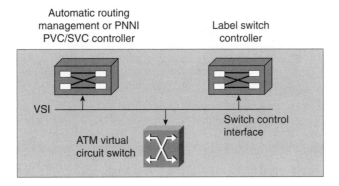

The MPLS control software is implemented in the LSC. Other VSI controllers may be software running on the switch control card. In the case of the BPX 8650 and MGX 8850, AutoRoute software, which controls PVCs, runs on the switch control card. PNNI control may be added to the BPX 8650 as a separate controller on the Service Expansion Shelf (SES). The LS1010 and 8540 MSR implement functionality similar to the VSI using internal software interfaces.

To ensure that the control planes can act independently, the VSI slave processes in the switch must allocate resources to the different control planes (MPLS or PNNI). In the BPX 8650, resources for AutoRoute PVCs are reserved in a similar way.

The resources partitioned in the different control planes include the following:

- **VPI/VCI space on trunks**—Each control plane gets a range of VPIs to use.
- **Bandwidth**—Each control plane is guaranteed a certain bandwidth for connection admission control (CAC) purposes. With soft partitioning, a pool of bandwidth can be shared between control planes for CAC purposes. Even with hard partitioning, spare bandwidth unused by a control plane is available on a cell-by-cell basis to other control planes.

- **Traffic queues**—MPLS traffic gets different traffic queues on the switch than the PVC and SVC traffic. This means that MPLS traffic can be handled by queues that directly support the MPLS classes of service (CoSs). The alternative is manually configured translations to ATM forum service types as used in IP over ATM implementations of QoS.

The configuration process for IP+ATM switches includes the assignment of the preceding resources to the different control planes. This involves creating different *partitions* of link resources for the different control planes, as shown in Figure 6-17.

Figure 6-17 *Partitioning of Resources on a Trunk*

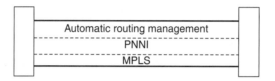

IP+ATM Networks

IP+ATM can be used to offer MPLS services, along with PVC and SVC services, on the same network. This means that some switches in the network act as both ATM LSRs and traditional ATM switches, as shown in Figure 6-18.

Traditional ATM services can also be used in conjunction with an MPLS service. Figure 6-18 shows the use of a PVC to connect ordinary IP traffic from a customer site to an ATM Edge LSR. A PVC used in this fashion is called an *MPLS Access PVC*.

Other PVCs are *traditional PVCs* that are part of a traditional end-to-end PVC service. The traffic from the Edge LSR can then be fed back through the ATM LSR function in the same switch that supports the MPLS access PVC, or alternatively through a different switch. In any case, the end-to-end data path for IP traffic can include both MPLS access PVCs and MPLS LVCs.

An integrated IP+ATM edge switch, such as the MGX 8850 or Cisco 6400, supports the ATM LSR function, as well as traditional access switch and PVC switching functions. In addition, the Edge LSR function is integrated into the device. In the MGX 8850, the routing function is supported by RPMs. Node Route Processor (NRP) modules are used in the Cisco 6400. Each RPM or NRP acts as an Edge LSR. In the MGX 8850, one of the RPMs simultaneously acts as an LSC and an Edge LSR.

Figure 6-18 *An IP+ATM Network*

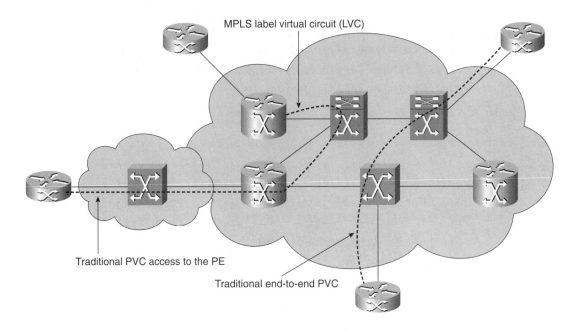

Packet-Based MPLS over ATM VPNs

Service providers that run IP over core ATM networks normally run an IP over ATM model. The ATM forum PVCs constitute the link layer for IP. The *router on a stick* model is still widely used. These ATM switches might or might not be MPLS-aware. LVCs are not built in such environments.

A migration plan is required to fully convert such networks to MPLS. Typically, the first step is to upgrade the router IOS to a stable version that supports MPLS and to configure packet-based MPLS over certain parts of the network. The second migration step entails cutting over the MPLS-capable ATM switches to ATM MPLS and running ATM MPLS. ATM forum PVCs can coexist with MPLS LVCs. This greatly helps with the migration. This step also entails cutting over the IP-based Frame Relay or ATM customers to managed IP MPLS VPN service. This section deals with the configuration of packet-based MPLS over an ATM backbone.

NOTE   The configuration of packet-based MPLS using ATM is similar to the VPN configuration discussed in Chapter 5, "Packet-Based MPLS VPNs." The basic steps are outlined in this chapter. This is followed by a case study.

Configuring Packet-Based MPLS over ATM VPNs

The network must be running the following Cisco IOS services before you configure VPN services:

- MPLS in provider backbone routers
- MPLS with VPN code in provider routers with VPN edge service (PE) routers
- BGP in all routers providing a VPN service
- CEF switching in every MPLS-enabled router
- CoS feature (optional)

Configuration of PE routers

You must perform the following tasks on the PE router to configure and verify MPLS VPN operation:

- Configure your ATM interfaces and IGP
- Define your VPNs
- Configure PE to PE routing sessions
- Configure PE to CE routing sessions. There are four ways to do this:
  — Static PE to CE routing configuration
  — RIPv2 PE to CE routing configuration
  — BGP4 PE to CE routing configuration
  — OSPF PE to CE routing configuration

Configuration of CE Routers

CE routers can be configured with one of four options:

- Static routing
- RIPv2 routing
- BGP4 routing
- OSPF routing

The PE router must be configured using the same routing protocol as the CE router.

Configuration of P Routers

The provider core routers (P routers) are LSRs that participate in the IGP routing protocol, such as OSPF or IS-IS. However, they do not take part in the multiprotocol IBGP process like the PEs would. In a packet-based ATM configuration, the P router concept is optional, and PE routers can communicate directly over ATM forum PVCs using a combination of the IGP and IBGP.

Case Study of a Packet-Based MPLS over ATM VPN

Consider the service provider shown in Figure 6-19. It has points of presence (PoPs) in Chicago, Seattle, San Diego, Miami, and Washington. The service provider can offer Layer 3 IP VPN services across its MPLS backbone. The service provider offers MPLS VPN services to three customers—A, B, and C. Backbone ATM switches have replaced the core P routers. The customers are each operating a single VPN.

Figure 6-19 *Case Study: Packet-Based MPLS over ATM VPN Configuration*

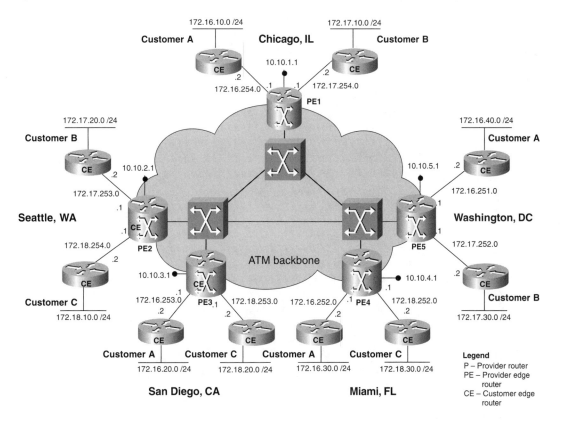

The service provider has provisioned the VPNs as shown in Table 6-2.

Table 6-2 *Case Study: VPN Deployment (PoP)*

	Customer A	Customer B	Customer C
Chicago, IL	VPN A	VPN B	
Seattle, WA		VPN B	VPN C
San Diego, CA	VPN A		VPN C
Miami, FL	VPN A		VPN C
Washington, DC	VPN A	VPN B	

The customer edge (CE) routers connect to the service provider's edge (PE) routers as shown in Table 6-3.

Table 6-3 *Case Study: PE Deployment*

	Customer A	Customer B	Customer C
Chicago, IL	PE1	PE1	
Seattle, WA		PE2	PE2
San Diego, CA	PE3		PE3
Miami, FL	PE4		PE4
Washington, DC	PE5	PE5	

Layer 3 Interior Gateway Routing protocols run across the backbone normally provide any-to-any connectivity for IBGP peers to communicate with each other, even though the IBGP peers (PE routers) are not directly connected to each other. Refer to Figure 6-20 for the PVC configuration in this case study.

Figure 6-20 *Case Study: PVC Configuration*

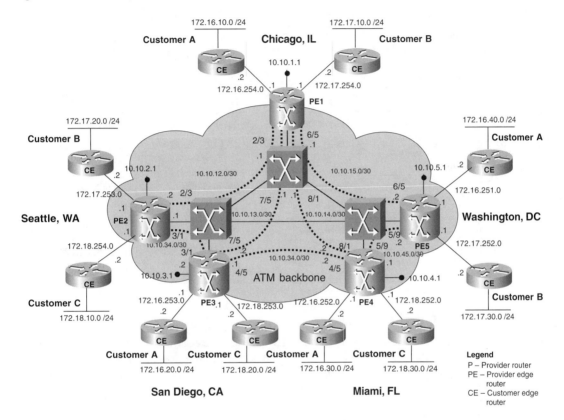

The IP addressing scheme used in the case study is explained in Table 6-4.

Table 6-4   *Case Study: VPN IP Address Architecture*

	PE Router	CE WAN Subnet	CE LAN Subnet
Customer A			
Chicago	10.10.1.1/32	172.16.254.0/24	172.16.10.0/24
Seattle	No presence	No presence	No presence
San Diego	10.10.3.1/32	172.16.253.0/24	172.16.20.0/24
Miami	10.10.4.1/32	172.16.252.0/24	172.16.30.0/24
Washington	10.10.5.1/32	172.16.251.0/24	172/16.40.0/24

continues

Table 6-4 *Case Study: VPN IP Address Architecture (Continued)*

	PE Router	CE WAN Subnet	CE LAN Subnet
Customer B			
Chicago	10.10.1.1/32	172.17.254.0/24	172.17.10.0/24
Seattle	10.10.2.1/32	172.17.253.0/24	172.17.20.0/24
San Diego	No presence	No presence	No presence
Miami	No presence	No presence	No presence
Washington	10.10.5.1/32	172.17.252.0/24	172/17.30.0/24
Customer C			
Chicago	No presence	No presence	No presence
Seattle	10.10.2.1/32	172.18.254.0/24	172.18.10.0/24
San Diego	10.10.3.1/32	172.18.253.0/24	172.18.20.0/24
Miami	10.10.4.1/32	172.18.252.0/24	172.18.30.0/24
Washington	No presence	No presence	No presence

Provider Edge Configuration

The PE router configurations for the ATM interfaces are shown in the following sections. The detailed configurations are similar to the PE configurations in Chapter 5. The ATM PVCs provide Layer 2 connectivity between the various PE routers. The PE routers run an IGP and multiprotocol IBGP within the cloud.

Chicago Configuration

Refer to Figure 6-20 for the Chicago area connectivity and addressing information. Chicago uses VPI/VCI 2/3 as a virtual circuit to establish Layer 2 connectivity with Seattle, VPI/VCI 7/5 to establish Layer 2 connectivity with San Diego, VPI/VCI 8/1 to establish Layer 2 connectivity with Miami, and VPI/VCI 6/5 to establish Layer 2 connectivity with Washington.

Chicago PE Configuration

The following is the Chicago PE configuration:

```
!
interface atm1/0/0
 no ip address
!
interface atm1/0/0.1 point-to-point
```

```
 description atm pvc to Seattle
 ip address 10.10.12.1 255.255.255.252
 pvc 2/3
 encapsulation aal5snap
 tag-switching ip
 !
interface atm1/0/0.2 point-to-point
 description atm pvc to San Diego
 ip address 10.10.13.1 255.255.255.252
 pvc 7/5
 encapsulation aal5snap
 tag-switching ip
 !
interface atm1/0/1
 no ip address
 !
interface atm1/0/1.1 point-to-point
 description atm pvc to Miami
 ip 10.10.14.1 255.255.255.252
 pvc 8/1
 encapsulation aal5snap
 tag-switching ip
 !
interface atm1/0/1.2 point-to-point
 description atm pvc to Washington
 ip 10.10.15.1 255.255.255.252
 pvc 6/5
 encapsulation aal5snap
 tag-switching ip
 !
```

Seattle Configuration

Refer to Figure 6-20 for the Seattle area connectivity and addressing information. Seattle uses VPI/VCI 2/3 as a virtual circuit to establish Layer 2 connectivity with Chicago and VPI/VCI 3/1 to establish Layer 2 connectivity with San Diego.

Seattle PE Configuration

The following is the Seattle PE configuration:

```
 !
interface atm1/0/0
 no ip address
 !
interface atm1/0/0.1 point-to-point
 description atm pvc to Chicago
 ip address 10.10.12.2 255.255.255.252
 pvc 2/3
```

continues

```
  encapsulation aal5snap
  tag-switching ip
 !
 interface atm1/0/0.2 point-to-point
  description atm pvc to Miami
  ip address 10.10.23.1 255.255.255.252
  pvc 3/1
  encapsulation aal5snap
  tag-switching ip
 !
```

San Diego Configuration

Refer to Figure 6-20 for the San Diego area connectivity and addressing information. San Diego uses VPI/VCI 3/1 as a virtual circuit to establish Layer 2 connectivity with Seattle, VPI/VCI 7/5 to establish Layer 2 connectivity with Chicago, and VPI/VCI 4/5 to establish Layer 2 connectivity with Miami.

San Diego PE Configuration

The following is the San Diego PE configuration:

```
 !
 interface atm1/0/0
  no ip address
 !
 interface atm1/0/0.1 point-to-point
  description atm pvc to Seattle
  ip 10.10.23.2 255.255.255.252
  pvc 3/1
  encapsulation aal5snap
  tag-switching ip
 !
 interface atm1/0/0.2 point-to-point
  description atm pvc to Chicago
  ip 10.10.13.2 255.255.255.252
  pvc 7/5
  encapsulation aal5snap
  tag-switching ip
 !
 interface atm1/0/0.3 point-to-point
  description atm pvc to Miami
  ip 10.10.34.1 255.255.255.252
  pvc 4/5
  encapsulation aal5snap
  tag-switching ip
 !
```

Miami Configuration

Refer to Figure 6-20 for the Miami area connectivity and addressing information. Miami uses VPI/VCI 4/5 as a virtual circuit to establish Layer 2 connectivity with San Diego, VPI/VCI 8/1 to establish Layer 2 connectivity with Chicago, and VPI/VCI 5/9 to establish Layer 2 connectivity with Washington.

Miami Configuration

The following is the Miami PE configuration:

```
!
interface atm1/0/0
 no ip address
!
interface atm1/0/0.1 point-to-point
 description atm pvc to San Diego
 ip 10.10.34.2 255.255.255.252
 pvc 4/5
 encapsulation aal5snap
 tag-switching ip
!
interface atm1/0/0.2 point-to-point
 description atm pvc to Chicago
 ip 10.10.14.2 255.255.255.252
 pvc 8/1
 encapsulation aal5snap
 tag-switching ip
!
interface atm1/0/0.3 point-to-point
 description atm pvc to Washington
 ip 10.10.45.1 255.255.255.252
 pvc 5/9
 encapsulation aal5snap
 tag-switching ip
!
```

Washington Configuration

Refer to Figure 6-20 for the Washington area connectivity and addressing information. Washington uses VPI/VCI 5/9 as a virtual circuit to establish Layer 2 connectivity with Miami and VPI/VCI 6/5 to establish Layer 2 connectivity with Chicago.

Washington PE Configuration

The following is the Washington PE configuration:

```
!
interface atm1/0/0
 no ip address
!
interface atm1/0/0.1 point-to-point
 description atm pvc to Miami
 ip 10.10.45.2 255.255.255.252
 pvc 5/9
 encapsulation aal5snap
 tag-switching ip
!
interface atm1/0/1
 no ip address
!
interface atm1/0/1.1 point-to-point
 description atm pvc to Chicago
 ip 10.10.15.2 255.255.255.252
 pvc 6/5
 encapsulation aal5snap
 tag-switching ip
!
```

ATM-Based MPLS VPNs

In an ATM-based MPLS configuration, ATM Forum PVCs are unnecessary. MPLS LVCs are automatically brought up after the switch has its resources partitioned for LVCs and other parameters have been appropriately set up.

The VPN feature of MPLS allows several sites to transparently interconnect through a service provider's network. One service provider network can support several different IP VPNs. Each of these VPNs appears to its users as a closed user group private network, separate from all other networks. Within a VPN, each site can send IP packets to any other site in the same VPN. Each VPN is associated with one or more VPN routing or forwarding instances (VRFs). A VRF consists of an IP routing table, a derived Cisco express forwarding (CEF) table, and a set of interfaces that use this forwarding table. The PE router maintains a separate routing and CEF table for each VRF. This prevents information from being sent outside the VPN and allows the same subnet to be used in several VPNs without causing duplicate IP address problems. The PE routers use Multiprotocol Interior Border Gateway Protocol (MP-IBGP) to distribute the VPN routing information using the BGP extended communities attributes.

NOTE	The MPLS VPN integration function resides only on the PE routers of the MPLS network. The MPLS cloud is composed of MPLS-aware ATM switches such as the BPX 8650, MGX 8850, 8540 MSR, or LightStream 1010. The Cisco Stratacom BPX 8650 is the recommended platform for industrial-strength core ATM switched networks. The PE feeder nodes could be a combination of MGX 8850s, 8540 MSRs, LS1010, 10000, 12000 GSRs, 7500, or 7200 ATM routers.

NOTE	If you plan to use the LightStream 1010 as an ATM MPLS switch, it is recommended that you use software version WA4.8d or higher.

Configuring ATM-Based MPLS VPNs

Your network must be running the following Cisco IOS and software services before you configure VPN operation:

- MPLS in provider backbone ATM switches
- MPLS with VPN code in provider routers with VPN edge service (PE) routers
- BGP in all routers providing a VPN service
- CEF switching in every MPLS-enabled router
- CoS feature (optional)

Configuration of PE Routers

The following tasks must be performed on the PE router to configure and verify MPLS VPN operation:

- Configure your ATM interfaces and IGP
- Define your VPNs
- Configure PE to PE routing sessions
- Configure PE to CE routing sessions. There are four ways to do so:
  - Static PE to CE routing configuration
  - RIPv2 PE to CE routing configuration
  - BGP4 PE to CE routing configuration
  - OSPF PE to CE routing configuration

Configuration of CE Routers

CE routers can be configured with one of four options:

- Static routing
- RIPv2 routing
- BGP4 routing
- OSPF routing

The PE router must be configured using the same routing protocol as the CE router.

Configuration of ATM MPLS Core Switches

The provider core devices are ATM LSRs that participate in the IGP routing protocol, such as OSPF or IS-IS. However, they do not take part in the multiprotocol IBGP process like the PEs would. In the ATM-based MPLS model, the P routers are implemented as LSCs working in conjunction with the ATM switches, providing Layer 3/MPLS control of the ATM switch using a VSI. This chapter focuses on the use of the BPX 8650 as an ATM MPLS core switch.

BPX 8650

The Cisco BPX 8600 series is a standards-based ATM switch with ATM and MPLS capabilities. The switch offers up to 20 Gbps of switching for multiple traffic types, data, voice, and video. The BPX 8600 series supports MPLS. This functionality can easily be added to any BPX switch already installed in the field with a software upgrade and the addition of a 7200 or 7500 LSC.

The BPX VSI allows controllers to set up and tear down virtual circuit converters through the BPX independent of the control protocol (PNNI, MPLS, SS7) and independent of whether the controller is internal or external to the chassis. Thus, the VSI allows multiple controllers to control the BPX. The controllers are optimized for the service to be delivered. The VSI manages the resource allocation, so the controllers are independent, and each service receives the QoS required.

The 7200 or 7500 LSC uses the VSI to provide MPLS control of the BPX. With a co-located Extended Services Processor (ESP), the BPX switch adds the capability to support ATM and Frame Relay SVCs and soft permanent virtual circuits (SPVCs). The ESP is an adjunct processor that is co-located with a BPX switch shelf. The ESP provides the signaling and Private Network-to-Network Interface (PNNI) routing for ATM and Frame Relay SVCs via BXM cards in the BPX switch and AUSM and FRSM cards in the MGX 8220. Frame Relay to ATM Interworking is performed in accordance with RFC 1490 and RFC 1483.

The BPX 8600 series switch is designed for high levels of reliability. All system components can be configured for 100-percent redundancy and are hot-swappable. Automatic Routing Management reroutes virtual circuits if a trunk fails. Software upgrades can be performed in the background, and the conversion to a new software release is achieved without interruption of traffic or loss of data. All broadband interfaces can be configured for 1:1 redundancy, and narrowband modules can be configured for 1:*n* redundancy.

The BPX 8600 series switch incorporates Stratacom technology implemented in custom silicon application-specific integrated circuits (ASICs) in the broadband switch modules (BXM). This supports traffic management, per-virtual-circuit queuing, CoS management, and multicasting. It also provides full virtual source/virtual destination (VS/VD) implementation of the ATM Forum's Traffic Management Specification V.4.0, as well as supporting explicit rate marking and explicit forward congestion indication (EFCI) tagging. The BPX supports Inverse ATM as well as virtual trunking, which provides the ability to define multiple trunks within a single physical trunk port interface. The configuration of the BPX 8650 and MGX 8850 core ATM MPLS switches is detailed in the following sections.

BPX 8650 Configuration

The BPX nodes need to be set up and configured in the ATM network, including links to other nodes, and so on. Following this, they may be configured for MPLS operation. In configuring the BPX nodes for operation, a virtual interface and associated partition are set up with the **cnfrsrc** command. The LSC is linked to the BPX with the **addshelf** command to allow the router's label switch controller function to control the MPLS operation of the BPX node. The partition's resources, such as bandwidth, VPI range, and the number of logical connection numbers (LCNs), may be distributed between the associated ports. The VPIs are of local significance, so they do not have to be the same for each port in a node, but it is generally convenient from a tracking standpoint to keep them the same for a given BPX node. In this example, it is assumed that a single external controller per node is supported, so the partition chosen is always 1. With the appropriate release of switch software, firmware, and IOS, service class templates are supported.

Step 1   Display the status of all cards as follows:

```
:dspcds
```

BXM cards that you are configuring should be *standby* or *active*. If they are not, perform a hard reset. For example, **resetcd 5 h** resets card 5.

Step 2   Check card connection capabilities using the **dspcd** command as follows:

```
:dspcd <card_number>
```

For example:

```
:dspcd 5
```

This elicits the following system response:

```
bpx2       TN    SuperUser      BPX 8620     9.2      Mar. 20 2001 16:10 EST

Detailed Card Display for BXM-155 in slot 5
```

continues

```
Status:              Active
Revision:            CD18
Serial Number:       783314
Fab Number:          28-2158-02
Queue Size:          228300
Support:             FST,4 Pts,OC3,Vc
Chnls:16320, PG[1}:7588, PG[2]:7588
PG [1} : 1,2,
PG [2] : 3,4,
Backcard Installed
  Type:        LM-BXM
  Revision:    BA
  Serial Number: 784533
  Supports: 4 pts, OC3, SMF Md


Last Command: dspcd 5


Next Command:
```

This example shows that ports 1 and 2 together have a total of 7588 connections or *channels* available for use. Ports 1 and 2 form a port group (PG). Similarly, ports 3 and 4 are a port group with a limit of 7588 connections.

NOTE   The connections just shown are used for PVCs, VSI connections, and internal signaling. Unless there is a good reason to do otherwise, it is best to leave many of the LCNs as spares. LCN connections can be allocated to MPLS on each port using the **cnfrsrc** command.

Step 3   Enable the BXM trunk interfaces as follows:

```
:uptrk slot.port.[virtual trk]
```

A BXM interface is a *trunk* if it connects to another BPX, MGX, or MGX 8220 (AXIS) feeder. The VSI connection to an LSC is also a *trunk*.

NOTE   The virtual trunk configuration is available from Release 9.2 onward. The **uptrk** command, for example, would be of the form **uptrk 9.1.1** for port interface 9.1, virtual trunk 1. Either ports or trunks can be active simultaneously on the same BXM.

The following is an example:

```
:uptrk 5.1
:uptrk 9.1
:uptrk 9.2
```

This elicits the following system response:

```
bpx2        TN   SuperUser      BPX 8620    9.2     Mar. 20 2001 16:20 EST

TRK         Type          Current Line Alarm Status          Other End
9.1         OC3           Clear  -  OK                        bpx1/9.1
9.2         OC3           Clear  -  OK                        bpx2/9.2
5.1         OC3           Clear  -  OK                        VSI(VSI)




Last Command: uptrk 9.2


Next Command:
```

In this example, trunk 5.1 is the link to the LSC controller, and trunks 9.1 and 9.2 are used as the broadband trunks to other BPX nodes on the network. Trunks 5.2 and 5.3 connect to PE routers and also need to be *upped*.

Step 4   Use the **cnfrsrc** command to configure partition resources for Automatic Routing Management PVCs or VSI-MPLS as follows:

```
:cnfrsrc <slot.port.{virtual trunk}> <maxpvclcns> <maxpvcbw> partitionID <e/d>
    <minvsilcns> <maxvsilcns> <vsistartvpi> <vsiendvpi> <vsiminbw> <vsimaxbw>
```

Table 6-5 describes the parameters used in the **cnfrsrc** command.

Table 6-5   cnfrsrc *Command Parameters*

Parameter	Description
slot.port	Specifies the slot and port number for the BXM card in the BPX.
virtual trunk	Specifies the virtual trunk number for the BXM slot and port in the BXM card.
maxpvclcns *a(x)*	The maximum number of LCNs allocated for AutoRoute PVCs for this port. For trunks, additional LCNs are allocated for AutoRoute that are not configurable. The **dspcd** *slot* command displays the maximum number of LCNs configurable via the **cnfrsrc** command for the given port. For trunks, configurable LCNs represent the LCNs remaining after the BCC has subtracted the additional LCNs needed. For a port card, a larger number is shown, as compared with a trunk card. Setting this field to 0 enables the configuration of all the configurable LCNs to the VSI. The variable *a(x)* is the mathematical representation of **maxpvclcns** in integer format.

continues

Table 6-5 **cnfrsrc** *Command Parameters (Continued)*

Parameter	Description
maxpvcbw	The maximum bandwidth of the port allocated for AutoRoute use.
partitionID	The partition number.
e/d	Enables or disables the VSI partition.
minvsilcns *n(x)*	The minimum number of LCNs guaranteed for this partition. The VSI controller guarantees at least this many connection endpoints in the partition, provided that there are sufficient free LCNs in the common pool to satisfy the request at the time the partition is added. When a new partition is added or the value is increased, existing connections might have depleted the common pool so that there are not enough free LCNs to satisfy the request. The BXM gives priority to the request when LCNs are freed. The net effect is that the partition might not receive all the guaranteed LCNs (min LCNs) until other LCNs are returned to the common pool.
	This value may not be decreased dynamically. All partitions in the same port group must be deleted first and reconfigured in order to reduce this value.
	The value may be increased dynamically. However, this might cause the deficit condition just described. The command-line interface warns the user when the action is invalid, except for the "deficit" condition. To avoid this deficit condition, which could occur with maximum LCN usage by a partition or partitions, it is recommended that you configure all partitions before adding connections. Also, it is recommended that you configure all partitions before adding a VSI controller via the **addshelf** command.
	The variable *n(x)* is the mathematical representation of **minvsilcns** in integer format.
maxvsilcns *m(x)*	The total number of LCNs that the partition is allowed for setting up connections. The min LCNs is included in this calculation. If max LCNs equals min LCNs, the max LCNs are guaranteed for the partition. Otherwise, $\max - \min$ or $\text{sum}(m(x)) - \text{sum}(n(x))$. LCNs are allocated from the common pool on a FIFO basis.
	If the common pool is exhausted, new connection setup requests are rejected for the partition, even though the max LCNs has not been reached. This value may be increased dynamically when there are enough unallocated LCNs in the port group to satisfy the increase.
	The value may not be decreased dynamically. All partitions in the same port group must be deleted first and reconfigured in order to reduce this value. Different types of BXM cards support different maximums. If you enter a value greater than the allowed maximum, a message is displayed with the allowable maximum.
	The variable *m(x)* is the mathematical representation of **maxvsilcns** in integer format.

Table 6-5   **cnfrsrc** *Command Parameters (Continued)*

Parameter	Description
vsistartvpi	By default, the LSC (7200 or 7500 series router) uses either a starting VSI VPI of 1 or 2 for Tag Switching—whichever is available. If both are available, a starting VSI VPI of 1 is used. The VPI range should be 2–15 on a BPX 8620 VSI. The VSI range for Tag Switching on the BPX 8620 is configured as a VSI partition—usually VSI partition 1. VSI VPI 1 is reserved for AutoRoute PVCs, so the VSI partition for Tag Switching should start at VPI 2. If VPI 2 is not to be used, the Tag Switching VPI interface configuration command can be used on the TSC to override the defaults.
vsiendvpi	Two VPIs are sufficient for the current release, although it might be advisable to reserve a larger range of VPIs for later expansion, such as VPIs 2–15.
vsiminbw	The minimum port bandwidth allocated to this partition in cells/sec. (Multiply by 400 based on 55 bytes per ATM cell to get approximate bits/sec.)
vsimaxbw	The maximum port bandwidth allocated to this partition. This value is used for VSI Qbin bandwidth scaling.

When you add a trunk, the entire bandwidth is allocated to Automatic Routing Management. The **cnfrsrc** command is used to change the allocation to provide resources for a VSI on the BPX switch. The VSIs need to partition the resources between competing controllers: Automatic Routing Management, MPLS, and PNNI. You can have different types of controllers splitting up a partition's assets—for example, Automatic Routing Management and MPLS or Automatic Routing Management and PNNI, but not PNNI and MPLS.

On each interface (port or trunk) of the BXM cards used for label switching, bandwidth and connection resources must be divided between traditional PVC connections and label switching connections. On each interface, space for connections is divided between traditional BPX switch PVC connections and LVCs.

The traditional PVC connections are configured directly on the BPX platform, and label switching connections are set up by the LSC using the VSI. As with all ATM switches, the BPX switch supports up to a specified number of connections. On the BPX switch, the number of connections supported depends on the number of port/trunk cards installed. When configuring the port using the **cnfrsrc** command, the term Logical Connection Number (LCN) is used in place of connection.

Each BXM card supports up to 16,384 connections in total, including PVCs, label switching VSI connections, and connections used for internal signaling. On the BXM, the ports are grouped, and each port group has a certain number of connections allocated to it, as shown in Table 6-6. For label switching, connections are allocated to VSI partitions, which are used to support the LSC.

Table 6-6   *BXM Card Connection Allocation*

BXM Card	Port Group	Port Group Size	LCN Limit Per Port	Average Connections Per Port
8-T3/E3	1	8 ports	16k	2048
12-T3/E3	1	12 ports	16k	1365
4-OC3	2	2 ports	8k	4096
8-OC3	2	4 ports	8k	2048
1-OC12	1	1 port	16k	16384
2-OC12	2	1 port	8k	8192

The various configurations of BXM port resources for label switching are described in this section. The first allocation example uses default allocations. The second allocation example describes more rigorous allocations in which default allocations are not applicable.

Table 6-7 shows the default allocation of LCNs.

Table 6-7   *Default Allocation of LCNs*

Connection Type	Variable	Default Value	cnfrsrc Parameter
AutoRoute LCNs	$a(x)$	256	**maxpvclcns**
Minimum VSI LCNs for partition 1	$n(x)$	512	**minvsilcns**
Maximum VSI LCNs for partition 1	$m(x)$	16384	**maxvsilcns**

NOTE   Different types of BXM cards support different maximums. If you enter a value greater than the allowed maximum, a message is displayed with the allowable maximum. The average *maximum* connections per port are shown in Table 6-7.

Rigorous allocations are possible when default values are not applicable. For example, the LCN allocations for a port group must satisfy the following equation:

g => sum($a(x)$) + sum($n(x)$) + $t \times 270$
g = The total number of LCNs available to the port group
$a(x)$ = AutoRoute LCNs
$n(x)$ = The minimum number of guaranteed VSI LCNs
t = The number of ports in the port group that are configured as AutoRoute trunks

Figure 6-21 shows the relationship of these elements.

Figure 6-21 *Port VSI Partition LCN Allocation Elements*

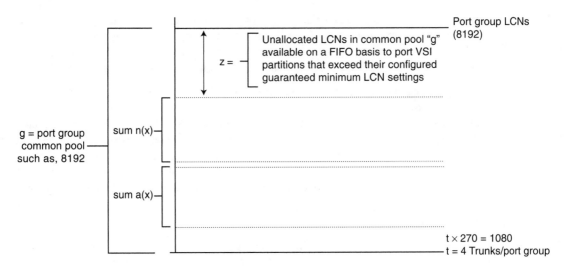

The 270 value reflects the number of LCNs that are reserved on each AutoRoute trunk for internal purposes. If the port is configured in port rather than trunk mode, t = 0, and t $\times$ 270 = 0.

Label switching can operate on a BXM card configured for either trunk (network) or port (service) mode. If a BXM card is configured for port (service) mode, all ports on the card are configured in port (service) mode. If a BXM card is configured for trunk (network) mode, all ports on the card are configured for trunk (network) mode. When the card is configured for *trunk* mode, the trunks reserve some connection bandwidth.

$z = g - \text{sum}(a(x)) - \text{sum}(n(x)) - t \times 270$
z = The number of unallocated LCNs in the common pool of LCNs available for use by the port VSI partitions
g = The total number of LCNs available to the port group
$a(x)$ = AutoRoute LCNs
$n(x)$ = The minimum number of guaranteed VSI LCNs
t = The number of ports in the port group that are configured as AutoRoute trunks

---

NOTE   For a BXM card with ports configured in *port* mode, t = 0, and the unallocated LCN equation becomes

$z = g - \text{sum}(a(x)) - \text{sum}(n(x))$

When a port partition has exhausted its configured guaranteed LCNs (min LCNs), it may draw LCNs for new connections on a FIFO basis from the unallocated LCNs, z, until its maximum number of LCNs, m(x), is reached or the pool, z, is exhausted.

No limit is actually placed on what may be configured for m(x), although m(x) is effectively ignored if it's larger than z + n. The value m(x) is a nonguaranteed maximum value of connection spaces that may be used for a new connection or shared by a number of connections at a given time if a sufficient number of unallocated LCNs are available in z.

The following is an example of a four-port OC-3 BXM configured in trunk mode. This example is for a four-port OC-3 BXM configured for trunk mode with all ports configured as trunks. Table 6-8 lists the configured connection space (LCN) allocations for each port with respect to a(x), n(x), and m(x). It also shows the unallocated LCN pool, z for each port group, and the total common pool access, g. The total number of LCNs available to the port group is g = 7588 for the four-port OC-3 BXM card. This value is obtained from the **dspcd** command output. Also, the number of trunks per port group is t = 2, which gives you the value of t × 270 = 540.

Table 6-8   *Example of LCN Allocation*

Port(x)	a(x)	n(x)	m(x)	Unallocated LCNs z = g – sum(a(x)) – sum(n(x)) – t × 270	Total LCNS Available to Port VSI Partition = min(z + n(x), m(x))
Port Group 1					
1	256	4096	7588	2184	6280
2	0	512	1024	2184	1024
Sum for Port 1 to 2	256	4608	N/A	N/A	N/A
Port Group 2					
3	0	3200	7588	648	3848
4	0	3200	7588	648	3848
Sum for Port 3 to 4	0	6400	N/A	N/A	N/A

The port groups in the example are ports 1–2 and 3–4, and the maximum number of connection spaces (LCNs) per port group is 7588 for this four-port OC-3 BXM card. The allocations for the port groups are shown in Figure 6-22.

Figure 6-22 *LCN Allocations for Port Group 1*

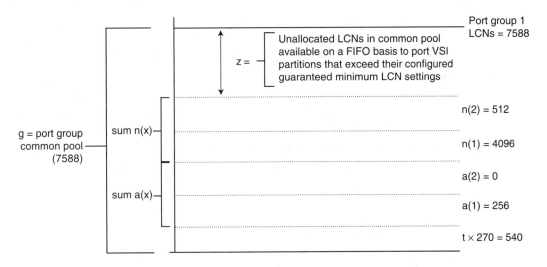

As shown in Figure 6-22 and Figure 6-23, g is the total number of connection spaces (LCNs) available to port group 1–2 and is equal to 7588 LCNs in this example. To find the number of unallocated LCNs available for use by port partitions that exhaust their assigned number of LCNs, proceed as follows:

Figure 6-23 *LCN Allocations for Port Group 2*

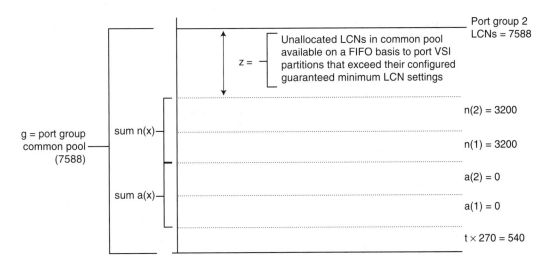

From g, subtract the sum of the AutoRoute connections, a(x), and the sum of minimum guaranteed LCNs, n(x). Also, because the ports in this example are configured in trunk mode, 270 LCNs per port are subtracted from g. Because there are two ports, t equals 2 in the expression t × 270. The unallocated LCNs in the pool (z) are available for use by ports 1–2 that exceed their minimum VSI LCN allocations n(x) for partition 1.

The maximum number of LCNs that a port partition can access on a FIFO basis from the unallocated pool z for new connections can only bring its total allocation up to either z + n(x) or m(x), whichever value is smaller. Also, because z is a shared pool, the value of z will vary as the common pool is accessed by other port partitions in the group.

The values shown in Table 6-8 are obtained as follows:

For ports 1–2:
$z = g - \text{sum}(a(x)) - \text{sum}(n(x)) - t \times 270$
$g = 7588$
$\text{sum}(a(x)) = 256$
$\text{sum}(n(x)) = 4608$
$t = 2$
Therefore, $z = 7588 - 256 - 4608 - (2 \times 270)$, which gives you the value of $z = 2184$ unallocated LCNs.

The values shown in Table 6-8 for the port group containing ports 1–2 may be summarized as follows:

Port 1 is guaranteed to be able to support 256 AutoRoute connections (PVCs) and 4096 label VCs (LVCs). It will not support more than 256 PVCs. It might be able to support up to 6280 LVCs, subject to the availability of unallocated LCNs z on a FIFO basis. Also, because z + n(1) of 6280 is less than m(1) of 7588, the maximum number of LVCs that can be supported is 6280.

Port 2 is guaranteed to be able to support 0 AutoRoute connections (PVCs) and 512 label VCs (LVCs). It might be able to support up to 1024 LVCs, subject to the availability of unallocated LCNs z on a FIFO basis. Also, because m(2) of 1024 is less than z + n(2) of 2696, the maximum number of LVCs that can be supported is 1024.

For ports 3–4:
$z = g - \text{sum}(a(x)) - \text{sum}(n(x)) - t \times 270$
$g = 7588$
$\text{sum}(a(x)) = 0$
$\text{sum}(n(x)) = 6400$
$t = 2$
Therefore, $z = 7588 - 0 - 6400 - (2 \times 270)$, which gives you the value of $z = 648$ unallocated LCNs.

The values shown in Table 6-8 for the port group containing ports 3–4 may be summarized as follows:

Port 3 is guaranteed to be able to support 0 AutoRoute connections (PVCs) and 3200 Label VCs (LVCs). It might be able to support up to 3848 LVCs, subject to the availability of unallocated LCNs z on a FIFO basis. Because z + n(3) of 3848 is less than m(3) of 7588, the maximum number of LVCs that can be supported is 3848.

Port 4 is guaranteed to be able to support 0 AutoRoute connections (PVCs) and 3200 Label VCs (LVCs). It might be able to support up to 3848 LVCs, subject to the availability of unallocated LCNs z on a FIFO basis. Because z + n(4) of 3848 is less than m(4) of 7588, the maximum number of LVCs that can be supported is 3848.

The following is an example of configuring resources on the VSI partition:

Configure the VSI partition for trunk 5.1 by entering the following command:

```
:cnfrsrc 5.1 256 26000 1 e 4096 7588 2 15 26000 100500
```

NOTE	In this example, AutoRoute PVCs a(x) = 256, VSI minimum LCNs n(x) = 4096, and VSI maximum LCNs m(x) = 7588. The m(x) value is derived from the output of the **dspcds** command. The output of the **dspcds** command provides a value for m(x), the maxvsilcns value. This value needs to be used with the **cnfrsrc** command.

The information in the preceding command line can also be entered individually:

```
cnfrsrc 5.1

PVC LCNs: [256]  [accept default value]
max PVC bandwidth: 26000
partition: 1
y   [to edit VSI parameters]
enabled: e
VSI min LCNs: 4096
VSI max LCNs: 7588
VSI start VPI: 2
VSI end VPI: 15
VSI min b/w: 26000
VSI max b/w: 100500
```

This elicits the following system response:

```
bpx2        TN    SuperUser     BPX 8620     9.2      Mar. 20 2001 16:33 EST


Port/Trunk : 5.1


Maximum PVC LCNS:            256       Maximum PVC Bandwidth:26000

Min Lcn(1) : 0 Min Lcn(2) : 0
Partition 1

Partition State :           Enabled
Minimum VSI LCNS:           4096
```

continues

```
Maximum VSI LCNS:         7588
Start VSI VPI:            2
End VSI VPI :             15
Minimum VSI Bandwidth :   26000     Maximum VSI Bandwidth :  100500




Last Command: cnfrsrc 5.1 256 26000 1 e 4096 7588 2 15 26000 100500


Next Command:
```

This example reserves space on the trunk for 256 AutoRoute PVCs. One VSI partition is supported, and it must be numbered 1. VSI min LCNs = 4096, and VSI max LCNs = 7588. This guarantees that MPLS can set up 4096 LVCs on this link but is allowed to use up to 7588, subject to the availability of LCNs.

VSI starting VPI = 2 and VSI ending VPI = 15. This reserves VPIs in the range of 2–15 for MPLS. Only one VP is really required, but a few more can be reserved to save for future use. AutoRoute uses a VPI range starting at 0, so MPLS should use higher values. It is best to always avoid using VPIs 0 and 1 for MPLS on the BPX 8650. VPIs are locally significant.

A different VPI value could be used for each of the three ports 5.1, 5.2, and 5.3. However, at each end of a trunk, the same VPI must be assigned. VSI min bandwidth = 26000, and VSI maximum = 100500. This guarantees that MPLS can use 26000 cells/sec (about 10 Mbps) on this link but allows it to use up to 100,500 cells/sec (about 40 Mbps) if bandwidth is available. More can be allocated if required.

The maximum PVC bandwidth has been configured with a value of 26000. This guarantees that PVCs can always use up to 26,000 cells per second (about 10 Mbps) on this link.

NOTE   Resource partitioning using the **cnfrsrc** command must be performed on all BXM trunks that will carry LVCs across them.

Step 5   Display the configuration of the specified Qbin on a BXM:

dspqbin *slot.port qbin number*

The **dspqbin** command displays the Qbin resources or CoS buffer resources on a selected trunk, port, or virtual trunk. It displays the Qbin parameters currently configured for an interface and shows whether the Qbin resources have been configured by the user or automatically by a template. It also displays whether the Qbin has EPD enabled or disabled.

The following is an example of displaying the Qbins on the BPX switch.

Display the MPLS queues on the BXM card on port 5.1 for Qbin 10:

```
dsqbin 5.1 10
```

NOTE   MPLS CoS uses Qbins 10–14. BPX software release 9.1 only uses Qbin 10.

This elicits the following system response:

```
bpx2        TN    SuperUser      BPX 8620     9.2      Mar. 20 2001 16:41 EST

Qbin Database 5.1 on BXM qbin 10

Qbin State:                Enabled
Minimum Bandwidth:         0
Qbin discard threshold:    65536
Low CLP/EPD threshold:     95%
High CLP/EPD threshold:    100%
EFCI threshold:            40%




Last Command: dspqbin 5.1 10


Next Command:
```

If preconfigured correctly, the display should show parameters similar to the preceding display.

Step 6   Use the **cnfqbin** command to configure the Qbin CoS buffers parameters on a selected BXM port or trunk as follows:

```
:cnfqbin <slot.port> <Qbin_number> <e/d> <y/n> <Qbin_discard_threshold>
   <Low_EPD_threshold> <High_CLP_Threshold> <EFCI_threshold>
```

Table 6-9 describes the parameters used in the **cnfqbin** command.

Label-switched VC connections are grouped into large buffers called Qbins. Qbins 10–14 are used for label-switched connections. MPLS for VSIs on a BXM card needs the default Qbin value to be adjusted. Qbin 10 is assigned to MPLS. The **cnfqbin** command is used to adjust the threshold for the traffic arriving in Qbin 10 of a given VSI interface as a way of fine-tuning traffic delay. If you use the **cnfqbin** command to set an existing Qbin to disabled, the egress of the connection traffic to the network is disabled. Reenabling the Qbin restores the egress traffic.

When a VSI interface is activated, the default template gets assigned to an interface. The corresponding Qbin template gets copied into the card Qbin data structure for that interface. Assigning new values using the **cnfqbin** command can change this. The Qbin is now user-configured as opposed to template-configured. This information is displayed on the **dspqbin** screen. It indicates whether the values in the Qbin are from the template assigned to the interface or whether the values have been changed to user-defined values.

Table 6-9 **cnfqbin** *Command Parameters*

Parameter	Description
slot.port	Specifies the slot and port number for the BXM.
Qbin_number	Specifies the ID number of the Qbin available for use by the LSC (MPLS controller) for VSI. The range is 0 to 255. 0 is the default. Always use 10 in BPX software releases 9.1 and 9.2.
e/d	Enables or disables the Qbin.
y/n	You enter **n** not to accept default values so that you can configure the following parameters.
Qbin_discard_threshold	Specifies the threshold in percentage for Qbin discard. The range is 0 to 100.
Low_EPD_threshold	Specifies the threshold in percentage for CLP low. The range is 0 to 100; 80% is the default.
High_CLP_threshold	Specifies a percentage of the Qbin depth. When the threshold is exceeded, the node discards cells with CLP = 1 in the connection until the Qbin level falls below the depth specified by CLP Lo. The range is 0 to 100; 80% is the default.
EFCI_threshold	Explicit Forward Congestion Indication. The percentage of Qbin depth that causes EFCI to be set. The range is 0 to 100; 30% is the default.

The following is an example of how to configure the Qbin values for the BPX:

```
:cnfqbin 5.1 10 e 0 65536 95 100 40
```

This elicits the following system response:

```
bpx2       TN    SuperUser    BPX 8620    9.2    Mar. 20 2001 16:45 EST


Qbin Database 5.1 on BXM qbin 10

Qbin State:                 Enabled
Minimum Bandwidth:          0
Qbin Discard threshold:     65536
Low CLP/EPD threshold:      95%
High CLP/EPD threshold:     100%
```

```
EFCI threshold:              40%



Last Command: cnfqbin 5.1 10 e 0 65536 95 100 40

Next Command:
```

Step 7   Add an ATM link between a BXM card on a BPX node and an MPLS controller
such as a series 6400, 7200, or 7500 router as follows:

```
addshelf <slot.port> <device-type> <control_id> <partition_id> <control_vpi>
    <control_vci_start>
```

NOTE   The link between the BXM card of the BPX node and the LSC must be free of major alarms
before you can add it with the **addshelf** command.

Table 6-10 describes the parameters used in the **addshelf** command.

Table 6-10   **addshelf** *Command Parameters*

Parameter	Description
slot.port	Specifies the BXM slot and port number of the trunk. You can configure the port for either trunk (network) or port (service) mode.
device-type	Specifies a virtual interface to an MPLS controller (LSC) such as a Cisco 6400, 7200, or 7500 series router. The value **vsi** is used for the MPLS Virtual Switch Interface.
control_id	Control IDs must be in the range of 1–32. These must be identical on the LSC and in the **addshelf** command. A control ID of 1 is the default used by the MPLS controller (LSC).
partition_id	Indicates the ID assigned to the VSI partition. A partition ID of 1 is the default used by the MPLS controller (LSC).

continues

Table 6-10 addshelf *Command Parameters (Continued)*

Parameter	Description
control_vpi	Starting VPI of the VSI control channels used for communication between the VSI master residing on the SES and VSI slaves residing on the BXM cards. There can be a total of 12 such channels—one for each slave residing on each BXM card.
	For a trunk interface with NNI header type:
	Valid values for this parameter are 0–4095
	For a trunk interface with UNI header type:
	Valid values for this parameter are 0–255.
	The default value is 0.
control_vci_start	Starting VCI of the VSI control channels. This VCI value is assigned to the first VSI control channel (between the VSI master and the VSI slave residing on the BXM card in slot 1). The last VSI control channel corresponding to communication with the VSI slave on slot 14 uses the VCI value of (<start_vci>+14-1).
	The valid values are 33–65521.
	The default value is 40.

The following is an example of adding the MPLS controller to the BPX.

Add an MPLS controller link to port 5.1 of the BXM card on the BPX node by entering the **addshelf** command as follows:

```
:addshelf 5.1 vsi 1 1
```

The first **1** after **vsi** is the VSI controller ID, which must be set the same on both the BPX 8650 and the LSC. The default controller ID on the LSC is 1. The second **1** after **vsi** is the partition ID, which indicates that this is a controller for partition 1.

This elicits the following system response:

```
bpx2      TN   SuperUser    BPX 8620    9.2     Mar. 20 2001 16:50 EST

                    BPX Interface Shelf Information

Trunk     Name     Type      Alarm
5.1       VSI      VSI       OK
```

```
This Command: addshelf 5.1 v 1 1

Next Command:
```

Label Switch Controller Configuration

The Label Switch Controller (LSC) is a Label-Switched Router (LSR) that controls the operation of a separate ATM switch. Together, the router and ATM switch function as a single ATM MPLS router (ATM-LSR). As shown in Figure 6-24, a Cisco 7200 or 7500 series router acts as the LSC, and a Cisco BPX 8600 service node acts as the VSI-controlled ATM switch. The LSC controls the ATM switch using the Virtual Switch Interface (VSI), which runs over an ATM link connecting the two.

Figure 6-24 *Label Switch Controller (LSC) and BPX*

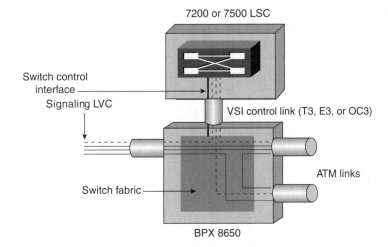

Before configuring the LSC for the label switch (MPLS) controlling function, you must perform the initial router configuration if this has not been done. As part of this configuration, you must enable and configure the ATM adapter interface and the extended ATM interface for label switching. On the LSC, the LC-ATM ports on the controlled switch are represented as an IOS interface type called extended label ATM (XmplsATM). You associate XmplsATM interfaces with particular physical interfaces on the controlled switch through the **extended-port** interface configuration command.

LSC as a Label Edge Device

The LSC can function simultaneously as a controller for an ATM switch and as a label edge device. Traffic can be forwarded between a router interface and an LC-ATM interface on the controlled switch as well as between two LC-ATM interfaces on the controlled switch. The LSC can perform the imposition and removal of labels and can serve as the head or tail of a Label-Switched Path (LSP) tunnel. However, when acting as a label edge device, the LSC is limited by the capabilities of its control link with the switch as follows:

- Total throughput between all other router interfaces and switch interfaces is limited by the bandwidth of the control link (that is, OC-3, 155 Mb per second).

- The number of VCs supported on the control link limits label space for LSC-terminated VCs.

The following steps outline the configuration process for the LSC:

Step 1 Enable IP routing on the LSC:

```
Router(config)#ip routing
```

Step 2 Enable the Cisco Express Forwarding (CEF) protocol:

```
Router(config)#ip cef switch
```

Step 3 Enable a physical interface link to BPX:

```
Router(config)#interface atm slot/adapter/port
```

Step 4 Remove any IP address assignment from the main ATM interface:

```
Router(config-if)#no ip address
```

Step 5 Enable the router ATM port as an LSC. The controller ID default is 1. Optional values are up to 32 for BPX.

```
Router(config-if)#tag-control-protocol vsi [controller ID]
```

Step 6 Create a logical XmplsATM virtual interface, and bind it to BPX port *SP*:

```
Router(config-if)#interface XtagATM SP
```

Step 7 Bind the extended port XtagATM *SP* to the BPX slave port *Slot.Port:*

```
Router(config-if)#extended-port <ATM slot/adapter/port> <BPX Slot.Port>
```

Step 8 Assign an IP address to XtagATM *SP*:

```
Router(config-if)#ip address ip_address mask
```

Step 9 Enable MPLS for Xmpls interface XtagATM *SP*:

```
Router(config-if)#tag-switching ip
```

NOTE	Extended label ATM interfaces differ from ordinary ATM interfaces in that MPLS is configured on the primary interface of an extended label ATM interface, whereas it is configured on an MPLS subinterface of an ordinary ATM interface.

Step 10 Set up the IGP routing process (OSPF or IS-IS) and other routing parameters.

Case Study of an ATM-Based MPLS VPN

Consider the service provider shown in Figure 6-25, with PoPs in Chicago, Seattle, San Diego, Miami, and Washington. The service provider can offer Layer 3 IP VPN services across its MPLS backbone. The service provider offers MPLS VPN services to three customers—A, B, and C—as shown in Table 6-11. MPLS-aware backbone ATM LSRs have replaced the core P routers. The customers are operating a single VPN each. Virtual circuits (PVCs, PVPs, SVCs, or soft PVCs) are not configured on the ATM switches.

The service provider has provisioned the VPNs as shown in Table 6-11.

Table 6-11   *Case Study: VPN Deployment (Point of Presence)*

	Customer A	Customer B	Customer C
Chicago, IL	VPN A	VPN B	
Seattle, WA		VPN B	VPN C
San Diego, CA	VPN A		VPN C
Miami, FL	VPN A		VPN C
Washington, DC	VPN A	VPN B	

The customer edge (CE) routers connect to the service provider's edge (PE) routers as shown in Table 6-12.

Table 6-12   *Case Study: PE Deployment*

	Customer A	Customer B	Customer C
Chicago, IL	PE1	PE1	
Seattle, WA		PE2	PE2
San Diego, CA	PE3		PE3
Miami, FL	PE4		PE4
Washington, DC	PE5	PE5	

Figure 6-25 *Case Study: ATM-Based MPLS VPN Configuration*

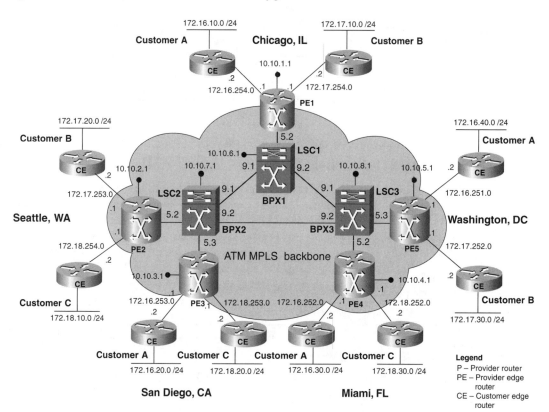

The core ATM MPLS LSRs are fully meshed in this example. However, this is not necessary. Layer 3 Interior Gateway Routing Protocol (IGRP) running across the backbone normally provides any-to-any connectivity for IBGP peers to communicate with each other, even though the IBGP peers (PE routers) are not directly connected to each other.

The IP addressing scheme used in this case study is explained in Table 6-13.

Table 6-13 *Case Study VPN IP Address Architecture*

	PE Router	CE WAN Subnet	CE LAN Subnet
Customer A			
Chicago	10.10.1.1/32	172.16.254.0/24	172.16.10.0/24
Seattle	No presence	No presence	No presence
San Diego	10.10.3.1/32	172.16.253.0/24	172.16.20.0/24
Miami	10.10.4.1/32	172.16.252.0/24	172.16.30.0/24

Table 6-13   *Case Study VPN IP Address Architecture (Continued)*

	PE Router	CE WAN Subnet	CE LAN Subnet
Washington	10.10.5.1/32	172.16.251.0/24	172/16.40.0/24
Customer B			
Chicago	10.10.1.1/32	172.17.254.0/24	172.17.10.0/24
Seattle	10.10.2.1/32	172.17.253.0/24	172.17.20.0/24
San Diego	No presence	No presence	No presence
Miami	No presence	No presence	No presence
Washington	10.10.5.1/32	172.17.252.0/24	172/17.30.0/24
Customer C			
Chicago	No presence	No presence	No presence
Seattle	10.10.2.1/32	172.18.254.0/24	172.18.10.0/24
San Diego	10.10.3.1/32	172.18.253.0/24	172.18.20.0/24
Miami	10.10.4.1/32	172.18.252.0/24	172.18.30.0/24
Washington	No presence	No presence	No presence

The customer MPLS VPNs could have overlapping IP address architectures. In the MPLS VPN model, each PE router maintains multiple VRF routing tables and a single global routing table. Each VRF routing table corresponds to the VPN routes for each customer.

Provider Edge Configuration

The PE router configurations for the ATM interfaces are shown in the following sections. The ATM LVCs provide MPLS connectivity between the various PE routers and ATM LSRs. The PE routers also run an IGP and multiprotocol IBGP within the cloud. The following configuration examples show the ATM configuration. The RD, VRF, and multiprotocol IBGP configurations are similar to the case study configurations detailed in Chapter 5.

Chicago Configuration

Refer to Figure 6-25 for the Chicago area connectivity and addressing information. Chicago uses the VPI range 2 to 10 to establish LVCs with the ATM LSR (LSC controlled BPX) and remote PE routers. The labels are carried in the VCI field of the ATM header.

Chicago PE Configuration

The following is the Chicago PE configuration for the ATM-based MPLS VPN:

```
!
interface Loopback 0
 ip address 10.10.1.1  255.255.255.255
 no ip directed-broadcast
!
interface atm 1/0/0
 no ip address
 no ip directed-broadcast
 no ip route-cache distributed
 no atm ilmi-keepalive
!
interface atm 1/0/0.1 tag-switching
 description ATM link to BPX1
 ip unnumbered Loopback0
 no ip directed-broadcast
 tag-switching atm vpi 2-10
 tag-switching ip
!
```

Seattle Configuration

Refer to Figure 6-25 for the Seattle area connectivity and addressing information. Seattle uses the VPI range 2 to 10 to establish LVCs with the ATM LSR (LSC controlled BPX) and remote PE routers. The labels are carried in the VCI field of the ATM header.

Seattle PE Configuration

The following is the Seattle PE configuration for the ATM-based MPLS VPN:

```
!
interface Loopback 0
 ip address 10.10.2.1  255.255.255.255
 no ip directed-broadcast
!
interface atm 1/0/0
 no ip address
 no ip directed-broadcast
 no ip route-cache distributed
 no atm ilmi-keepalive
!
interface atm 1/0/0.1 tag-switching
 description ATM link to BPX2
 ip unnumbered Loopback0
 no ip directed-broadcast
 tag-switching atm vpi 2-10
 tag-switching ip
!
```

San Diego Configuration

Refer to Figure 6-25 for the San Diego area connectivity and addressing information. San Diego uses the VPI range 2 to 10 to establish LVCs with the ATM LSR (LSC controlled BPX) and remote PE routers. The labels are carried in the VCI field of the ATM header.

San Diego PE Configuration

The following is the San Diego PE configuration for the ATM-based MPLS VPN:

```
!
interface Loopback 0
 ip address 10.10.3.1  255.255.255.255
 no ip directed-broadcast
!
interface atm 1/0/0
 no ip address
 no ip directed-broadcast
 no ip route-cache distributed
 no atm ilmi-keepalive
!
interface atm 1/0/0.1 tag-switching
 description ATM link to BPX2
 ip unnumbered Loopback0
 no ip directed-broadcast
 tag-switching atm vpi 2-10
 tag-switching ip
!
```

Miami Configuration

Refer to Figure 6-25 for the Miami area connectivity and addressing information. Miami uses the VPI range 2 to 10 to establish LVCs with the ATM LSR (LSC controlled BPX) and remote PE routers. The labels are carried in the VCI field of the ATM header.

Miami PE Configuration

The following is the Miami PE configuration for the ATM-based MPLS VPN:

```
!
interface Loopback 0
 ip address 10.10.4.1  255.255.255.255
 no ip directed-broadcast
!
interface atm 1/0/0
 no ip address
 no ip directed-broadcast
 no ip route-cache distributed
```

continues

```
 no atm ilmi-keepalive
!
interface atm 1/0/0.1 tag-switching
 description ATM link to BPX3
 ip unnumbered Loopback0
 no ip directed-broadcast
 tag-switching atm vpi 2-10
 tag-switching ip
!
```

Washington Configuration

Refer to Figure 6-25 for the Washington area connectivity and addressing information. Washington uses the VPI range 2 to 10 to establish LVCs with the ATM LSR (LSC controlled BPX) and remote PE routers. The labels are carried in the VCI field of the ATM header.

Washington PE Configuration

The following is the Washington PE configuration for the ATM-based MPLS VPN:

```
!
interface Loopback 0
 ip address 10.10.5.1   255.255.255.255
 no ip directed-broadcast
!
interface atm 1/0/0
 no ip address
 no ip directed-broadcast
 no ip route-cache distributed
 no atm ilmi-keepalive
!
interface atm 1/0/0.1 tag-switching
 description ATM link to BPX3
 ip unnumbered Loopback0
 no ip directed-broadcast
 tag-switching atm vpi 2-10
 tag-switching ip
!
```

Label Switch Controller Configuration

The LSC router configurations for the BPX switches are shown in the following sections. The LSC routers run an IGP such as OSPF or IS-IS within the cloud. In this example, the LSCs are running OSPF with a process ID (PID) of 66. The ATM interface to the BPX slave does not have an IP address and is configured for VSI control. This enables the creation and configuration of logical extended MPLS ATM ports.

LSC1 Configuration

Refer to Figure 6-25 for LSC1 connectivity and addressing information. The following is the LSC1 configuration for the ATM-based MPLS VPN:

```
!
hostname lsc1
!
ip cef
!
interface Loopback0
 ip address 10.10.6.1 255.255.255.255
 no ip directed-broadcast
!
interface ATM1/0
 no ip address
 no ip directed-broadcast
 tag-control-protocol vsi
 no atm ilmi-keepalive
!
interface XTagATM51
 IP unnumbered Loopback0
 no IP directed-broadcast
 extended-port ATM1/0 bpx 5.1
tag-switching IP
!
interface XTagATM91
 IP unnumbered Loopback0
 no IP directed-broadcast
 extended-port ATM1/0 bpx 9.1
 tag-switching IP
!
interface XTagATM92
 IP unnumbered Loopback0
 no IP directed-broadcast
 extended-port ATM1/0 bpx 9.2
 tag-switching IP
!
router ospf 66
 network 10.10.6.1 0.0.0.0 area 0
!
```

LSC2 Configuration

Refer to Figure 6-25 for LSC2 connectivity and addressing information. The following is the LSC2 configuration for the ATM-based MPLS VPN:

```
!
hostname lsc2
!
ip cef
!
interface Loopback0
 ip address 10.10.7.1 255.255.255.255
 no ip directed-broadcast
!
interface ATM1/0
 no ip address
 no ip directed-broadcast
 tag-control-protocol vsi
 no atm ilmi-keepalive
!
interface XTagATM51
 IP unnumbered Loopback0
 no IP directed-broadcast
 extended-port ATM1/0 bpx 5.1
 tag-switching IP
!
interface XTagATM52
 IP unnumbered Loopback0
 no IP directed-broadcast
 extended-port ATM1/0 bpx 5.2
 tag-switching IP
!
interface XTagATM91
 IP unnumbered Loopback0
 no IP directed-broadcast
 extended-port ATM1/0 bpx 9.1
 tag-switching IP
!
interface XTagATM92
 IP unnumbered Loopback0
 no IP directed-broadcast
 extended-port ATM1/0 bpx 9.2
 tag-switching IP
!
router ospf 66
 network 10.10.7.1 0.0.0.0 area 0
!
```

LSC3 Configuration

Refer to Figure 6-25 for LSC3 connectivity and addressing information. The following is the LSC3 configuration for the ATM-based MPLS VPN:

```
!
hostname lsc3
!
ip cef
!
interface Loopback0
 ip address 10.10.8.1 255.255.255.255
 no ip directed-broadcast
!
interface ATM1/0
 no ip address
 no ip directed-broadcast
 tag-control-protocol vsi
 no atm ilmi-keepalive
!
interface XTagATM51
 IP unnumbered Loopback0
 no IP directed-broadcast
 extended-port ATM1/0 bpx 5.1
 tag-switching IP
!
interface XTagATM52
 IP unnumbered Loopback0
 no IP directed-broadcast
 extended-port ATM1/0 bpx 5.2
 tag-switching IP
!
interface XTagATM91
 IP unnumbered Loopback0
 no IP directed-broadcast
 extended-port ATM1/0 bpx 9.1
 tag-switching IP
!
interface XTagATM92
 IP unnumbered Loopback0
 no IP directed-broadcast
 extended-port ATM1/0 bpx 9.2
 tag-switching IP
!
router ospf 66
 network 10.10.8.1 0.0.0.0 area 0
!
```

BPX Switch Configuration

The partition's BPX switch resources must be distributed between the associated BXM trunk ports. This is set up with the **cnfrsrc** command. The Qbin CoS buffer parameters on the BXM trunks are set up using the **cnfqbin** command. Finally, the LSC is linked to the BPX with the **addshelf** command to allow the router's LSC function to control the MPLS operation of the BPX node.

BPX1 Configuration

Refer to Figure 6-25 for BPX1 connectivity and addressing information. In this case study, BPX1 has a four-port BXM 155-4 in slot 5 with an SMF LM 155-8 back card. A two-port BXM 622-2 is installed in slot 9 with an SMF LM 622-2 back card. Two BCC-4 broadband controller cards are installed in slots 7 and 8 with LM-BCCs installed as back cards. The Alarm Service Module (ASM) card with its associated back card (LM-AMS) is installed in slot 15. Refer to Table 6-14 for the BPX port assignment.

Table 6-14 *BPX Port Assignment*

	BPX1	BPX2	BPX3
BPX1		9.1	9.1
BPX2	9.1		9.2
BPX3	9.2	9.2	
PE1	5.2		
PE2		5.2	
PE3		5.3	
PE4			5.2
PE5			5.3
LSC	5.1	5.1	5.1

The following steps provide the basic configuration commands required by the BPX to achieve operational readiness.

Step 1

Perform the initial BPX configuration as follows:

1 Configure the node name using the **cnfname** command.

2 Configure the time zone using the **cnftmzn** command.

3 Configure the date using the **cnfdate** command.

4 Configure the LAN interface using the **cnflan** command.

5 Configure the IP Relay address using the **cnfnwip** command.

6 Configure the auxiliary or terminal ports to support any necessary external devices such as a local printer or modem using the **cnfprt**, **cnfterm**, and **cnftermfunc** commands.

NOTE   Refer to the *Cisco BPX 8600 Series Installation and Configuration Guide* for detailed information on the initial setup procedures.

Step 2

Display the status of all cards, and verify Active status:

```
:dspcds
```

Step 3

Check the logical connection capabilities of the four-port OC3 BXM-155 card in slot 5 using the **dspcd** command:

```
:dspcd 5
```

The following is the output:

```
bpx1        TN   SuperUser     BPX 8620    9.2    Mar. 20 2001 16:10 EST

Detailed Card Display for BXM-155 in slot 5
Status:            Active
Revision:          CD18
Serial Number:     783314
Fab Number:        28-2158-02
Queue Size:        228300
Support:           FST,4 Pts,OC3,Vc
Chnls:16320, PG[1}:7588, PG[2]:7588
PG [1} : 1,2,
PG [2] : 3,4,
Backcard Installed
  Type:         LM-BXM
  Revision:     BA
  Serial Number: 784533
  Supports: 4 pts, OC3, SMF Md


Last Command: dspcd 5


Next Command:
```

This example shows that ports 1 and 2 together have a total of 7588 connections or channels available for use. Ports 1 and 2 form a port group (PG). Similarly, ports 3 and 4 are a port group with a limit of 7588 connections.

Step 4

Enable the BXM trunk interfaces:

```
:uptrk 5.1
:uptrk 5.2
:uptrk 9.1
:uptrk 9.2
```

The following is the output:

```
bpx1        TN    SuperUser      BPX 8620     9.2     Mar. 20 2001 16:20 EST

TRK         Type           Current Line Alarm Status        Other End
9.1         OC3            Clear  -  OK                      bpx1/9.1
9.2         OC3            Clear  -  OK                      bpx2/9.2
5.1         OC3            Clear  -  OK                      VSI(VSI)




Last Command: uptrk 9.2


Next Command:
```

In this example, trunk 5.1 is the link to the LSC controller, and trunks 9.1 and 9.2 are used as the broadband trunks to other BPX nodes on the network. Trunk 5.2 connects to the Chicago PE router and also needs to be *upped*.

Step 5

Use the **cnfrsrc** command to configure partition resources for AutoRoute PVCs and VSI-MPLS. The four-port OC-3 BXM is configured in trunk mode with all ports configured as trunks. Table 6-15 lists the configured connection space (LCN) allocations for each port with respect to a(x), n(x), and m(x). It also shows the unallocated LCN pool, z for each port group, and the total common pool access, g. The total number of LCNs available to the port group is g = 7588 for the four-port OC-3 BXM card. This value is obtained from the **dspcd** command output. Also, the number of trunks per port group is t = 2, which gives you the value of $t \times 270 = 540$.

Table 6-15   *LCN Allocations for Port Groups*

Port(x)	a(x)	n(x)	m(x)	Unallocated LCNs $z = g - \text{sum}(a(x)) - \text{sum}(n(x)) - t \times 270$	Total LCNS Available to Port VSI Partition = min(z + n(x), m(x))
Port Group 1					
1	256	4096	7588	2184	6280
2	0	512	1024	2184	1024
Sum for Port 1 to 2	256	4608	N/A	N/A	
Port Group 2					
3	0	3200	7588	648	3848
4	0	3200	7588	648	3848
Sum for Port 3 to 4	0	6400	N/A	N/A	

The values shown in Table 6-15 are obtained as follows:

For ports 1–2:
$z = g - \text{sum}(a(x)) - \text{sum}(n(x)) - t \times 270$
$g = 7588$
$\text{sum}(a(x)) = 256$
$\text{sum}(n(x)) = 4608$
$t = 2$
Therefore, $z = 7588 - 256 - 4608 - (2 \times 270)$, which gives you the value of $z = 2184$ unallocated LCNs.

For ports 3–4:
$z = g - \text{sum}(a(x)) - \text{sum}(n(x)) - t \times 270$
$g = 7588$
$\text{sum}(a(x)) = 0$
$\text{sum}(n(x)) = 6400$
$t = 2$
Therefore, $z = 7588 - 0 - 6400 - (2 \times 270)$, which gives you the value of $z = 648$ unallocated LCNs.

In this case study, AutoRoute PVCs a(x) = 256, VSI minimum LCNs n(x) = 4096, and VSI maximum LCNs m(x) = 7588. The maximum PVC bandwidth = 26000 cells/sec, minimum VSI bandwidth = 26000 cells/sec, and maximum VSI bandwidth = 100500 cells/sec.

The starting VPI is 2, and the ending VPI is 15:

```
:cnfrsrc 5.1 256 26000 1 e 4096 7588 2 15 26000 100500
```

The information in the preceding command line can be entered individually using the BPX command menu prompt:

```
cnfrsrc 5.1

PVC LCNs: [256]  [accept default value]
max PVC bandwidth: 26000
partition: 1
y   [to edit VSI parameters]
enabled: e
VSI min LCNs: 4096
VSI max LCNs: 7588
VSI start VPI: 2
VSI end VPI: 15
VSI min b/w: 26000
VSI max b/w: 100500
```

```
bpx1        TN   SuperUser    BPX 8620    9.2    Mar. 20 2001 16:33 EST

Port/Trunk : 5.1


Maximum PVC LCNS:          256      Maximum PVC Bandwidth:26000

Min Lcn(1) : 0 Min Lcn(2) : 0
Partition 1

Partition State :          Enabled
Minimum VSI LCNS:          4096
Maximum VSI LCNS:          7588
Start VSI VPI:             2
End VSI VPI :              15
Minimum VSI Bandwidth :    26000    Maximum VSI Bandwidth :   100500



Last Command: cnfrsrc 5.1 256 26000 1 e 4096 7588 2 15 26000 100500


Next Command:
```

Repeat this command for all BXM trunks that will carry MPLS LVCs.

Step 6

Display the configuration of Qbin 10 on BPX port 5.1:

```
:dsqbin 5.1 10
```

```
bpx1         TN    SuperUser      BPX 8620     9.2     Mar. 20 2001 16:41 EST


Qbin Database 5.1 on BXM qbin 10

Qbin State:                 Enabled
Minimum Bandwidth:          0
Qbin discard threshold:     65536
Low CLP/EPD threshold:      95%
High CLP/EPD threshold:     100%
EFCI threshold:             40%




Last Command: dspqbin 5.1 10


Next Command:
```

If preconfigured correctly, the display should show parameters similar to the preceding display. If the configuration needs modification, go to Step 5.

Step 7

Configure the Qbin CoS buffer parameters on BXM trunk 5.1:

`:cnfqbin 5.1 10 e 0 65536 95 100 40`

```
bpx1         TN    SuperUser      BPX 8620     9.2     Mar. 20 2001 16:45 EST


Qbin Database 5.1 on BXM qbin 10

Qbin State:                 Enabled
Minimum Bandwidth:          0
Qbin Discard threshold:     65536
Low CLP/EPD threshold:      95%
High CLP/EPD threshold:     100%
EFCI threshold:             40%




Last Command: cnfqbin 5.1 10 e 0 65536 95 100 40

Next Command:
```

Step 8

Add an MPLS controller link to port 5.1 of the BXM card on the BPX node:

```
:addshelf 5.1 vsi 1 1
```

```
bpx1        TN    SuperUser       BPX 8620      9.2      Mar. 20 2001 16:50 EST

                             BPX Interface Shelf Information

Trunk     Name      Type        Alarm
5.1       VSI       VSI         OK




This Command: addshelf 5.1 v 1 1

Next Command:
```

NOTE   Repeat this procedure for BPX2 and BPX3. The configurations for BPX2 and BPX3 are similar to the BPX1 configuration.

Summary

Service providers that currently operate ATM or Frame Relay networks over an ATM backbone can leverage the benefits provided by MPLS. They can utilize their existing infrastructure to provide VPN services using MPLS. This is possible if the ATM switches are MPLS-aware. For non-MPLS ATM switches, MPLS can be configured on MPLS-aware routers. The underlying ATM virtual circuits will be considered ATM links.

The operation of MPLS over ATM PVCs results in an overlay model. MPLS is configured on ATM routers, which perform provider (P) and provider edge (PE) router functionality. This model does not realize the full advantages of the underlying ATM QoS. However, for service providers running core ATM networks with non-MPLS ATM switches, MPLS can still be deployed to create VPNs or leverage the advantages of traffic engineering.

The operation of MPLS over native ATM using ATM LSRs as PE routers and WAN switched ATM LSRs as P routers offers service providers the QoS levels guaranteed by ATM core networks and completely alleviates the scalability problem posed by the ATM overlay model.

In an ATM environment, the label switching forwarding function is carried out similarly to normal switching. The label information needed for label switching is carried in the VCI field within one or a small number of VPs.

The control component of MPLS consists of link-state IP routing protocols running in conjunction with MPLS label allocation and maintenance procedures. The control component is responsible for setting up label forwarding paths along IP routes. ATM LSRs use the downstream-on-demand allocating mechanism. Each ATM-LSR maintains a label forwarding information base (LFIB) that contains a list of all IP routes that the ATM LSR uses.

ATM virtual circuits (VCs) established for MPLS are called Label Virtual Circuits (LVCs). A link between two ATM LSRs, or between an ATM Edge LSR and an ATM LSR, is an ordinary ATM link. Because ATM MPLS uses the VCI fields of a few separate VPIs to carry a label, each label on a link corresponds to a different LVC.

The Label Switch Controller (LSC) manages the control and forwarding component of the ATM LSR. Using information provided by the IGP, LDP establishes labels (such as VCs) on links connected to the ATM LSR. When the LSC has established incoming and outgoing labels for the same route in its LFIB, it instructs the switch fabric to set up a connection with the parameters (incoming interface, incoming label VCI, outgoing interface, outgoing label VCI). The LSC can be implemented in integrated switch software or using an external router platform.

A Virtual Switch Interface (VSI) provides a standard interface so that a controller other than the built-in BPX controller card can control a resource in the BPX switch. External controllers such as the LSC are usually implemented as an external 7200 or 7500 router.

The MPLS VPN integration function resides only on the PE routers of the MPLS network. The MPLS cloud is composed of MPLS-aware ATM switches such as the BPX 8650, MGX 8850, 8540 MSR, and LightStream 1010. The BPX 8650 is the recommended platform for industrial-strength core ATM switched networks. The PE feeder nodes can be a combination of MGX 8850s, 8540 MSRs, LS1010, 10000, 12000 GSRs, 7500, or 7200 ATM routers.

This chapter covers the following topics:

- **The Need for Traffic Engineering on the Internet**—Through the deployment of traffic engineering, the traffic flowing across the service provider's backbone can be optimized, and traffic flows over underutilized paths can be optimized.

- **Unequal-Cost Load Balancing via Metric Manipulation**—This technique allows routers to take advantage of load sharing over multiple unequal-cost paths to a given destination. This can be achieved by manipulating the parameters that determine the routing metrics for protocols such as OSPF, IS-IS, and EIGRP.

- **Advantages of MPLS Traffic Engineering**—This section describes the features provided by MPLS traffic engineering that replicate and expand upon the traffic engineering capabilities of Layer 2 WAN technologies.

- **MPLS Traffic Engineering Elements**—This section describes the various elements of MPLS traffic engineering and their relationships, which together constitute MPLS TE and allow the various elements and functions of traffic engineering to be completely under the control of IP.

- **MPLS Traffic Engineering Configuration**—This section describes the actual configuration steps of MPLS traffic engineering on headend network elements such as MPLS enabled Layer 3 devices.

- **Configuration Case Study of an MPLS Traffic-Engineered Network (IS-IS)**— This case study presents an MPLS traffic-engineered network configured using IS-IS as the Interior Gateway Protocol within the autonomous system.

- **Configuration Case Study of an MPLS Traffic-Engineered Network (OSPF)**— This case study presents an MPLS traffic-engineered network configured using OSPF as the Interior Gateway Protocol within the autonomous system.

CHAPTER 7

MPLS Traffic Engineering

The Need for Traffic Engineering on the Internet

A widespread consensus is that the Internet will transform into a multiservice medium leading to the convergence of voice, video, and data communications. Internet traffic is rising in a geometric progression, with compounded traffic growth. Although the Internet's long-term market performance is difficult to predict, one constant remains—phenomenal growth. Large Internet service providers have responded to the challenge of Internet growth by implementing three complementary initiatives: scalable network architectures, capacity expansion, and traffic engineering (TE).

Internet service providers are ever more challenged to provide the reliability that users have become accustomed to with PSTN and TDM networks. There is also a need to deploy service differentiation in the networks so that ISPs can provide various classes of service at different tariffs. In order to provide such capabilities in the network, the basic traffic-forwarding archetype of the present-day Internet must be enhanced to support traffic engineering. Traffic engineering encompasses many aspects of network performance. These include the provisioning of a guaranteed hard quality of service (QoS), improving the utilization of network resources by distributing traffic evenly across network links, and providing for quick recovery when a node or link fails.

For a service provider to truly and successfully implement commercial Voice over IP (VoIP), a hard QoS with guaranteed delivery of voice packets is required. This can be accomplished by deploying MPLS traffic engineering across the core backbone.

The Internet can be modeled as a collection of autonomous systems communicating with each other using an Exterior Gateway Protocol (EGP). An Interior Gateway Protocol (IGP) is run within the autonomous system to provide any-to-any connectivity. Link-state protocols such as Intermediate System-to-Intermediate System (IS-IS) and Open Shortest Path First (OSPF) typically provide IGP functionality. The EGP currently in use is BGP4. However, Border Gateway Protocol (BGP) is also run within the autonomous system to provide full-mesh Interior Border Gateway Protocol (IBGP) communication between IBGP peers. The IBGP peers might not be directly connected to each other. This is precisely why you need an IGP such as OSPF or IS-IS to provide destination or next-hop routing information for IBGP.

Link-state IGP routing protocols are used to distribute information about all links in the network. Consequently, every IGP router within the autonomous system obtains a complete picture of all the links and routers in the network. Each router then uses this information to compute the shortest path to every possible target subnet in the network using a shortest-path algorithm. The router then builds a forwarding table, associating an address prefix with the next-hop link.

When a packet arrives at a router, the forwarding table is consulted, and the packets are forwarded out on the appropriate link based on the destination IP address. This approach works very well in networks that have a sparse topology. In a network with a densely connected topology, this approach might cause disproportionate network loading. Links that are not on the shortest-path tree remain underutilized despite the presence of heavy traffic loads.

This leads to wasted and underutilized bandwidth on service provider trunks that could otherwise be put to good use.

This issue is currently addressable to some extent by manipulating the link metric used by the routing protocols and forcing unequal-cost load balancing across links. However, these methods do not provide dynamic redundancy and do not consider the characteristics of offered traffic and network capacity constraints when making routing decisions.

In Figure 7-1, the service provider is running an IGP (for example, OSPF). Based on the cumulative-path cost metric, path R1-R2-R6-R8 is determined to be the best path. All traffic traversing the backbone from R1 to R8 is routed over this path. This leaves the (OC3) links R1-R4-R8 and the mixed high-bandwidth links R1-R2-R5-R7-R8 within the backbone underutilized. Meanwhile, the single OC48 path bears the entire traffic load, making it heavily overutilized.

Figure 7-1 *Underutilized Paths in a Service Provider Backbone*

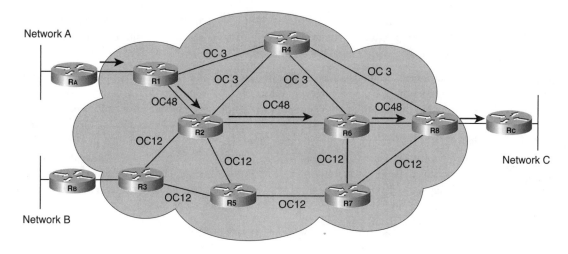

Through the deployment of traffic engineering, the traffic flowing across the service provider's backbone can be optimized. The routes R1-R4-R8 and R1-R2-R5-R7-R8 can be utilized to load-share the traffic traversing the route between R1 and R8. Figure 7-2 illustrates optimized backbone link utilization for traffic flows between R1 and R8.

Figure 7-2   *Optimized Backbone Link Utilization*

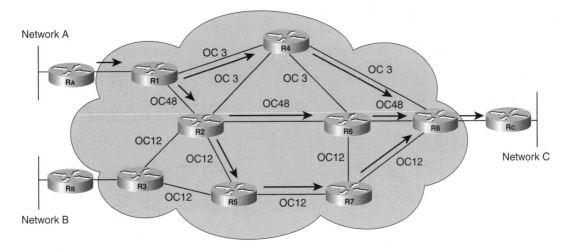

Unequal-Cost Load Balancing via Metric Manipulation

Unequal-cost load balancing is a concept that allows routers to take advantage of load sharing over multiple unequal-cost paths to a given destination. This can be achieved by manipulating the parameters that determine the routing metrics for protocols such as OSPF, IS-IS, and EIGRP.

OSPF Unequal-Cost Load Balancing

Open Shortest Path First (OSPF) uses the cost metric to calculate the best path to a destination network. The path cost is the cumulative sum of the costs assigned to all interfaces that forward traffic along the path to the destination. OSPF calculates the cost based on the link's bandwidth. In general, the path cost in routers is calculated using the formula 10^8/bandwidth (in bps).

OSPF defaults to equal-cost load balancing. In other words, it load-shares across equal-cost links only. In order to enable OSPF unequal-cost load balancing, you use the **bandwidth** command on the interface. This command might not represent the actual speed of the link, so it can be used to manipulate how data is load-shared over different links with varying speeds. For OSPF to load-share across links with varying speeds, the **bandwidth** command can be used to set the same value (in bps) across these links. The physical throughput, however, is unchanged, and the command is used only to represent or manipulate the link speed.

For example, in Figure 7-3, there are three ways for Router A to get to Network 10.1.1.0/24:

- A-H-G with a path cost of 84
- A-B-C-G with a path cost of 31
- A-D-E-G with a path cost of 94

Figure 7-3   *OSPF Unequal-Cost Load Balancing*

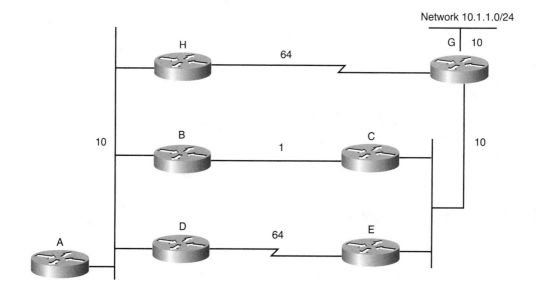

You can set the **bandwidth** statements on the interfaces such that the path cost for all three paths is equal. The **ip ospf cost** *cost* command can also be used to change the default cost assigned to a link. This command serves the same purpose as the **bandwidth** command.

| NOTE | When changing the path cost using either command, you must be careful that the cost value set conforms to the lowest-speed link. If the value is set according to the highest-speed link, traffic flow will overwhelm the slow links. |

EIGRP Unequal-Cost Load Balancing

Most routing protocols support equal-cost-path load balancing. IGRP and EIGRP also support unequal-cost-path load balancing, which is known as *variance*. The **variance** *n* command instructs the router to include routes with a metric smaller than *n* times the minimum metric route for that destination. Traffic is also distributed among the links with respect to the metric.

NOTE   According to the EIGRP routing protocol, if a path isn't a feasible successor, it isn't used in load balancing.

Now look at an example. In Figure 7-4, there are three ways to get to Network 10.1.1.0/24:

* A-H-G with a metric of 40
* A-B-C-G with a metric of 31
* A-D-E-G with a metric of 130

Figure 7-4   *EIGRP Unequal-Cost Load Balancing*

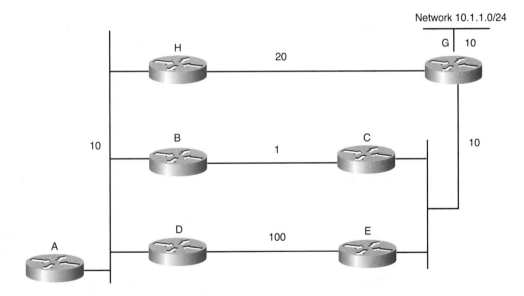

Router A selects the second path, A-B-C-G, with a metric of 31, because 31 is better than 40 or 130. In order to instruct EIGRP to select the path A-H-G as well, configure variance with a multiplier of 2:

```
router eigrp asn
 network network-number
 variance 2
```

This increases the minimum metric to 62 (2 × 31 = 62). EIGRP includes all the routes that have a metric less than 62 as feasible successors. In the preceding configuration, EIGRP now uses two paths to get to Network 10.1.1.0/24—A-B-C-G and A-H-G—because both paths have a metric less than 62. EIGRP doesn't use path A-D-E-G because it has a metric of 130 and is not a feasible successor.

NOTE   EIGRP is currently not supported as an IGP for traffic engineering. The only two link-state IGPs supported by MPLS TE are IS-IS and OSPF. The purpose of the preceding discussion is to demonstrate existing methods of unequal-cost load balancing. EIGRP has a large following in the enterprise community, and the preceding example can be used as a guide to configure unequal-cost load balancing for an EIGRP network.

Metric Manipulation Versus MPLS Traffic Engineering

IP networks exhibit poor efficiency, because the only mechanism for redirecting traffic is to change the link metrics presented to a link-state IGP such as OSPF. However, changing a link's metric can potentially change the path of all packets traversing the link. Also, these methods do not provide dynamic redundancy and do not consider the characteristics of offered traffic and network capacity constraints when making routing decisions.

In an MPLS traffic-engineered network, any Label-Switched Path (LSP) can be dynamically shifted from a congested path to an alternative path. This represents an efficiency improvement over the traditional operational methods for IP networks, because the network managers can run their networks at much higher capacity under normal circumstances, secure in the knowledge that before congestion occurs, some of the traffic can easily be shifted away from the congestion point. Furthermore, network managers can make use of global optimization algorithms that provide a mapping from the traffic demand to the physical links that could not otherwise be achieved using only local optimization. The net result is that a service provider can achieve a much higher degree of link utilization throughout the network, thereby providing services at a lower cost.

MPLS traffic engineering allows service providers to define explicit paths, similar to source routing, across their network and steer traffic over these paths. Redundant explicit paths can be configured, thereby providing a fallback mechanism. Furthermore, a final fallback can be configured. This is typically a dynamic path selected by the IGP. Traffic engineering can also perform Cisco Express Forwarding (CEF)-based unequal-cost load balancing across tunnels. This combination of manual automatic tuning helps realize the goals of capacity planning and helps optimize network utilization on backbone trunks.

Advantages of MPLS Traffic Engineering

MPLS traffic engineering features allow an MPLS backbone to replicate and expand upon the traffic engineering capabilities of Layer 2 ATM and Frame Relay networks. Traffic engineering is essential for service provider and Internet service provider backbones. Both backbones must support a high use of transmission capacity, and the networks must be very resilient so that they can withstand link or node failures. The following are the advantages of MPLS traffic engineering:

- With MPLS, traffic engineering capabilities are integrated into Layer 3, which optimizes the routing of IP traffic given the constraints imposed by backbone capacity and topology.

- It routes IP traffic flows across a network based on the resources the traffic flow requires and the resources available in the network.

- It utilizes *constraint-based routing,* in which the path for a traffic flow is the shortest path that meets the resource requirements or constraints in terms of bandwidth requirements, media requirements, and the traffic flow's priority.

- It dynamically recovers from link or node failures that change the backbone's topology by adapting to a new set of constraints even if several primary paths are precalculated offline.

- It enables unequal-cost load sharing and permits the use of paths other than IGP learned paths.

- It accounts for link bandwidth and for the size of the traffic flow when determining explicit routes across the backbone.

- It replaces the need to manually configure the network devices to set up explicit routes. Instead, you can rely on the MPLS traffic engineering functionality to understand the backbone topology and the automated signaling process.

MPLS Traffic Engineering Elements

The overlay model in which IP is run over an ATM or Frame Relay network results in distinct Layer 2 and Layer 3 networks. The IP network operates over a virtual topology in which every other router is one hop away. This causes difficulties and slows the network's responses to events such as link or node failures. MPLS allows the elements of traffic engineering to be completely under the control of IP. This results in a one-tier network that can offer IP services that now can be achieved only by overlaying a Layer 3 network on a Layer 2 network. This provides a way to achieve the same traffic engineering benefits of the overlay model without needing to run a separate network and without needing a nonscalable full mesh of router interconnects.

MPLS traffic engineering uses Resource Reservation Protocol (RSVP) to automatically establish and maintain a tunnel across the backbone. The path used by a given tunnel at any point in time is determined based on the tunnel resource requirements and network resources, such as bandwidth. Available resource information is flooded via extensions to a link–state–based IGP such as OSPF or IS-IS.

Tunnel paths are calculated at the tunnel head (source router) based on a fit between required and available resources (constraint-based routing). The IGP automatically routes the traffic into these tunnels. Typically, a packet crossing the MPLS traffic-engineering backbone travels on a single tunnel that connects the ingress point to the egress point.

NOTE	A traffic trunk is an aggregation of microflows that are forwarded along a common path within a service provider's backbone network from PoP to PoP. These flows normally share a common QoS requirement.

The various elements of MPLS traffic engineering are discussed in the following sections.

LSP Tunnels

LSP tunnels provide the mechanism for steering packets through the MPLS network. They are built using an Integrated Services signaling protocol such as RSVP. LSP tunnels share many of the characteristics of ATM VCs. They are explicitly set up and routed and have a rich set of QoS mechanisms. The RSVP *path* message carries the explicit route to be followed and is used in the interim to allocate resources along the path. The *reservation* message sent in response establishes the label operations and turns the interim allocation into a permanent reservation. When using RSVP, the full QoS offerings of Integrated Services are made available. LSP tunnels are unidirectional. The source router is referred to as the *headend,* and the destination router is the *tail end*. The forward and return paths for an IP flow are independent. Thus, the unidirectional nature of LSP tunnels fits well with traffic engineering of IP traffic.

NOTE	The MPLS header contains 3 experimental bits that are used to represent different Differentiated Services (DiffServ) code points in the future. This results in 2^3 or 8 different DiffServ code points available over a single LSP tunnel.

Distribution of Constraint-Based Routing Information

The distribution of constraint-based information must be performed in order to find appropriate paths through the network. LSP traffic-engineered tunnels must be routed with an understanding of the traffic load they need to carry. The constraint information must be distributed across the MPLS network in a consistent way. The flooding mechanism used by link-state routing protocols such as OSPF and IS-IS can help create an integrated constraint and forwarding database.

Distance vector (DV) protocols such as RIP are not well-suited for the job due to their limited perception of the network that is confined to just their immediate neighbors. Path determination using DV protocols gets extremely complex, because DV routing tables don't have enough information to calculate alternative paths used by traffic engineering.

This is illustrated in Figures 7-5 and 7-6. Figure 7-5 depicts the network from R1's link state perspective, and Figure 7-6 depicts the network from R1's distance vector perspective.

Figure 7-5   *R1's Link State View of the Network*

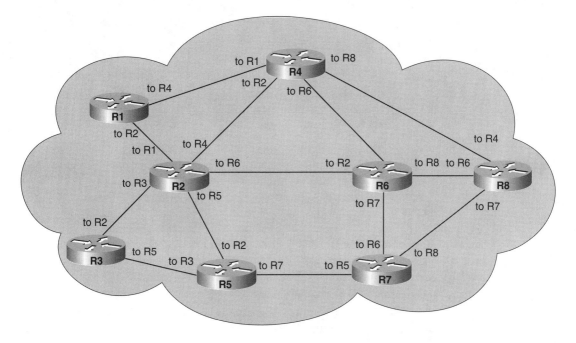

OSPF and IS-IS have been extended to carry link constraint information without the need for a separate Layer 2 routing protocol such as ATM Private Network Node Interface (PNNI). MPLS tunnels are not advertised, and updates are not flooded over them. In the overlay model, a single physical link normally carries many virtual circuits (VCs). The failure of a single physical link appears as a failure of multiple links to IP. With MPLS, a single physical link failure appears as a single link failure, thereby reducing flooding and convergence time.

Figure 7-6 *R1's Distance Vector View of the Network*

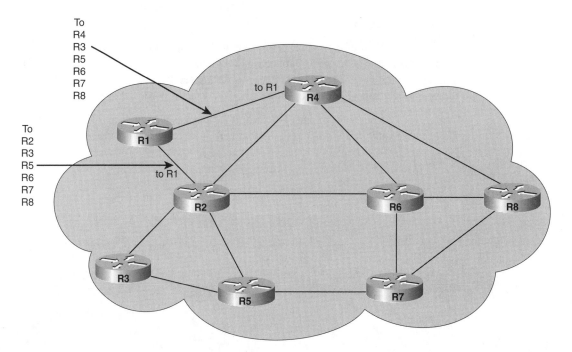

NOTE   For more information on the flooding service from the OSPF IGP, refer to the document on opaque Link State Advertisements (LSAs) for OSPF, draft-katz-yeung-ospf-traffic-04.txt, available at www.ietf.org/internet-drafts/draft-katz-yeung-ospf-traffic-04.txt.

For more information on the flooding service from the IS-IS IGP, refer to the document on new wide TLVs for IS-IS. draft-ietf-isis-traffic-03.txt available at http://www.ietf.org/internet-drafts/draft-ietf-isis-traffic-03.txt

Assigning Traffic to Tunnels

The integrated routing feature accomplishes automatic assignment of traffic to tunnels using a modified Shortest Path First (SPF) algorithm. The conventional SPF algorithm runs by iteratively placing contending paths on a *tentative* list, selecting the shortest path from that list, and adding that path and destination node to its forwarding tree. The root node is added to the SPF tree and then adds the one-hop paths to each of its directly connected neighbors to the tentative list. On each iteration, it adds the current shortest path to its tree and then extends those paths via the links connected to the last node of that path. Routing tables are derived from this shortest-path tree. The routing tables contain ordered sets of destination and first-hop information. If a router does normal hop-by-hop routing, the first hop is a physical interface attached to the router.

Traffic engineering algorithms calculate explicit routes to one or more nodes in the network. These explicit routes are viewed as logical interfaces by the originating router.

These explicit routes are represented by LSPs and are called traffic engineering tunnels (TE tunnels). Link-state IGPs can install routes in the routing table that point to these TE tunnels. These tunnels use explicit routes, and the router that is the headend of the tunnel controls the path taken by a TE tunnel. In the absence of errors, TE tunnels are guaranteed not to loop, but routers must agree on how to use the TE tunnels. Otherwise, traffic might loop through two or more tunnels.

To automatically route traffic onto tunnels, the SPF algorithm is modified as follows: When the endpoint of a tunnel is reached, the next hop to that node is set to the tunnel interface. As the algorithm proceeds, nodes downstream of the tunnel endpoint inherit that tunnel's interface as their next hop. This process continues until the algorithm encounters another node to which it has a tunnel.

This ensures loop-free routing of traffic and provides the same degree of loop prevention provided by link-state routing protocols.

Traffic can also be assigned to LSP tunnels based on BGP next hop or using class of service (CoS) parameters. RSVP defines aggregation over tunnels. LSP tunnels may be used in this way, with the added benefit that they may be routed to where the resources exist if the normal IP route has insufficient resources for the request.

Rerouting

Traffic-engineered networks must be able to respond to changes in network topology and maintain stability. Any link or node failure should not disrupt high-priority network services, especially the higher classes of service. Fast rerouting is a mechanism that minimizes service disruptions for traffic flows affected by an outage, and optimized rerouting reoptimizes traffic flows affected by a change in topology.

Fast Rerouting

In MPLS, splicing and stacking techniques are utilized to enable local repair of LSP tunnels.

Splicing Technique

In this technique, an alternative LSP tunnel is preestablished from the point of protection to the destination via a path that bypasses the downstream network elements being protected. Upon detection of a failure, the forwarding entry for the protected LSP tunnel is updated to use the label and interface of the bypass LSP tunnel.

Stacking Technique

In this technique, a single alternative LSP tunnel, acting as the replacement for the failed link, is created. It bypasses the protected link. The local router maintains a label that represents the bypass tunnel.

NOTE   The alternative LSP tunnel can also be used as a *hop* by another tunnel. Pushing the bypass label onto the stack of labels for packets flowing on the rerouted tunnels does this.

When the protected link fails, all tunnels using that link are updated to use the bypass tunnel. The label forwarding information is updated to first do its normal swap and then push on a label for the bypass tunnel and send the packet out the interface for the bypass tunnel. The label stack is popped at the next-to-last hop of the bypass tunnel. This delivers the labels expected by the next router of the protected LSP tunnel.

Optimized Rerouting

Fast rerouting can result in suboptimal traffic-engineered paths. The key is to dynamically respond to failure as well as to new or restored paths. Thus, when a failure is detected, it is necessary to also notify the headend of the LSP tunnel. The headend can then compute a more optimal path. Traffic can then be diverted to the new LSP tunnel. This can be done without further disruption.

Often missing from Layer 2 networks is a feature called *bridge-and-roll* or *make-before-break*. This is the capability to always set up a new VC while maintaining the current VC. The problem to overcome is this: Suppose the new and existing paths for a tunnel require resources from common links. However, one or more of these links does not have sufficient capacity to admit the second path. The tunnel must first be torn down and then reestablished on the new path. However, if the links can recognize the second path as a replacement for the existing path, the path can be admitted.

RSVP has a reservation style called *shared explicit*. This instructs network elements to use the same capacity to service multiple explicitly named sources. In traffic engineering's use of RSVP, a second path for a tunnel is represented as a different *source* by carrying a path ID as part of the source identification. When a source (the tunnel's headend) wants to reroute, it sends a path message just as it would for a new tunnel. This message names the same tunnel, but with a new path ID. For links not in common, this appears as a new request. For links that are in common, no new resources need to be allocated. The tail end then sends a reserve message for both paths (senders) using the shared explicit style. The two sender objects are included, and separate label operations are associated with each. As soon as the new path is created, updating the forwarding table diverts traffic. This occurs without service disruption. The old path can then be removed. The presence of the second path message on shared links prevents the cleanup process from removing resources used by the new path.

MPLS Traffic Engineering Configuration

MPLS traffic engineering has certain basic requirements. For example, it is supported by Cisco IOS versions 12.0S, 12.1, 12.1T, and higher service provider IOS images.

The minimum traffic engineering transit configuration tasks are outlined in the following sections.

Configuring a Device to Support MPLS TE Tunnels

To configure a device to support MPLS TE tunnels, do the following:

Step 1   Set up your network with the usual configuration. It is mandatory to set up a loopback interface with a mask of 32 bits. This address is used by the routing protocol for the setup of the MPLS network and TE. This loopback must be in the IGP and must be reachable via the global routing table.

```
Router(config)#interface Loopback n
Router(config-if)#ip address ip-address mask
```

Step 2   Turn on the CEF feature that is necessary for MPLS TE:

```
Router(config)#ip cef
```

NOTE   The command **ip cef distributed** can be used on only certain platforms, such as the 7500 and 12000 Gigabit Switch Router, which support distributed processing.

Step 3   Enable the MPLS traffic engineering tunnel feature on the device:

```
Router(config)#mpls traffic-eng tunnels
```

Configuring the Interface(s) to Support RSVP Signaling and IGP Flooding

To configure the interface(s) to support RSVP signaling and IGP flooding, do the following:

Step 1 Enable the MPLS traffic engineering tunnel feature on all traffic-engineered interfaces to support. This command is needed on both ends of any link an LSP could pass over.

```
Router(config-if)#mpls traffic-eng tunnels
```

Step 2 Configure all MPLS TE interfaces to support RSVP:

```
Router(config-if)#ip rsvp bandwidth [x-interface-kbps] [y-interface-kbps]
```

The *interface-kbps* argument is optional. It lets you specify the amount of bandwidth in Kbps on the interface to be reserved. The range is 1 to 10,000,000.

x = Maximum reservable bandwidth (default is 75% of available bandwidth)

y = Maximum reservable bandwidth for a single LSP (default is 100% of available bandwidth)

Configuring MPLS Tunnels

MPLS traffic engineering tunnels are unidirectional and are configured at the source router to create an LSP headend. The steps to configure MPLS traffic engineering tunnels are as follows:

Step 1 Configure a tunnel interface, and enter interface configuration mode:

```
Router(config)#interface Tunnel0
```

Step 2 Configure the headend to use the IP address of the loopback interface. IOS will not route IP across an interface without an IP address.

```
Router(config-if)#ip unnumbered Loopback0
```

Step 3 Specify the tunnel mode for MPLS traffic engineering. Other choices for a tunnel encapsulation include GRE and IPSec, which are normally used for VPNs.

```
Router(config-if)#tunnel mode mpls traffic-eng
```

Step 4 The destination address specifies the tunnel's tail-end router. The address specified for the destination must be the router ID (RID) or loopback interface IP address of the tail-end router.

```
Router(config-if)#tunnel destination IP-address
```

Step 5   Specify the tunnel's path calculation method. The tunnel has two path setup options—a preferred explicit path and a backup dynamic path. This command configures the tunnel to use a named IP explicit path or a path dynamically calculated from the traffic engineering topology database. A dynamic path is used if an explicit path is currently unavailable.

```
Router(config-if)# tunnel mpls traffic-eng path-option number
{dynamic | explicit {name path-name | path-number}} [lockdown]
```

Explicit path configuration:

```
Router(config)#interface Tunnel0
Router(config-if)#tunnel mpls traffic-eng path-option priority
explicit {id|name} ID|NAME
```

Dynamic path configuration is as follows. A backup dynamic path can be calculated from the traffic engineering topology database:

```
Router(config-if)tunnel mpls traffic-eng path-option priority dynamic
```

Explicit Path Configuration

A preferred explicit path is set up manually by creating explicit path entries. Each entry indicates a hop to the destination. Each hop specified is a RID or the next-hop interface address of the next-hop router. To enter the subcommand mode for IP explicit paths to create or modify the named path, use the **ip explicit-path** command. An IP explicit path is a list of IP addresses, each representing a node or link in the explicit path. The configuration is as follows:

```
Router(config)# ip explicit-path {name WORD | identifier number} [{enable | disable}]
Router(cfg-ip-expl-path)#next-address next hop RID
Router(cfg-ip-expl-path)#next-address next hop RID
. . .
Router(cfg-ip-expl-path)#next-address next hop RID
Router(cfg-ip-expl-path)#exit
```

Configuring an MPLS TE Tunnel for IGP Use

To configure an MPLS traffic engineering tunnel that an IGP can use, perform these steps in interface configuration mode. If these steps are not executed, the tunnel will come up but will not be used.

Step 1   Configure an interface type, and enter interface configuration mode:

```
Router(config-if)# interface tunnel0
```

Step 2   Announce the tunnel tail-end reachability to the Routing Information
Base (RIB). This causes the IGP to use the tunnel in its enhanced SPF
calculation.

```
Router(config-if)#tunnel mpls traffic-eng autoroute announce
```

Configuring IS-IS for MPLS TE

Recently, new extensions have been designed and implemented for the IS-IS routing
protocol. These extensions serve multiple purposes. One goal is to remove the 6-bit limit
on link metrics. A second goal is to allow for interarea IP routes. A third goal is to allow
IS-IS to carry different kinds of information for the purpose of traffic engineering. In the
future, more extensions might be needed. To serve these purposes, two new TLVs have been
defined. (TLV stands for type, length, and value object.) The first new TLV (TLV 22)
describes links (or, rather, adjacencies). The second new TLV (TLV 135) describes reachable
IP prefixes. Both new TLVs have a fixed-length part followed by optional sub-TLVs. The
metric space in these new TLVs has been enhanced from 6 bits to 24 or 32 bits. The sub-
TLVs allow you to add new properties to links and prefixes. Traffic engineering is the first
technology to make use of this ability to describe new properties of a link.

IS-IS Migration Solution 1

One solution when you are migrating from old-style TLVs toward new-style TLVs is to
advertise the same information twice—once in old-style TLVs and once in new-style TLVs.
This ensures that all routers have the opportunity to understand what is advertised.
However, this approach has two obvious drawbacks:

- **The size of the LSPs**—During transition, the LSPs grow roughly two times in size.
  This might be a problem in networks where the LSPDB is large. An LSPDB can be
  large because there are many routers and thus LSPs. Or, the LSPs are large because of
  many neighbors or IP prefixes per router. A router that advertises a lot of information
  causes the LSPs to be fragmented. A large network in transition pushes the limits of
  LSP flooding and SPF scaling. During the transition, you can expect some extra
  network instability. During this time, you especially do not want to test how far you
  can push an implementation. There is also the possibility that the traffic engineering
  extensions might cause LSPs to be reflooded more often. For a large network, this
  solution could produce unpredictable results.

- **The problem of ambiguity**—If you choose this solution, you might get an ambiguous
  answer to a question such as this: What should a router do if it encounters different
  information in the old-style TLVs and new-style TLVs?

This problem can largely be solved easily by using all information in old-style and new-style TLVs in an LSP. The router uses the adjacency with the lowest link metric if an adjacency is advertised more than once. The main benefit is that network administrators can use new-style TLVs before all routers in the network can understand them.

IS-IS Migration Solution 1 Transition Steps

Here are some steps you can follow when transitioning from using IS-IS with old-style TLVs to new-style TLVs:

Step 1   Advertise and use only old-style TLVs if all routers run old software.

Step 2   Upgrade some routers to newer software.

Step 3   Configure some routers with new software to advertise both old-style and new-style TLVs. They accept both styles of TLVs. Configure other routers (with old software) to keep advertising and using only old-style TLVs.

Step 4   Test traffic engineering in parts of the network. However, wider metrics cannot be used yet.

Step 5   If the whole network needs to migrate, upgrade and configure all remaining routers to advertise and accept both styles of TLVs.

Step 6   Configure all routers to advertise and accept only new-style TLVs.

Step 7   Configure metrics larger than 63.

IS-IS Migration Solution 2

Routers advertise only one style of TLV at the same time but can understand both types of TLVs during migration. One benefit is that LSPs stay roughly the same size during migration. Another benefit is that there is no ambiguity between the same information advertised twice inside one LSP.

The drawback is that all routers must understand the new-style TLVs before any router can start advertising new-style TLVs. So, this transition scheme is useful when transitioning the whole network (or a whole area) to use wider metrics. It does not help solve the second problem, in which network administrators want to use the new-style TLVs for traffic engineering while some routers can still understand only old-style TLVs.

IS-IS Migration Solution 2 Transition Steps

Here are some steps you can follow when transitioning from using IS-IS with old-style
TLVs to a combination of old- and new-style TLVs:

Step 1 Advertise and use only old-style TLVs if all routers run old software.

Step 2 Upgrade all routers to newer software.

Step 3 Configure all routers one-by-one to advertise old-style TLVs and to
accept both styles of TLVs.

Step 4 Configure all routers one-by-one to advertise new-style TLVs and to
accept both styles of TLVs.

Step 5 Configure all routers one-by-one to advertise and accept only new-style
TLVs.

Step 6 Configure metrics larger than 63.

Configuring IS-IS for MPLS TE Within the AS   IS-IS routing must be properly
configured for IP within the autonomous system as the IGP using a proper IP architecture.
Do the following to accomplish this:

Step 1 Enable IS-IS routing, and specify an IS-IS process for IP, which places
you in router configuration mode:

```
Router(config)#router isis
```

Step 2 Turn on MPLS traffic engineering for IS-IS level 1 or 2:

```
Router(config-router)#mpls traffic-eng level [1 | 2]
```

NOTE Currently, MPLS traffic engineering does not support level 2 IS-IS. Most ISP backbones
are either all level 1 or all level 2.

Step 3 Specify the traffic engineering router identifier for the node to be the IP
address associated with interface loopback0:

```
Router(config-router)#mpls traffic-eng router-id loop0
```

Step 4 Configure the router to generate and accept only new-style TLVs:

```
Router(config-router)#metric-style wide
```

Configuring OSPF for MPLS TE

To configure OSPF for MPLS TE, follow these steps:

NOTE	OSPF uses type 10 LSAs (also called opaque LSAs).

Step 1 Enable the OSPF process on the router and specify the Process ID (PID), which places you in router configuration mode:

```
Router(config)#router ospf pid
```

Step 2 Configuring OSPF for MPLS requires traffic engineering to be configured in an area:

```
Router(config-router)#mpls traffic-eng area area
```

NOTE	Currently, OSPF supports MPLS traffic engineering in only a single area—typically, the backbone or Area 0.

Step 3 Explicitly configure the RID. The IP address of the loopback interface is used as the RID.

```
Router(config-router)#mpls traffic-eng area router-id loop0
```

Configuring MPLS Tunnel Unequal-Cost Load Balancing

Unequal-cost load balancing can be configured between two or more MPLS traffic engineering tunnels with the same destination tail end. The bandwidth parameter used for load balancing is specified in kilobits per second. The default bandwidth is 0.

```
Router(config)#interface Tunnel0
Router(config-if)#tunnel destination destination IP address
Router(config-if)#tunnel mpls traffic-eng bandwidth x

Router(config)#interface Tunnel1
Router(config-if)#tunnel destination destination IP address
Router(config-if)#tunnel mpls traffic-eng bandwidth y
```

Verifying MPLS Traffic Engineering Operation

The following steps show you how to verify MPLS traffic engineering operation:

Step 1 Display information about the MPLS TE tunnels using the **show mpls traffic-eng tunnel** command:

```
show mpls traffic-eng tunnel [tunnel_interface | destination address |
source-id {ip-address | 0-MAX | name name role
```

{**all** | **head** | **middle** | **tail** | **remote**} | {**up** | **down**}}] [**brief**]

The following example shows a sample output from the **show mpls traffic-eng tunnel brief** command:

```
R1#show mpls traffic-eng tunnel brief

Signaling Summary:
    LSP Tunnels Process:            running
    RSVP Process:                   running
    Forwarding:                     enabled
    Periodic reoptimization:        every 180 seconds, next in 108 seconds
TUNNEL NAME                         DESTINATION     STATUS      STATE
R1_t0                               10.10.10.8      up/up       up/up
R1_t1                               10.10.10.8      up/up       up/up
...
Displayed 2 (of 2) heads, 0 (of 0) midpoints, 1 (of 1) tails
```

The detailed configuration of any tunnel can be seen using the following:

```
R1#show mpls traffic-eng tunnels name R1_t0

Name: R1_t0                    (Tunnel0) Destination: 10.10.10.8
Status:
Admin: up        Oper: up     Path: valid     Signaling: connected
    path option 1, type explicit low (Basis for Setup, path weight 40)
Config Parameters:
Bandwidth:  120000 kbps  Priority: 2  2   Affinity: 0x0/0xFFFF
AutoRoute:  enabled   LockDown: disabled
InLabel  :  -
OutLabel : atm4/0/0.1, 17
RSVP Signaling Info:
Src 10.10.10.1, Dst 10.10.10.8, Tun_Id 0, Tun_Instance 1601
RSVP Path Info:
My Address: 10.10.10.1
Explicit Route: 10.10.12.2 10.10.25.2 10.10.57.2 10.10.78.2
Record   Route:  NONE
Tspec:av rate=120000 kbits, burst=8000 bytes,peak rate=120000 kbits
RSVP Resv Info:
Record   Route:  NONE
Fspec: av rate=120000 kbits, burst=8000bytes, peak rate=84974967 kbits
History:
Current LSP:
Uptime: 3 hours, 33 minutes
Selection: reoptimation
Prior LSP:
ID: path option 1 [1600]
Removal Trigger: configuration changed
```

In the preceding case, the path is explicit and specified in the RSVP message. (The field that carries the path is also known as the Explicit Route Object [ERO].) If this path cannot be followed, the MPLS TE engine uses the next path option, which can be another explicit route or a dynamic route.

Step 2   Display RSVP information about the interfaces using the **show ip rsvp interface** command:

```
show ip rsvp interface
```

In the following output, on R4, four reservations are made, each of 30000K:

```
R4#show ip rsvp interface
interface     allocated   i/f max   flow max pct UDP   IP   UDP_IP   UDP M/C
atm4/0/0      0M          0M        0M       0   0    0    0        0
atm4/0/0.1    30000K      30000K    30000K   30  0    1    0        0
atm4/0/1      0M          0M        0M       0   0    0    0        0
atm4/0/1.1    30000K      30000K    30000K   30  0    1    0        0
atm4/0/2      0M          0M        0M       0   0    0    0        0
atm4/0/2.1    30000K      30000K    30000K   30  0    1    0        0
atm4/0/3      0M          0M        0M       0   0    0    0        0
atm4/0/3.1    30000K      30000K    30000K   30  0    1    0        0
```

Step 3   Display the TE path that will be used for a particular destination (and a particular bandwidth) without creating a tunnel:

```
show mpls traffic-eng topology path destination dest-ip-address
bandwidth bandwidth-in-kbps
```

The following is an example:

```
R1#show mpls traffic-eng topology path destination 10.10.10.8 bandwidth 200000
Query Parameters:
  Destination: 10.10.10.8
   Bandwidth: 200000
  Priorities: 0 (setup), 0 (hold)
    Affinity: 0x0 (value), 0xFFFFFFFF (mask)
Query Results:
  Min Bandwidth Along Path: 622000  (kbps)
  Max Bandwidth Along Path: 2500000 (kbps)
  Hop  0: 10.10.12.1  : affinity 00000000, bandwidth 2500000(kbps)
  Hop  1: 10.10.25.1  : affinity 00000000, bandwidth 622000 (kbps)
  Hop  2: 10.10.57.1  : affinity 00000000, bandwidth 622000 (kbps)
  Hop  2: 10.10.78.1  : affinity 00000000, bandwidth 620000 (kbps)
  Hop  3: 10.10.10.8
```

Step 4   To display a log of 20 entries of MPLS traffic engineering IS-IS adjacency changes, use the **show isis mpls traffic-eng adjacency-log** EXEC command:

```
show isis mpls traffic-eng adjacency-log
```

Example 7-1   *Step 4 – Example 1*

```
R1#show isis mpls traffic-eng adjacency-log

IS-IS RRR log
When        Neighbor ID       IP Address       Interface Status Level
04:52:52    0000.0024.0004.02 0.0.0.0          Et0/2     Up     level-1
04:52:50    0000.0026.0001.00 170.1.1.2        PO1/0/0   Up     level-1
04:52:37    0000.0024.0004.02 0.0.0.0          Et0/2     Up     level-1
```

Step 5   To display RSVP terminal point information for receivers or senders, use the **show ip rsvp host** EXEC command:

```
show ip rsvp host {host {receivers | senders} | installed | interface |
neighbor | request | reservation | sender}
```

Example 7-2   *Step 5 – Example 1*

```
R1# show ip rsvp host receivers
To           From          Pro DPort Sport Next Hop     I/F   Fi Serv BPS Bytes
10.0.0.11    10.1.0.4      0   10011 1                        SE LOAD 100K  1K
```

Step 6   To display the last flooded record from MPLS traffic engineering, use the **show isis mpls traffic-eng advertisements** EXEC command:

```
show isis mpls traffic-eng advertisements
```

Example 7-3   *Step 6 – Example 1*

```
R1#show isis mpls traffic-eng advertisements

System ID:dtp-5.00
  Router ID:5.5.5.5
  Link Count:1
    Link[1]
      Neighbor System ID:dtp-5.01 (broadcast link)
      Interface IP address:172.21.39.5
      Neighbor IP Address:0.0.0.0
      Admin. Weight:10
      Physical BW:10000000 bits/sec
      Reservable BW:1166000 bits/sec
      BW unreserved[0]:1166000 bits/sec, BW unreserved[1]:1166000 bits/sec
      BW unreserved[2]:1166000 bits/sec, BW unreserved[3]:1166000 bits/sec
      BW unreserved[4]:1166000 bits/sec, BW unreserved[5]:1166000 bits/sec
      BW unreserved[6]:1166000 bits/sec, BW unreserved[7]:1153000 bits/sec
      Affinity Bits:0x00000000
```

Step 7   To show summary information about tunnels, use the **show mpls traffic-eng tunnel summary** command:

```
show mpls traffic-eng tunnel summary
```

Example 7-4   *Step 7 – Example 1*

```
R1# show mpls traffic-eng tunnel summary

Signalling Summary:
    LSP Tunnels Process:            running
    RSVP Process:                   running
    Forwarding:                     enabled
    Head: 1 interfaces, 1 active signalling attempts, 1 established
          1 activations, 0 deactivations
    Midpoints: 0, Tails: 0
    Periodic reoptimization:        every 3600 seconds, next in 3436 seconds
```

Step 8   To show the MPLS traffic engineering global topology as currently known at this node, use the **show mpls traffic-eng topology** privileged EXEC command:

```
show mpls traffic-eng topology [A.B.C.D | igp-id {isis nsapaddr |
ospf A.B.C.D}] [brief]
```

Example 7-5   *Step 8 – Example 1*

```
R1#show mpls traffic-eng topology

My_System_id: 0000.0025.0003.00

IGP Id: 0000.0024.0004.00, MPLS TE Id:24.4.4.4 Router Node
      link[0 ]:Intf Address: 150.1.1.4
              Nbr IGP Id: 0000.0024.0004.02,
            admin_weight:10, affinity_bits:0x0
            max_link_bw:10000 max_link_reservable: 10000
            allocated    reservable       allocated    reservable
            ---------    ----------       ---------    ----------
      bw[0]: 0            10000        bw[1]: 0          10000
      bw[2]: 0            10000        bw[3]: 0          10000
      bw[4]: 0            10000        bw[5]: 0          10000
      bw[6]: 0            10000        bw[7]: 0          10000
```

Configuration Case Study of an MPLS Traffic-Engineered Network (IS-IS)

Consider a service provider that has the network topology shown in Figure 7-7. In this example, the network is running over an ATM backbone, and the link-state routing protocol being used is IS-IS. The links between R1-R2-R6-R8 are OC48 (2.5 Gbps). The rest of the links within the service provider cloud are OC3 (155 Mbps) and OC12 (622 Mbps). Based on the link-state routing algorithm, traffic traversing from Network A to Network C is routed across the best path determined on the basis of an IS-IS metric. Therefore, the path across R1-R2-R6-R8 is selected for routing this traffic because it has the lowest cumulative path cost. Similarly, traffic between Network B and Network C is routed through Routers R3-R2-R6-R8, leaving the other links within the cloud underutilized. The underutilized paths in the backbone are R1-R4-R8 and R1-R2-R5-R7-R8 for traffic flowing between Network A and Network C, and the links R3-R5-R7-R8 and R3-R2-R4-R8 are underutilized for traffic flowing between Network B and Network C.

Figure 7-7   *MPLS TE Case Study Topology and Traffic Flow R1-R3 to R8*

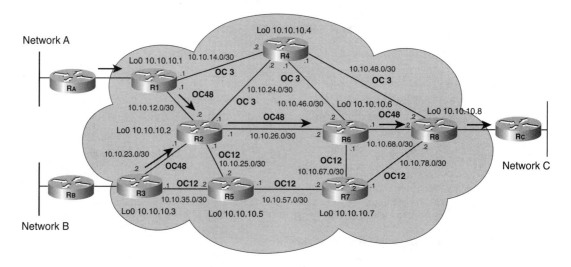

Implementing MPLS traffic engineering can optimize network resource utilization and evenly spread traffic across the underutilized links.

R1 Traffic Engineering Policy

R_A uses the IGP selected path R1-R2-R6-R8 by default in order to access R_C. As shown in Figure 7-8, MPLS traffic engineering tunnels Tunnel0 and Tunnel1 steer traffic through the underutilized paths R1-R2-R5-R7-R8 and R1-R4-R8, respectively. Tunnel0 has been configured to utilize R1-R2-R5-R7-R8 (the OC12 path) as its first path (in order of priority) and R1-R4-R8 (the OC3 path) as its second path (in order of priority). The dynamic path is the fallback path if the first and second paths are unavailable due to link or node failure. The dynamic path is normally the IGP derived path. In this case study, the IGP used is IS-IS.

Figure 7-8   *R1 to R8 Traffic Engineering Tunnels*

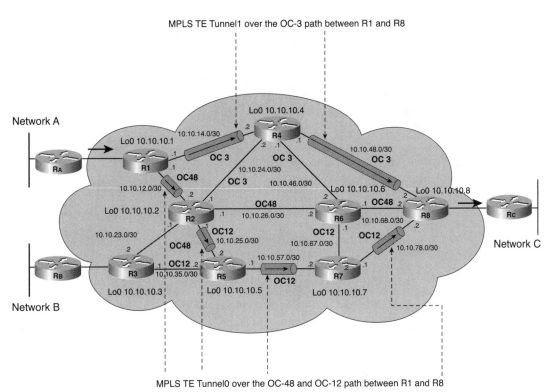

MPLS TE Tunnel1 over the OC-3 path between R1 and R8

MPLS TE Tunnel0 over the OC-48 and OC-12 path between R1 and R8

Tunnel1 has been configured to utilize R1-R4-R8 (the OC3 path) as its first path (in order of priority) and R1-R2-R5-R7-R8 (the OC12 path) as its second path (in order of priority). It uses the dynamic path in the same way as Tunnel0.

The network has also been traffic-engineered to load-balance across Tunnel0 and Tunnel1. The load balancing is achieved by configuring bandwidth statements within each tunnel interface. The ratio of these values is used by CEF to make load-balancing decisions.

R1 Configuration (IS-IS)

The configuration of R1 is as follows:

```
!
hostname R1
!
ip cef
mpls traffic-eng tunnels
!
```

continues

```
interface Loopback0
 ip address 10.10.10.1 255.255.255.255
 ip router isis
!
interface Tunnel0
 ip unnumbered Loopback0
 tunnel destination 10.10.10.8
 tunnel mode mpls traffic-eng
 tunnel mpls traffic-eng autoroute announce
 tunnel mpls traffic-eng priority 1 1
 tunnel mpls traffic-eng bandwidth 120000
 tunnel mpls traffic-eng path-option 10 explicit name r1r8_oc12path
 tunnel mpls traffic-eng path-option 20 explicit name r1r8_oc3path
 tunnel mpls traffic-eng path-option 30 dynamic
!
interface Tunnel1
 ip unnumbered Loopback0
 tunnel destination 10.10.10.8
 tunnel mode mpls traffic-eng
 tunnel mpls traffic-eng autoroute announce
 tunnel mpls traffic-eng priority 2 2
 tunnel mpls traffic-eng bandwidth 30000
 tunnel mpls traffic-eng path-option 10 explicit name r1r8_oc3path
 tunnel mpls traffic-eng path-option 20 explicit name r1r8_oc12path
 tunnel mpls traffic-eng path-option 30 dynamic
!
interface atm4/0/0
 no ip address
 no ip directed broadcast
 no atm ilmi-keepalive
!
interface atm4/0/0.1 point-to-point
 description OC48 to R2
 bandwidth 2500000
 ip address 10.10.12.1 255.255.255.252
 ip router isis
 tag-switching ip
 mpls traffic-eng tunnels
 pvc 2/5
 encapsulation aal5snap
 ip rsvp bandwidth 500000 500000
!
interface atm4/0/1
 no ip address
 no ip directed broadcast
 no atm ilmi-keepalive
!
interface atm4/0/1.1 point-to-point
 description OC3 to R4
 bandwidth 155000
 ip address 10.10.14.1 255.255.255.252
 ip router isis
```

```
  tag-switching ip
  mpls traffic-eng tunnels
  pvc 3/5
  encapsulation aal5snap
  ip rsvp bandwidth 30000 30000
 !
 router isis
  net 49.0001.0000.0000.0001.00
  is-type level-1
  metric-style wide
  mpls traffic-eng router-id Loopback0
  mpls traffic-eng level-1
 !
 ip classless
 !
 ip explicit-path name oc12path enable
  next-address 10.10.12.2
  next-address 10.10.25.2
  next-address 10.10.57.2
  next-address 10.10.78.2
 !
  ip explicit-path name oc3path enable
  next-address 10.10.14.2
  next-address 10.10.48.2
 !
 end
```

R3 Traffic Engineering Policy

R_B uses the IGP selected path R3-R2-R6-R8 by default in order to access R_C. In Figure 7-9, MPLS traffic engineering tunnels Tunnel0 and Tunnel1 steer traffic through the underutilized paths R3-R5-R7-R8 and R3-R2-R4-R8, respectively. Tunnel0 has been configured to utilize R3-R5-R7-R8 (the OC12 path) as its first path (in order of priority) and R3-R2-R4-R8 (the OC3 path) as its second path (in order of priority). The dynamic path is the fallback path if the first and second paths are unavailable due to link or node failure. The dynamic path is normally the IGP derived path. In this case study, the IGP used is IS-IS.

Tunnel1 has been configured to utilize R3-R2-R4-R8 (the OC3 path) as its first path (in order of priority) and R3-R5-R7-R8 (the OC12 path) as its second path (in order of priority). It uses the dynamic path in the same way as Tunnel0.

The network has also been traffic-engineered to load-balance across Tunnel0 and Tunnel1. The load balancing is achieved by configuring bandwidth statements within each tunnel interface. The ratio of these values is used by CEF to make load-balancing decisions.

Figure 7-9 *R3 to R8 Traffic Engineering Tunnels*

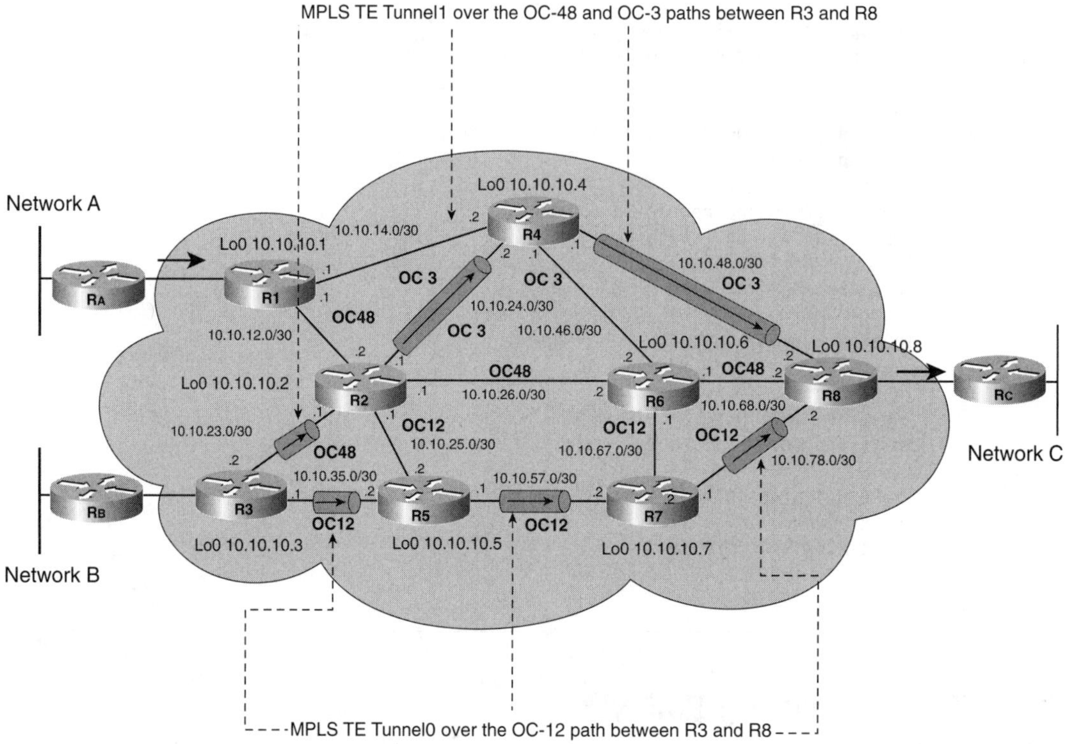

R3 Configuration (IS-IS)

The configuration of R3 is as follows:

```
!
hostname R3
!
ip cef
mpls traffic-eng tunnels
!
interface Loopback0
 ip address 10.10.10.3 255.255.255.255
 ip router isis
!
interface Tunnel0
 ip unnumbered Loopback0
 tunnel destination 10.10.10.8
```

```
 tunnel mode mpls traffic-eng
 tunnel mpls traffic-eng autoroute announce
 tunnel mpls traffic-eng priority 1 1
 tunnel mpls traffic-eng bandwidth 120000
 tunnel mpls traffic-eng path-option 10 explicit name r3r8_oc12path
 tunnel mpls traffic-eng path-option 20 explicit name r3r8_oc3path
 tunnel mpls traffic-eng path-option 30 dynamic
!
interface Tunnel1
 ip unnumbered Loopback0
 tunnel destination 10.10.10.8
 tunnel mode mpls traffic-eng
 tunnel mpls traffic-eng autoroute announce
 tunnel mpls traffic-eng priority 2 2
 tunnel mpls traffic-eng bandwidth 30000
 tunnel mpls traffic-eng path-option 10 explicit name r3r8_oc3path
 tunnel mpls traffic-eng path-option 20 explicit name r3r8_oc12path
 tunnel mpls traffic-eng path-option 30 dynamic
!
interface atm4/0/0
 no ip address
 no ip directed broadcast
 no atm ilmi-keepalive
!
interface atm4/0/0.1 point-to-point
 description OC48 to R2
 bandwidth 2500000
 ip address 10.10.23.2 255.255.255.252
 ip router isis
 tag-switching ip
 mpls traffic-eng tunnels
 pvc 4/6
 encapsulation aal5snap
 ip rsvp bandwidth 500000 500000
!
interface atm4/0/1
 no ip address
 no ip directed broadcast
 no atm ilmi-keepalive
!
interface atm4/0/1.1 point-to-point
 description OC12 to R5
 bandwidth 622000
 ip address 10.10.35.1 255.255.255.252
 ip router isis
 tag-switching ip
 mpls traffic-eng tunnels
 pvc 5/8
 encapsulation aal5snap
 ip rsvp bandwidth 120000 120000
!
router isis
```

continues

```
 net 49.0003.0000.0000.0003.00
 is-type level-1
 metric-style wide
 mpls traffic-eng router-id Loopback0
 mpls traffic-eng level-1
 !
ip classless
 !
ip explicit-path name r3r8_oc12path enable
 next-address 10.10.35.2
 next-address 10.10.57.2
 next-address 10.10.78.2
 !
 ip explicit-path name r3r8_oc3path enable
 next-address 10.10.23.1
 next-address 10.10.24.2
 next-address 10.10.48.2
end
```

R8 Traffic Engineering Policy

Figure 7-10 shows the default traffic flows between Network C and Network A or B. R_C uses the IGP selected path R8-R6-R2-R1 by default in order to access R_A and uses R8-R6-R2-R3 to access R_B.

In Figure 7-11, MPLS traffic engineering tunnels Tunnel0 and Tunnel1 steer traffic between R_C and R_A through the underutilized paths R8-R7-R5-R2-R1 and R8-R4-R1, respectively. Tunnel0 has been configured to utilize R8-R7-R5-R2-R1 (the OC12 path) as its first path (in order of priority) and R8-R4-R1 (the OC3 path) as its second path (in order of priority). The dynamic path is the fallback path if the first and second paths are unavailable due to link or node failure.

Tunnel1 has been configured to utilize R8-R4-R1 (the OC3 path) as its first path (in order of priority) and R8-R7-R5-R2-R1 (the OC12 path) as its second path (in order of priority). The dynamic path is the fallback path if the first and second paths are unavailable due to link or node failure. The dynamic path is normally the IGP derived path. In this case study, the IGP used is IS-IS.

Similarly, as shown in Figure 7-12, Tunnel2 and Tunnel3 steer traffic between R_C and R_B through the underutilized paths R8-R7-R5-R3 and R8-R4-R2-R3, respectively. Tunnel2 has been configured to utilize R8-R7-R5-R3 (the OC12 path) as the first path (in order of priority) and R8-R4-R2-R3 (the OC3 path) as the second path (in order of priority). The dynamic path is the fallback path if the first and second paths are unavailable due to link or node failure.

Figure 7-10 *MPLS TE Case Study Topology and Traffic Flow R8 to R1-R3*

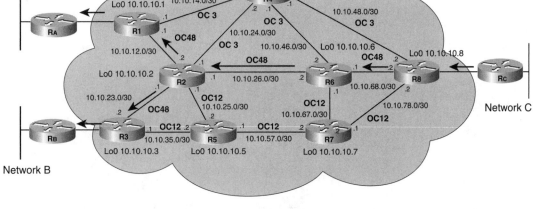

Figure 7-11 *R8 to R1 Traffic Engineering Tunnels*

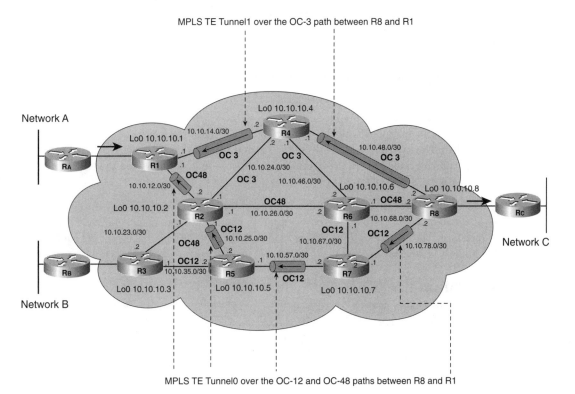

Figure 7-12 *R8 to R3 Traffic Engineering Tunnels*

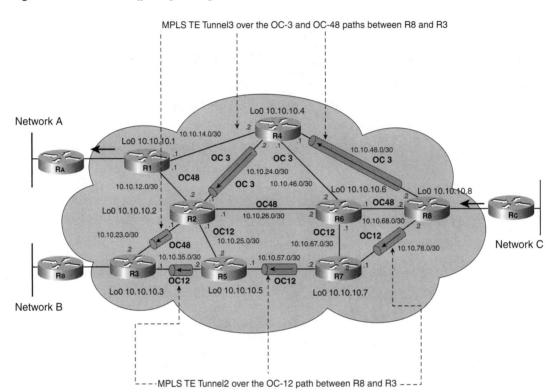

Tunnel3 has been configured to utilize R8-R4-R2-R3 (the OC3 path) as the first path (in order of priority) and R8-R7-R5-R3 (the OC12 path) as the second path (in order of priority). The dynamic path is the fallback path if the first and second paths are unavailable due to link or node failure. The dynamic path is normally derived from the IGP, which, in this case, is IS-IS.

The network has also been traffic-engineered to load-balance across Tunnel2 and Tunnel3. The load balancing is achieved by configuring bandwidth statements within each tunnel interface. The ratio of these values is used by CEF to make load-balancing decisions.

R8 Configuration (IS-IS)

The configuration of R8 is as follows:

```
!
hostname R8
!
```

```
ip cef
mpls traffic-eng tunnels
!
interface Loopback0
 ip address 10.10.10.8 255.255.255.255
 ip router isis
!
interface Tunnel0
 ip unnumbered Loopback0
 tunnel destination 10.10.10.1
 tunnel mode mpls traffic-eng
 tunnel mpls traffic-eng autoroute announce
 tunnel mpls traffic-eng priority 1 1
 tunnel mpls traffic-eng bandwidth 120000
 tunnel mpls traffic-eng path-option 10 explicit name oc12pathR1
 tunnel mpls traffic-eng path-option 20 explicit name oc3pathR1
 tunnel mpls traffic-eng path-option 30 dynamic
!
interface Tunnel1
 ip unnumbered Loopback0
 tunnel destination 10.10.10.1
 tunnel mode mpls traffic-eng
 tunnel mpls traffic-eng autoroute announce
 tunnel mpls traffic-eng priority 2 2
 tunnel mpls traffic-eng bandwidth 30000
 tunnel mpls traffic-eng path-option 10 explicit name oc3pathR1
 tunnel mpls traffic-eng path-option 20 explicit name oc12pathR1
 tunnel mpls traffic-eng path-option 30 dynamic
!
interface Tunnel2
 ip unnumbered Loopback0
 tunnel destination 10.10.10.3
 tunnel mode mpls traffic-eng
 tunnel mpls traffic-eng priority 1 1
 tunnel mpls traffic-eng bandwidth 120000
 tunnel mpls traffic-eng path-option 10 explicit name oc12pathR3
 tunnel mpls traffic-eng path-option 20 explicit name oc3pathR3
 tunnel mpls traffic-eng path-option 30 dynamic
!
interface Tunnel3
 ip unnumbered Loopback0
 tunnel destination 10.10.10.3
 tunnel mode mpls traffic-eng
 tunnel mpls traffic-eng autoroute announce
 tunnel mpls traffic-eng priority 2 2
 tunnel mpls traffic-eng bandwidth 30000
 tunnel mpls traffic-eng path-option 10 explicit name oc3pathR3
 tunnel mpls traffic-eng path-option 20 explicit name oc12pathR3
 tunnel mpls traffic-eng path-option 30 dynamic
!
interface atm4/0/0
 no ip address
```

continues

```
 no ip directed broadcast
 no atm ilmi-keepalive
!
interface atm4/0/0.1 point-to-point
 description OC48 to R6
 bandwidth 2500000
 ip address 10.10.68.2 255.255.255.252
 ip router isis
 tag-switching ip
 mpls traffic-eng tunnels
 pvc 6/9
 encapsulation aal5snap
 ip rsvp bandwidth 500000 500000
!
interface atm4/0/1
 no ip address
 no ip directed broadcast
 no atm ilmi-keepalive
!
interface atm4/0/1.1 point-to-point
 description OC12 to R7
 bandwidth 622000
 ip address 10.10.78.2 255.255.255.252
 ip router isis
 tag-switching ip
 mpls traffic-eng tunnels
 pvc 7/9
 encapsulation aal5snap
 ip rsvp bandwidth 120000 120000
!
interface atm4/0/2
 no ip address
 no ip directed broadcast
 no atm ilmi-keepalive
!
interface atm4/0/2.1 point-to-point
 description OC3 to R4
 bandwidth 155000
 ip address 10.10.48.2 255.255.255.252
 ip router isis
 tag-switching ip
 mpls traffic-eng tunnels
 pvc 8/9
 encapsulation aal5snap
 ip rsvp bandwidth 30000 30000
!
router isis
 net 49.0008.0000.0000.0008.00
 is-type level-1
 metric-style wide
 mpls traffic-eng router-id Loopback0
 mpls traffic-eng level-1
```

```
!
ip classless
!
ip explicit-path name oc12pathR1 enable
 next-address 10.10.78.1
 next-address 10.10.57.1
 next-address 10.10.25.1
 next-address 10.10.12.1
!
ip explicit-path name oc3pathR1 enable
 next-address 10.10.48.1
 next-address 10.10.14.1
!
ip explicit-path name oc12pathR3 enable
 next-address 10.10.78.1
 next-address 10.10.57.1
 next-address 10.10.35.1
!
 ip explicit-path name oc3pathR3 enable
  next-address 10.10.48.1
  next-address 10.10.24.1
  next-address 10.10.23.1
!
end
```

R2 Configuration (IS-IS)

The configuration of R2 is as follows:

```
!
hostname R2
!
ip cef
mpls traffic-eng tunnels
!
interface Loopback0
 ip address 10.10.10.2 255.255.255.255
 ip router isis
!
interface atm4/0/0
 no ip address
 no ip directed broadcast
 no atm ilmi-keepalive
!
interface atm4/0/0.1 point-to-point
 description OC48 to R1
 bandwidth 2500000
 ip address 10.10.12.2 255.255.255.252
 ip router isis
```

continues

```
 tag-switching ip
 mpls traffic-eng tunnels
 pvc 2/5
 encapsulation aal5snap
 ip rsvp bandwidth 500000 500000
!
interface atm4/0/1
 no ip address
 no ip directed broadcast
 no atm ilmi-keepalive
!
interface atm4/0/1.1 point-to-point
 description OC48 to R3
 bandwidth 2500000
 ip address 10.10.23.1 255.255.255.252
 ip router isis
 tag-switching ip
 mpls traffic-eng tunnels
 pvc 4/6
 encapsulation aal5snap
 ip rsvp bandwidth 500000 500000
!
interface atm4/0/2
 no ip address
 no ip directed broadcast
 no atm ilmi-keepalive
!
interface atm4/0/2.1 point-to-point
 description OC3 to R4
 bandwidth 155000
 ip address 10.10.24.1 255.255.255.252
 ip router isis
 tag-switching ip
 mpls traffic-eng tunnels
 pvc 6/5
 encapsulation aal5snap
 ip rsvp bandwidth 30000 30000
!
interface atm4/0/3
 no ip address
 no ip directed broadcast
 no atm ilmi-keepalive
!
interface atm4/0/3.1 point-to-point
 description OC48 to R6
 bandwidth 2500000
 ip address 10.10.26.1 255.255.255.252
 ip router isis
 tag-switching ip
 mpls traffic-eng tunnels
 pvc 7/9
 encapsulation aal5snap
```

```
  ip rsvp bandwidth 500000 500000
 !
 interface atm4/0/4
  no ip address
  no ip directed broadcast
  no atm ilmi-keepalive
 !
 interface atm4/0/4.1 point-to-point
  description OC12 to R5
  bandwidth 622000
  ip address 10.10.25.1 255.255.255.252
  ip router isis
  tag-switching ip
  mpls traffic-eng tunnels
  pvc 8/5
  encapsulation aal5snap
  ip rsvp bandwidth 120000 120000
 !
 router isis
  net 49.0002.0000.0000.0002.00
  is-type level-1
  metric-style wide
  mpls traffic-eng router-id Loopback0
  mpls traffic-eng level-1
 !
 ip classless
 !
 end
```

R4 Configuration (IS-IS)

The configuration of R4 is as follows:

```
 !
 hostname R4
 !
 ip cef
 mpls traffic-eng tunnels
 !
 interface Loopback0
  ip address 10.10.10.4 255.255.255.255
  ip router isis
 !
 interface atm4/0/0
  no ip address
  no ip directed broadcast
  no atm ilmi-keepalive
 !
 interface atm4/0/0.1 point-to-point
```

continues

```
 description OC3 to R1
 bandwidth 155000
 ip address 10.10.14.2 255.255.255.252
 ip router isis
 tag-switching ip
 mpls traffic-eng tunnels
 pvc 3/5
  encapsulation aal5snap
 ip rsvp bandwidth 30000 30000
!
interface atm4/0/1
 no ip address
 no ip directed broadcast
 no atm ilmi-keepalive
!
interface atm4/0/1.1 point-to-point
 description OC3 to R2
 bandwidth 155000
 ip address 10.10.24.2 255.255.255.252
 ip router isis
 tag-switching ip
 mpls traffic-eng tunnels
 pvc 6/5
  encapsulation aal5snap
 ip rsvp bandwidth 30000 30000
!
interface atm4/0/2
 no ip address
 no ip directed broadcast
 no atm ilmi-keepalive
!
interface atm4/0/2.1 point-to-point
 description OC3 to R6
 bandwidth 155000
 ip address 10.10.46.1 255.255.255.252
 ip router isis
 tag-switching ip
 mpls traffic-eng tunnels
 pvc 10/7
  encapsulation aal5snap
 ip rsvp bandwidth 30000 30000
!
interface atm4/0/3
 no ip address
 no ip directed broadcast
 no atm ilmi-keepalive
!
interface atm4/0/3.1 point-to-point
 description OC3 to R8
 bandwidth 155000
 ip address 10.10.48.1 255.255.255.252
 ip router isis
```

```
 tag-switching ip
 mpls traffic-eng tunnels
 pvc 12/3
 encapsulation aal5snap
 ip rsvp bandwidth 30000 30000
!
router isis
 net 49.0004.0000.0000.0004.00
 is-type level-1
 metric-style wide
 mpls traffic-eng router-id Loopback0
 mpls traffic-eng level-1
!
ip classless
!
end
```

R5 Configuration (IS-IS)

The configuration of R5 is as follows:

```
!
hostname R5
!
ip cef
mpls traffic-eng tunnels
!
interface Loopback0
 ip address 10.10.10.5 255.255.255.255
 ip router isis
!
interface atm4/0/0
 no ip address
 no ip directed broadcast
 no atm ilmi-keepalive
!
interface atm4/0/0.1 point-to-point
 description OC12 to R3
 bandwidth 622000
 ip address 10.10.35.2 255.255.255.252
 ip router isis
 tag-switching ip
 mpls traffic-eng tunnels
 pvc 5/8
 encapsulation aal5snap
 ip rsvp bandwidth 120000 120000
!
interface atm4/0/1
```

continues

```
 no ip address
 no ip directed broadcast
 no atm ilmi-keepalive
!
interface atm4/0/1.1 point-to-point
 description OC12 to R2
 bandwidth 622000
 ip address 10.10.25.2 255.255.255.252
 ip router isis
 tag-switching ip
 mpls traffic-eng tunnels
 pvc 8/5
 encapsulation aal5snap
 ip rsvp bandwidth 120000 120000
!
interface atm4/0/2
 no ip address
 no ip directed broadcast
 no atm ilmi-keepalive
!
interface atm4/0/2.1 point-to-point
 description OC12 to R7
 bandwidth 622000
 ip address 10.10.57.1 255.255.255.252
 ip router isis
 tag-switching ip
 mpls traffic-eng tunnels
 pvc 15/1
 encapsulation aal5snap
 ip rsvp bandwidth 120000 120000
!
router isis
 net 49.0005.0000.0000.0005.00
 is-type level-1
 metric-style wide
 mpls traffic-eng router-id Loopback0
 mpls traffic-eng level-1
!
ip classless
!
end
```

R6 Configuration (IS-IS)

The configuration of R6 is as follows:

```
!
hostname R6
!
ip cef
```

```
mpls traffic-eng tunnels
!
interface Loopback0
 ip address 10.10.10.6 255.255.255.255
 ip router isis
!
interface atm4/0/0
 no ip address
 no ip directed broadcast
 no atm ilmi-keepalive
!
interface atm4/0/0.1 point-to-point
 description OC48 to R2
 bandwidth 2500000
 ip address 10.10.26.2 255.255.255.252
 ip router isis
 tag-switching ip
 mpls traffic-eng tunnels
 pvc 7/9
 encapsulation aal5snap
 ip rsvp bandwidth 500000 500000
!
interface atm4/0/1
 no ip address
 no ip directed broadcast
 no atm ilmi-keepalive
!
interface atm4/0/1.1 point-to-point
 description OC12 to R7
 bandwidth 622000
 ip address 10.10.67.1 255.255.255.252
 ip router isis
 tag-switching ip
 mpls traffic-eng tunnels
 pvc 17/7
 encapsulation aal5snap
 ip rsvp bandwidth 120000 120000
!
interface atm4/0/2
 no ip address
 no ip directed broadcast
 no atm ilmi-keepalive
!
interface atm4/0/2.1 point-to-point
 description OC3 to R4
 bandwidth 155000
 ip address 10.10.46.2 255.255.255.252
 ip router isis
 tag-switching ip
 mpls traffic-eng tunnels
 pvc 10/7
 encapsulation aal5snap
```

continues

```
 ip rsvp bandwidth 30000 30000
!
interface atm4/0/3
 no ip address
 no ip directed broadcast
 no atm ilmi-keepalive
!
interface atm4/0/3.1 point-to-point
 description OC48 to R8
 bandwidth 2500000
 ip address 10.10.68.1 255.255.255.252
 ip router isis
 tag-switching ip
 mpls traffic-eng tunnels
 pvc 8/9
  encapsulation aal5snap
 ip rsvp bandwidth 500000 500000
!
router isis
 net 49.0006.0000.0000.0006.00
 is-type level-1
 metric-style wide
 mpls traffic-eng router-id Loopback0
 mpls traffic-eng level-1
!
ip classless
!
end
```

R7 Configuration (IS-IS)

The configuration of R7 is as follows:

```
!
hostname R7
!
ip cef
mpls traffic-eng tunnels
!
interface Loopback0
 ip address 10.10.10.7 255.255.255.255
 ip router isis
!
interface atm4/0/0
 no ip address
 no ip directed broadcast
 no atm ilmi-keepalive
!
interface atm4/0/0.1 point-to-point
 description OC12 to R5
```

```
   bandwidth 622000
   ip address 10.10.57.2 255.255.255.252
   ip router isis
   tag-switching ip
   mpls traffic-eng tunnels
   pvc 15/1
   encapsulation aal5snap
   ip rsvp bandwidth 120000 120000
 !
interface atm4/0/1
 no ip address
 no ip directed broadcast
 no atm ilmi-keepalive
 !
interface atm4/0/1.1 point-to-point
 description OC12 to R6
 bandwidth 622000
 ip address 10.10.67.2 255.255.255.252
 ip router isis
 tag-switching ip
 mpls traffic-eng tunnels
 pvc 17/7
 encapsulation aal5snap
 ip rsvp bandwidth 120000 120000
 !
interface atm4/0/2
 no ip address
 no ip directed broadcast
 no atm ilmi-keepalive
 !
interface atm4/0/2.1 point-to-point
 description OC12 to R8
 bandwidth 622000
 ip address 10.10.78.1 255.255.255.252
 ip router isis
 tag-switching ip
 mpls traffic-eng tunnels
 pvc 11/4
 encapsulation aal5snap
 ip rsvp bandwidth 120000 120000
 !
router isis
 net 49.0007.0000.0000.0007.00
 is-type level-1
 metric-style wide
 mpls traffic-eng router-id Loopback0
 mpls traffic-eng level-1
 !
ip classless
 !
end
```

Configuration Case Study of an MPLS Traffic-Engineered Network (OSPF)

In this case study, the same network has been reconfigured to run OSPF as the IGP. The configurations for R1, R3, and R8 are included in this section. The MPLS tunnel headend configurations are similar, except for the OSPF configuration.

NOTE   Currently, the Cisco IOS 12.0(s), 12.1, and 12.1T MPLS traffic engineering implementations for OSPF support only single-area OSPF networks.

R1 Configuration (OSPF)

The configuration of R1 is as follows:

```
!
hostname R1
!
ip cef
mpls traffic-eng tunnels
!
interface Loopback0
 ip address 10.10.10.1 255.255.255.255
!
interface Tunnel0
 ip unnumbered Loopback0
 tunnel destination 10.10.10.8
 tunnel mode mpls traffic-eng
 tunnel mpls traffic-eng autoroute announce
 tunnel mpls traffic-eng priority 1 1
 tunnel mpls traffic-eng bandwidth 120000
 tunnel mpls traffic-eng path-option 10 explicit name r1r8_oc12path
 tunnel mpls traffic-eng path-option 20 explicit name r1r8_oc3path
 tunnel mpls traffic-eng path-option 30 dynamic
!
interface Tunnel1
 ip unnumbered Loopback0
 tunnel destination 10.10.10.8
 tunnel mode mpls traffic-eng
 tunnel mpls traffic-eng autoroute announce
 tunnel mpls traffic-eng priority 2 2
 tunnel mpls traffic-eng bandwidth 30000
 tunnel mpls traffic-eng path-option 10 explicit name r1r8_oc3path
 tunnel mpls traffic-eng path-option 20 explicit name r1r8_oc12path
 tunnel mpls traffic-eng path-option 30 dynamic
!
interface atm4/0/0
 no ip address
```

```
   no ip directed broadcast
   no atm ilmi-keepalive
 !
 interface atm4/0/0.1 point-to-point
   description OC48 to R2
   bandwidth 2500000
   ip address 10.10.12.1 255.255.255.252
   tag-switching ip
   mpls traffic-eng tunnels
   pvc 2/5
   encapsulation aal5snap
   ip rsvp bandwidth 500000 500000
 !
 interface atm4/0/1
   no ip address
   no ip directed broadcast
   no atm ilmi-keepalive
 !
 interface atm4/0/1.1 point-to-point
   description OC3 to R4
   bandwidth 155000
   ip address 10.10.14.1 255.255.255.252
   tag-switching ip
   mpls traffic-eng tunnels
   pvc 3/5
   encapsulation aal5snap
   ip rsvp bandwidth 30000 30000
 !
 router ospf 1
   network 10.0.0.0 0.255.255.255 area 0
   mpls traffic-eng area 0
   mpls traffic-eng router-id loop0
 !
 ip classless
 !
 ip explicit-path name r1r8_oc12path enable
   next-address 10.10.12.2
   next-address 10.10.25.2
   next-address 10.10.57.2
   next-address 10.10.78.2
 !
   ip explicit-path name r1r8_oc3path enable
   next-address 10.10.14.2
   next-address 10.10.48.2
 !
 end
```

R3 Configuration (OSPF)

The configuration of R3 is as follows:

```
!
hostname R3
!
ip cef
mpls traffic-eng tunnels
!
interface Loopback0
 ip address 10.10.10.3 255.255.255.255
!
interface Tunnel0
 ip unnumbered Loopback0
 tunnel destination 10.10.10.8
 tunnel mode mpls traffic-eng
 tunnel mpls traffic-eng autoroute announce
 tunnel mpls traffic-eng priority 1 1
 tunnel mpls traffic-eng bandwidth 120000
 tunnel mpls traffic-eng path-option 10 explicit name r3r8_oc12path
 tunnel mpls traffic-eng path-option 20 explicit name r3r8_oc3path
 tunnel mpls traffic-eng path-option 30 dynamic
!
interface Tunnel1
 ip unnumbered Loopback0
 tunnel destination 10.10.10.8
 tunnel mode mpls traffic-eng
 tunnel mpls traffic-eng autoroute announce
 tunnel mpls traffic-eng priority 2 2
 tunnel mpls traffic-eng bandwidth 30000
 tunnel mpls traffic-eng path-option 10 explicit name r3r8_oc3path
 tunnel mpls traffic-eng path-option 20 explicit name r3r8_oc12path
 tunnel mpls traffic-eng path-option 30 dynamic
!
interface atm4/0/0
 no ip address
 no ip directed broadcast
 no atm ilmi-keepalive
!
interface atm4/0/0.1 point-to-point
 description OC48 to R2
 bandwidth 2500000
 ip address 10.10.23.2 255.255.255.252
 tag-switching ip
 mpls traffic-eng tunnels
 pvc 4/6
 encapsulation aal5snap
 ip rsvp bandwidth 500000 500000
!
interface atm4/0/1
 no ip address
 no ip directed broadcast
```

```
  no atm ilmi-keepalive
 !
 interface atm4/0/1.1 point-to-point
  description OC12 to R5
  bandwidth 622000
  ip address 10.10.35.1 255.255.255.252
  tag-switching ip
  mpls traffic-eng tunnels
  pvc 5/8
  encapsulation aal5snap
  ip rsvp bandwidth 120000 120000
 !
 router ospf 1
  network 10.0.0.0 0.255.255.255 area 0
  mpls traffic-eng area 0
  mpls traffic-eng router-id loop0
 !
 ip classless
 !
 ip explicit-path name r3r8_oc12path enable
  next-address 10.10.35.2
  next-address 10.10.57.2
  next-address 10.10.78.2
 !
  ip explicit-path name r3r8_oc3path enable
  next-address 10.10.23.1
  next-address 10.10.24.2
  next-address 10.10.48.2
 !
 end
```

R8 Configuration (OSPF)

The configuration of R8 is as follows:

```
 !
 hostname R8
 !
 ip cef
 mpls traffic-eng tunnels
 !
 interface Loopback0
  ip address 10.10.10.8 255.255.255.255
 !
 interface Tunnel0
  ip unnumbered Loopback0
  tunnel destination 10.10.10.1
  tunnel mode mpls traffic-eng
  tunnel mpls traffic-eng autoroute announce
```

continues

```
 tunnel mpls traffic-eng priority 1 1
 tunnel mpls traffic-eng bandwidth 120000
 tunnel mpls traffic-eng path-option 10 explicit name r8r1_oc12path
 tunnel mpls traffic-eng path-option 20 explicit name r8r1_oc3path
 tunnel mpls traffic-eng path-option 30 dynamic
!
interface Tunnel1
 ip unnumbered Loopback0
 tunnel destination 10.10.10.1
 tunnel mode mpls traffic-eng
 tunnel mpls traffic-eng autoroute announce
 tunnel mpls traffic-eng priority 2 2
 tunnel mpls traffic-eng bandwidth 30000
 tunnel mpls traffic-eng path-option 10 explicit name r8r1_oc3path
 tunnel mpls traffic-eng path-option 20 explicit name r8r1_oc12path
 tunnel mpls traffic-eng path-option 30 dynamic
!
interface Tunnel2
 ip unnumbered Loopback0
 tunnel destination 10.10.10.3
 tunnel mode mpls traffic-eng
 tunnel mpls traffic-eng priority 1 1
 tunnel mpls traffic-eng bandwidth 120000
 tunnel mpls traffic-eng path-option 10 explicit name r8r3_oc12path
 tunnel mpls traffic-eng path-option 20 explicit name r8r3_oc3path
 tunnel mpls traffic-eng path-option 30 dynamic
!
interface Tunnel3
 ip unnumbered Loopback0
 tunnel destination 10.10.10.3
 tunnel mode mpls traffic-eng
 tunnel mpls traffic-eng autoroute announce
 tunnel mpls traffic-eng priority 2 2
 tunnel mpls traffic-eng bandwidth 30000
 tunnel mpls traffic-eng path-option 10 explicit name r8r3_oc3path
 tunnel mpls traffic-eng path-option 20 explicit name r8r3_oc12path
 tunnel mpls traffic-eng path-option 30 dynamic
!
interface atm4/0/0
 no ip address
 no ip directed broadcast
 no atm ilmi-keepalive
!
interface atm4/0/0.1 point-to-point
 description OC48 to R6
 bandwidth 2500000
 ip address 10.10.68.2 255.255.255.252
 tag-switching ip
 mpls traffic-eng tunnels
 pvc 8/9
 encapsulation aal5snap
 ip rsvp bandwidth 500000 500000
```

```
!
interface atm4/0/1
 no ip address
 no ip directed broadcast
 no atm ilmi-keepalive
!
interface atm4/0/1.1 point-to-point
 description OC12 to R7
 bandwidth 622000
 ip address 10.10.78.2 255.255.255.252
 tag-switching ip
 mpls traffic-eng tunnels
 pvc 11/4
 encapsulation aal5snap
 ip rsvp bandwidth 120000 120000
!
interface atm4/0/2
 no ip address
 no ip directed broadcast
 no atm ilmi-keepalive
!
interface atm4/0/2.1 point-to-point
 description OC3 to R4
 bandwidth 155000
 ip address 10.10.48.2 255.255.255.252
 tag-switching ip
 mpls traffic-eng tunnels
 pvc 12/3
 encapsulation aal5snap
 ip rsvp bandwidth 30000 30000
!
router ospf 1
 network 10.0.0.0 0.255.255.255 area 0
 mpls traffic-eng area 0
 mpls traffic-eng router-id loop0
!
ip classless
!
ip explicit-path name r8r1_oc12path enable
 next-address 10.10.78.1
 next-address 10.10.57.1
 next-address 10.10.25.1
 next-address 10.10.12.1
!
ip explicit-path name r8r1_oc3path enable
 next-address 10.10.48.1
 next-address 10.10.14.1
!
ip explicit-path name r8r3_oc12path enable
 next-address 10.10.78.1
 next-address 10.10.57.1
```

continues

```
 next-address 10.10.35.1
!
ip explicit-path name r8r3_oc3path enable
 next-address 10.10.48.1
 next-address 10.10.24.1
 next-address 10.10.23.1
!
end
```

Summary

For a service provider to truly and successfully implement commercial IP services, a hard QoS with guaranteed delivery of packets is required. This can be accomplished by deploying MPLS traffic engineering across the core backbone. Traffic engineering encompasses many aspects of network performance. These include the provisioning of a guaranteed hard QoS, improving the utilization of network resources by distributing traffic evenly across network links, and providing for quick recovery when a node or link fails.

Unequal-cost load balancing is a concept that allows routers to take advantage of load sharing over multiple unequal-cost paths to a given destination. This can be achieved by manipulating the parameters that determine the routing metrics for protocols such as OSPF, IS-IS, and EIGRP. However, changing a link's metric can potentially change the path of all packets traversing the link. These methods do not provide dynamic redundancy and do not consider the characteristics of offered traffic and network capacity constraints when making routing decisions.

MPLS traffic engineering allows an MPLS backbone to replicate and expand upon the traffic engineering capabilities of Layer 2 ATM and Frame Relay networks. Traffic engineering is essential for service provider and Internet service provider backbones. Both backbones must support a high use of transmission capacity, and the networks must be very resilient so that they can withstand link or node failures.

MPLS traffic engineering allows service providers to define explicit paths, similar to source routing, across their network and steer traffic over these paths. Redundant explicit paths can be configured, thereby providing a fallback mechanism. Furthermore, a final fallback could be configured. This is typically a dynamic path selected by the IGP. Traffic engineering can also perform CEF-based unequal-cost load balancing across tunnels.

MPLS traffic engineering uses RSVP to automatically establish and maintain a tunnel across the backbone. The path used by a given tunnel at any point in time is determined based on the tunnel resource requirements and network resources, such as bandwidth. Available resource information is flooded via extensions to a link-state-based IGP such as OSPF or IS-IS. The integrated routing feature accomplishes automatic assignment of traffic to tunnels using a modified SPF algorithm.

Fast rerouting is a mechanism that minimizes service disruptions for traffic flows affected by an outage, while allowing optimized rerouting servers to reoptimize traffic flows affected by a change in topology. In MPLS, the splicing and stacking techniques are utilized to enable local repair of LSP tunnels.

This chapter covers the following topics:

- **Quality of Service**—Service providers that offer IP services over an MPLS backbone must support IP quality of Service (QoS) over their MPLS infrastructure. This means supporting IP QoS over MPLS VPNs or MPLS traffic-engineered paths. MPLS can help service providers offer IP QoS services more efficiently over a wider range of platforms, such as ATM LSRs.

- **Integrated Services**—Integrated Services (IntServ) refers to an overall QoS architecture developed by the Internet Engineering Task Force (IETF). IntServ specifies a number of service classes designed to meet the needs of different application types. IntServ also specifies various signaling protocols.

- **IP Precedence**—This section discusses IP Precedence, which classifes packets at the edge of the network into one of eight different classes. This is accomplished by setting three precedence bits in the ToS (type of service) field of the IP header. IP precedence closely resembles differentiated service code point (DSCP) and serves as a prestandard DSCP implementation.

- **Differentiated Services**—The DiffServ model divides traffic into a small number of classes and allocates resources on a per-class basis. This model is similar to the IP precedence model. A 6-bit differentiated service code point (DSCP) marks the packet's class in the IP header.

- **Modular QoS CLI**—The Modular QoS command-line interface (MQC) is a provisioning mechanism in IOS software that allows for separation of packet classification configured using class maps, from policies configured using policy maps applied on the defined classes, and from the application of those policies on interfaces and subinterfaces configured using service policies.

- **MPLS Implementation of DiffServ**—This section examines the MPLS implementation of DiffServ. MPLS LSRs do not examine the contents of the IP header and the value of its DSCP field, as required by DiffServ. This means that the appropriate PHB must be determined from the label value.

- **MPLS VPN Support of QoS**—This section discusses the two models used to describe QoS in the VPN context—the pipe model and the hose model. Various MPLS QoS classes of service should be available on a per-VPN basis, and applications should receive various classes of service within the VPN.

- **MPLS QoS Implementation**—This section discusses MPLS QoS enhancements that allow service providers to classify packets according to their type, input interface, and other factors by marking each packet within the MPLS experimental field without changing the IP precedence/DSCP field.

- **Configuring QoS for MPLS VPNs**—The Modular QoS CLI is used to configure QoS on ingress PE routers. It allows users to specify a traffic class independently of QoS policies. The Modular QoS CLI configures traffic classes to classify IP packets according to various criteria using class maps. It utilizes service policies implemented using policy maps and associates input interfaces with the service policies.

- **MPLS QoS Case Study**—This section discusses a case study that considers an MPLS VPN configured with Modular QoS CLI.

CHAPTER 8

MPLS Quality of Service

Quality of Service

The Internet is changing every aspect of our day-to-day lives—including the way we work, study, and entertain ourselves. A major factor in the success of the Internet is its universal accessibility, ease of use, and the practical convenience of Web-related technologies.

Consider a user who has subscribed to low-cost long distance with a carrier providing voice over IP (VoIP) phone service. The person placing the VoIP call would expect that call to emulate a traditional long-distance call. Transparency of the underlying technology is the key to success for the VoIP service provider. If the user perceives the voice quality as being inferior to what she is used to with conventional phone service, and she experiences severe distortion on a regular basis, she would be reluctant to renew her contract with the VoIP service provider. It is up to the service provider in this example to ensure that the VoIP call suffers little or no jitter (variable delay), that the one-way delay is within 150 milliseconds, and that the guaranteed bandwidth for the VoIP flow is within the range of 8 to 12 Kbps, assuming that G.729 compression is used on the CODEC.

Other examples of applications that have stringent requirements in terms of bandwidth and other network resources include real-time videoconferencing, streaming video, distance learning, secure financial transactions, ERP, Business-to-Business (B2B) commerce applications, and other low-bandwidth, session-sensitive applications. Each of these applications has varying needs for delay, delay variation (jitter), bandwidth, packet loss, and availability. These parameters form the basis of QoS. The IP network should be designed to provide the QoS required by these applications.

Many service providers offer premium services defined by Service-Level Agreements (SLAs) to expedite traffic from certain customers or applications. QoS in IP networks gives devices the intelligence to preferentially handle traffic as dictated by the SLA and ensuing network policy. QoS is defined as those mechanisms that let network managers control the mix of bandwidth, delay, jitter, and packet loss in the network. QoS is not a device feature; it is an end-to-end system architecture. A robust QoS solution includes a variety of technologies that interoperate to deliver scalable, media-independent services throughout the network, with system-wide performance monitoring capabilities. IP QoS capabilities allow providers to prioritize service classes, allocate bandwidth, and avoid congestion.

Service providers that offer IP services over an MPLS backbone must support IP QoS over their MPLS infrastructure. This means supporting IP QoS over MPLS VPNs or MPLS traffic-engineered paths. MPLS can help service providers offer IP QoS services more efficiently over a wider range of platforms, such as ATM LSRs. Certain useful QoS capabilities such as guaranteed-bandwidth LSPs can be supported over MPLS networks.

The Internet Engineering Task Force (IETF) has defined two models for IP QoS implementation: Integrated Services (IntServ) and Differentiated Services (DiffServ). IntServ follows the signaled QoS model, in which the end hosts signal their QoS need to the network for reservation of bandwidth and device resources. DiffServ works on the provisioned QoS model, in which network elements are set up to service multiple classes of traffic with varying QoS requirements. The IntServ and DiffServ models can be driven off a policy base using the COPS (Common Open Policy Server) protocol.

QoS in a tangible sense is implemented by various mechanisms. The Resource Reservation Protocol (RSVP) is an IntServ signaling protocol, and Committed Access Rate (CAR), Generic Traffic Shaping (GTS), and Frame Relay Traffic Shaping (FRTS) are policing and shaping mechanisms. Weighted Fair Queuing (WFQ), Class-Based Queuing (CBQ), Weighted Random Early Detection (WRED), Priority Queuing, and Custom Queuing are examples of congestion-management mechanisms. Compressed Real-Time Protocol (CRTP) and Link Fragmentation and Interleaving (LFI) are examples of link efficiency mechanisms.

Integrated Services

IntServ provides for an end-to-end QoS solution by way of end-to-end signaling, state maintenance (for each RSVP flow and reservation), and admission control at each network element. The term Integrated Services (IntServ) refers to an overall QoS architecture developed by the IETF. IntServ specifies a number of service classes designed to meet the needs of different application types. IntServ also specifies various signaling protocols. RSVP is an IntServ signaling protocol that is used to make requests for QoS using the IntServ service classes.

IntServ has defined a traffic specification called Tspec, which specifies the kind of application traffic that ingresses the network. IntServ requires network elements such as routers and switches to perform functions such as policing and verifying that traffic conforms to its Tspec. If the traffic does not conform to Tspec values, the nonconforming packets are dropped.

IntServ also defines a reservation specification called Rspec, which requests specific QoS levels and the reservation of network resources. IntServ requires network elements such as routers and switches to perform functions such as admission control, which checks to see if there are enough resources to meet a QoS request. If resources are scarce, the request for QoS is denied.

IntServ also requires network elements to perform classification of packets, which need specific QoS levels as well as queuing and scheduling mechanisms.

IntServ Service Classes

IntServ defines two service classes—guaranteed service and controlled load. These service classes can be requested via RSVP (assuming that all network devices support RSVP along the path from the source to the destination).

Guaranteed Service

The guaranteed service class provides for hard bounds on end-to-end delay and assured bandwidth for traffic that conforms to the reserved specifications. Guaranteed service requires every flow using the service to be queued separately, which often results in low network utilization.

Controlled Load

The controlled load service class provides for a better-than-best effort and low delay service under light to moderate network loads. Thus, it is possible in theory to provide the requisite QoS for every flow in the network, provided that it is signaled using RSVP and the resources are available.

RSVP

RSVP is the IntServ signaling protocol that lets applications signal QoS requirements to the network. The network then acknowledges the QoS request with a success or failure reply. RSVP carries classification information, including the source and destination IP addresses and UDP port numbers, so that flows with particular QoS requirements can be recognized within the network. RSVP also carries Tspecs, Rspecs, and information on the service class desired. RSVP carries this information from the application to each and every network element along the path from sender to receiver.

As shown in Figure 8-1, RSVP carries its information using two message types: PATH and RESV messages. PATH messages travel from the sender to one or more receivers and include Tspecs and classification information provided by the sender. Multiple receivers are possible because RSVP was designed for multicast applications. When the receiver gets the PATH message, it sends a RESV message back to the sender, identifying the session for which the reservation is to be made. It includes an Rspec indicating the level of QoS required by the receiver. It may also include some information regarding which senders are permitted to utilize the resources allocated for the flow.

Figure 8-1   *PATH and RESV Message Flow*

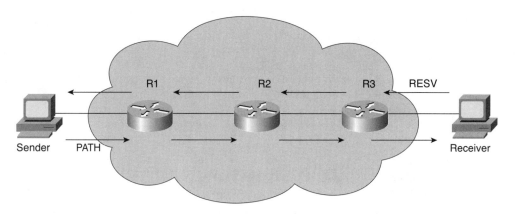

NOTE   The RSVP reservation is unidirectional. If bidirectional reservation were required, an additional PATH and RESV message flow in the opposite direction would be required, as shown in Figure 8-2.

Figure 8-2   *Bidirectional PATH and RESV Message Flow*

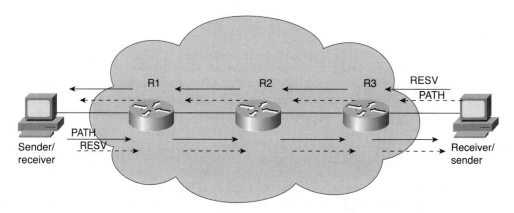

When a reservation is established, routers along the path can identify the packets that belong to the reservation by inspecting up to five fields in the IP and transport protocol headers: destination IP address, destination port, protocol number, source IP address, and source port. A set of packets identified in this way is called a *reserved flow*. Packets in a reserved flow are usually policed to ensure that the flow is not generating more traffic than advertised in the Tspec. These packets also receive appropriate queuing and scheduling to meet the desired QoS.

RSVP was designed to support resource reservation for individual application microflows. It is possible in theory to provide the requisite QoS for every flow in the network, provided it is signaled using RSVP and the resources are available. However, there are several practical downsides to this approach. Every network element along a packet's path, including the end systems, needs to be fully aware of RSVP and capable of signaling the required QoS. State information for each reservation needs to be maintained by each network element along the path. This can result in potential scalability with hundreds of thousands of flows through a network core.

Reservations in each device along the path are *soft,* which means they need to be refreshed periodically, thereby adding to the traffic on the network and increasing the chance that the reservation might time out if refresh packets are lost. Although some mechanisms alleviate this problem, it adds to the complexity of the RSVP solution. Maintaining soft states in each router, combined with admission control at each hop, adds to the complexity of each network element along the path, along with increased memory requirements, to support a large number of reservations.

However, RSVP can make reservations for aggregated traffic. This forms the basis of the MPLS implementation of RSVP, wherein packets belonging to a *reserved flow* can be defined as belonging to a particular Forwarding Equivalence Class (FEC). Label bindings can be created that associate labels with FEC instances. These labels can then be distributed using LDP or extended routing protocols.

MPLS Implementation of IntServ

MPLS can be enabled on LSRs by associating labels with flows that have RSVP reservations. Packets for which an RSVP reservation has been made can be considered FECs. A label can identify each FEC. Bindings created between labels and the RSVP flows must be distributed between the LSRs.

As shown in Figure 8-3, on receipt of an RSVP PATH message, the host responds with a standard RSVP RESV message. LSR3 receives the RESV message, allocates a label from its pool of free labels, and sends out an RESV message with a LABEL object and the value of the label (7) to LSR2. It also assigns label 7 as the incoming label in its LFIB. LSR2 in turn creates an entry in its LFIB with label 7 as the outgoing label. It then allocates a new label (3) to use as the incoming label, which is sent upstream to LSR1. As the RESV message with the LABEL object proceeds upstream, an LSP is established along the RSVP path, and each LSR can associate QoS resources with the LSP.

In operational mode, when LSR2 receives a packet from LSR1 with a label value of 3, it can look up the label in its LFIB and recognize all the QoS-related mechanisms associated with the packet, such as policing and queuing. The IP or transport layer headers need not be examined.

Figure 8-3 *MPLS PATH and RESV Message Flow*

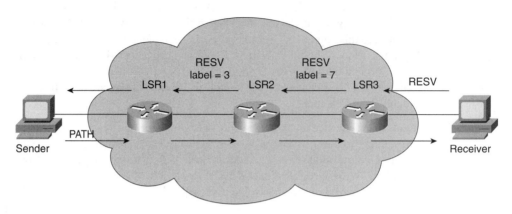

In Figure 8-3, LSR1 can associate all packets associated with a FEC and assign them to a particular LSP. For example, all packets destined for a particular destination prefix can be assigned to a particular LSP. This way, a single LSP can provide a QoS guarantee for a large aggregate of traffic flows. MPLS also defines a LABEL_REQUEST object, which could be carried in an RSVP PATH message initiated by LSR1. This object can tell LSR3 to send back an RESV message to establish the LSP as well as set up end-to-end LSPs.

Guaranteed Bandwidth LSPs

RSVP extensions can be used to distribute labels as part of the resource reservation process and establish an LSP with reserved resources. Such an LSP is known as a *guaranteed bandwidth LSP*.

As shown in Figure 8-4, if a reservation were established along a path from LSR1 to LSR3, LSR1 would consult its link-state database and select a path to LSR3 before sending a PATH message to node LSR3. This path would need to meet the bandwidth requirement constraint across all the links to support the reservation, as well as have adequate buffer space on intermediate nodes to accommodate bursts for the reserved traffic flow. After obtaining the path, LSR1 would insert an Explicit Route Object into the PATH message, ensuring that the LSP will be established along the selected path.

Figure 8-4   *Guaranteed Bandwidth LSP*

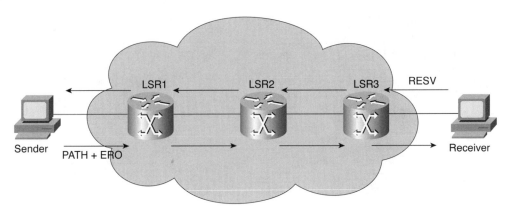

IP Precedence

The IntServ RSVP per-flow approach to QoS described in the preceding section is clearly not scalable and leads to complexity of implementation. IP precedence defined by the IETF has simplified the approach to IP QoS by adopting an aggregate model for flows by classifying various flows into aggregated classes and providing the appropriate QoS for the classified flows.

Packets are classified at the edge of the network into one of eight different classes. This is accomplished by setting three precedence bits in the ToS (type of service) field of the IP header, as shown in Figure 8-5. The three precedence bits are mainly used to classify packets at the edge of the network into one of the eight possible categories listed in Figure 8-5.

As shown in Table 8-1, packets can assume up to eight levels of precedence. Packets of lower precedence are dropped in favor of higher precedence when there is congestion on a network. Furthermore, each packet may be marked to receive one of two levels of delay, throughput, and reliability (the DTS bits) in its forwarding (RFC-791). However, RFC-1349 redefines these three bits and adds the seventh bit in the byte for designating the ToS request for the packet, in addition to its priority.

As soon as packets are marked with the appropriate IP precedence bits, any network node along the packet's path knows the relative priority level of the packet and can apply preferential forwarding to packets of higher priority levels.

The IP precedence scheme allows only the specification of a packet's relative priority. It has no provisions to specify different drop precedence for packets of a similar priority level. For example, if SMTP and Telnet are assigned the same class, there is no provision to drop the Telnet packets in the event of network congestion in favor of the SMTP packets.

Figure 8-5 *Type of Service Field in the IP Header*

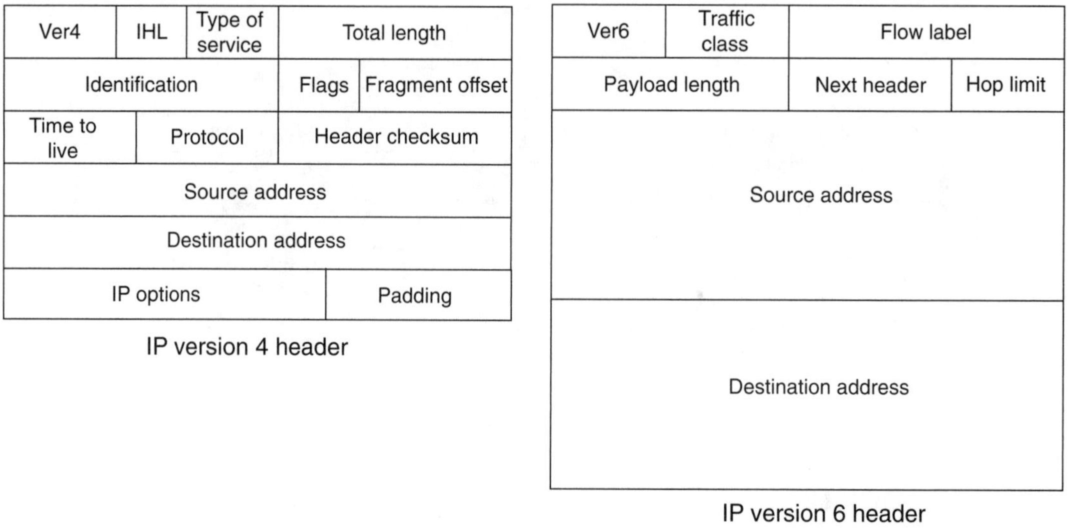

Ver4	IHL	Type of service	Total length		
Identification			Flags	Fragment offset	
Time to live		Protocol	Header checksum		
Source address					
Destination address					
IP options			Padding		

IP version 4 header

Ver6	Traffic class	Flow label	
Payload length		Next header	Hop limit
Source address			
Destination address			

IP version 6 header

Table 8-1 *IP Precedence Values*

Number	Name
0	Routine
1	Priority
2	Immediate
3	Flash
4	Flash override
5	Critical
6	Internet control
7	Network control

The 3 bits restrict the number of possible priority classes to eight. Furthermore, two IP precedence classes are reserved for network control and internetwork control.

This reduces the number of usable classes for production traffic to 6. There is no consistent vendor implementation of the IP precedence or the DTS bits. Furthermore, RFC-1349 redefines the ToS subfield by utilizing bits 3, 4, 5, and 6, and eliminating the DTS concept. This leads to interoperability issues while implementing end-to-end QoS.

Differentiated Services

The DiffServ model divides traffic into a small number of classes and allocates resources on a per-class basis. This model is similar to the IP precedence model discussed in the previous section.

A 6-bit *differentiated services code point* (DSCP) marks the packet's class in the IP header. The DSCP is carried in the ToS byte field in the IP header. 6 bits can result in the implementation of 64 different classes; however, in practice, only a few classes are normally implemented. As shown in Table 8-2, IP precedence levels can be mapped to fixed DSCP classes. RFC 2474 and RFC 2475 define the DiffServ architecture and the general use of bits within the DS field. This supersedes the IPv4 ToS octet definitions of RFC 1349.

Table 8-2   *IP Precedence-to-DSCP Mapping*

IP Precedence	DSCP
IP precedence 0	DSCP 0
IP precedence 1	DSCP 8
IP precedence 2	DSCP 16
IP precedence 3	DSCP 24
IP precedence 4	DSCP 32
IP precedence 5	DSCP 40
IP precedence 6	DSCP 48
IP precedence 7	DSCP 56

Per-Hop Behavior (PHB)

As shown in Figure 8-6, network elements or *hops* along the path examine the value of the DSCP field and determine the QoS required by the packet. This is known as a *per-hop behavior* (PHB). Each network element has a table that maps the DSCP found in a packet to the PHB that determines how the packet is treated. The DSCP is a number or value carried in the packet, and PHBs are well-specified behaviors that apply to packets.

A collection of packets that have the same DSCP value in them, and crossing a network element in a particular direction, is called a Behavior Aggregate (BA). PHB refers to the packet scheduling, queuing, policing, or shaping behavior of a node on any given packet belonging to a BA.

Figure 8-6 *PHB Based on DSCP Value*

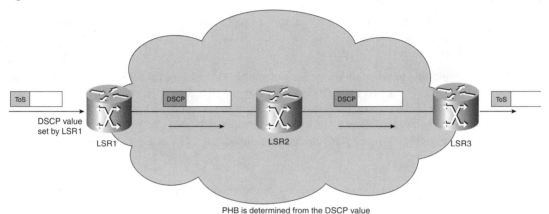

PHB is determined from the DSCP value

To date, four standard PHB implementations of DiffServ are available:

- Default PHB
- Class-selector PHB
- Expedited Forwarding (EF) PHB
- Assured Forwarding (AF) PHB

Default PHB

The default PHB results in a standard best-effort delivery of IP packets. Packets marked with a DSCP value of 000000 get the traditional best-effort service from a DS-compliant node. Also, if a packet arrives at a DS-compliant node and its DSCP value is not mapped to any of the other PHBs, it is mapped to the default PHB.

Class-Selector PHB

Many current implementations of IP QoS use *IP precedence* due to its simplicity and ease of implementation. In order to preserve backward compatibility with the IP precedence scheme, DSCP values of the form *xxx*000 are defined (where *x* equals 0 or 1). Such codepoints are called class-selector codepoints. The default codepoint 000000 is a class-selector codepoint. The PHB associated with a class-selector codepoint is a class-selector PHB. These PHBs retain almost the same forwarding behavior as nodes that implement IP precedence-based classification and forwarding. As an example, packets that have a DSCP value of 101000 (IP precedence 101) have a preferential forwarding treatment as compared to packets that have a DSCP value of 011000 (IP precedence 011). These PHBs ensure that DS-compliant nodes can coexist with IP precedence-aware nodes, with the exception of the DTS bits.

Expedited Forwarding (EF) PHB

The DSCP marking of EF results in expedited forwarding with minimal delay and low loss. These packets are prioritized for delivery over others. The EF PHB in the DiffServ model provides for low packet loss, low latency, low jitter, and guaranteed bandwidth service. Applications such as VoIP, video, and online e-commerce require such guarantees. EF can be implemented using priority queuing, along with rate limiting on the class. Although EF PHB when implemented in a DiffServ network provides a premium service, it should be specifically targeted toward the most critical applications, because if congestion exists, it is not possible to treat all or most traffic as high-priority. According to RFC 2474, the recommended DSCP value for EF is 101110.

Assured Forwarding (AF) PHB

The DSCP marking of AF packets specifies an AF *class* and *drop preference* for IP packets. Packets with different drop preferences within the same AF class are dropped based on the their relative drop precedence values within the AF class. RFC 2587 recommends 12 AF PHBs representing four AF classes with three drop-preference levels in each.

The Assured Forwarding PHB defines a method by which BAs can be given different forwarding assurances. The AFxy PHB defines four classes: AF1y, AF2y, AF3y, and AF4y. Each class is assigned a certain amount of buffer space and interface bandwidth, dependent on the customer's SLA with the service provider. Within each AFx class, it is possible to specify three drop precedence values. If there is congestion in a DiffServ network element on a specific link, and packets of a particular AFx class need to be dropped, packets are dropped such that dp(AFx1) <= dp(AFx2) <= dp(AFx3), where dp(AFxy) is the probability that packets of the AFxy class will be dropped.

The subscript y in AFxy denotes the drop precedence within an AFx class. For example, packets in AF23 get dropped before packets in AF22 and before packets in AF21. Table 8-3 shows the DSCP values for each class, and the drop precedence. According to RFC 2597, an AFx class can be denoted by the DSCP xyzab0, where xyz is 001, 010, 011, or 100, and ab represents the drop precedence bits.

Table 8-3 *DiffServ AF Codepoint Table*

Drop Precedence	Class 1	Class 2	Class 3	Class 4
Low drop precedence	(AF11)	(AF21)	(AF31)	(AF41)
	001010	010010	011010	100010
Medium drop precedence	(AF12)	(AF22)	(AF32)	(AF42)
	001100	010100	011100	100100
High drop precedence	(AF13)	(AF23)	(AF33)	(AF43)
	001110	010110	011110	100110

Differentiated Services Architecture

The DiffServ (DS) region is composed of one or more DS domains. Each DS domain in turn is configured using the DSCP and the different PHBs. The entire IP path that a packet travels must be DiffServ-enabled. A DS domain itself is made up of DS ingress nodes, DS internal nodes in the core, and DS egress nodes.

A DS ingress or egress node might be a DS boundary node, connecting two DS domains. Typically, the DS boundary node performs traffic conditioning. As shown in Figure 8-7, a traffic conditioner typically classifies the incoming packets into predefined aggregates based on the content of some portion of the packet header, meters them to check compliance to traffic parameters or marks them appropriately by writing or rewriting the DSCP, and finally shapes (buffers to achieve a target flow rate) or drops the packet in case of congestion. A DiffServ internal node enforces the appropriate PHB by employing policing or shaping techniques and sometimes by remarking out-of-profile packets, depending on the policy.

Figure 8-7   *DiffServ Traffic Conditioner Block (TCB)*

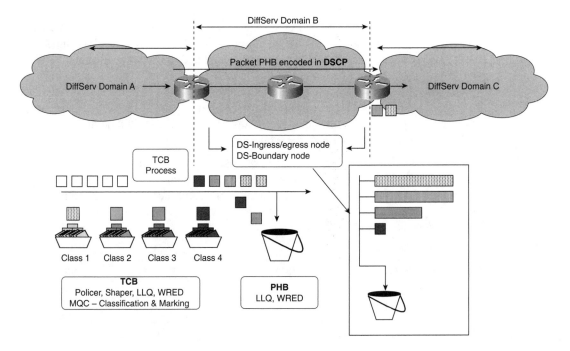

DiffServ Mechanisms

The DiffServ model only defines the use of the DSCP and the PHBs. The PHBs simply describe the forwarding behavior of a DiffServ-compliant node. The model does not specify how these PHBs may be implemented. A variety of queuing, policing, metering, and shaping techniques may be used to affect the desired traffic conditioning and PHB.

Traffic Policing

Committed Access Rate (CAR) is used for traffic conditioning and in providing PHB for AF classes at the edge and in the core of a DS domain. Packets are metered, and different actions are taken, depending on whether the packet in question conforms to, violates, or exceeds the configured average rate, committed burst (Bc), or excess burst (Be). Traffic that is within the token bucket parameter Bc in an interval is within the configured access rate. Traffic between Bc and Be is excess traffic. Traffic that is more than Bc + Be is dropped. A packet can be transmitted, dropped, or remarked with a different DSCP value (moving it into a lower AF class or changing its drop precedence value), depending on the configured policy.

Traffic Shaping

Generic Traffic Shaping (GTS) and Frame Relay Traffic Shaping (FRTS) buffer packets rather than simply dropping them in the case of congestion. This can be done generically by configuring an average rate, Bc, and Be. FRTS can also be employed to make the traffic slow down when congestion is reported by the Frame Relay switch.

PHB Enforcement

PHB is enforced on core routers depending on the DSCP value marked on the packet. EF is implemented using Low Latency Queuing (LLQ), and AF can be implemented using a combination of CBWFQ (Class-Based Weighted Fair Queuing) and WRED or CAR.

LLQ for the AF PHB

LLQ offers strict priority queuing for delay-sensitive traffic such as VoIP along the data path. LLQ must be implemented at each hop. This priority queue is policed in order to ensure that excess delay-sensitive traffic does not interfere with traffic of other classes.

CBWFQ and WRED for the AF PHB

CBWFQ lets you slice up bandwidth among the various classes defined. Bandwidth may be allocated to each class on an absolute basis or as a percentage of the interface or subinterface bandwidth to which this policy will be applied. Within an AF class, packets can be dropped based on the drop precedence scheme using WRED.

Traffic Policing for the AF PHB

CAR can be used to implement the PHB in the core as well as for traffic conditioning and in providing PHB for AF classes in the core of a DS domain.

Even if packets of a class are policed at the edge of a network, the core will have many streams of a particular class merging from its numerous input interfaces, and hence will need to police the class further at a higher aggregate rate. Packets are metered, and different actions are taken, depending on whether the packet in question conforms to, violates, or exceeds the configured average rate, Bc, or Be.

Modular QoS CLI

The Modular QoS command-line interface (MQC) is a provisioning mechanism in IOS software that allows for separation of packet classification configured using class maps, from policies configured using policy maps applied on the defined classes, and from the application of those policies on interfaces and subinterfaces configured using service policies. As shown in Figure 8-8, the MQC forms the basis for provisioning DiffServ, and all the QoS mechanisms are part of the class maps (classification) or policy maps (policing, shaping, queuing, congestion avoidance, packet marking, or Layer 2 CoS marking).

Figure 8-8 *Modular QoS CLI Mechanisms*

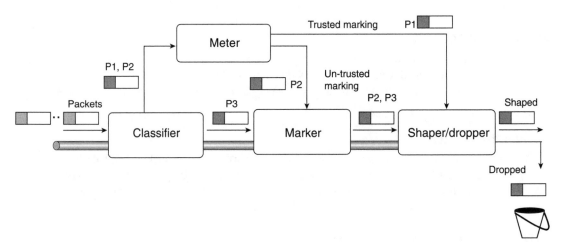

Packets entering a DiffServ domain (DS domain) can be metered, marked, shaped, or policed to implement traffic policies. In IOS software, classifying and marking are done using the MQC's class maps. Metering is done using a token bucket algorithm, shaping is done using GTS or FRTS, and policing is done using class-based policing or CAR.

In addition, statistics for each class can be extracted from the per-class accounting MIB for network management purposes. In order to implement DiffServ using IOS software, class maps may be defined to classify packets into one or more BAs. Policy maps can be created using the defined class maps. Finally, the policies can be applied to the desired interfaces (or subinterfaces) in either the incoming or outgoing direction. The policy-based mechanism is a much simpler, cleaner, and more scalable way to implement DiffServ. Network-Based Application Recognition (NBAR) is another method used in IOS software to identify traffic streams that use variable TCP/UDP ports.

In addition to providing all the core DiffServ functionality, IOS software makes it possible to define arbitrary DSCP values (local use) and associate almost any kind of policy with them. For example, Telnet flows between two subnets may be categorized into a BA with a DSCP value of 100011 and provided 100 Kbps of bandwidth end-to-end. The IETF has divided the possible 64 DSCP values into three pools, as described in RFC-2598 and shown in Table 8-4. Any value from Pool 1, 2, or 3 can be used.

Table 8-4   *DSCP Pools*

Pool	Codepoint Space	Assignment Policy
1	XXXXX0	Standard action (EF, AFxy, default, class-selector codepoints)
2	XXXX11	Experimental/local usage
3	XXXX01	Experimental/local usage/future standards

NOTE   On the Cisco 7500 platforms, VIP-based distributed CAR, LLQ, GTS, WRED, and FRTS are available to offload these algorithms from the main processor and achieve high-end scalability.

MPLS Implementation of DiffServ

MPLS LSRs do not examine the contents of the IP header and the value of its DSCP field as required by DiffServ. This means that the appropriate PHB must be determined from the label value. The MPLS shim header has a 3-bit field called Exp. It was originally defined for experimental use. This field supports eight different values and is used for MPLS support of up to eight DiffServ classes.

NOTE   The Exp field of the MPLS shim header was originally defined to accommodate the 3 bits
           used in IP precedence. The DiffServ DSCP field is 6 bits and can support up to 64 classes
           of service (CoSs).

As shown in Figure 8-9, the IP precedence bits or the first 3 bits of the DSCP field are
copied into the MPLS Exp field at the edge of the network. Each LSR along the LSP
maps the Exp bits to a PHB. The service provider can also set an MPLS packet's CoS to a
different value, as determined by a service offering. This feature allows the service provider
to set the MPLS Exp field instead of overwriting the value in the customer's IP precedence
field. This leaves the IP header intact and available for the customer's use. The customer-
configured CoS is not changed as the packet travels through the MPLS backbone. The LSPs
created this way are known as E-LSPs or Exp-LSPs. E-LSPs can support up to eight PHBs
per LSP.

Figure 8-9   *MPLS E-LSP*

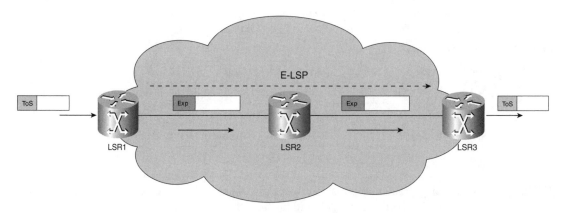

As shown in Figure 8-10, if more than 8 PHBs are needed in the MPLS network, L-LSPs
(Label LSPs) are used, in which case the PHB of the LSR is inferred from the label. However, as shown in Figure 8-11, in the case of ATM where the shim header is not used, the
PHB is inferred from the label carried in the VCI field. The label-to-PHB mapping is
signaled. Only one PHB per L-LSP is possible, except for DiffServ AF.

In the case of DiffServ AF, packets sharing a common PHB can be aggregated into a FEC,
which can be assigned to an LSP. This is known as a *PHB scheduling class*. The drop
preferences are encoded in the Exp bits of the shim header, as shown in Figure 8-10.

However, in case of ATM, the drop preferences are encoded in the CLP bit, as shown in
Figure 8-11.

Figure 8-10 *MPLS L-LSP*

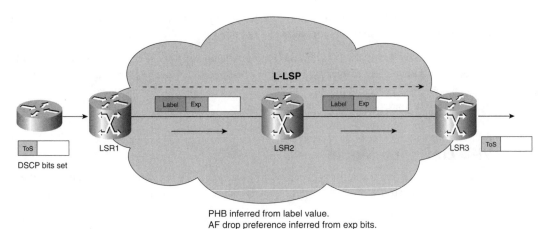

PHB inferred from label value.
AF drop preference inferred from exp bits.

Figure 8-11 *ATM MPLS L-LSP*

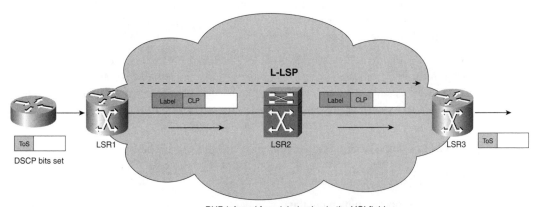

PHB inferred from label value in the VCI field.
AF drop preference inferred from ATM CLP bit.

E-LSPs are more efficient than L-LSPs, because the E-LSP model is similar to the standard DiffServ model. Multiple PHBs can be supported over a single E-LSP. The total number of LSPs created can be limited, thus saving label space.

MPLS VPN Support of QoS

A VPN is defined as a closed user group sharing a public network infrastructure with a set of administrative policies that control both connectivity and QoS among sites.

The various MPLS QoS CoSs should be available on a per-VPN basis. Applications should receive various CoSs within the VPN. For example, real-time applications such as VoIP could receive a preferential CoS versus a file transfer. Two models are used to describe QoS in the VPN context—the *pipe* model and the *hose* model.

MPLS VPN QoS Pipe Model

In the pipe model, the service provider provides the VPN customer with certain QoS guarantees for traffic flows between one CE router and another within the same VPN.

This model can be represented as a pipe between two CE routers. Any traffic that enters this pipe gets certain QoS guarantees, such as a guaranteed minimum bandwidth between the two CE routers. The PE router at the headend of the pipe can specify request traffic flows permitted to use the pipe. The MPLS QoS pipe model is similar to the QoS model that VPN customers are accustomed to with ATM or Frame Relay. However, ATM or Frame Relay connections are bidirectional, whereas the pipe model is unidirectional. The unidirectional nature of the pipe model permits traffic pattern asymmetry, which allows for different traffic rates in either direction, between CE routers.

As shown in Figure 8-12, a service provider provides VPN1 with a pipe that guarantees 30 Mbps for traffic from site 1 to site 3, another pipe that guarantees 10 Mbps for traffic from site 1 to site 2, and yet another pipe that guarantees 5 Mbps for traffic from site 2 to site 3. There is also a pipe that guarantees 45 Mbps for traffic flows from site 3 to site 2. This asymmetry is possible due to the unidirectional nature of MPLS QoS pipes.

VPN2 has symmetrical pipes that guarantee 20 Mbps for traffic from site 1 to site 2, and vice versa. The preceding example shows that it is possible for a CE router to have more than one pipe originating from it or terminating at it.

In order to properly implement the pipe model, the customer must have a good idea of his or her traffic model and must perform a network traffic analysis with proper capacity planning. The pipe model closely resembles the IntServ model for QoS and can provide hard guarantees.

Figure 8-12 *Example of MPLS VPN QoS: Pipe Model*

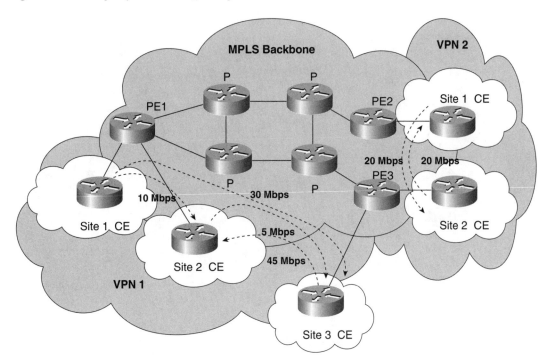

Guaranteed bandwidth LSPs are used to support the pipe model. These LSPs originate and terminate at PE routers and provide guaranteed bandwidth for all the CE-to-CE pipes between them. There is no need to configure guaranteed bandwidth LSPs for each of the CE-to-CE pipes. As shown in Figure 8-13, the service provider has configured a 15 Mbps pipe for VPN1 from VPN1-site3 to VPN1-site1. Another 30 Mbps pipe is configured for VPN2 from VPN2-site 3 to VPN2-site 2. In order to support these two pipes, a guaranteed bandwidth LSP is configured between PE3 and PE1. The bandwidth reserved on the guaranteed bandwidth LSP is equal to the sum of the bandwidth of the two CE-to-CE pipes. In this example, the guaranteed bandwidth LSP has a guaranteed bandwidth of up to 45 Mbps. When PE3 receives a packet destined for VPN1-site1 or VPN2-site 3, it determines whether the packet must receive a CoS. If so, it forwards the packet along the guaranteed bandwidth LSP to PE1.

Figure 8-13 *Guaranteed Bandwidth LSP: Pipe Model*

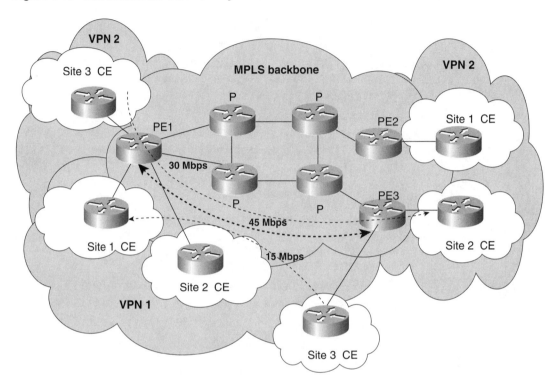

The guaranteed bandwidth LSP mechanism improves the scalability of MPLS VPN QoS, because service providers do not have to configure CE-to-CE pipes for individual customer site pairs.

MPLS VPN QoS Hose Model

In the hose model, the service provider supplies a customer with certain guarantees for the traffic that a particular CE router would send to and receive from other CE routers in the same VPN. It is easy for a customer to implement the hose model for MPLS QoS within the VPN, because the customer does not have to perform a detailed traffic analysis or capacity planning and specify the traffic distribution between various CE routers.

The two parameters used in the hose model are the Ingress Committed Rate (ICR) and the Egress Committed rate (ECR). The ICR is the traffic rate at which the CEs in the VPN can receive from a particular CE, and the ECR is the traffic rate at which the CEs in the VPN can send traffic to a particular CE router. The ICR and ECR values are independent of each other and need not be the same.

In Figure 8-14, a service provider supplies VPN1 with certain guarantees of up to 30 Mbps for traffic received by site 2 and site 3 from site 1 (site 1 ICR = 30 Mbps). This traffic could be directed to site 2 or site 3 or could be distributed in an arbitrary way between site 2 and site 3.

Figure 8-14 *Example of MPLS VPN QoS: Hose Model*

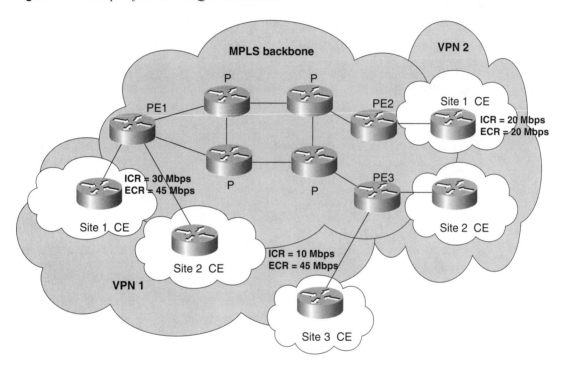

The service provider also supplies VPN1 with certain guarantees of up to 45 Mbps for traffic sent by site 2 and site 3 to site 1 (site 1 ECR = 45 Mbps). This traffic could be directed to site 1 from site 2 or site 3 or distributed in an arbitrary way between site 2 and site 3 and sent to site 1. In VPN2, the service provider supplies certain guarantees of up to 20 Mbps for traffic sent by site 1 to site 2 (site 1 ICR = 20 Mbps). Site 1 also has an ECR of 20 Mbps, which means that site 2 can send traffic to site 1 with a guaranteed bandwidth of up to 20 Mbps.

The hose model closely resembles the DiffServ model for QoS, which supports multiple CoSs. These CoSs differ from each other in their relative performance characteristics. The different CoSs within the hose model are supported using DiffServ mechanisms.

A service provider can offer a VPN customer the pipe model, hose model, or a combination of both. The PE routers at the ingress determine which traffic receives a particular CoS, depending on the incoming interface, IP source and destination addresses, IP precedence,

TCP port numbers, or a combination of these values. The ingress PE routers can also police incoming traffic and mark packets that are out-of-rate, based on the SLA drawn with the customer. These packets can be marked differently and dropped in case of congestion.

MPLS QoS Implementation

Consider a case in which a customer sends IP traffic from one CE site to another. The IP precedence field (the first 3 bits of the DSCP field in the header of an IP packet) specifies the CoS. Based on the IP precedence marking, the packet is given the desired treatment, such as the latency or the percent of bandwidth allowed. The IP precedence bits are copied into the MPLS Exp field at the edge of the network. However, the service provider might want to set an MPLS packet's QoS to a different value determined by the service offering.

This feature allows the service provider to set the MPLS Exp field instead of overwriting the value in the customer's IP precedence field. This way, the IP header remains available for the customer's use, and the IP packet's marking is not changed as the packet travels through the MPLS network.

MPLS QoS enhancements allow service providers to classify packets according to their type, input interface, and other factors by marking each packet within the MPLS Exp field without changing the IP precedence/DSCP field. For example, service providers can classify packets with or without considering the rate of the packets that an ingress PE receives. If the rate is a consideration, the service provider marks in-rate packets differently from out-of-rate packets. Customers can differentiate traffic within their network and need not buy multiple grades of service from the service provider. The MPLS experimental bits allow you to specify the QoS for an MPLS packet, and the IP precedence/DSCP bits allow you to specify the QoS for an IP packet. Currently, Cisco's implementation of MPLS QoS supports the following services:

- **Committed Access Rate (CAR)**—Classifies packets according to input or output transmission rates. This allows you to set the MPLS experimental bits or the IP precedence/DSCP bits, whichever is appropriate.

- **Weighted Random Early Detection (WRED)**—Monitors network traffic to prevent congestion by dropping packets based on the IP precedence/DSCP bits or the MPLS Exp field.

- **Class-Based Weighted Fair Queuing (CBWFQ)**—An automated scheduling system that uses a queuing algorithm to ensure bandwidth allocation to different classes of network traffic.

NOTE   In order to implement MPLS QoS, the network must support MPLS and CEF switching (on every MPLS-enabled router in the network). This must be configured prior to configuring QoS.

MPLS Experimental Field

Setting the value of the MPLS Exp field fulfills the requirement of service providers who do not want the value of the IP precedence field modified within IP packets transported through their networks. By selecting different values for the MPLS Exp field, you can mark packets based on their characteristics, such as rate or type, so that packets have the priority they require during periods of congestion.

Packet Prioritization

IP packets can be classified according to their source address, destination address, port, protocol identification, or class of service field. Packet classification is important, because a packet's priority is determined by how it is classified or marked. A packet's priority affects how the packet is treated during periods of congestion. For example, service providers have Service-Level Agreements (SLAs) with customers. The agreement specifies how much traffic the service provider has agreed to deliver. To comply with the agreement, the customer must not transmit more than the agreed-upon rate. Packets are considered in-rate or out-of-rate. If there is congestion in the network, out-of-rate packets might be dropped more aggressively.

Ingress PE Router Configuration

The ingress PE is configured in order to classify IP packets. Packets are received at the ingress router as IP packets and are transmitted as MPLS packets. To perform the configuration, use either of the following:

- Modular Quality of Service command-line interface (Modular QoS CLI)
- Committed Access Rate (CAR)

NOTE The Modular QoS CLI method is the preferred procedure to configure MPLS QoS on PE routers for MPLS QoS.

Configuring QoS for MPLS VPNs

The Modular QoS CLI is used to configure QoS on ingress PE routers. It allows users to specify a traffic class independently of QoS policies. The Modular QoS CLI involves the following three steps:

- Configure traffic classes to classify IP packets according to various criteria using class maps.
- Configure service policies using policy maps.
- Configure the input interface to attach the service policy.

Traffic Class Configuration

The **class-map** command is used to create a traffic class. In order to create a traffic class containing match criteria, the **class-map** command is used to specify the traffic class name, and a **match** command is used in class map configuration mode.

The **class-map** syntax is as follows:

```
class-map [match-any | match-all] class-name
no class-map [match-any | match-all] class-name
```

The **class-map match-all** command is used when all of the match criteria in the traffic class must be met in order for a packet to match the specified traffic class. The **class-map match-any** command is used when the first possible match criterion from a list of match criteria must be met for a packet to match the specified traffic class. If neither **match-all** nor **match-any** is specified, the traffic class behaves in a manner consistent with the **class-map match-all** command. The **match not** command is used to specify a match criterion that prevents a packet from being classified as a member of the class.

The following steps assign traffic flows to various classes using class maps:

Step 1   Specify the class map to which packets will be matched:

```
Router(config)# class-map class-map-name
```

Step 2   Specify the packet characteristics that will be matched to the class:

```
Router(config-cmap)# match criteria
```

The various match criteria include the following:

— **match access-group** *access-group*—Configures the match criteria for a class map based on the specified ACL number.

— **match any**—Configures the match criteria for a class map to be a successful match criteria for all packets.

— **match class-map** *class-map-name*—Configures the match criteria for a class map based on a classification policy.

— **match cos** *cos-value* [*cos-value cos-value cos-value*] —Configures the match criteria for a class map based on a Layer 2 CoS marking.

— **match destination-address mac** *address*—Configures the match criteria for a class map based on the destination MAC address.

— **match input-interface** *interface-name*—Configures the match criteria for a class map based on the specified input interface.

— **match ip dscp** *dscp-value* [*dscp-value dscp-value dscp-value dscp-value dscp-value dscp-value dscp-value*]—Configures the match criteria for a class map based on a specific IP differentiated service code point (DSCP) value. Up to eight IP DSCP values can be matched in one **match** statement. The DSCP value ranges between 0 and 63.

— **match ip precedence** *precedence-value* [*precedence-value precedence-value precedence-value*]—Configures the match criteria for a class map based on IP precedence values. Up to four precedence values can be matched in one **match** statement. The IP precedence values range from 0 to 7.

— **match ip rtp** *starting-port-number port-range*—Configures the match criteria for a class map based on the Real-Time Protocol (RTP) port. The starting RTP port number value ranges from 2000 to 65535. The RTP port number value ranges from 0 to 16383.

— **match mpls experimental** *number*—Configures the match criteria for a class map based on the value of the Exp field. The Exp value ranges from 0 to 7.

— **match not**—Configures the match criteria for a class map based on an unsuccessful match criterion.

— **match protocol** *protocol*—Configures the match criteria for a class map based on the specified protocol.

— **match qos-group** *qos-group-value*—Configures the match criteria for a class map based on the QoS group value. The QoS group value ranges from 0 to 99 and has no mathematical significance. The QoS group value is local to the router and is used as a marker. The treatment of these packets is defined by the user through the setting of QoS policies in policy map class configuration mode.

— **match source-address mac** *address*—Configures the match criteria for a class map based on the source MAC address.

Step 3 Exit class map configuration mode:

```
Router(config-cmap)# end
```

For example, use the following code to configure a class map so that all packets that contain IP precedence 5 are matched by the class map name critical:

```
Router(config)# class-map critical
Router(config-cmap)# match ip precedence 5
Router(config-cmap)# end
```

Service Policy Configuration

A service policy is configured using the **policy-map** command to specify a service policy name. The traffic class is associated with the service policy with the **class** command.

The QoS policies for the service policy are defined in policy map submode. The QoS policies that can be applied in the service policy in policy map submode are detailed in this section.

The **policy-map** syntax is as follows:

```
policy-map policy-name
no policy-map policy-name
```

The **class** command syntax is as follows:

```
class class-name
no class class-name
```

If a default class is configured, all traffic that fails to meet the matching criteria belongs to the default class.

Step 1   Create a policy map that can be attached to one or more interfaces to specify a service policy:

```
Router(config)# policy-map policy-map-name
```

Step 2   Specify the name of the class map previously designated in the **class-map** command:

```
Router(config-pmap)# class class-map-name
```

Step 3   Specify the default class to be created as part of the service policy:

```
Router(config-pmap)# class class-default
```

NOTE   Steps 4 through 15 are the policy map class submode configuration options.

Step 4   Specify a minimum bandwidth guarantee to a traffic class. A minimum bandwidth guarantee can be specified in kilobits per second or by a percentage of the overall available bandwidth:

```
Router(config-pmap-c)# bandwidth {bandwidth-kbps | percent percent}
```

Step 5   Set a command to its default value:

```
Router(config-pmap-c)# default command
```

Step 6   Specify the number of queues to be reserved for the class:

```
Router(config-pmap-c)# fair-queue number-of-queues
```

Step 7 Specify a maximum bandwidth usage by a traffic class through the use of a token bucket algorithm:

```
Router(config-pmap-c)# police bps burst-normal burst-max
conform-action action exceed-action action violate-action action
```

The following action is enforced by the **police** command on incoming packets:

— **drop**—Drops the packet.

— **set-prec-transmit** *new-prec*—Sets the IP precedence and transmits the packet.

— **set-qos-transmit** *new-qos*—Sets the QoS group and transmits the packet.

— **set-dscp-transmit**—Sets the DSCP value and transmits the packet.

— **set-atm-clp**—Sets the ATM CLP bit from 0 to 1 on the packet.

— **transmit**—Transmits the packet.

Step 8 Specify the guaranteed allowed bandwidth (in Kbps or percentage) for priority traffic. The optional *bytes* argument controls the size of the burst allowed to pass through the system without being considered in excess of the configured Kbps rate:

```
Router(config-pmap-c)# priority {kbps | percent percent} [bytes]
```

Step 9 Specify the maximum number of packets queued for a traffic class (in the absence of the **random-detect** command):

```
Router(config-pmap-c)# queue-limit packets
```

Step 10 Enable a WRED drop policy for a traffic class that has a bandwidth guarantee:

```
Router(config-pmap-c)# random-detect
```

Step 11 Set the ATM cell loss priority bit to 1:

```
Router(config-pmap-c)# set atm-clp
```

Step 12 Specify a CoS value or values to associate with the packet. The number is in the range 0–7:

```
Router(config-pmap-c)# set cos cos-value
```

Step 13 Specify the IP DSCP of packets within a traffic class. The IP DSCP value can be any value between 0 and 63:

```
Router(config-pmap-c)# set ip dscp ip-dscp-value
```

Step 14 Specify the IP precedence of packets within a traffic class. The IP precedence value can be any value between 0 and 7:

```
Router(config-pmap-c)# set ip precedence ip-precedence-value
```

Step 15 Designate the value to which the MPLS bits are set if the packets match the specified policy map:

```
Router(config-pmap-c)# set mpls experimental value
```

Step 16 Exit policy map configuration mode:

```
Router(config-pmap-c)# end
```

For example, use the following code to configure a policy map so that the value in the MPLS experimental field of each packet that is matched by the class map critical is set to 4:

```
Router(config)# policy-map set_experimental_4
Router(config-pmap)# class critical
Router(config-pmap-c)# set mpls experimental 4
Router(config-pmap-c)# end
```

Configure the Service Policy to Attach to an Interface

The **service-policy** interface configuration command is used to attach the service policy to an interface and to specify the direction in which the policy should be applied. The **service-policy** command syntax is as follows:

```
service-policy {input | output} policy-map-name
no service-policy {input | output} policy-map-name
```

Step 1 Designate the input interface:

```
Router(config)# interface interface-name
```

Step 2 Attach the specified policy map to the input interface:

```
Router(config-int)# service-policy input policy-map-name
```

Step 3 Exit interface configuration mode:

```
Router(config-int)# end
```

For example, use the following code to attach the service policy set_experimental_4 to the Ethernet input interface:

```
Router(config)# interface ethernet 1/0/0
Router(config-int)# service-policy input set_experimental_4
Router(config-int)# end
```

Verify the Modular QoS CLI Configuration

Verify the Modular QoS CLI configuration using the following steps:

Step 1 Display all traffic class information:

```
Router# show class-map
```

Step 2 Display the traffic class information for the user-specified traffic class:

```
Router# show class-map class-name
```

Step 3 Display all configured service policies:

```
Router# show policy-map
```

Step 4 Display the user-specified service policy:

```
Router# show policy-map policy-map-name
```

Step 5 Display configuration and statistics for all input and output policies that are attached to an interface:

```
Router# show policy-map interface
```

Step 6 Display the configuration and statistics for the input and output policies attached to a particular interface:

```
Router# show policy-map interface interface-spec
```

Step 7 Display the configuration and statistics for the input policy attached to an interface:

```
Router# show policy-map interface interface-spec input
```

Step 8 Display the configuration and statistics for the output policy attached to an interface:

```
Router# show policy-map interface interface-spec output
```

Step 9 Display the configuration and statistics for the class name configured in the policy:

```
Router# show policy-map [ interface [interface-spec [input | output]
   [ class class-name]]]
```

CAR Configuration of the Ingress PE

The Committed Access Rate for classification of IP packets can be used for MPLS networks if the ingress rate needs to be policed. The MPLS Exp bits can be set based on the conform action of the CAR policing.

- Configure an IP rate-limit access list on the ingress PE for classifying IP packets according to their IP precedence.

- Configure a rate limit on an input interface to set MPLS packets by writing the packet's classification into the MPLS Exp field.

Configure a Rate-Limit Access List for Classifying IP Packets

Configure a rate limit access list that will classify IP packets for throttle back:

Step 1 Specify the criteria to be matched:

```
Router(config)# access-list rate-limit acl-index precedence
```

Step 2 Exit configuration mode:

```
Router(config)# end
```

For example, use the following code to configure a rate-limit access list 25 to match all packets that contain IP precedence 5:

```
Router(config)# access-list rate-limit 25 5
Router(config)# end
```

Configure a Rate Limit on an Input Interface to Set MPLS Packets

Configure a rate limit on the input interface that will throttle back the preclassified IP packets:

Step 1 Designate the input interface:

```
Router(config)# interface interface-name
```

Step 2 Specify the action to take on packets during label imposition:

```
Router(config-int)# rate-limit input [access-group
[rate-limit] acl-index] bps burst-normal burst-max
conform-action set-mpls-exp-transmit exp exceed-action
set-mpls-exp-transmit exp
```

Step 3 Exit interface configuration mode:

```
Router(config-int)# end
```

Here is an example. The experimental field for the output MPLS packet is set to 4 if the input IP packets match the access list and conform to the rate. The MPLS experimental field is set to 0 if packets match access list 25 and exceed the input rate:

```
Router(config)# interface ethernet 1/0/0
Router(config-int)# rate-limit input access-group rate-limit 25
    64000 64000 64000 conform-action set-mpls-exp-transmit 4
    exceed-action set-mpls-exp-transmit 0
Router(config-int)# end
```

NOTE The output IP packet's QoS is determined by the IP header information, and the MPLS experimental field in the topmost label determines the output MPLS packet's QoS.

MPLS QoS Case Study

This case study considers an MPLS VPN configured with Modular QoS CLI. The CE routers have the option of setting the IP precedence/DSCP bits. These bits are mapped to the MPLS CoS Exp bits in the label header at the PE routers, and E-LSPs are constructed across the MPLS backbone. At the various P routers along the LSP path, a per-hop behavior (PHB) is implemented based on the value of the Exp bits carried in the label header.

The following steps are covered in detail in this section:

Step 1   Create traffic classes.

Step 2   Create service policies and associate the traffic classes with them.

Step 3   Attach the service policies to the input interfaces.

Step 1: Create Traffic Classes

Create QoS traffic classes on ingress PE LSRs for the MPLS VPN.

PE1 Configuration

Figure 8-15 shows an MPLS VPN defined using an ATM LSR backbone. Customers A, B, C, and D have been provided MPLS QoS for various classes of traffic. The QoS traffic classes are configured on ingress PE LSRs.

On PE1, notice that Customer A uses S0/0/0 as its ingress interface into the MPLS backbone, whereas Customer B uses S0/0/1 as its ingress interface. This helps the service provider differentiate between packets from Customers A and B and apply appropriate QoS policy mechanisms for them. These packets are classified as belonging to VPN_A and VPN_B.

```
PE1(config)# class-map VPN_A
PE1(config-cmap)# match input interface serial0/0/0
PE1(config-cmap)# end

PE1(config)# class-map VPN_B
PE1(config-cmap)# match input interface serial0/0/1
PE1(config-cmap)# end
```

Figure 8-15 *MPLS QoS Case Study*

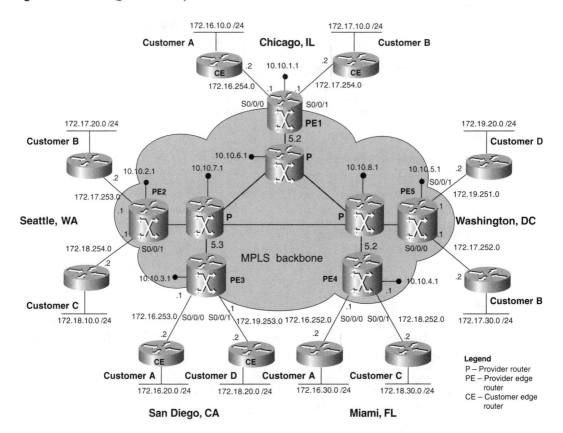

PE2 Configuration

On PE2, Customer B uses S0/0/0 on as its ingress interface into the MPLS backbone. These packets are classified as belonging to VPN_B. Customer C uses S0/0/1 as its ingress interface. Customer C maintains its own internal IP QoS policies using the IP precedence ToS bits in the IP header. These policies have to be mapped to MPLS Exp bit settings on the backbone. These packets are classified as VPN_C. The **match-all** keyword matches both criteria for packets to qualify for traffic class VPN_C.

```
PE2(config)# class-map VPN_B
PE2(config-cmap)# match input interface serial0/0/0
PE2(config-cmap)# end
```

```
PE2(config)# class-map match-all VPN_C
PE2(config-cmap)# match input interface serial0/0/0
PE2(config-cmap)# match ip precedence 5
PE2(config-cmap)# end
```

PE3 Configuration

On PE3, Customer A uses S0/0/0 as its ingress interface into the MPLS backbone, and Customer D uses S0/0/1 as its ingress interface. This helps the service provider differentiate between packets from Customers A and D and apply appropriate QoS policy mechanisms for them. These packets are classified as belonging to VPN_A and VPN_D.

```
PE3(config)# class-map VPN_A
PE3(config-cmap)# match input interface serial0/0/0
PE3(config-cmap)# end

PE3(config)# class-map VPN_D
PE3(config-cmap)# match input interface serial0/0/1
PE3(config-cmap)# end
```

PE4 Configuration

On PE4, Customer A uses S0/0/0 as its ingress interface into the MPLS backbone; these packets are classified as belonging to VPN_A. Customer C uses S0/0/1 as its ingress interface. Customer C maintains its own internal IP QoS policies using the IP precedence ToS bits in the IP header. These policies have to be mapped to MPLS Exp bit settings on the backbone. These packets are classified as VPN_C. The **match-all** keyword matches both criteria for packets to qualify for traffic class VPN_C.

```
PE4(config)# class-map VPN_A
PE4(config-cmap)# match input interface serial0/0/0
PE4(config-cmap)# end

PE4(config)# class-map match-all VPN_C
PE4(config-cmap)# match input interface serial0/0/1
PE4(config-cmap)# match ip precedence 5
PE4(config-cmap)# end
```

PE5 Configuration

On PE5, Customer B uses S0/0/0 as its ingress interface into the MPLS backbone, and Customer D uses S0/0/1 as its ingress interface. This helps the service provider differentiate between packets from Customers B and D and apply appropriate QoS policy mechanisms for them. These packets are classified as belonging to VPN_B and VPN_D.

```
PE5(config)# class-map VPN_B
PE5(config-cmap)# match input interface serial0/0/0
PE5(config-cmap)# end

PE5(config)# class-map VPN_D
PE5(config-cmap)# match input interface serial0/0/1
PE5(config-cmap)# end
```

P-LSR Configuration

The core MPLS LSRs have up to seven classes of traffic, which can be awarded a QoS based on the MPLS Exp bits contained in the label header. Four classes are defined in this case study. A match is performed on the value of the MPLS Exp or CoS bits to determine the resources required for the traffic flow. The PHBs are configured on the core P-LSRs.

```
P(config)# class-map class1
P(config-cmap)# match mpls experimental 5
P(config-cmap)# end

P(config)# class-map class2
P(config-cmap)# match mpls experimental 4
P(config-cmap)# end

P(config)# class-map class3
P(config-cmap)# match mpls experimental 3
P(config-cmap)# end

P(config)# class-map class4
P(config-cmap)# match mpls experimental 2
P(config-cmap)# end
```

NOTE   The traffic classes *class1, class2, class3,* and *class4* are configured on all P-LSRs—in this case study, P1, P2, and P3.

Step 2: Create Service Policies and Associate the Traffic Classes with Them

Create service policies for the traffic classes on the various VPNs.

Service Policy for VPN A

Specify a minimum bandwidth guarantee of 256 Kbps to all traffic in traffic class VPN_A to be delivered in the event of congestion. The queue reserved for this class can queue up to 60 packets before tail drop is enacted. When the policy map containing this class is attached to the interface to stipulate the service policy for that interface, available bandwidth is assessed, taking into account all configured class policies and RSVP. Designate the value of the MPLS Exp bits as 4 if the packets match the traffic class requirements associated with policy map VPN_A_policy.

A policy is configured for the *class-default* default class included in the policy map VPN_A_policy. The *class-default* default class has been configured for 20 hashed queues for traffic that does not meet the match criteria of other classes associated with policy map VPN_A_policy and a maximum of 40 packets per queue before tail drop is enacted to handle additional enqueued packets.

```
PE(config)# policy-map VPN_A_policy
PE(config-pmap)# class VPN_A
PE(config-pmap-c)# bandwidth 256
PE(config-pmap-c)# queue-limit 60
PE(config-pmap-c)# set mpls experimental 4
PE(config-pmap-c)# exit
PE(config-pmap)# class class-default
PE(config-pmap-c)# fair-queue 20
PE(config-pmap-c)# queue-limit 40
PE(config-pmap-c)# end
```

NOTE   The service policy for traffic class VPN_A is implemented on all PE LSRs where VPN A has a presence—in this case study, PE1, PE3, and PE4.

Service Policy for VPN B

Specify a minimum bandwidth guarantee of 128 Kbps to all traffic in traffic class VPN_B to be delivered in the event of congestion. For congestion avoidance, WRED packet drop is used instead of tail drop, and a weight factor of 10 is used to calculate the average queue size. When the policy map containing this class is attached to the interface to stipulate the service policy for that interface, available bandwidth is assessed, taking into account all configured class policies and RSVP. Designate the value of the MPLS Exp bits as 4 if the packets match the traffic class requirements associated with policy map VPN_B_policy.

A policy is configured for the *class-default* default class included in the policy map VPN_B_policy. The *class-default* default class has been configured for 20 hashed queues for traffic that does not meet the match criteria of other classes associated with policy map VPN_B_policy. For congestion avoidance, WRED packet drop is used instead of tail drop, and a weight factor of 15 is used to calculate the average queue size.

```
PE(config)# policy-map VPN_B_policy
PE(config-pmap)# class VPN_B
PE(config-pmap-c)# bandwidth 128
PE(config-pmap-c)# random-detect exponential-weighting-constant 10
PE(config-pmap-c)# set mpls experimental 3
PE(config-pmap-c)# exit
PE(config-pmap)# class class-default
PE(config-pmap-c)# fair-queue 20
PE(config-pmap-c)# random-detect exponential-weighting-constant 15
PE1(config-pmap-c)# end
```

NOTE   The service policy for traffic class VPN_B is implemented on all PE LSRs where VPN B has a presence—in this case study, PE1, PE2, and PE5.

Service Policy for VPN C

Specify a minimum bandwidth guarantee of 512 Kbps to all traffic in traffic class VPN_C to be delivered in the event of congestion. The queue reserved for this class can queue up to 90 packets before tail drop is enacted. When the policy map containing this class is attached to the interface to stipulate the service policy for that interface, available bandwidth is assessed, taking into account all configured class policies and RSVP. Designate the value of the MPLS Exp bits as 5 if the packets match the traffic class requirements associated with policy map VPN_C_policy.

A policy is configured for the *class-default* default class included in the policy map VPN_C_policy. The *class-default* default class has been configured for 20 hashed queues for traffic that does not meet the match criteria of other classes associated with policy map VPN_C_policy and a maximum of 40 packets per queue before tail drop is enacted to handle additional queued packets.

```
PE(config)# policy-map VPN_C_policy
PE(config-pmap)# class VPN_C
PE(config-pmap-c)# bandwidth 512
PE(config-pmap-c)# queue-limit 90
PE(config-pmap-c)# set mpls experimental 5
PE(config-pmap-c)# exit
PE(config-pmap)# class class-default
PE(config-pmap-c)# fair-queue 20
PE(config-pmap-c)# queue-limit 40
PE(config-pmap-c)# end
```

NOTE   The service policy for traffic class VPN_C is implemented on all PE LSRs where VPN C has a presence—in this case study, PE2 and PE4.

Service Policy for VPN D

Specify the maximum bandwidth usage by traffic class VPN_D through the use of a token bucket algorithm. The policer sets the average rate to 64000, the normal burst to 16384 bytes, and the excess burst size to 20480 bytes. Packets that conform to the rate limit are transmitted, and packets that don't conform to the rate limit are dropped. Designate the value of the MPLS Exp bits as 2 if the packets match the traffic class requirements associated with policy map VPN_D_policy.

A policy is configured for the *class-default* default class included in the policy map VPN_D_policy. The *class-default* default class has been configured for 20 hashed queues for traffic that does not meet the match criteria of other classes associated with policy map VPN_D_policy and a maximum of 40 packets per queue before tail drop is enacted to handle additional queued packets.

```
PE(config)# policy-map VPN_D_policy
PE(config-pmap)# class VPN_D
PE(config-pmap-c)# police bandwidth 64000 16384 20480 conform-action
    transmit exceed-action drop
PE(config-pmap-c)# set mpls experimental 2
PE(config-pmap-c)# exit
PE(config-pmap)# class class-default
PE(config-pmap-c)# fair-queue 20
PE(config-pmap-c)# queue-limit 40
PE(config-pmap-c)# end
```

NOTE   The service policy for traffic class VPN_D is implemented on all PE LSRs where VPN D has a presence—in this case study, PE3 and PE5.

Service Policy for the P-LSRs

Configure service policies for the various traffic classes traversing the core P-LSRs.

Service Policy for Traffic Class class1

Specify a minimum bandwidth guarantee of 512 Kbps to all traffic in traffic class class1. The queue reserved for this class can queue up to 90 packets before tail drop is enacted. The default class has been configured for 20 hashed queues with a maximum of 40 packets per queue before tail drop is enacted.

Service Policy for Traffic Class class2

Specify a minimum bandwidth guarantee of 256 Kbps to all traffic in traffic class class2. The queue reserved for this class can queue up to 60 packets before tail drop is enacted. The default class has been configured for 20 hashed queues with a maximum of 40 packets per queue before tail drop is enacted.

Service Policy for Traffic Class class3

Specify a minimum bandwidth guarantee of 128 Kbps to all traffic in traffic class class3. The queue reserved for this class can queue up to 30 packets before tail drop is enacted. The default class has been configured for 20 hashed queues with a maximum of 40 packets per queue before tail drop is enacted.

Service Policy for Traffic Class class4

Specify a minimum bandwidth guarantee of 64 Kbps to all traffic in traffic class class4. The queue reserved for this class can queue up to 30 packets before tail drop is enacted. The default class has been configured for 20 hashed queues with a maximum of 40 packets per queue before tail drop is enacted.

```
P(config)# policy-map class_PHB_policy
P(config-pmap)# class class1
P(config-pmap-c)# bandwidth 512
P(config-pmap-c)# queue-limit 90
P(config-pmap-c)# exit
P(config-pmap)# class class2
P(config-pmap-c)# bandwidth 256
P(config-pmap-c)# queue-limit 60
P(config-pmap-c)# exit
P(config-pmap)# class class3
P(config-pmap-c)# bandwidth 128
P(config-pmap-c)# queue-limit 30
P(config-pmap-c)# exit
P(config-pmap)# class class4
P(config-pmap-c)# bandwidth 64
P(config-pmap-c)# queue-limit 30
P(config-pmap-c)# exit
P(config-pmap)# class class-default
P(config-pmap-c)# fair-queue 20
P(config-pmap-c)# queue-limit 40
P(config-pmap-c)# end
```

NOTE   The service policy for traffic class class_PHB_policy is implemented on all P-LSRs—in this case study, P1, P2, and P3.

Step 3: Attach the Service Policies to the Input Interfaces

Associate the service policies with the input interfaces.

PE1 Configuration

```
PE1(config)# interface serial0/0/0
PE1(config-int)# service-policy input VPN_A_policy
PE1(config-int)# exit
PE1(config)# interface serial0/0/1
PE1(config-int)# service-policy input VPN_B_policy
PE1(config-int)# end
```

PE2 Configuration

```
PE2(config)# interface serial0/0/0
PE2(config-int)# service-policy input VPN_B_policy
PE2(config-int)# exit
PE2(config)# interface serial0/0/1
PE2(config-int)# service-policy input VPN_C_policy
PE2(config-int)# end
```

PE3 Configuration

```
PE3(config)# interface serial0/0/0
PE3(config-int)# service-policy input VPN_A_policy
PE3(config-int)# exit
PE3(config)# interface serial0/0/1
PE3(config-int)# service-policy input VPN_D_policy
PE3(config-int)# end
```

PE4 Configuration

```
PE4(config)# interface serial0/0/0
PE4(config-int)# service-policy input VPN_A_policy
PE4(config-int)# exit
PE4(config)# interface serial0/0/1
PE4(config-int)# service-policy input VPN_C_policy
PE4(config-int)# end
```

PE5 Configuration

```
PE5(config)# interface serial0/0/0
PE5(config-int)# service-policy input VPN_B_policy
PE5(config-int)# exit
PE5(config)# interface serial0/0/1
PE5(config-int)# service-policy input VPN_D_policy
PE5(config-int)# end
```

P1 Configuration

```
P1(config)# interface serial0/0/0
P1(config-int)# service-policy input class_PHB_policy
P1(config-int)# exit
P1(config)# interface serial0/0/1
P1(config-int)# service-policy input class_PHB_policy
P1(config-int)# exit
P1(config)# interface serial0/0/2
P1(config-int)# service-policy input class_PHB_policy
P1(config-int)# end
```

P2 Configuration

```
P2(config)# interface serial0/0/0
P2(config-int)# service-policy input class_PHB_policy
P2(config-int)# exit
P2(config)# interface serial0/0/1
P2(config-int)# service-policy input class_PHB_policy
P2(config-int)# exit
P2(config)# interface serial0/0/2
P2(config-int)# service-policy input class_PHB_policy
P2(config-int)# exit
P2(config)# interface serial0/0/3
P2(config-int)# service-policy input class_PHB_policy
P2(config-int)# end
```

P3 Configuration

```
P3(config)# interface serial0/0/0
P3(config-int)# service-policy input class_PHB_policy
P3(config-int)# exit
P3(config)# interface serial0/0/1
P3(config-int)# service-policy input class_PHB_policy
P3(config-int)# exit
P3(config)# interface serial0/0/2
```

```
P3(config-int)# service-policy input class_PHB_policy
P3(config-int)# exit
P3(config)# interface serial0/0/3
P3(config-int)# service-policy input class_PHB_policy
P3(config-int)# end
```

Summary

Integrated Services (IntServ) provides for an end-to-end QoS solution by way of end-to-end signaling, state maintenance (for each RSVP flow and reservation), and admission control at each network element. The term IntServ refers to an overall QoS architecture developed by the IETF. RSVP is an IntServ signaling protocol.

MPLS can be enabled on LSRs by associating labels with flows that have RSVP reservations. Packets for which an RSVP reservation has been made can be considered FECs. A label can identify each FEC. Bindings created between labels and the RSVP flows must be distributed between the LSRs.

IP precedence has simplified the approach to IP QoS by adopting an aggregate model for flows by classifying various flows into aggregated classes and providing the appropriate QoS for the classified flows.

The DiffServ model divides traffic into a small number of classes and allocates resources on a per-class basis. This model is similar to the IP precedence model. A 6-bit differentiated services code point (DSCP) marks the packet's class in the IP header. The DSCP is carried in the type of service (ToS) byte field in the IP header. 6 bits can result in the implementation of 64 different DSCP classes.

Network elements or *hops* along the path examine the value of the DSCP field and determine the QoS required by the packet. This is known as a *per-hop behavior* (PHB). Each network element has a table that maps the DSCP found in a packet to the PHB that determines how the packet is treated. The DSCP is a number or value carried in the packet, whereas PHBs are well-specified behaviors that apply to packets.

MPLS LSRs do not examine the contents of the IP header and the value of its DSCP field, as required by DiffServ. This means that the appropriate PHB must be determined from the label value. The MPLS shim header has a 3-bit field called the Exp field. It was originally defined for experimental use. This field supports eight different values and is used for MPLS support of up to eight DiffServ classes.

If more than eight PHBs are needed in the MPLS network, L-LSPs (Label LSPs) are used, in which case the PHB of the LSR is inferred from the label. In the case of ATM, where the shim header is not used, the PHB needs to be inferred from the label carried in the VCI field. The label-to-PHB mapping is signaled. Only one PHB per L-LSP is possible, except for DiffServ AF.

In the pipe model, the service provider provides the VPN customer with certain QoS guarantees for traffic flows between one CE router and another within the same VPN. In the hose model, the service provider supplies a customer with certain guarantees for the traffic that a particular CE router sends to and receives from other CE routers in the same VPN.

The Modular QoS CLI is used to configure QoS on ingress PE routers for MPLS VPNs. It allows users to specify a traffic class independently of QoS policies. The Modular QoS CLI has the following three steps: configure traffic classes to classify IP packets according to various criteria using class maps, configure service policies using policy maps, and configure the input interface to attach the service policy.

This chapter covers the following topics:

- **MPLS VPN Design and Topologies**—The various design approaches to practical MPLS VPN deployment are described in this section. MPLS VPNs can be implemented in a variety of ways, using a combination of packet-based and ATM MPLS Label-Switched Routers (LSRs).

- **Migrating MPLS into an ATM network**—This section describes how MPLS can be deployed into a traditional ATM network gradually, starting with just a single pair of ATM LSRs in an otherwise purely ATM network. MPLS can be deployed across non-MPLS-capable switches using VP connections over traditional ATM switches. Core ATM switches may be phased out or converted to ATM LSRs, leading to full deployment of ATM MPLS.

- **ATM MPLS design criteria**—Several design criteria must be evaluated prior to deploying MPLS. This section examines the implementation of MPLS on high-end ATM switches. The design criteria for selecting ATM Edge LSRs and ATM LSRs is discussed here.

- **Designing MPLS Networks**—The MPLS network must be designed before it is installed in order to ensure that it will operate reliably and optimally. Customer traffic must be properly estimated, because IP traffic is inherently connectionless and indeterministic. This section discusses various MPLS network design options in detail.

- **Additional MPLS Design Considerations**—This secion discusses additional MPLS design considerations that pertain to the size of Internet routing tables, traffic engineering constraints, virtual path tunnel constraints, and LVC exhaustion.

CHAPTER 9

MPLS Design and Migration

MPLS VPN Design and Topologies

MPLS Virtual Private Networks (VPNs) can be implemented in a variety of ways, using a combination of packet-based and ATM MPLS Label-Switched Routers (LSRs). The various design approaches to practical MPLS VPN deployment are described in this section.

Packet-Based MPLS VPNs

Figure 9-1 shows a packet-based MPLS VPN network deployed using a router-based backbone. The links between the core P routers, PE to core P routers, and PE to CE routers can be any mix of conventional Layer 2 technologies. The MPLS header is carried as a shim header in the case of a legacy Layer 2 header or in the VPI/VCI field in the case of ATM. The MPLS backbone need not be fully meshed. However, the IGP (OSPF or IS-IS) should have full connectivity, and there should be a full MP-IBGP mesh between all MB-IBGP peers. The PE routers would act as the points of presence (PoPs) and could be co-located at the service provider's facilities or data center/CO. Packet-based MPLS design follows design rules similar to those used by standard IP routing.

ATM-Based MPLS VPNs

ATM-based MPLS VPNs use ATM LSRs in the core and a combination of ATM routers or other ATM LSRs (performing the Edge LSR or PE function) at the various points of presence. The various combinations are shown in Figure 9-2. The core ATM LSRs use Label Virtual Circuits (LVCs) to communicate with other core LSRs and the PE ATM routers. In Figure 9-2, you might notice that the core ATM LSRs are BPX 8650s with 7200 or 7500 Label Switch Controllers (LSCs). The LSC in the service provider's PoP-1 can also function as an Edge LSR. This eliminates the need for a separate ATM PE router to be co-located along with the core ATM LSR.

Figure 9-1   *Packet-Based MPLS VPN*

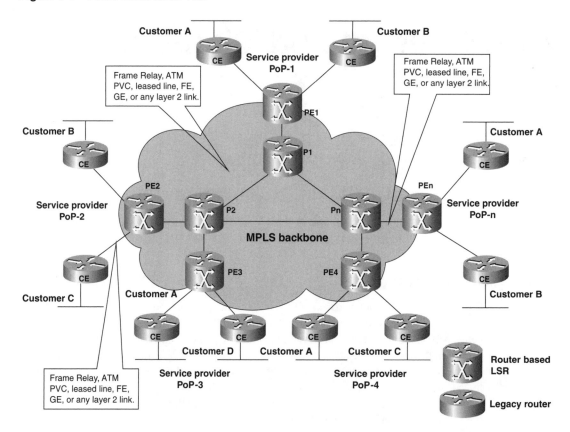

Traffic at the service provider's PoP-2 from customers B and C can be aggregated using an MGX 8220 AXIS shelf and can be backhauled over ATM PVCs to the nearest ATM Edge LSR. In this case, the closest Edge LSR is PE3. ATM MPLS networks with router-based Edge LSRs may also use separate access devices such as the MGX 8220 if access is required through a device that does not support MPLS services. This might be required if access is required to both IP services and ATM PVC services through a non-MPLS access or for the support of higher densities of low-bandwidth access lines than would be possible by simply using an Edge LSR. Customer traffic is carried through the access device to the Edge LSR. Between the access device and the Edge LSR, there is a different logical link for each customer. This may be a Frame Relay or ATM PVC, or a PPP link.

At PoP-*n,* the customers terminate on an MGX 8800. In the MGX 8850, router cards called Route Processor Modules (RPMs) act as Edge LSRs. One of the RPMs also acts as a label switch controller, giving ATM LSR functionality to the MGX 8800. All these functions are combined in a single chassis. The 6400 access switch has similar capabilities.

Figure 9-2 *ATM-Based MPLS VPN*

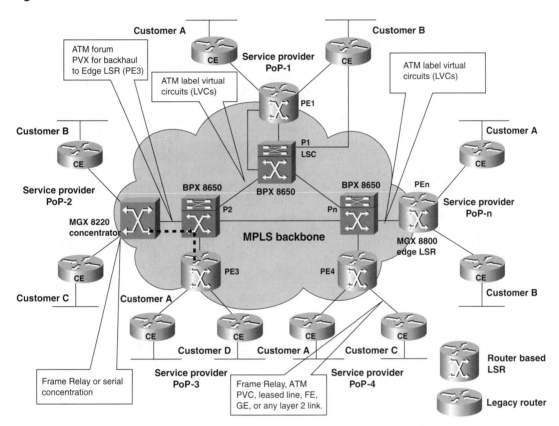

Hybrid ATM and Packet-Based MPLS VPNs

A hybrid ATM and packet-based MPLS network uses a combination of ATM LSRs, ATM Edge LSRs, and packet-based Edge LSRs. It is possible to mix ATM MPLS and packet-based MPLS on one network with ATM LSRs in the core, ATM Edge LSRs on the distribution layer, and packet-based LSRs in tail circuits of the access layer. An example of this is shown in Figure 9-3. In a network such as this, some links run packet-based MPLS, and others run ATM MPLS. The devices that interface between packet-based MPLS and ATM MPLS are the same routers that act as ATM Edge LSRs. These could be anything from a 3600 up to a 12000.

Figure 9-3 *Hybrid MPLS VPN*

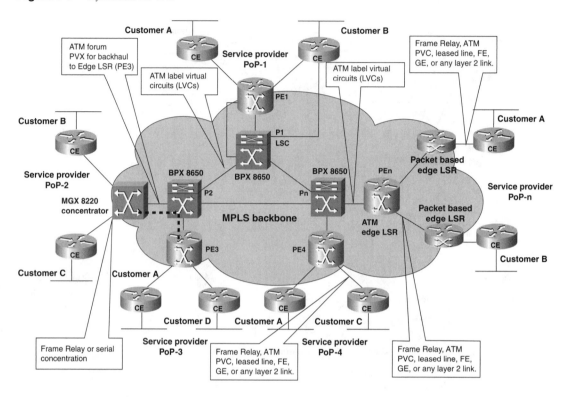

Migrating MPLS into an ATM Network

Many service providers currently operate ATM backbones and offer ATM and Frame Relay services to their customers. From a Closed User Group (CUG) perspective, the Frame Relay or ATM services are a Layer 2 VPN. Most customers run IP over ATM or Frame Relay. In some cases, the service provider supplies Managed IP services over its ATM or Frame Relay infrastructure. These topologies possess most of the disadvantages of traditional IP-over-ATM networks—notably, reduced router peering scaling and meager bandwidth efficiency.

MPLS VPNs are an excellent alternative. They offer superior scalability and bandwidth efficiency along with traffic engineering capabilities and QoS. MPLS can be deployed into a traditional ATM network gradually, starting with just a single pair of ATM LSRs in an otherwise purely ATM network. MPLS can be deployed across non-MPLS-capable switches using VP connections through the traditional ATM switches. These VP connections are called *VP tunnels* because they allow MPLS to tunnel through traditional ATM switches. VP tunnels provide for easy migration to a full MPLS integration, although they do have several disadvantages.

The following steps provide a plan for migrating MPLS into an ATM network:

Step 1   Configure and install Edge ATM router-based LSRs using PVPs or PVCs across the ATM backbone. These PVPs or PVCs must be configured on the ATM switches using standard PCP configuration methods. A feasible migration strategy starting point for introducing MPLS into an existing ATM network is shown in Figure 9-4.

Figure 9-4 shows a starting position with routers connected by PVPs through an ATM cloud. This has most of the disadvantages of traditional IP-over-ATM networks, including scalability and bandwidth efficiency issues. However, it can support MPLS VPN services.

Figure 9-4   *Migration Phase 1*

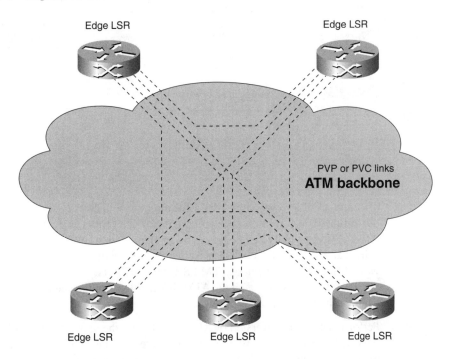

Step 2   Introduce ATM LSRs into the network core, as shown in Figure 9-5. You can convert traditional ATM switches such as the BPX 8650 to ATM LSRs by adding a 7200 or 7500 Label Switch Controller (LSC) and configuring resources for the MPLS partition. This results in the control of the ATM switch by the MPLS controller as well as the PNNI controller. The details of this procedure are explained in Chapter 6,

"ATM-Based MPLS VPNs." ATM LSRs also support traditional ATM services. Take care to work around existing customer ATM PVCs or PVPs. Reserve VPIs 2 through 15 for LVC use. This might involve reprovisioning certain customer VCs. You must give ATM customers adequate forewarning in the event of circuit reprovisioning.

Figure 9-5 *Migration Phase 2*

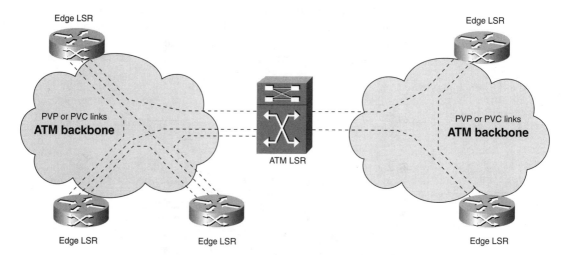

The number of PVPs to each Edge LSR might be reduced to one (two if dual-homed), and in some cases to zero, if an Edge LSR is adjacent to an ATM LSR. Adjacent Edge LSRs can be configured with LVCs. The ATM LSRs can be interconnected with ordinary ATM switches in a variety of ways. Careful deployment of ATM LSRs and PVPs can be used to make the PVP mesh closely match the ATM link topology and hence improve bandwidth efficiency.

Step 3 Perform a phased conversion of ATM switches on the network edge to ATM LSRs, as shown in Figure 9-6. Adequate care must be applied not to disrupt services to ATM or Frame Relay customers in the interim. Most of the configuration can be performed online during the conversion process. However, it is prudent to announce minor outage windows during cutovers.

Figure 9-6   *Migration Phase 3*

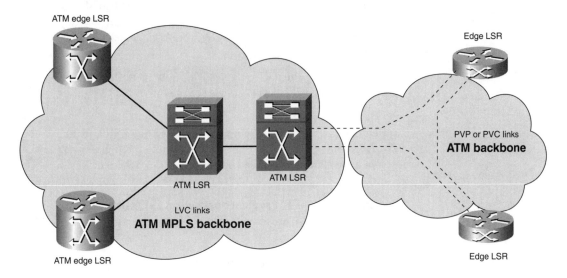

ATM edge LSR

Edge LSR

PVP or PVC links
ATM backbone

ATM LSR

ATM LSR

LVC links
ATM MPLS backbone

ATM edge LSR

Edge LSR

Step 4   Phase out all the remaining ATM switches in the core in favor of ATM
LSRs. Core ATM switches may be phased out or converted to ATM
LSRs, leading to full deployment of ATM MPLS, as shown in Figure 9-7.
The use of PVPs is no longer required. LVCs will be used throughout the
core and between core ATM LSRs and Edge LSRs.

Figure 9-7   *Migration Phase 4*

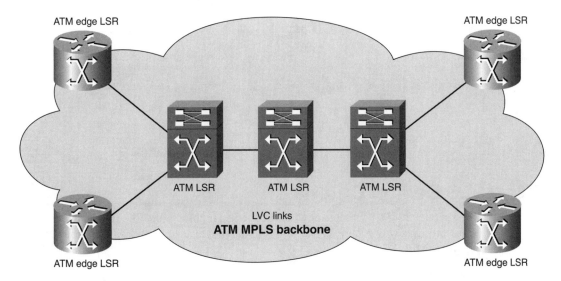

ATM edge LSR

ATM edge LSR

ATM LSR

ATM LSR

ATM LSR

LVC links
ATM MPLS backbone

ATM edge LSR

ATM edge LSR

MPLS networks can use traditional ATM equipment as a migration step in introducing MPLS to an existing ATM network. Traditional ATM switches can be used in three ways, as shown in Figure 9-8. These uses of traditional ATM equipment have disadvantages, as explained earlier, and must be used with care:

— **Backhauling when the access device is remote from the Edge LSR**—PVCs connect the access device to the Edge LSR in the ATM network.

— **Tunneling through ATM switches between an Edge LSR and an ATM LSR**—In this case, the Edge LSR does not need to be adjacent to an ATM LSR but can be connected through an ATM network.

— **Tunneling through ATM switches between ATM LSRs**—In this case, the core network uses traditional ATM switches as well as ATM switches.

Figure 9-8 *Use of Traditional ATM Switches in an MPLS Network*

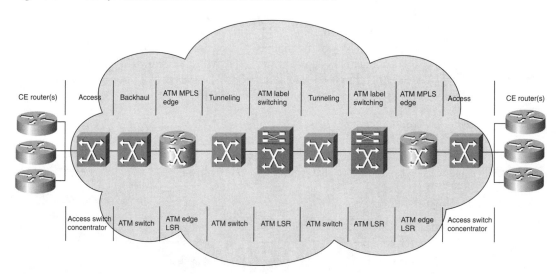

ATM MPLS Design Criteria

Cisco supports MPLS on most or all midrange and high-end routers, ATM switches, and access products with routing capability. You must evaluate several design criteria before deploying MPLS.

Design Criteria for Selecting ATM Edge LSRs

There are four main considerations when selecting ATM MPLS edge equipment:

- **The service type that will be offered**—This can be Managed IP services, ATM services, or a combination of both. Service providers with an existing ATM infrastructure will prefer a phased migration to MPLS.

- **The different types of access lines and associated protocols**—The line cards must use a technology and protocol that will interface with the majority of CE routers, such as serial, serial/Frame Relay, ISDN up to E1/T1, 10 Mbps Ethernet, Fast Ethernet, Gigabit Ethernet, HSSI, high-speed serial, ATM, packet-over-SONET/SDH, and others.

- **The number of access lines and the concentration of these lines**—For example, the MGX 8220 can concentrate up to 80 T1 or E1 lines on a single shelf and has one OC3 trunk uplink to the BPX. As another example, a Cisco 7206 router has six card slots and can nominally support 48 Ethernet ports (or eight per slot). However, when you use the Cisco 7206 router as an ATM Edge LSR, at least one slot must be used for an ATM interface to the ATM LSR. Therefore, the actual Ethernet port capacity of a Cisco 7206 ATM Edge LSR is 40 Ethernet ports.

- **Requirements for redundancy and reliability**—Other factors that influence the selection of the Edge LSRs include hot standby capabilities, online insertion and removal (hot-swappable modules or cards), multi-homing of customer sites, and processor redundancy. For example, the MGX 8800 has hot-standby 1:n redundancy capability for customer access lines, hot-standby control for PVCs, and hot-standby trunks.

Design Criteria for Selecting ATM LSRs

There are five main considerations when selecting ATM LSRs:

- The different types of trunks supported by the ATM LSR
- The number of trunks supported by the switch
- The number of connections supported
- VC merge capability
- Requirements for redundancy and reliability

Designing MPLS Networks

MPLS network design must be accomplished prior to network installation in order to ensure that the network will operate reliably and optimally. Customer traffic must be properly estimated, because IP traffic is inherently connectionless, and customers will not be able to tell the service provider exactly which traffic they want to send where. This leads to a situation in which the network must be approximately sized with the option for scalability.

The following design steps must be taken into account:

- PoP design
- MPLS backbone link sizing
- Layer 3 routing design
- MPLS LVC sizing
- Fine-tuning the evolving network

PoP Design

Point of presence (PoP) design constraints include the choice of access line type and equipment for the network.

The location of PoPs is largely determined by user traffic and the location of population centers. Proper capacity planning must be performed prior to PoP design. The capacity-planning phase should make proper estimates and approximations for future traffic growth based on the existing customer base and anticipated customer growth and corresponding traffic growth. Oversubscription should not be factored in for baseline traffic planning.

Single ATM Edge LSR

A single Edge LSR PoP design, illustrated in Figure 9-9, is used if the node can support the number and types of access lines required by customer CE routers in the PoP location. The single Edge LSR is susceptible to scalability issues. These issues can be avoided if the ATM Edge LSR is co-located with the ATM LSR and additional Edge LSRs can be added to ATM ports on the core ATM LSR.

Multiple Edge LSRs and an ATM LSR

If multiple access lines are to be supported at a PoP, the PoP might require more than one Edge LSR at that location. Alternatively, different types of Edge LSRs might be required due to different types of access lines that might have to be supported. It is strongly recommended that you co-locate an ATM LSR if there are several Edge LSRs in a PoP.

This topology is shown in Figure 9-10.

Figure 9-9   *Single ATM Edge LSR*

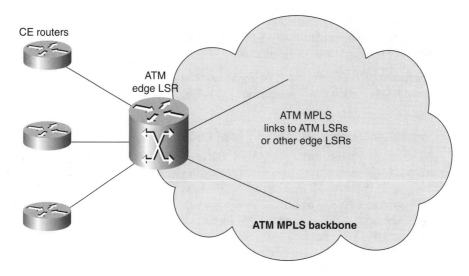

CE routers

ATM
edge LSR

ATM MPLS
links to ATM LSRs
or other edge LSRs

ATM MPLS backbone

Figure 9-10   *Multiple Edge LSRs*

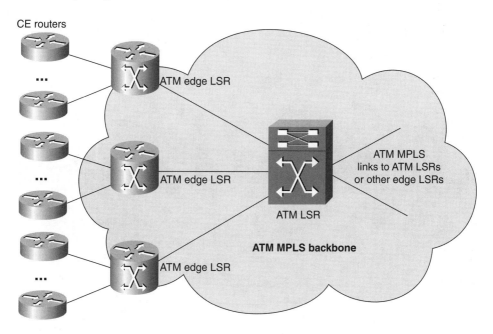

CE routers

ATM edge LSR

...

ATM edge LSR

...

ATM MPLS
links to ATM LSRs
or other edge LSRs

ATM LSR

ATM MPLS backbone

ATM edge LSR

...

The ATM LSR locally switches traffic going between different Edge LSRs in the PoP. It can also concentrate traffic going from the PoP onto a single set of ATM MPLS links. Routing scalability is improved, because only one IP routing protocol peering is required from the ATM LSR to other points in the MPLS network. Without the ATM LSR, separate peering would be required from all Edge LSRs.

Redundant pairs of links could be used between the Edge LSRs and the ATM LSR, depending on reliability requirements.

Access Concentrator, Edge LSR, and an ATM LSR

Access concentrators such as the MGX 8220 can be used in addition to Edge LSRs and an ATM LSR for concentrating user traffic and backhauling to an Edge LSR. An example of this type of PoP uses MGX 8220 access shelves; 6400, 7200, or 7500 Edge LSRs; and a BPX 8650 as a core ATM LSR. This topology is shown in Figure 9-11. IP traffic from access concentrators is carried in ATM PVCs to Edge LSRs. These may be carried through the same BPX 8650 that acts as the ATM LSR, because the BPX is an IP+ATM switch. As shown in Figure 9-11, LSR PE1 must have at least two ATM interfaces—one for access PVCs from the access concentrator, and one for ATM MPLS traffic.

There may also be Edge LSRs in the PoP that do not handle access PVCs at all and that have only directly connected access lines. The LSC could have such a configuration if provisioned to terminate CE routers.

Figure 9-11 *Multiple Edge LSRs*

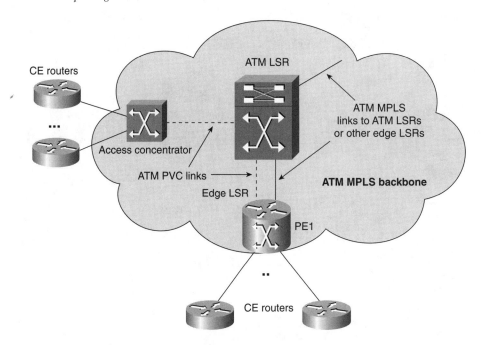

| NOTE | The LSC in the BPX 8650 can act as an Edge LSR simultaneously while performing its LSC function. However, use of an LSC as an Edge LSR is not recommended for providers who consider the separation of MPLS control functions from data forwarding functions vital. |

The number of Edge LSRs required in the PoP depends on the total number of access lines and the total bandwidth of the access lines, calculated from the average utilization. For example, if the sum of the access lines' bandwidths were 1 Gbps, the utilization might not exceed 500 Mbps. The capacity of a 6400, 7200, or 7500 router running MPLS Edge functions is roughly the same as its ordinary IP capacity using Cisco Enhanced Forwarding (CEF). For example, a 7200 router with an NPE 200 processor can support close to 200 Mbps of MPLS Edge traffic at normal IP packet sizes.

If additional Edge QoS functions such as MQC policing, metering, and traffic shaping are used, performance might be affected. In these circumstances, the routers' performance should be verified for the particular combination of features to be used.

Multiservice Access Concentrator as an Edge LSR

Multiservice access concentrators such as the MGX 8850 and Cisco 6400 can integrate the access, Edge LSR, and ATM LSR functions described in the previous example into a single device, as illustrated in Figure 9-12. It consists of a multiservice access concentrator with various types of Frame Relay and ATM access lines, circuit emulation lines, and one or more Edge LSRs. Each Edge LSR is an RPM card in the case of the MGX 8850 or a node route processor (NRP) card in the case of the 6400. The number of RPMs or NRPs acting as Edge LSRs depends on the total number of access lines and the total bandwidth of the access lines, downrated according to the utilization. For example, if the sum of the access lines' bandwidth were 1 Gbps, the utilization might not exceed 500 Mbps.

The RPM with an NPE150 processor can support an MPLS edge function for up to 700 access lines. It can support up to 150 Mbps of MPLS edge traffic at normal IP packet sizes. However, the performance should be verified with the particular combination of edge functions such as QoS to be used in addition to MPLS edge functions. The NRP capabilities are similar to those of the RPM. The 6400 and MGX 8850 also have IP+ATM capability. In the MGX 8850, one of the RPM cards acts as a label switch controller. It may perform both LSC functions and Edge LSR functions simultaneously, if desired. The use of an RPM for simultaneous LSC and Edge LSR is not recommended for providers who consider the separation of MPLS control functions from data forwarding functions vital. In the Cisco 6400, the main node switch processor also acts as an LSC.

Figure 9-12 *Multiservice Access Concentrator*

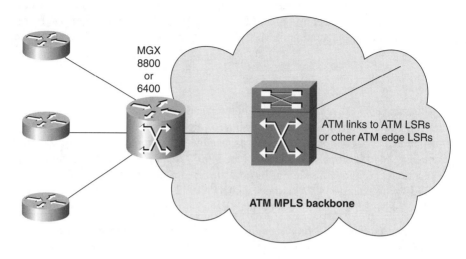

Single LSR PoP

A single LSR PoP site usually performs an ATM switching role to terminate customers using ATM router CEs. Such a site consists of a single ATM LSR, as shown in Figure 9-13, or possibly a redundant pair of ATM LSRs. The ATM LSR is typically a BPX 8650. The CE ATM router can terminate directly on the LSC using a TDM circuit or get switched over an ATM PVC provisioned in the BPX and terminate on an ATM Edge LSR or the LSC itself. However, true scalability can be achieved only by using ATM and a router-based LSR.

Figure 9-13 *Single LSR PoP*

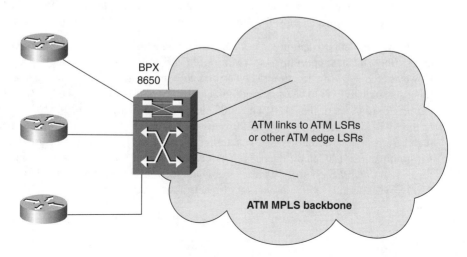

MPLS Backbone Link Sizing

The following steps detail the procedures involved with MPLS backbone link sizing:

Step 1   Design points of presence.

Step 2   Estimate traffic from each point of presence.

Step 3   Estimate the unidirectional traffic matrix.

Step 4   Estimate the bidirectional traffic matrix.

Step 5   Design the backbone trunk topology.

Step 6   Calculate estimated link bandwidths.

Step 7   Assign link capacity.

Step 8   Adjust redundancy.

Step 9   Verify equipment selection.

Step 1: Design Points of Presence

The first step in MPLS network design is to select the size, type, and layout of the PoPs according to the considerations described in the previous section.

The edge PoPs shown in Figure 9-14 are chosen based on the estimated customer link demand shown in the figure. 7500 ATM router-based Edge LSRs have been selected as PE routers, with BPX 8650 core ATM LSRs co-located at all PoP sites.

Step 2: Estimate Traffic from Each Point of Presence

The sum of the total customer access line bandwidths is considered, and an estimate of the total traffic sent from customers to each PoP can be made. A peak-traffic period estimate should be used, such as the rate during the busiest minute of the day.

This ensures adequate dimensioning. A maximum estimate would be the total of the access line bandwidths at the PoP, as shown in Figure 9-14. However, it is often reasonable to take a somewhat lower estimate, such as 60 percent of the total access bandwidth, as shown in Figure 9-15.

Figure 9-14 *Total Access Line Bandwidths*

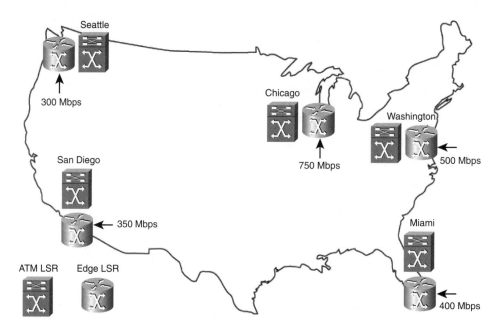

Figure 9-15 *Modified Access Line Bandwidths*

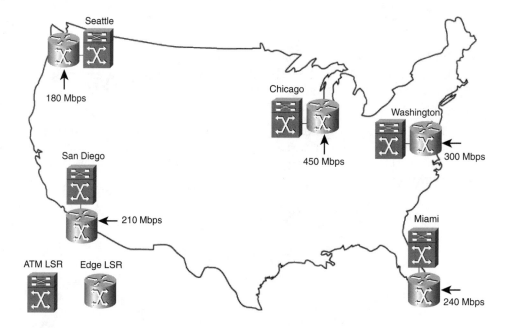

Step 3: Estimate the Unidirectional Traffic Matrix

This step estimates the volume of traffic flow from PoP to PoP based on a variety of factors, including customer population distribution and modified access line bandwidth per PoP. Another factor is the presence of co-located applications such as Web servers in the case of a service provider who is also an ASP. The exact procedure for this step varies from network to network. For interstate business IP traffic, a reasonable first approximation might be that 33 percent of traffic will go to Chicago, 22 percent to Washington, 13 percent to Seattle, 15 percent to San Diego, and 17 percent to Miami. An existing service provider would probably already have estimates for traffic patterns for its region. Based on the estimated traffic distribution percentages and the total PoP traffic from Step 2, a traffic matrix can be estimated. The traffic matrix for this example is shown in Table 9-1.

Table 9-1   *Unidirectional Traffic Distribution Matrix*

Destination	Source					Distribution
	Chicago	**Washington**	**Miami**	**San Diego**	**Seattle**	
Chicago	100	175	125	100	60	33%
Washington	250	50	75	65	25	22%
Miami	50	25	20	10	20	17%
San Diego	30	20	10	20	35	15%
Seattle	20	30	10	15	40	13%
Total	450	300	240	210	180	100%

In a typical network, this matrix will be very roughly symmetrical. For example, in Table 9-1, the traffic from Washington to Chicago is 175 Mbps, but the traffic from Chicago to Washington is 250 Mbps. If the traffic were more asymmetrical than about 2:1 or 3:1, there might be an error in traffic estimates or modeling, so this must be verified.

Step 4: Estimate the Bidirectional Traffic Matrix

In IP networks, traffic from node A to node B often flows along the same path, but in the reverse direction, as traffic from node B to node A. Although numerous routing protocol features and traffic engineering can override this, it might be useful to assume that this will happen, predominantly in small networks. Working from this assumption, it might be easier to use bidirectional traffic flows rather than unidirectional flows in an initial network design.

The estimated bidirectional flows for the sample network are shown in Table 9-2. The bidirectional traffic bandwidth between Washington and Chicago, for example, is taken to be 250 Mbps, which is the maximum of the unidirectional bandwidth from Washington to Chicago (175 Mbps) and the bandwidth from Chicago to Washington (250 Mbps). Forming bidirectional flows in this way tends to slightly overestimate the traffic in the network. However, this is useful as a conservative first approximation, and it ensures a degree of bandwidth scalability.

Table 9-2   *Bidirectional Traffic Distribution Matrix*

	Source				
Destination	**Chicago**	**Washington**	**Miami**	**San Diego**	**Seattle**
Chicago	100	N/A	125	100	60
Washington	250	50	75	65	N/A
Miami	N/A	N/A	20	10	20
San Diego	N/A	N/A	N/A	20	35
Seattle	N/A	30	N/A	N/A	40

Step 5: Design the Backbone Trunk Topology

The backbone trunk topology layout depends on a number of factors:

- Node location and layout from a geographical perspective. This includes the availability of lit and dark fiber and the presence of a centralized distribution point such as an Internet Network Access Point (NAP). In this example, the Chicago NAP serves as a distribution and aggregation point for the long-haul fiber trunks.

- Secure facilities with proper electrical and environmental characteristics are required to house the ATM LSR nodes. These facilities should also be scalable in the physical sense to accommodate Edge LSRs and additional shelves upon network growth.

- Network-level redundancy by virtue of having multiple paths to each destination is of prime importance. This ensures that all nodes have alternative paths to each other.

- The fiber trunks must be fully redundant from a Layer 1 fiber and card module/node perspective. The BPX provides for 1:1 BCC processor card redundancy and n:1 line card redundancy within the chassis, which is a very nice feature.

The network layout selected in this example is shown in Figure 9-16. Many alternative layouts are possible. The one selected consists of a ring configured as a partial mesh. This design provides a good degree of network-level redundancy, with at least two paths between each pair of nodes. It is not essential to have redundant trunks, because it is possible to reroute MPLS LVCs. In conventional ATM connection-oriented networks, rerouting of virtual circuits is a last resort, to be used only when all other redundancy mechanisms have failed. This is because it inevitably involves disruption of customer traffic for many seconds or minutes as all circuits are rerouted. In IP networks, however, rerouting is a much less severe issue, because packet flows can be switched from one link to another almost instantaneously as soon as the IP routing protocol has converged. MPLS networks lie between these two extremes. Rerouting in MPLS networks is particularly feasible if VC merge is used, for two reasons: VC merge reduces the number of VCs that are used in the network, and it reduces the scope of changes required in connections when rerouting does occur. Most trunks in this example are nonredundant for economy. However, a redundant pair of trunks is used for the Washington-to-Chicago link, because this path is expected to have the heaviest utilization.

Figure 9-16 *Network Link Design*

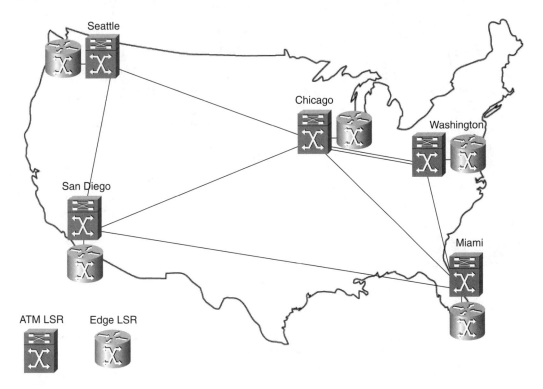

Step 6: Calculate Estimated Link Bandwidths

The network link bandwidths can be calculated based on the bidirectional traffic distribution matrix shown in Table 9-2. Assume that Layer 3 IP routing protocols operating over equal-bandwidth links will select a minimum-hop path unless administrative costs are used.

This results in equal-cost load balancing of traffic when there are two or more minimum-hop paths.

The process of calculating link flows for the traffic in Table 9-2 is detailed in Figure 9-17.

Figure 9-17 *Network Link Bandwidth Calculation*

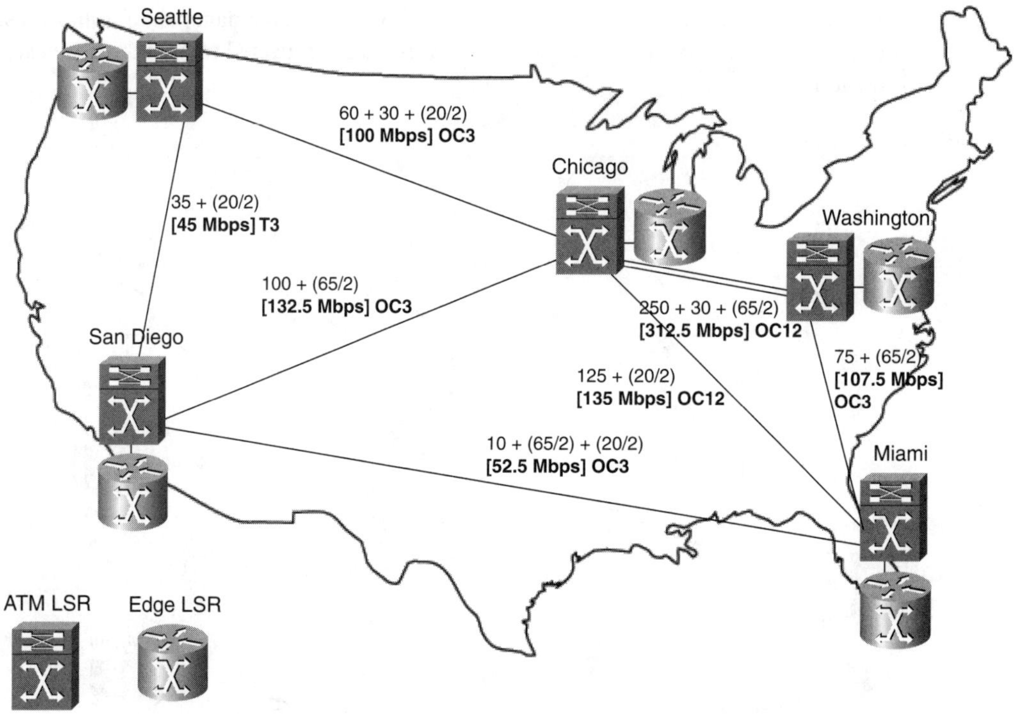

Seattle

60 + 30 + (20/2)
[100 Mbps] OC3

Chicago

35 + (20/2)
[45 Mbps] T3

Washington

100 + (65/2)
[132.5 Mbps] OC3

250 + 30 + (65/2)
[312.5 Mbps] OC12

San Diego

75 + (65/2)
**[107.5 Mbps]
OC3**

125 + (20/2)
[135 Mbps] OC12

10 + (65/2) + (20/2)
[52.5 Mbps] OC3

Miami

ATM LSR   Edge LSR

As an example, the bandwidth requirement between San Diego and Chicago is 100 Mbps, and the bandwidth requirement between San Diego and Washington is 65 Mbps. However, there are two equal-cost paths from San Diego to Washington—namely, San Diego-Chicago-Washington and San Diego-Miami-Washington. Load balancing across these paths results in 65/2 Mbps shared across these paths.

Step 7: Assign Link Capacity

The estimated link bandwidths calculated in Step 6 can be assigned to the links in the network. This involves selecting the next-larger standard link size than the estimated link flow calculated earlier. This is shown in Figure 9-17.

Step 8: Adjust Redundancy

The network relies on Layer 3 rerouting in the event of link failure, because redundant trunks are not being used across all links. It is good design practice to upwardly adjust link bandwidths to ensure that there is sufficient bandwidth capacity on alternative paths to deal with link failures.

For example, if the link between San Diego and Seattle failed, the OC3 between San Diego and Chicago would end up with 132.5 + 45, or 177.5 Mbps, which clearly exceeds the OC3 rate of 155 Mbps between San Diego and Chicago. Therefore, an OC12 or multiple OC3 links would be required for this link.

The final allocation of link bandwidths is shown in Figure 9-18.

Figure 9-18 *Link Bandwidth with Redundancy Considerations*

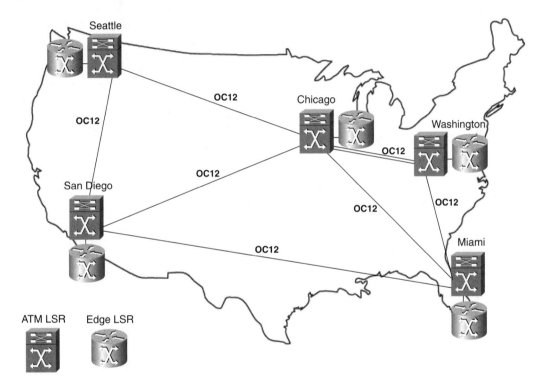

Step 9: Verify Equipment Selection

Verify whether the PoP equipment selected can support the interface types and support the bandwidth requirements.

This involves checking with your Cisco Systems SE to see if the selected PoP equipment can support the number and size of links chosen in the network design. CCO has product specifications and interface details for all equipment with MPLS support. The network in this example would pass this check.

Due to the requirements of multiple OC12s at each site, if a PoP had used an MGX 8850 instead of a BPX 8680, the PoP would need to be redesigned by using a BPX 8680 instead of an MGX 8850.

ATM Link Redundancy

There are three main ways of achieving changeover for a redundant pair of ATM links:

- Data link-level changeover using Automatic Protection Switching (APS). SONET APS changeovers result in no change to the interfaces, as seen by connection routing, and no loss of connection state.

- Inverse multiplexing over ATM (IMA) by distributing cells across the links in round-robin fashion. This offers both redundancy and data link-level load sharing across links. IMA is available only for low-speed links—groups of T1 or E1 links.

- Network-layer rerouting using IP or PNNI routing.

NOTE   ATM MPLS networks should use inverse multiplexing for redundancy of low-speed trunks. Otherwise, if the network uses VC merge, parallel links with network-layer changeover should be used, in order to make the full network capacity available for use. Finally, if VC merge is unavailable, data link redundancy should be used.

Layer 3 Routing Design

MPLS uses link-state routing protocols such as OSPF and IS-IS to determine the routes for IP traffic and LVCs. LSRs run IP routing protocols in the same way that regular IP routers do. Designing IP routing in an MPLS network is almost exactly the same process as designing IP routing for an ordinary IP network. The network can be depicted in a logical topology, and a routing topology can be ascertained.

By looking at the routing topology, you can divide the network into areas, design route summarization, and so on.

The physical design perspective represents the physical devices and links in a network. An example is shown in Figure 9-19.

The logical design perspective shows the network as it is seen by an IP routing protocol. An example of the logical perspective of the physical design is shown in Figure 9-20. Layer 2 PVC switches and PVC switching functions are transparent to IP routing. If a PVC connects a customer site to a router, the PVC is a one-hop direct connection from an IP routing perspective. A label switch controller and a switch together form a single routing node.

Figure 9-19 *MPLS Network Physical Perspective*

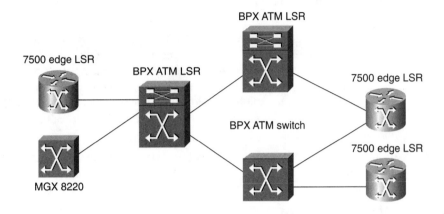

Figure 9-20 *MPLS Network Logical Perspective*

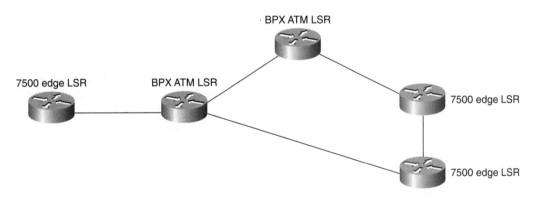

MPLS Layer 3 Routing Design Criteria

The following steps detail the design procedures involved in MPLS Layer 3 routing:

- The IGP used in MPLS backbones should be a link-state routing protocol such as OSPF or IS-IS. IS-IS is currently supported on most Cisco MPLS equipment, but not on the LS1010 and 8540 MSR. EIGRP can also be used, but it does not support MPLS Traffic Engineering, because it is a hybrid distance-vector routing protocol. IGRP or RIP also work with MPLS, but not with MPLS TE, so they are not recommended.

- Use unnumbered IP links wherever possible. This reduces the number of IP destinations known to the LSRs and hence reduces the number of LVCs used in the network.

- If route summarization is required in an ATM MPLS network, it must be performed on an ATM Edge LSR. An ATM LSR may be used on an OSPF or IS-IS Area Border Router (ABR), but only if no summarization is done at the ABRs. This is due to the fact that ATM LSRs cannot examine IP addresses. ATM LSRs, such as the BPX 8650, have a limited ability to examine IP addresses by sending the packets to an Edge LSR in the LSC. However, this can be done only for a small minority of the traffic flowing through the ATM LSR.

- If the MPLS network needs to peer with an external autonomous system, an ATM Edge LSR may be configured as a BGP4 Autonomous System Boundary Router. However, ATM LSRS may not.

- MPLS traffic engineering works in backbones that contain a single OSPF or IS-IS area. MPLS Traffic Engineering/Routing with Resource Reservation (TE/RRR) may not be used in multiple area networks where the ABRs are ATM LSRs. This restriction will be eased in later versions of RRR and IOS.

- Currently it is not possible to use MPLS TE/RRR in a network where the ABRs are ATM LSRs. A future RRR release will allow TE/RRR tunnels to pass through ABRs, allowing TE/RRR to be used in networks where the ABRs are ATM LSRs.

- Summarization cannot be performed in the interior of an MPLS VPN network. The interior of an MPLS network supporting VPNs may have multiple OSPF or IS-IS areas, but summarization should not be used. The restrictions on summarization exist because summarization restricts some types of label-switched paths from being set up end-to-end.

MPLS LVC Sizing

An ATM switch can support only a limited number of active VCs. Multiple ATM services such as MPLS, PNNI, and Autoroute share the resources of the links in an IP+ATM network. Hence, a sufficient number of VCs must be reserved for use as LVCs on each link. The design problem is to determine the number of LVCs required. The required number of LVCs depends on the number of IP destinations in the network, the relationship between IP destinations and LVCs, VC merge, and the paths selected by IP routing.

Destination Prefixes

The following steps detail the criteria involved in MPLS LVC sizing:

- The number of LVCs used in a particular area of a network depends on the number of IP destination prefixes known in that area.

- The loopback address of all Edge LSRs and ATM LSRs in the area is a destination prefix.

- The subnet address prefix of any numbered point-to-point link, or any other subnet, is a destination prefix. This stresses the need to use unnumbered links in MPLS networks.

- Addresses summarized into a single address at an Edge LSR ABR or ASBR are counted as a single destination prefix.

- Any other address prefixes advertised into the area must be counted as well.

NOTE   VPN customer destination prefixes are not advertised into the core of the network and do not count toward the LVC count. This is one of the keys to the scalability of MPLS VPNs.

LVCs and VC Merge

Each Edge LSR and LSC asks a neighboring MPLS node for LVCs for the destination prefixes it knows about. If MPLS class of service (CoS) is used, it may ask for up to four LVCs for each destination prefix. The requests for LVCs flow through the network according to the paths selected by IP routing. If VC merge is not used, there may be many LVCs per link, as shown in Figure 9-21.

Figure 9-21 *LVCs Without VC Merge*

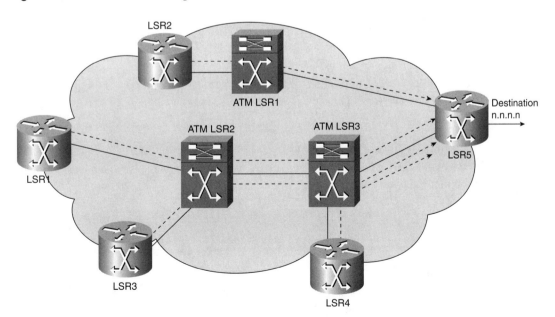

With VC merge, the LVCs to each destination are merged at each ATM LSR. This means that on each link, there is at most one LVC per destination in the area. This is shown in Figure 9-22. If MPLS CoS is used, the number of classes multiplies the number of destinations in order to get the number of LVCs.

Figure 9-22 *LVCs with VC Merge*

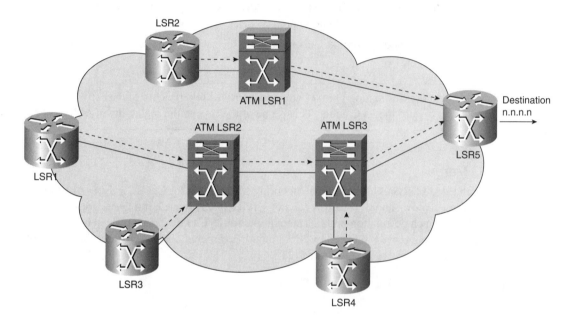

Design Calculations for Edge LSRs

For ATM Edge LSRs, the number of LVCs used per link depends on whether VC merge is being used in the network.

Equation 1

If d is the number of destination prefixes known in an area, and c is the number of CoSs used in the network, and VC merge is used, the number of LVCs used per link l is as follows:

$$l <= cd$$

Equation 2

If VC merge is not being used in the network, there are three dependencies:

- The number of LSCs in the area
- The number of Edge LSRs in the area
- The number of destinations that are directly reachable through the Edge LSR in question

If *d* is the number of destination prefixes known in an area, and *c* is the number of CoSs used in the network, and *de* is the number of destinations that are reachable through a particular ATM Edge LSR (this often equals 1, due to summarization), and the total number of ATM Edge LSRs and LSCs in the area is *n,* the number of LVCs used per link is as follows:

$$l <= c\ (d - de) + (c)(n)(de)$$

Equation 3

A simpler equation applies in the particular case where all these conditions exist:

- VC merge is not used
- There is one destination prefix per Edge LSR or LSC
- All links are unnumbered
- There are no address prefixes from outside the area

These conditions often apply in the core of MPLS networks supporting VPNs, but not using VC merge.

The number of LVCs used per link on the ATM Edge LSR in this case is given by:

$$l < 2cn$$

Equation Guidelines: Equations 1 Through 3

One of the preceding three equations is then used to check whether a sufficient number of LVCs is available on the equipment, as shown in Table 9-3. Table 9-4 shows the LVC capacity of Cisco ATM Edge LSR interfaces.

Table 9-3   *Edge LSR LVC Limits*

Device	Situation	Key Parameter	Equation
Edge LSR	The network uses VC merge.	Number of active VCs supported per ATM link	Equation 1
Edge LSR	The network does not use VC merge. There is one destination prefix per LSR or Edge LSR, all links are unnumbered, and there are no out-of-area routes.	Number of active VCs supported per ATM link	Equation 3
Edge LSR	The network does not use VC merge. All other situations apply.	Number of active VCs supported per ATM link	Equation 2

Table 9-4   *ATM Edge LSR LVC Capacity*

Device	Interface	Number of Active LVCs Supported	Notes
3600	NM-1A ATM network modules	1024	
4700	NP-1A ATM network processor module	1023	
7200, 7500	PA-A1 or standard ATM port adapter	2048	
Cat 5500, 7200, 7500	PA-A3 ATM port adapter	4096	
6400	Node Route Processor (NRP)	2048	Capacity is reduced by one LVC for each active PVC that terminates on the NRP.
MGX 8850 IP+ATM switch	Route Processor Module (RPM)	4096	Capacity is reduced by one LVC for each active PVC that terminates on the RPM. In addition, the PXM is limited to 16 K LVCs. This is unlikely to be a problem unless more than three RPMs are used in an MGX 8850 shelf.
12000 series routers	4xOC-3 ATM line card	2047	The 2047 active VCs are shared between all four ports. Network capacity is reduced by one destination prefix for every second and subsequent route chosen for each destination according to equal-cost multipath routing if the extra routes are on the same card.
12000 series routers	1xOC-12 ATM line card	2047	

Design Case Study 1

Consider a network in which VC merge and one CoS are being used. If all Edge LSRs are 7500 series routers with PA-A1 port adapters, how many IP destination prefixes can safely be supported in the area?

Solution to Design Case Study 1   VC merge is being used, so Table 9-3 indicates that Equation 1 should be used. One CoS is being used, so $c = 1$. Table 9-4 states that the PA-A1 port adapter supports 2048 LVCs, so $l = 2048$. Substituting these into Equation 1 results in the following:

$$l <= cd$$
$$2048 <= (1)(d)$$
$$d => 2048$$

This means that 2048 destination prefixes can be supported within the area, provided that the ATM LSRs do not impose a tighter limit.

Design Case Study 2

Consider a network in which VC merge is not used and four CoSs are in use. This network is the core of an MPLS VPN service, and there is one destination prefix per LSR or Edge LSR. All links are unnumbered. No out-of-area routes are injected into the interior routing protocol. The Edge LSRs are 7200 and 3600 series routers with PA-A3 ATM port adapters and NM-1A ATM network modules.

What is the largest number of LSRs that can be used if the network consists of a single area? Assume that the ATM LSRs support a sufficiently large number of LVCs.

Solution to Design Case Study 2   According to the conditions given, Table 9-3 indicates that Equation 3 should be used. Four CoSs are used, so $c = 4$. Table 9-4 shows that the 7200 ATM interfaces support 4096 LVCs and that the 3600 ATM interfaces support 1024 LVCs. 1024 LVCs make a tighter design constraint, so $l = 1024$. Substituting these into Equation 3 results in the following:

$$l < 2cn$$
$$1024 < 2\ (4)(n)$$
$$8n > 1024$$
$$n > 128$$

This means that a maximum of 128 LSRs (Edge LSRs or ATM LSRs) may be used in the area, provided that the IP routing protocol supports that many routers in that area.

Design Case Study 3

Consider a network in which VC merge is not used. Four CoSs are in use, and the network is the core of an MPLS VPN service. There is one destination prefix per ATM LSR or Edge LSR. All links are unnumbered. The network has multiple areas, and there are at most 50 ATM LSRs and LSRs in each area. The Edge LSRs are 3600s with NM-1A ATM network modules, and the ATM LSRs support a sufficiently large number of LVCs. How many LSRs can be used in the entire network?

Solution to Design Case Study 3 There are multiple areas, so there will be out-of-area routes in each area. Table 9-3 indicates that Equation 2 should be used in this case. Four CoSs are used, so $c = 4$. Table 9-4 says that $l = 1024$. There are at most 50 ATM LSRs and LSRs in each area, so use $n = 50$.

There is one route per Edge LSR. In the worst case, all out-of-area routes are accessed through a single LSR. This concentrates the LVC requirements on the links to that single LSR.

In this case:

$$de = (d - 50)$$
$$d = de + 50$$
$$d - de = 50$$

Substituting these variables into Equation 2 results in the following:

$$l <= c(d\text{–}de) + (c)(n)(de)$$
$$1024 <= 4\ (50) + (4)\ (50)\ (d - 50)$$
$$1024 <= 200 + 200\ (d - 50)$$
$$1024 + 10000 - 200 <= 200d$$
$$d => 54$$

This means that only 54 LSRs can be used in the network.

NOTE   Using multiple areas can have major disadvantages in ATM MPLS networks without VC merge. The preceding examples indicate that ATM LSRs without VC merge typically can't be used in networks larger than a few hundred nodes. A workaround is to use the same switches with MPLS-over-PVCs instead of ATM MPLS.

Design Calculations for ATM LSRs with VC Merge

With VC merge, the LVCs to each destination are merged at each ATM LSR. This means that there is at most one LVC per destination on each link, as shown in Figure 9-22. If MPLS COS is used, the number of classes multiplies the number of LVCs.

Equation 4

If d is the number of destination prefixes known in an area, and c is the number of CoSs used, the number of LVCs used per link l is as follows:

$$l < cd$$

Equation 5

Another important issue in switches that support VC merge is the number of LVCs that must be merged in the switch, *m*. This depends on the number of links into the switch, *k*. The limit is:

$$m < cd\,(k-1)$$

Equation Guidelines: Equations 4 and 5

These equations are then used to check whether a sufficient number of LVCs are available on the equipment, as shown in Table 9-5. Both equations must be checked.

Table 9-5 *ATM LSR LVC Limits with VC Merge*

Device	Key Parameters	Check Against
ATM LSR with VC Merge	1. Number of active VCs supported per ATM link	Equation 4
	2. Number of merging LVCs supported per switch or per port card—whichever is applicable to the switch architecture	Equation 5

NOTE A per-switch limit applies to shared-memory switches such as the LS1010 or 8540 MSR, and a per-port card limit applies to crosspoint matrix switches such as the BPX 8650.

Table 9-6 details the LVC capacities for various ATM switches.

Table 9-6 *ATM LSR LVC Capacity with VC merge*

Device	Interface Hardware	Number of Active LVCs Supported	Number of Active Merging LVCs Supported
LS1010	Any ATM port hardware	4096 per OC-3 port, 16 K per OC-12 port, 16 K per OC-48 port	64 K per switch
6400	Any ATM port hardware	4096 per OC-3 port, 16K per OC-12 port, 16 K per OC-48 port	256 K per switch
8540 MSR	Any ATM port adapters	4096 per OC-3 port, 16K per OC-12 port, 16 K per OC-48 port	256 K per switch
BPX 8650 or 8680	BXM-E cards	32 K per BXM, shared among up to 12 interfaces	32 K per BXM, with a maximum of 16K per port on OC-3 BXM cards and 2xOC-12 BXM cards. T3/E3 BXM cards and 1xOC-12 BXM cards have a limit of 32 K per port.
MGX 8800 with PXM-45	AXSM cards	128 K per AXSM, shared among up to 16 interfaces	128 K per AXSM

NOTE   In Table 9-6, the numbers of active LVCs supported are maximums. The actual limits depend on configurations. In a BPX 8650, for example, the actual number of active LVCs supported per link must be downrated by a minimum of 270 lines per interface if AutoRoute is enabled on that interface. On all switches, the VC space reserved for PVCs, SVCs, and so on, must be subtracted from the available VC space.

Design Case Study 4

A network uses BPX 8650 ATM LSRs with VC merge. Four CoSs are used. Each BPX 8650 has three one-port OC-12/STM-4 BXM cards, with each port used to link to another ATM LSR or Edge LSR. What limit do these ATM LSRs put on the number of IP destination prefixes that can be supported inside an area?

Solution to Design Case Study 4   Table 9-5 shows that both Equation 4 and Equation 5 must be checked. Two CoSs are used, so $c = 4$. Each switch has three ports, so $k = 3$. Looking up the BPX 8650 in Table 9-6 shows that BXM cards support 32 K active LVCs. In this case, each BXM card has one port, so each link supports 32 K LVCs, or $l = 32768$. Table 9-6 shows that 32 K LVCs can be merged into a one-port OC-12 BXM card, so $m = 32768$.

Substituting these parameters into Equation 4 results in the following:

$$l < cd$$
$$32768 < 4d$$
$$d > 8192$$

Also, using Equation 5, you get this:

$$m < cd\,(k - 1)$$
$$32768 < (4)(d)(3 - 1)$$
$$32768 < 8d$$
$$d > 4096$$

The limit from Equation 5 is tighter, which means that the limit imposed by the ATM LSRs is 4096 destination prefixes in the area. However, the Edge LSRs might impose a tighter limit.

Design Case Study 5

A network uses BPX 8650 ATM LSRs with VC merge. Four CoSs are used. Each BPX has four eight-port OC-3/STM-1s, with each port used to link to another ATM LSR or Edge LSR. What limit do these ATM LSRs put on the number of IP destination prefixes that can be supported inside an area?

Solution to Design Case Study 5   Table 9-5 shows that both Equation 4 and Equation 5 must be checked. Four CoSs are used, so $c = 4$. Each switch has 32 ports, so $k = 32$. Looking up the BPX in Table 9-6 shows that the eight-port OC-3 BXM cards support (32768/8) or 4096 LVCs per port, or $l = 4096$. Similarly, Table 9-6 shows that the BPX supports 32768 merging VCs per BXM. The worst case is when all LVCs try to merge into the same port, so use $m = 16384$.

Substituting these parameters into Equation 4 results in the following:

$l < cd$
$4096 < 4d$
$d > 1024$

Also, using Equation 5, you get this:

$m < cd\,(k - 1)$
$16384 < 4d\,(32 - 1)$
$124d > 16384$
$d > 132$

The limit from Equation 5 is tighter, which means that the limit imposed by the ATM LSRs is 132 destination prefixes in the area. However, the Edge LSRs might impose a tighter limit. This example clearly shows the effects on destination prefix support of having a large number of links (32 OC-3s in this case study) with multiple CoSs.

Design Case Study 6

A network uses BPX 8650 ATM LSRs with VC merge. Two CoSs are used. Each BPX 8650 has eight OC-3/STM-1 ports, on two four-port OC-3/STM-1 BXM cards and two OC-12/STM-4 ports on two one-port OC-12/STM-1 BXM cards. Each port is used to link to another ATM LSR or Edge LSR. What limit do these ATM LSRs put on the number of IP destination prefixes that can be supported inside an area?

Solution to Design Case Study 6   Table 9-5 shows that both Equation 4 and Equation 5 must be checked. Four CoSs are used, so $c = 4$. Each switch has ten ports in all, so $k = 10$. Looking up the BPX 8650 in Table 9-6 shows that each BXM card supports 32 K active LVCs. In this case, each OC-3 BXM card has four ports, so you can assume that each OC-3 link supports 32 K/4 LVCs, or $l(1) = 8192$. The OC-12 BXM card has only one port, so $l(2) = 32768$. $l(1)$ provides a tighter design constraint, so $l = 8192$. Table 9-6 shows that the maximum number of active merging LVCs is 32768 for the one-port OC-12 card. Table 9-6 also shows that four-port OC-3 BXM cards can support 32 K merging VCs, with a maximum of 16 K per port. The tighter design constraint is when all LVCs try to merge into the same OC-3 port, so use $m = 16384$.

Substituting these parameters into Equation 4 results in the following:

$l < cd$
$8192 < 4d$
$d > 2048$

Also, using Equation 5, you get this:

$m < cd\ (k - 1)$
$16384 < 4d\ (10 - 1)$
$36d > 16384$
$d > 455$

The limit from Equation 5 is tighter, which means that the limit imposed by the ATM LSRs is 455 destination prefixes in the area. However, the Edge LSRs might impose a tighter limit.

Design Calculations for ATM LSRs Without VC Merge

The following equations need to be satisfied for ATM LSRs without VC merge.

Equation 6

Without VC merge, there may be many VCs per destination on each link, as shown in Figure 9-21. If the total number of ATM Edge LSRs and LSCs in the area is n, there may be up to $c(n - 1)$ LVCs per destination on each link.

The number of LVCs used per link will then be as follows:

$l < cd\ (n - 1)$

Equation 7

A tighter limit applies in the particular case where VC merge is not used; there is one destination prefix per Edge LSR or LSC, all links are unnumbered, and there are no address prefixes from outside the area. These conditions often apply in the core of MPLS networks supporting VPNs but not using VC merge.

The number of LVCs used in this case is given by

$l <= c\ (n^2 / 2)$

Equation Guidelines: Equations 6 and 7

Either Equation 6 or Equation 7 is then used to check whether a sufficient number of LVCs is available on the equipment, as shown in Table 9-7. Table 9-8 shows the limits of Cisco ATM LSRs without VC merge capability.

Table 9-7   *ATM LSR LVC Limits Without VC Merge*

Device	Situation	Key Parameter	Check Against
ATM LSR without VC merge	There is one destination prefix per LSR or Edge LSR, all links are unnumbered, and there are no out-of-area routes	Number of active VCs supported per ATM link	Equation 3
ATM LSR without VC merge	All other situations	Number of active VCs supported per ATM link	Equation 2

Table 9-8   *ATM LSR LVC Capability Without VC Merge*

Device	Interface Hardware	Number of Active LVCs Supported Per Link
BPX 8650	Older BXM cards (or pre-9.3.x software)	16 K per BXM, shared among up to 12 interfaces

NOTE   In Table 9-8, the numbers of active LVCs supported are maximums. The actual limits depend on configurations. In a BPX 8650, for example, the actual number of active LVCs supported per link must be downrated by a minimum of 270 lines per interface if AutoRoute is enabled on that interface. On all switches, the VC space reserved for PVCs, SVCs, and so on, must be subtracted from the available VC space.

Design Case Study 7

A network uses BPX 8650 ATM LSRs without VC merge. Four CoSs are used. Each BPX 8650 has one eight-port OC-3/STM-1 BXM card, with each port used to link to another ATM LSR or Edge LSR. There is one destination prefix per LSR or Edge LSR. All links in the area are unnumbered, and no out-of-area routes are known. What limit do these ATM LSRs put on the number of LSRs or Edge LSRs that can be supported inside an area?

Solution to Design Case Study 7   Table 9-7 shows that Equation 7 should be checked in this case. Four CoSs are used, so $c = 4$. Looking up the BPX 8650 in Table 9-8 shows that the pre-9.3.x software release BXM cards support a total of 16 K active LVCs. In this case, each BXM card has eight ports, so each link supports 16384 / 8 LVCs, or $l = 2048$.

Substituting these parameters into Equation 7 results in the following:

$$l <= c \ (n^2 / 2)$$
$$2048 <= 4 \ (n^2 / 2)$$
$$2n^2 => 2048$$
$$n => 32$$

This means that the limit imposed by the ATM LSRs is 32 LSRs or Edge LSRs.

NOTE   This example indicates that ATM LSRs without VC merge typically cannot be used in networks of larger than a few hundred nodes. An alternative that works around these limitations is to use the same switches while using MPLS-over-PVCs instead of ATM MPLS.

Design Case Study 8

A network uses BPX 8650 ATM LSRs without VC merge. Four CoSs are used. Each BPX 8650 has five one-port OC-12/STM-4 BXM cards, with each port used to link to another ATM LSR or Edge LSR. What limit do these ATM LSRs put on the number of IP destination prefixes that can be supported inside an area?

Solution to Design Case Study 8   You don't have any information available on the relationship between devices and routes. However, Table 9-7 shows that Equation 6 should be checked. Two CoSs are used, so $c = 4$. Looking up the BPX 8650 in Table 9-8 shows that BXM cards support 16 K active LVCs. In this case, each BXM card has one port, so each link supports 16 K LVCs, or $l = 16384$.

Substituting these parameters into Equation 6 results in the following:

$$l < cd \ (n - 1)$$
$$16384 < 4d \ (n - 1)$$
$$d(n - 1) > 4096$$

Because n, the number of LSRs in the area, has not been given, the answer cannot be explicitly derived. However, if you assumed that $n = 50$, this would give an indicative value of d = 83. In other words, the number of destination prefixes that may be supported depends on the number of LSRs in the area. For example, you have a limit of 83 destination prefixes if there are 50 LSRs in the area.

NOTE   This design example provides a what-if scenario and a relationship between the destination prefixes and the number of LSRs. The derivation can be used to simulate various possible scenarios.

Fine-Tuning the Evolving Network

Fine-tuning and engineering the network design is an ongoing process. As soon as an MPLS network is deployed, continuing design activities are required to verify the assumptions used in the initial design. The network must also be fine-tuned as new customers and PoPs are added. The ongoing process involves the following steps:

- Perform regular traffic measurements and analysis. Measure actual PoP and link traffic, and compare these measurements against the predicted traffic and link capacities.

- The network traffic model continuously evolves. Regular baselining of traffic must be performed, and the traffic distribution model must be constantly updated. The traffic distribution matrix is a starting point for any network redesign.

- As new customers are added and provisioned, traffic will increase. You must review the initial design to add new Edge LSRs to PoPs and higher-bandwidth links. The routing parameters must be adjusted, and the LVC limitations must not be exceeded in the network core.

Additional MPLS Design Considerations

This section discusses additional MPLS design considerations, including the size of Internet routing tables, traffic engineering constraints, virtual path tunnel constraints, and LVC exhaustion.

Internet Routing Tables

The destination prefix limits in MPLS networks do not restrict MPLS networks from handling Internet routes.

Full Internet routes are nearing the 120,000-route mark. However, ATM MPLS can still be used in networks with full Internet routing, by use of an MPLS feature known as BGP Next-Hop Labeling. BGP Next-Hop Labeling allows BGP Autonomous System Boundary Routers to exchange the full Internet routing tables with each other by way of BGP, while re-advertising only a limited subset of these addresses (or none at all) into the IGP (OSPF or IS-IS) areas through which they are connected. Because only a limited set of destination prefixes is known within the IGP in the MPLS network, the destination prefix limit values can be respected.

Traffic Engineering Constraints

The design limits for ATM LSRs apply when MPLS traffic engineering is not used. If traffic engineering is used, one LVC is used for each traffic engineering tunnel on each link, in addition to the limits discussed in Equations 4 through 7.

Virtual Path Tunnel Constraints

VP tunnels involve several logical links terminating on a single physical interface on an LSR or ATM LSR. When VP tunnels are terminated on an interface, the LVCs on all VP tunnels must be taken into account. For example, if four VP tunnels terminate on a logical interface that supports 2000 LVCs, an average of only 500 LVCs will be available per VP tunnel.

LVC Exhaustion

The proper design of an ATM MPLS network takes into account the number of LVCs, destination prefixes, classes of service, Edge and core LSRs, merged LVCs, and links into the switch. However, these design limits have large tolerances, and in some cases they might be exceeded—especially if VC merge is not being used. It is difficult to calculate exactly how many LVCs will be required. This depends on the exact shape and state of the network and the exact paths chosen by IP routing. If this can be analyzed, taking into account such things as failed links and multipath routing, fewer LVCs could be safely reserved on each link.

When a link runs out of LVCs, traffic is transmitted over the default (0,32) LVCs in the case of standard IP traffic. This traffic is then forwarded around the links by the LSC processors, not the ATM switch fabrics. Network stability can be maintained if MPLS QoS is configured to give precedence to the routing and LDP traffic. However, large traffic flow volume, especially on a busy core backbone, might overwhelm the LSC when it exceeds the LSC's packet-forwarding capacity. In the case of MPLS VPNs, the packets that would otherwise use the failed paths are discarded. It is imperative that the MPLS network not exhaust LVCs over links. The design must allocate switch resources so that a sufficient number of LVCs are available on each link.

Summary

Packet-based MPLS VPN networks use a router-based backbone. The links between the core P routers, PE to core P routers, and PE to CE routers can be any mix of conventional Layer 2 technologies. The MPLS header is carried as a shim header in the case of a legacy Layer 2 header or in the VPI/VCI field in the case of ATM.

ATM-based MPLS VPNs use ATM LSRs in the core and a combination of ATM routers or other ATM LSRs (performing the Edge LSR or PE function) at the various PoPs. The core ATM LSRs use LVCs to communicate with other core LSRs and the PE ATM routers.

MPLS can be deployed into a traditional ATM network gradually, starting with just a single pair of ATM LSRs in an otherwise purely ATM network. MPLS can be deployed across non-MPLS-capable switches using VP connections through the traditional ATM switches.

These VP connections are called VP tunnels because they allow MPLS to tunnel through traditional ATM switches.

MPLS networks can use traditional ATM equipment as a migration step in introducing MPLS to an existing ATM network. Traditional ATM switches can be used to backhaul traffic from a CE router to an Edge ATM LSR or to tunnel traffic between ATM LSRs.

The main considerations when selecting ATM LSRs include the different types and number of trunks supported by the ATM LSR switch, the number of connections supported, VC merge capability, and redundancy and reliability requirements. The design steps for ATM MPLS design include PoP design, MPLS backbone link sizing, IP routing design, MPLS LVC sizing, and eventually fine-tuning the evolving network.

This chapter covers the following topics:

- **Optical Networking**—This section discusses the requirement for fiber-optic network infrastructures in which switches and routers have integrated optical interfaces and are directly connected by fiber or optical network elements, such as Dense Wavelength Division Multiplexers (DWDMs). Conventional fiber-optic systems and DWDM technology are also discussed.

- **Optical Transport Network Elements**—Technical details of Optical Transport Network (OTN) elements such as optical amplifiers, wavelength converters, Optical Add Drop Multiplexers (OADMs), and optical cross-connect switches are discussed in this section.

- **Multiprotocol Lambda Switching**—Multiprotocol Lambda Switching (MPλS) is the optical analogy of MPLS. This section compares MPλS with MPLS and examines the MPLS control plane, which performs all crucial control functions for MPLS data networks as applied to optical networks.

- **Optical UNI**—The Optical UNI defines a link for communicating control, signaling, and data packets between the optical client and adjacent optical transport-networking devices. This section discusses the O-UNI, which was created so that carriers can offer an open interface for accessing circuit-based services across an Optical Transport Network (OTN).

- **Unified Control Plane**—The Unified Control Plane (UCP) incorporates extensions to the MPLS traffic-engineering standard that are called Multiprotocol Lambda Switching (MPλS). This section discusses the Cisco UCP architecture that lets a single management layer manage and provision elements that were previously independently managed.

CHAPTER 10

Advanced MPLS Architectures

Optical Networking

The power of the Internet and the World Wide Web resides in its content. Retrieval of high-quality content from application servers such as Web servers and e-commerce sites in the shortest possible time has driven the "need for speed" for individual and corporate end users alike. Users are demanding affordable high-speed access services such as xDSL and cable modem access while the enterprise market pushes toward high-speed managed IP VPN services with Internet access. In an effort to retain their customer base, service providers are forced to cater to their subscribers' requests for fear of losing them as customers to the next start-up company that can lure them away with offers of low-cost bundled voice and data services with high-speed Internet access. Increased aggregation at the access layer creates the need for bandwidth at the network's distribution and core. This exponential growth has fueled the need for extremely scalable high-bandwidth core technologies.

Technology has seen the limits of bandwidth and transmission speeds over traditional TDM media and headend systems. Traditional networks have been built using a combination of circuit-switched TDM technology and a TDM-capable SONET/SDH infrastructure. Traffic flows over fiber-optic circuits, which terminate or get switched in an electrical device, have to undergo optoelectronic conversion, electrical switching, and an electro-optical conversion process known as OEO conversion, which typically results in latency at the node. The ultimate goal of true optical switching is to eliminate the need for optoelectronic conversion and perform true end-to-end optical switching.

The concept of running data directly over an optical transport network has been fueled by the premise that elimination of unnecessary network layers will lead to a vast reduction in the cost and complexity of the network. Packet-over-SONET is an example of a technology where IP can be directly encapsulated in a SONET frame and can run over a SONET infrastructure without the need for ATM. An example of this elimination of layers is shown in Figure 10-1.

Optical internetworking as defined by the Optical Internetworking Forum (OIF) is a data-optimized network infrastructure in which switches and routers have integrated optical interfaces and are directly connected by fiber or optical network elements, such as dense wavelength division multiplexers (DWDMs).

Figure 10-1 *Elimination of Layers*

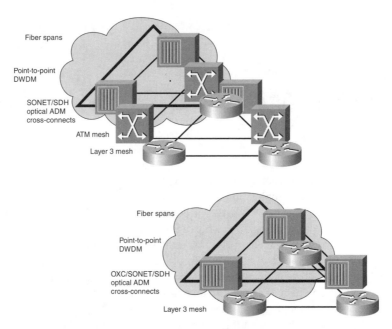

Dense Wavelength Division Multiplexing

Conventional fiber-optic systems use a single wavelength or color injected by an optical transmitter that is a light-emitting diode (LED) in the case of multimode fiber (MMF) or a laser diode in the case of single-mode fiber (SMF). Laser diodes or LEDs perform an electrical-to-optical (EO) conversion of the electrical signal. The light is injected at a precise angle into the core of the fiber-optic cable using a lens, which has a higher refractive index than the cladding. Light pulses are transmitted along the fiber-optic line due to the principle of total internal reflection, which states that when the angle of incidence exceeds a critical value, light cannot leave the core. Instead, the light reflects inward toward the core and bounces back in as a result. Figure 10-2 shows conventional fiber-optic cable types.

The fiber-optic core is the photonic carrier element at the center of the optical fiber. It is commonly made from a combination of silica and germania. Single-mode fiber has a much smaller core than multimode fiber, typically 5 to 10 microns. This uses a graded index scheme in which the refractive index diminishes gradually from the center axis out toward the cladding.

Figure 10-2 *Conventional Fiber-Optic Cable Types*

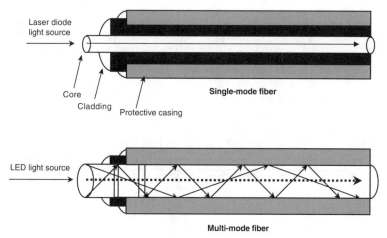

Multimode fiber core diameters typically are 50, 62.5, or 100 micrometers. MMF uses a step index scheme in which there is a distinct refractive index difference between the core and the cladding. Surrounding the core is the optic cladding, made of pure silica. This combination makes the principle of total internal reflection possible. This creates a waveguide effect, which guides the light signal to its destination, where it is detected by a photodetector. The photodetector performs an optical-to-electric (OE) conversion of the signal.

MMF cable segments have a typical distance limitation of 2 km, and intermediate-reach (IR) SMF segments have a distance limitation of 20 km. Long-reach (LR) SMF segments have a typical distance limitation of 40 km. Signal attenuation and degradation are caused primarily by the dispersion and scattering of light within the cable itself. This necessitates the use of fiber-optic amplifiers between rated segments.

DWDM is the process of multiplexing signals of different wavelengths onto a single fiber. This operation creates many virtual fibers, each capable of carrying a different signal. A schematic of a DWDM system is shown in Figure 10-3.

DWDM employs wavelengths to transmit data parallel-by-bit or serial-by-character, which increases the fiber's capacity by assigning incoming optical signals to specific frequencies (wavelength, lambda) within a designated frequency band and then multiplexing the resulting signals out onto one fiber. Each signal can be carried at a different rate (such as OC-3/12/48) and in a different format (SONET, ATM, data, and so on). This can increase the capacity of existing networks without the need for expensive recabling and can tremendously reduce the cost of network infrastructure upgrades. DWDM supports point-to-point, ring, and mesh topologies. Existing fiber in a SONET fiber plant can be easily migrated to DWDM.

Figure 10-3 *DWDM Schematic*

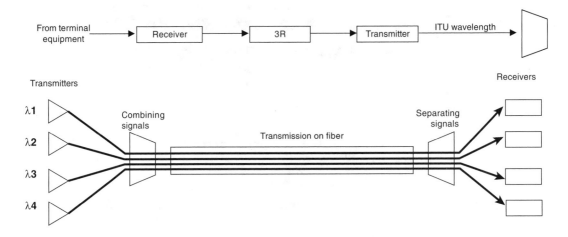

Most DWDM systems support standard SONET/SDH short-reach optical interfaces to which any SONET/SDH-compliant client device can attach. There are two kinds of DWDM systems—metro DWDM and long-haul DWDM. In today's long-haul DWDM systems, the interfaces are most often OC-48c/STM-16c interfaces operating at the 1310 nm wavelength. In addition, other interfaces important in metropolitan areas and access networks are commonly supported: Ethernet, Fast Ethernet, Gigabit Ethernet, ESCON, Sysplex Timer, Sysplex Coupling Facility Links, and Fibre Channel. The new 10 Gigabit Ethernet standard is supported using a very-short-reach (VSR) OC-192 interface over MMF between 10 Gigabit Ethernet and DWDM equipment.

On the client side, there can be SONET/SDH terminals or ADMs, ATM switches, or routers. By converting incoming optical signals into the precise ITU-standard wavelengths to be multiplexed, transponders are currently a key determinant of the openness of DWDM systems. A schematic of the DWDM system with transmission elements is illustrated in Figure 10-4.

The DWDM system performs the following main functions:

- **Generating the signal**—The source, a solid-state laser, must provide stable light within a specific, narrow bandwidth that carries the digital data, modulated as an analog signal. Stability of a light source is a measure of how constant its intensity and wavelength are. The distributed feedback (DFB) laser is well-suited for DWDM applications, because it emits a nearly monochromatic light, is capable of high speeds, and has a favorable signal-to-noise ratio. It has center frequencies in the region around 1310 nm, and from 1520 to 1565 nm. The latter wavelength range is compatible with Erbium Doped Fiber Amplifier (EDFA) fiber-optic amplifiers.

- **Combining the signals**—DWDM systems employ multiplexers to combine the signals. Some inherent loss is associated with multiplexing and demultiplexing. This loss depends on the number of channels, but it can be mitigated with optical amplifiers, which boost all the wavelengths at once without electrical conversion. Arrayed Waveguide Grating (AWG) devices perform multiplexing and demultiplexing operations simultaneously and are also suited for large channel counts.

- **Transmitting the signals**—The effects of crosstalk and optical signal degradation or loss must be reckoned with in fiber-optic transmission. Controlling variables such as channel spacings, wavelength tolerance, and laser power levels can minimize these effects. Over a transmission link, the signal might need to be optically amplified.

- **Separating the received signals**—At the receiving end, the multiplexed signals must be separated or demultiplexed. Demultiplexing must be performed before the light is detected, because photodetectors are inherently broadband devices that cannot selectively detect a single wavelength. An AWG is used for demultiplexing.

- **Receiving the signals**—The demultiplexed signal is received by a photodetector. Two types of photodetectors are widely deployed—the positive-intrinsic-negative (PIN) photodiode and the avalanche photodiode (APD).

Figure 10-4 *DWDM System*

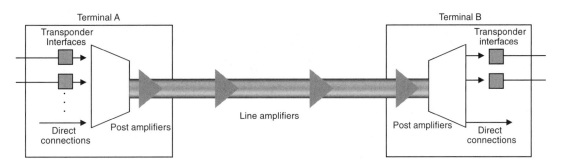

In addition to these functions, a DWDM system must also be equipped with client-side interfaces to receive the input signal. This function is performed by transponders. On the DWDM side are interfaces to the optical fiber that links DWDM systems.

Within the DWDM system, a transponder converts the client optical signal back to an electrical signal and performs the 3R (reshape, retime, retransmit) functions. This electrical signal is then used to drive the WDM laser. Each transponder within the system converts its client's signal to a slightly different wavelength. The wavelengths from all the transponders in the system are then optically multiplexed. In the receive direction of the DWDM system, the reverse process takes place.

Optical Transport Network Elements

The Optical Transport Network (OTN) system is comprised of network elements such as optical amplifiers, wavelength converters, Optical Add Drop Multiplexers (OADMs), and optical cross-connect switches.

Optical Amplifiers

Optical amplifiers are doped fiber strands used to amplify attenuated optical signals with the aim of generating a good signal. They operate in the optical domain without converting the signal into electrical pulses. They are usually found in long-haul networks, where the cumulative loss is huge. Doping a small strand of fiber with an earth metal such as Erbium gives the fiber strand its amplification properties. The noise figure, automatic gain control, bandwidth, and gain flatness characterize the optical amplifier used in a system. EDFA is a common amplifier found in most networks. In practice, signals can travel up to 74 miles (120 km) between amplifiers. At longer distances of 372 to 620 miles (600 to 1000 km), the signal must be regenerated. That is because the optical amplifier merely amplifies the signals and does not perform the 3R functions (reshape, retime, retransmit).

Wavelength Converters

Wavelength converters convert data on an input wavelength onto a different output wavelength within the system's operation bandwidth. This component is used in the routing devices when the wavelength that marks the route to be followed is to be changed.

Optical Add Drop Multiplexer

The OADM is the optical subsystem that facilitates the add and drop of wavelengths into the physical fiber without having to regenerate all the WDM channels. Rather than combining or separating all wavelengths, the OADM can remove some while passing others on. No conversion of the signal from optical to electrical takes place. The system maintains each connection as sequential ports and performs manipulations on them. The wavelengths or channels to be added or dropped can be either preassigned or reconfigured automatically based on the type of implementation. The former is called fixed OADM, and the latter is known as reconfigurable or programmable OADM. Optical amplification components might or might not be present in an OADM, depending on its design.

NOTE	The SONET/SDH Optical Add Drop Multiplexer (ADM) should not be confused with the OADM. The SONET ADM is an OEO device that performs optical-to-electronic conversion before adding or dropping channels into SONET frames. The ADM provides TDM subchannel switching within the wavelength. It then converts the electronic signal back to the wavelength. SONET extends the TDM DS1/DS3 to the OC*n* hierarchy with practical scalability up to OC768 (10 Gbps).

Optical Cross-Connect

The Optical Cross-Connect (OXC) is a DWDM system component that provides cross-connect switching functionality between *n* input ports and *n* output ports, each handling a bundle of multiplexed single-wavelength signals. The OXC permits bandwidth management and supports network reconfiguration. The OXC lets service providers transport and manage wavelengths efficiently at the optical layer. An OXC contains a bit-rate and format-independent optical switch that helps it cross-connect over multiple bit rates such as OC-3, OC-12, OC-48, and OC-192 and formats such as SONET and ATM. The OXC also performs network management, signal monitoring, provisioning and grooming, and restoration at the optical layer. The OXC might also combine the function of the OADM and control plane functionality, depending on its design. The OXC will eventually support full standards-based Multiprotocol Lambda Switching (MPλS).

Optical Gateways

The optical gateway is the device that performs an interface function between electrically encoded protocols and the optical layer. It is also called a transducer or transponder. It provides a common transport structure for the grooming of traffic entering the optical layer. These blocks are essential for maintaining protocol transparency and ensuring maximum bandwidth capacity. The emerging basic format for high-speed transparent transport is ATM, and optical gateways will allow a mix of standard SONET and ATM services.

Multiprotocol Lambda Switching

Multiprotocol Lambda Switching (MPλS) is the optical analogy of MPLS. The MPLS control plane performs all crucial control functions for MPLS data networks. MPLS RSVP-TE extensions or CR-LSDP extensions can be applied to optical networks to unify the control plane for optical network elements.

MPλS approaches the design of control planes for OXC switches and other integrated multifunctional optical switches that leverage existing control-plane techniques developed for MPLS traffic engineering. This combines advances in MPLS traffic engineering control-plane constructs with OXC technology to provide a framework for real-time provisioning of optical channels and to allow the use of uniform semantics for network management and operations control in hybrid networks consisting of OXCs and label-switching routers.

The term OXC is used in the rest of this chapter to indicate an optical switching device.

The current MPLS TE control plane supports these features:

- The ability to disseminate information about both the network topology and available resources

- Constraint-based routing (the ability to compute a path based on a combination of some optimization criteria and a set of constraints)

- The ability to support both resource-related constraints (such as unreserved bandwidth) and administrative constraints

- The ability to resolve contention for available resources via preemption (where a new LSP could preempt an established LSP)

- The ability to have path protection via a combination of primary and secondary (hot standby) LSPs

- The ability to use Layer 1 indications to detect faults

- The ability to specify a path via configuration rather than using constraint-based routing for path computation

The current MPLS TE control plane has most of the functionality needed to control not only routers and ATM LSRs, but also SONET/SDH ADMs and OXCs. Therefore, it forms a firm basis for the UCP.

Labels in MPLS can be viewed as analogous to optical channels in optical networks. LSRs are viewed as analogous to OXCs. The data plane of an LSR uses the label-swapping paradigm to transfer a labeled packet from an input port to an output port. The data plane of an OXC uses a switching matrix to connect an optical channel (OCh) trail from an input port to an output port.

An LSR performs label switching by first establishing a relationship between an <input port, input label> tuple and an <output port, output label> tuple. Likewise, an OXC provisions OCh trails by first establishing a relationship between an <input port, input optical channel> tuple and an <output port, output optical channel> tuple. MPLS uses the label-forwarding information base (LFIB), and MPλS uses the analogous wavelength forwarding information base (WFIB).

The functions of the control plane for both LSRs and OXCs include resource discovery, distributed routing control, and connection management. In particular, the control plane of the LSR is used to discover, distribute, and maintain relevant state information associated with the MPLS network and to initiate and maintain Label-Switched Paths (LSPs) under various MPLS traffic-engineering rules and policies. An LSP is the path through one or more LSRs, followed by a specific forwarding equivalence class. An explicit LSP is one whose route is defined at its origination node.

The control plane of the OXC, on the other hand, is used to discover, distribute, and maintain relevant state information associated with the OTN and to establish and maintain OCh trails under various optical traffic engineering rules and policies. An OCh trail provides a point-to-point optical connection between two access points. At each intermediate OXC along the route of an OCh trail, the OXC switch fabric connects the trail from an input port to an output port.

A distinction between OXCs and LSRs is that the former do not perform packet-level processing in the data plane, but the latter perform datagram devices, which might perform certain packet-level operations in the data plane. A significant conceptual difference is that with LSRs, the forwarding information is carried explicitly as part of the labels appended to data packets, whereas with OXCs, the switching information is implied from the wavelength or optical channel.

Each OXC transmits messages over a signaling network to neighboring OXCs. MPλS then adds additional information to internal gateway protocols such as OSPF to propagate information about optical network topology and resource availability. A constraint-based routing algorithm uses the network topology and state information to compute routes through the network for optical connections. As soon as a route is selected, MPλS uses a similar message set to that of explicit routing in an MPLS signaling protocol (RSVP and/or CR-LDP) to affect cross-connects along the selected route. One notable feature is that OXCs do not support label stacking in the current standard. Because an OXC cannot perform label push-pop operations, the start/end of a nested LSP must be on an edge router. In this situation, the wavelength of the *container* OCh trail itself constitutes the outermost label.

Originally proposed to the Internet Engineering Task Force (IETF) as MPλS, the standards body has progressed to the point where the proposal is now incorporated into drafts under the heading of Generalized MPLS (GMPLS). However, collectively, these are often called Multiprotocol Lambda Switching.

Optical UNI

The Optical Internetworking Forum (OIF) is the standards body that is developing an Optical User Network Interface (O-UNI), which provides an interface between optical clients and an optical network. The O-UNI defines a link for communicating control, signaling, and data packets between the optical client (such as an IP router) and the adjacent optical transport-networking device (such as an OXC). The O-UNI was created so that carriers could offer a simple, open, external interface for accessing circuit-based services across an Optical Transport Network (OTN). The O-UNI defines only the interface and protocol interactions between the client and an adjacent optical device. An O-UNI can be static, meaning that only control information (such as checking the identity and state of UNI links and devices) is exchanged between the client and OXC device. An O-UNI can also be dynamic, where a source client generates signaling information, subsequently sending it over the UNI to dynamically establish an optical connection with a target client.

A client can be an IP router, ATM switch, SONET/SDH Add-Drop Multiplexer (ADM), or any optical client device that requests services from the OTN. The actions that can be invoked over the O-UNI include light-path creation, deletion, modification, and status inquiry. A client also might want to register or deregister its identity with the adjacent OXC.

In contrast to the implied peer model of MPλS, which calls for routing protocol exchanges, including topology information between adjacent devices, the O-UNI model requires only a topology subset in which the OTN topology is hidden from an overlay network of attached client devices. The UCP does not restrict a carrier or service provider to choosing only one of these implementations. UCP takes advantage of the fact that MPλS and O-UNI are similar in that both employ the same protocol mechanism incorporating extensions being defined within the IETF, including RSVP and Constraint-Based Label Distribution Protocol (CR-LDP) for signaling and the Link Management Protocol (LMP) for link management and discovery between adjacent nodes. Both protocols let the client, source, or edge device request through signaling a dynamically established optical connection with a target device.

The Label Distribution Protocol (LDP) has been defined for distributing labels among LSRs in an MPLS network. Two LSRs that directly communicate using LDP to exchange labels are called *LDP peers*. An *LDP session* is realized over a TCP connection required between peer LSRs. LDP procedures permit LSRs to establish LSPs through an MPLS network by mapping network layer routing information directly to data link layer switched paths.

RSVP with Traffic Engineering extensions (RSVP-TE) has been defined for establishing LSPs subject to routing constraints in an MPLS network. The RSVP-TE definition includes additional procedures, message, and object formats over the base RSVP definition. GMPLS signaling extends basic MPLS signaling procedures and abstract messages to cover different types of switching applications such as circuit switching, wavelength switching, and the like.

The basic difference between the IETF MPλS and OIF O-UNI standards approaches is the amount of information exchanged between client and OTN. A phased deployment of the major components of both protocols within the UCP will let carriers and providers alike implement the solution most suitable to their needs.

Unified Control Plane

MPLS operates on a forwarding plane and a control plane. The control plane for MPLS can be extended to the optical layer. This forms the basis of the Unified Control Plane (UCP).

Existing packet-oriented control planes, such as those used by MPLS, were designed to encompass devices that could recognize packet and/or cell boundaries. The header contents are processed in order to create the LSP and make forwarding decisions. However, within OTNs, devices and their constituent protocols make their forwarding decisions based on time slots (TDM), wavelengths (lambda), or physical ports (fiber) and are therefore unable to forward data based on the information carried in either packet or cell headers. By providing protocol extensions to the control plane to support the OTN devices that are TDM-, lambda-, and fiber switch-capable, the UCP provides a standardized signaling interface between the optical layer and the higher data service layers such as IP, ATM, and SONET/SDH. The various layers covered by the UCP are shown in Figure 10-5.

Figure 10-5 *Unified Control Plane*

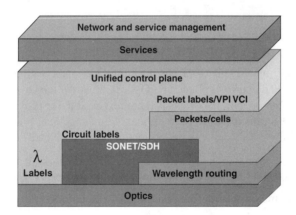

The UCP is based on two key protocols: IP and MPLS. One of the fundamental benefits of MPLS is the separation of the control and forwarding planes. This simple concept is at the heart of the value of MPLS, because it creates a network provisioning and engineering framework that is independent of the network elements themselves. This significantly simplifies network design and operation, radically increases service velocity, and significantly reduces provisioning costs.

The independent forwarding plane allows a variety of mechanisms to establish the network topology map. This is performed predominantly by using IP routing protocols such as OSPF or Intermediate System-to-Intermediate System (IS-IS). When the basic network is in place, flexible control of topology constraints enables the provisioning of Virtual Private Networks (VPNs), traffic engineering, restoration, and so on. A forwarding database, based on labels, is constructed from the topology and policy information. This is known as the forwarding information base (FIB). An independent forwarding plane lets this forwarding information be implemented on almost any type of device, from IP routers to ATM switches to optical cross-connects. The same control mechanism provisions transport and services independent of the switching platform. The implementation on each device takes advantage of the native forwarding capabilities of the underlying switch. This complements the underlying native forwarding capabilities of the device.

UCP adds several powerful elements to network operations, including the ability to provision new services in large-scale carrier networks. This new service architecture is best described through a comparison with the service architecture of a contemporary service provider.

The unified control plane allows a single management group to provision services in the network from end to end. Figure 10-5 shows the application of UCP in the delivery of end-to-end services.

UCP incorporates extensions to the MPLS traffic-engineering standard that are referred to as MPλS.

UCP Management and Control Architecture

The Unified Control Plane (UCP) architecture provides a comprehensive and open management and control architecture. Optical network elements (NEs) within an optical network contain operating systems that are responsible for providing the network control functions, data transmission functions, and NE management functions for those elements. For the purposes of discussion, these functions can be divided into three categories:

- **Control plane**—Includes functions related to networking control capabilities such as routing, signaling, and provisioning, as well as resource and service discovery.

- **Data plane**—Includes functions related to data forwarding and transmission.

- **Management plane**—Includes functions related to the management of NE, networking layers, and network services.

Complex telecommunications networks consist of many layer networks, including IP, ATM, SONET/SDH, and optical. Each of these has client/server relationships. For management and operational reasons, the layer independence has been carefully guarded to allow one layer to be modified without impacting the layers above or below it. Each layer has a control plane that is responsible for all the network control functions within the layer.

The UCP provides capabilities, such as bandwidth on demand and interlayer protection schemes, that consequently require communication among the network layers. This interlayer communication can be described as a layer control plane, but it does not fully control any of the layer networks. Instead, it provides signaling and other communications between the existing network layer control planes. Within the UCP, IP, ATM, SONET/SDH, and optical control planes, gateway interfaces are provided for signaling across the interlayer control plane. The UCP management schematic is shown in Figure 10-6.

Figure 10-6 *Unified Control Plane Management*

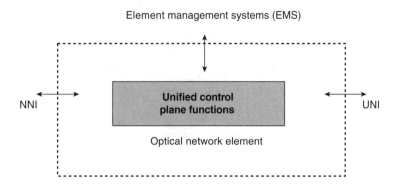

Standards bodies, including the IETF and OIF, are working toward specification of these gateway interfaces to allow all vendors to include the control and management functions for light-path provisioning and management. This will allow carriers to integrate their existing management and operation support systems, thus speeding up the deployment of the optical network technology. These control functions will be accessible via an NMS interface, an NE management plane interface, UNI, and Network-to-Network Interface (NNI). An example of an element management system (EMS) is Cisco Transport Manager (CTM), as shown in Figure 10-7.

Figure 10-7 *CTM Element Management Model for OTN*

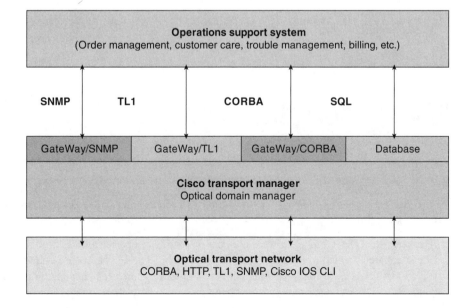

CTM has inherent support for SONET/SDH and DWDM, as well as IP and Ethernet, providing an integrated optical transport domain management. CTM enables Operations Support System (OSS) automation by functioning as a mediator of management information and functionality through open Transaction Language 1 (TL-1) and Simple Network Management Protocol (SNMP) interfaces. The SNMP interface forwards traps to an SNMP NMS, whereas the TL-1 interface supports autonomous alarm, event, and performance data reporting, as well as full command and response in the native syntax of the managed NEs.

NOTE   Common Object Request Broker Architecture (CORBA) has emerged as the accepted technology standard for integrating the components of the next generation of OSSs. CORBA will be implemented in future releases of CTM.

UCP Overlay Model

In the overlay model, the basic premise is that there are two very distinct control planes, as shown in Figure 10-8. The routers at the edge of the network have the primary intelligence and communicate with the optical transport network via a signaling interface.

Figure 10-8 *UCP Overlay Model*

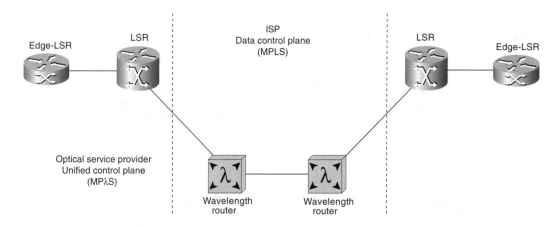

The routing, topology distribution, and signaling protocols for the router and optical network are different.

IP routers and OTN OXC equipment are contained in two separate administrative domains. IP routers are attached to the nearest OXC over a UNI. The IP routers are unaware of the OTN topology and form adjacencies with each other over the OTN-provided optical connections; they can subsequently exchange topology information regarding the IP network. In short, the IP network and OTN each maintain their own set of signaling and routing protocols (control plane), maintaining separate topologies and exchanging little or no topology information. This does not inhibit the routing function of the IP network, because the IP routers can still request (signal for) the OTN to establish an optical connection with other IP routers.

Providers who initially want to keep the OTN and IP (or other client network) separate are expected to deploy the overlay model. Common reasons for this include existing administrative control or the fact that their OTN currently offers billing for circuit-based services connecting a variety of different client types (including IP routers, ATM switches, and SONET/SDH ADMs).

UCP Peer Model

The peer model has essentially one control plane (UCP). Within this model, the Layer 3 devices and the OXC act as true peers, as shown in Figure 10-9. The IP and optical networks share a common routing protocol with optics-based extensions. This allows a router to compute an end-to-end path across an optical infrastructure, because the IP routers can signal for an optical connection with other IP routers—including the OXC equipment within the OTN. The peer model provides a unified control plane for IP and optical NEs— one that is optimized for IP-based services, with all the IP routers and OXC devices sharing a common view of the entire network topology.

Figure 10-9 *UCP Peer Model*

The peer model has the following characteristics:

* IP routers and OTN OXC equipment are within a single administrative domain.

* IP routers and directly attached OXC neighbors form adjacencies to exchange topology information. This is possible because the IP routers and OXCs run a common set of routing and signaling protocols and use a single addressing scheme.

Deployment Options

IP-based service providers who own and manage their own router, fiber, and OTN infrastructure are more inclined to go with a peer model implementation of MPλS.

Providers who offer multiple services over their OTN will probably choose an overlay solution. As noted earlier, providers have the flexibility to use any combination. For example, a provider could configure a domain of IP routers and OXCs all running an MPLS- or MPλS-based control plane to support ISP services. Some OXCs might also support external O-UNIs that allow client devices to request and receive connection-oriented services. MPλS protocols in the backbone can handle the routing and signaling of O-UNI connection requests. If desired, the provider can also use more traditional, centralized NMS-based tools for provisioning certain service-specific connections.

The transitions from the overlay model to a peer model, and from independent protection to coordinated restoration, can be scheduled, depending on service requirements (service upgrade, legacy equipment, new build, and so on). Network engineers and operators can choose the number of data-plane layers and restoration techniques and control the entire network using UCP. Money is saved, because large-scale network upgrades are not required. A UCP with both O-UNI and MPλS adherence supports a timely and cost-effective migration. The phased approach for UCP deployment is illustrated in Figure 10-10.

Figure 10-10 *UCP Phased Deployment*

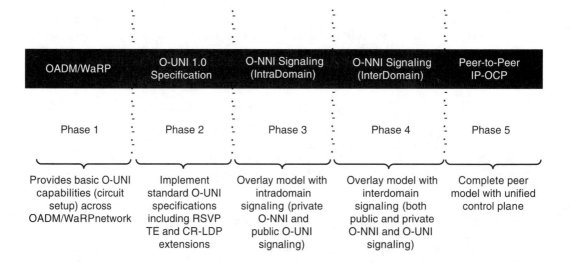

Phase 1: SONET DCC Channels

Phase 1 of the UCP deployment recommends using the SONET Data Country Code (DCC) channel for end-to-end connection of SONET-based optical equipment, as shown in Figure 10-11. The ONS 15000 series supports the SONET/SDH DCC channel and, in addition, the capabilities of an IP stack over the same channels. This provides an end-to-end channel between the Cisco 12000 series routers, connected via OC-48, either directly to or through metro optical transport Cisco ONS 15454 optical network systems. These can then be carried through the DCC in an ONS 15000 wavelength-routed OTN, enabling a channel capable of carrying both data and control information. In Phase 1 of the UCP, the control information is passed through this channel, thereby being labeled as in-fiber and in-band. The Phase 1 deployment approach is illustrated in Figure 10-12.

Figure 10-11 *Phase 1: SONET DCC Channels*

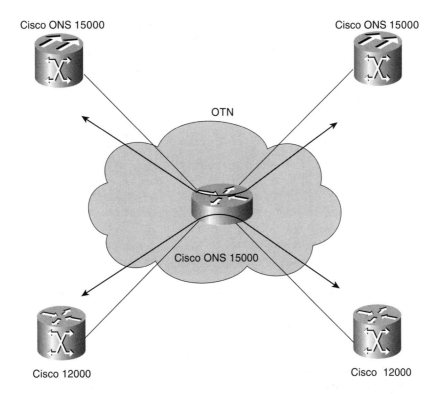

Cisco ONS 15000

Cisco ONS 15000

OTN

Cisco ONS 15000

Cisco 12000

Cisco 12000

Such an implementation also maintains the operations, administration, maintenance, and provisioning (OAM&P) capabilities in the network, providing the ability to maintain or deploy automated or manual end-to-end configuration and provisioning through existing standard and enhanced interfaces. The UCP solution, combined with a wavelength-routed core network, reduces the layering of equipment, thereby removing functional overlap and enabling an optical transport that complements IP.

Figure 10-12 *Phase 1: Optical UNI*

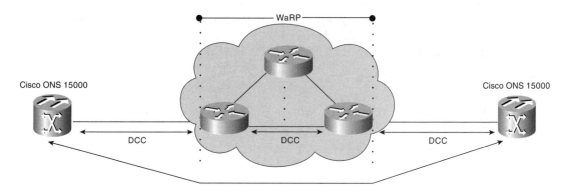

<table>
<tr><td>NOTE</td><td>The Wavelength router network is controlled by a dynamic routing protocol known as the Wavelength Routing Protocol (WaRP). WaRP is a prestandard version of an optical control plane built on the well-known and tested implementations of OSPF and PNNI. WaRP provides an immediate solution to build optical networks that can be provisioned easily and restored rapidly. Each instance of WaRP in the network is completely upgradeable to the O-UNI or optical NNI (O-NNI) standards via software upgrades as the standards are completed. WaRP supports mesh restoration. WaRP is currently supported on certain ONS 15000 models.</td></tr>
</table>

Phase 2: O-UNI with Static NNI

Phase 2 describes an overlay model in which the client—typically a router/switch-based network—communicates its requirements with the OTN network via the standard OIF-derived UNI. This creates a network where the client or outer NEs (routers and switches) are not aware of inner NEs (OTN components).

The outer elements (UNI-C) treat the inner network (UNI-N) as a static circuit, or static NNI. Topology information concerning the inner transport network is not published to the outer UNI-capable elements. However, these outer elements can discover each other through or across the inner transport network and its elements. The procedures for discovery, label routing, and resource allocations are outlined in the OIF UNI Specification, which is based on CR-LDP and RSVP. Figure 10-13 illustrates a Phase 2 deployment.

Phase 2 maintains a consistent UCP management view of all NEs, especially for the purpose of reporting accurate network topology. Unlike the previous phase, Phase 2 allows visibility and management of devices within each domain, based on standards.

Figure 10-13 *Phase 2: O-UNI with Static NNI*

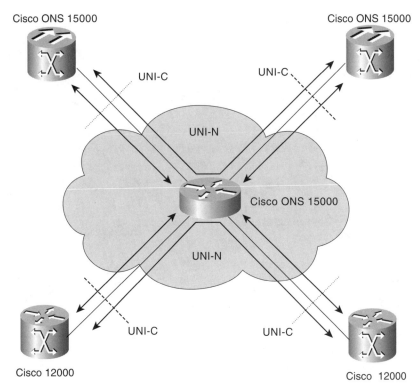

Phase 3: Intradomain NNI

Phase 3 describes an overlay model with the addition of signaling between dissimilar NEs. This introduces the concept of an NNI. The NNI provides a method whereby a standard signaling protocol is used within a carrier's OTN. There are two models for the NNI: public and private. Phase 3 includes the provision for an intradomain or intracarrier NNI. Figure 10-14 illustrates a Phase 3 deployment.

The distinction between the private interfaces and the public interfaces is necessary because the two types of interfaces have different levels of access and security trust. The interfaces between the carrier's optical network and its clients are public UNI (PUB-UNI), and the interfaces between optical networks of different operators are the public NNI (PUB-NNI)— a capability that is available in Phase 4. Phase 3 allows the outer (client, or edge device) elements of the network to request resources from the inner OTN elements, even if the inner and outer elements do not share a common control plane. These are the first steps toward a common (peer) control plane, with an implementation based on emerging standards. Phase 3 also features a consistent UCP management view of all NEs.

Figure 10-14 *Phase 3: Intradomain NNI*

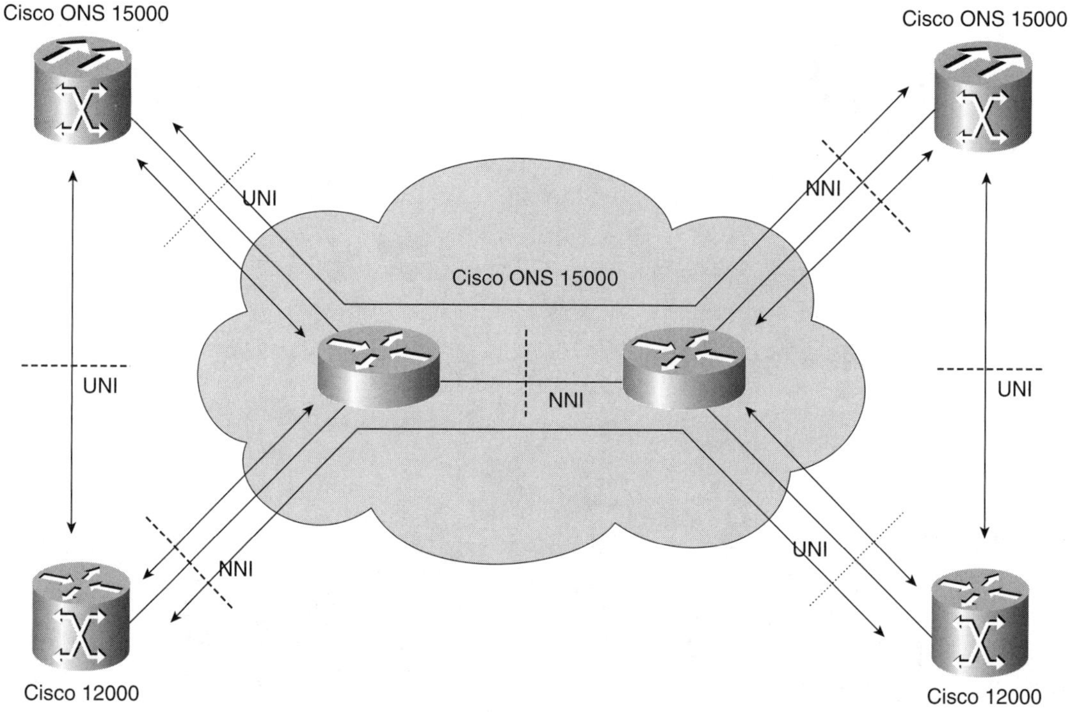

Phase 4: Interdomain NNI

Phase 4 continues the overlay model from Phase 3 but adds the important capability of interdomain and, hence, intercarrier signaling. This is known as the interdomain NNI. An example of Phase 4 deployment is shown in Figure 10-15. Phase 4 also features a consistent UCP management view of all NEs.

Phase 5: Unified Control Plane

The final phase of UCP deployment delivers a complete peer-to-peer network capability to span multiple carrier and provider networks. This functionality enables seamless internetworking between customer and carrier networks alike. The peer-to-peer model provides the ability to dynamically request and create a light path between a customer's remotely located devices through multiple carrier networks. An example of a full UCP-compliant architecture is shown in Figure 10-16.

Figure 10-15 *Phase 4: Interdomain NNI*

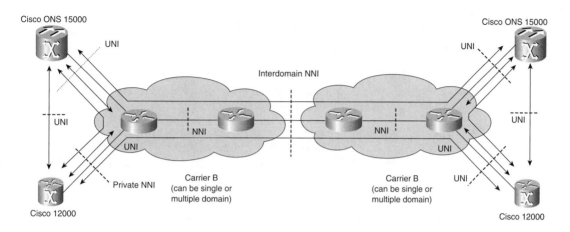

Figure 10-16 *Phase 5: Unified Control Plane Architecture*

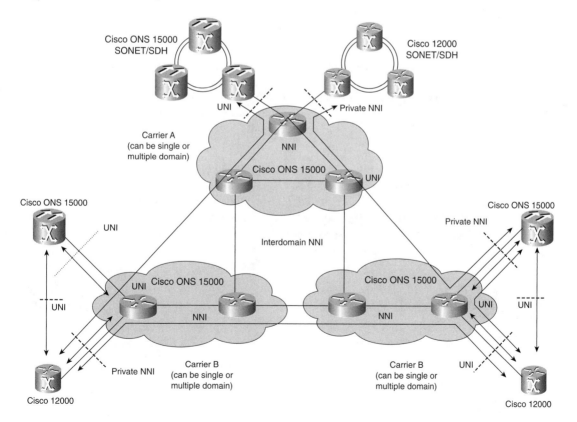

In this complete solution, carriers can deliver services over network architectures optimized for IP, or multiservice backbones.

Summary

Dense wavelength division multiplexing (DWDM) is the process of multiplexing signals of different wavelengths onto a single fiber. Through this operation, many virtual fibers are created, each capable of carrying a different signal.

Multiprotocol Lambda Switching (MPλS) is the optical analogy of MPLS. The MPLS control plane performs all crucial control functions for MPLS data networks. MPLS RSVP-TE extensions or CR-LSDP extensions can be applied to optical networks to unify the control plane for optical network elements (NEs).

The Unified Control Plane (UCP) describes an architecture that extends the MPLS control plane to the optical layer. It is a model of distributed intelligence that incorporates the NEs themselves, which contain much of the information and functions that are necessary to accomplish the control-plane tasks. The deployment and scope of UCP is across multiple platforms and includes devices such as traditional routers and optical platforms. All the NEs within the administrative domain share control information based on standard protocols and extensions, ensuring interoperability.

The Cisco UCP architecture allows a single management layer to manage and provision elements that were previously independently managed. Although existing protocols continue to be used, the availability of both O-UNI and MPλS control-plane models within the UCP on network elements provides a unified solution for new networks and a migration path for established operators seeking to simplify and move to an efficient and scalable IP+optical architecture.

UCP is the key enabler of mesh networking. UCP and mesh networks offer a unified management layer and flexible end-to-end provisioning, along with the bandwidth engineering efficiencies of mesh networking. Mesh architectures improve upon current methods for bandwidth engineering through efficient routing of "working" traffic and efficient mesh restoration schemes.

MPLS Command Reference

This MPLS command reference provides tables that document the commonly used MPLS commands. Cisco's prestandard equivalent tag-switching commands are provided, along with their MPLS counterparts. Sample usage of many of these commands can be found in the case studies and examples throughout this book. For sample usage of the remaining commands listed here, refer to the IOS Command Reference and Configuration Guide. These documents are available on Cisco's documentation CD-ROM and on Cisco Connection Online.

Table A-1 displays various generic MPLS commands, which are used to configure MPLS on label-switched routers.

Table A-1 *MPLS Commands*

MPLS Command	Tag-Switching Command	Description
ip cef	**ip cef**	Enables Cisco Express Forwarding. (Global mode)
ip cef distributed	**ip cef distributed**	Enables Distributed Cisco Express Forwarding for modules that support distributed processing, such as the Versatile Interface Processor (VIP). (Global mode)
clear mpls traffic-eng auto-bw timers	No equivalent tag-switching command	Reinitializes the automatic bandwidth adjustment feature on a platform. (Exec mode)
mpls atm control-vc	**tag-switching atm control-vc**	Configures the VPI and VCI to be used for the initial link to the label-switching peer device. (Interface mode)
mpls atm vpi	**tag-switching atm vpi**	Configures the range of values to be used in the VPI field for label VCs (LVCs). (Interface mode)
mpls ip (global configuration)	**tag-switching ip (global configuration)**	Enables MPLS forwarding of IPv4 packets along normally routed paths for the platform. (Global mode)

continues

Table A-1 *MPLS Commands (Continued)*

MPLS Command	Tag-Switching Command	Description
mpls ip (interface configuration)	**tag-switching ip (interface configuration)**	Enables MPLS forwarding of IPv4 packets along normally routed paths for a particular interface. (Interface mode)
mpls ip default-route	**tag-switching ip default-route**	Enables the distribution of labels associated with the IP default route. (Global mode)
mpls ip propagate-ttl	**tag-switching ip propagate-ttl**	Sets the time-to-live (TTL) value when an IP packet is encapsulated in MPLS. (Exec mode)
mpls ip ttl-expiration pop	No equivalent tag-switching command	Specifies how a packet with an expired TTL value is forwarded. Forwards packets using the global IP routing table or the original label stack, determined by the number of labels in the packet. (Privileged Exec mode)
mpls label protocol (global configuration)	No equivalent tag-switching command	Specifies the default label distribution protocol for the platform. (Global mode)
mpls label protocol (interface configuration)	No equivalent tag-switching command	Specifies the label distribution protocol to be used on a given interface. (Interface mode)
mpls label range	**tag-switching tag-range downstream**	Configures the range of local labels available for use on packet interfaces. (Global mode)
mpls ldp address-message	No equivalent tag-switching command	Specifies the advertisement of platform addresses to a label-controlled ATM (LC-ATM) LDP peer. (Interface mode)
mpls ldp advertise-labels	**tag-switching advertise-tags**	Controls the distribution of locally assigned (incoming) labels via the Label Distribution Protocol (LDP). (Global mode)
mpls ldp advertise-labels old-style	No equivalent tag-switching command	Causes the interpretation of the **for prefix-access-list** parameter for **mpls ldp advertise-labels** commands to be interpreted according to the method used in earlier software versions. (Global mode)
mpls ldp atm control-mode	**tag-switching atm allocation-mode**	Controls the mode used for handling label binding requests on LC-ATM interfaces. (Global mode)
mpls ldp atm vc-merge	**tag-switching atm vc-merge**	Controls whether vc-merge (multipoint-to-point) capability is supported for unicast label VCs. (Global mode)

Table A-1   *MPLS Commands (Continued)*

MPLS Command	Tag-Switching Command	Description
mpls ldp backoff	No equivalent tag-switching command	Configures parameters for the LDP backoff mechanism. (Global mode)
mpls ldp discovery	**tag-switching tdp discovery**	Configures the interval between transmission of consecutive LDP discovery hello messages, or the hold time for a discovered LDP neighbor, or the neighbors from which requests for targeted hello messages may be honored. (Global mode)
mpls ldp discovery transport-address	No equivalent tag-switching command	Specifies the transport address advertised in LDP Discovery Hello messages sent on an interface. (Interface mode)
mpls ldp explicit-null	No equivalent tag-switching command	Causes a router to advertise an Explicit Null label in situations where it would normally advertise an Implicit Null label. (Global mode)
mpls ldp holdtime	**tag-switching tdp holdtime**	Changes the time for which an LDP session is maintained in the absence of LDP messages from the session peer. (Global mode)
mpls ldp loop-detection	No equivalent tag-switching command	Enables the LDP optional loop-detection mechanism. (Global mode)
mpls ldp maxhops	**tag-switching atm maxhops**	Limits the number of hops permitted in an LSP established by the downstream-on-demand method of label distribution. (Global mode)
mpls ldp neighbor	No equivalent tag-switching command	Configures a password key for use with the TCP Message Digest 5 (MD5) Signature Option for the session TCP connection with the specified neighbor. (Global mode)
mpls ldp router-id	No equivalent tag-switching command	Specifies a preferred interface for determining the LDP router ID. (Global mode)
mpls ldp targeted-sessions	No equivalent tag-switching command	Configures the use of LDP for "targeted" sessions. (Global mode)
mpls mtu	**tag-switching mtu**	Sets the per-interface maximum transmission unit (MTU) for labeled packets. (Interface mode)

continues

Table A-1   *MPLS Commands (Continued)*

MPLS Command	Tag-Switching Command	Description
mpls traffic-eng auto-bw timers	No equivalent tag-switching command	Enables automatic bandwidth adjustment for a platform and starts output rate sampling for tunnels configured for automatic bandwidth adjustment. (Global mode)
No equivalent MPLS command	**tag-control-protocol vsi**	Configures the use of VSI on a particular master control port. (Interface mode)
No equivalent MPLS command	**tag-switching atm multi-vc**	Configures a router subinterface to create one or more tag VCs over which packets of different classes are sent. (ATM subinterface submode)
No equivalent MPLS command	**tag-switching atm vp-tunnel**	Specifies an interface or a subinterface as a VP tunnel. (Interface mode)
No equivalent MPLS command	**tag-switching cos-map**	Creates a class map that specifies how classes map to label VCs when combined with a prefix map. (Global mode)
No equivalent MPLS command	**tag-switching prefix-map**	Configures a router to use a specified CoS map when a label destination prefix matches the specified access list. (ATM subinterface submode)
show mpls atm-ldp bindings	**show tag-switching atm-tdp bindings**	Displays specified entries from the ATM label-binding database. (Exec mode)
show mpls atm-ldp capability	**show tag-switching atm-tdp capability**	Displays the ATM MPLS capabilities negotiated with LDP neighbors for LC-ATM interfaces. (Exec mode)
show mpls forwarding-table	**show tag-switching forwarding-table**	Displays the contents of the MPLS label forwarding information base (LFIB). (Exec mode)
show mpls interfaces	**show tag-switching interfaces**	Displays information about one or more interfaces that have been configured for label switching. (Exec mode)
show mpls ip binding	No equivalent tag-switching command	Displays information about label bindings learned by LDP. (Exec mode)
show mpls label range	No equivalent tag-switching command	Displays the range of local labels available for use on packet interfaces. (Exec mode)

Table A-1   *MPLS Commands (Continued)*

MPLS Command	Tag-Switching Command	Description
show mpls ldp backoff	No equivalent tag-switching command	Displays information about the configured session setup backoff parameters and any potential LDP peers with which session setup attempts are being throttled. (Privileged Exec mode)
show mpls ldp bindings	**show tag-switching tdp bindings**	Displays the contents of the label information base (LIB). (Privileged Exec mode)
show mpls ldp discovery	**show tag-switching tdp discovery**	Displays the status of the LDP discovery process or a list of interfaces over which the LDP discovery is running. (Privileged Exec mode)
show mpls ldp neighbor	**show tag-switching tdp neighbor**	Displays the status of Label Distribution Protocol (LDP) sessions. (Privileged Exec mode)
show mpls ldp parameters	**show tag-switching tdp parameters**	Displays the available LDP (TDP) parameters. (Exec mode)
No equivalent MPLS command	**show tag-switching tsp-tunnels**	Displays information about the configuration and status of selected tunnels. (Privileged Exec mode)
No equivalent MPLS command	**show xtagatm cross-connect**	Displays information about the LSC's view of the cross-connect table on the remotely controlled ATM switch. (Exec mode)
No equivalent MPLS command	**show xtagatm vc**	Displays information about terminating VCs on extended label ATM (XTagATM) interfaces. (Exec mode)
debug mpls adjacency	**debug tag-switching adjacency**	Displays changes to label-switching entries in the adjacency database. (Exec mode)
debug mpls atm-ldp api	**debug tag-switching atm-tdp api**	Displays information about the VCI allocation of label VCs, label-free requests, and cross-connect requests. (Exec mode)
debug mpls atm-ldp routes	**debug tag-switching atm-tdp routes**	Displays information about the state of the routes for which VCI requests are being made. (Exec mode)
debug mpls atm-ldp states	**debug tag-switching atm-tdp states**	Displays information about LVC state transitions as they occur. (Exec mode)

continues

Table A-1   *MPLS Commands (Continued)*

MPLS Command	Tag-Switching Command	Description
debug mpls events	**debug tag-switching events**	Displays information about significant MPLS events. (Privileged Exec mode)
debug mpls ldp advertisements	**debug tag-switching tdp advertisements**	Displays information about the advertisement of labels and interface addresses to LDP peers. (Privileged Exec mode)
debug mpls ldp bindings	**debug tag-switching tdp bindings**	Displays information about addresses and label bindings learned from LDP peers by means of LDP Downstream Unsolicited label distribution. (Privileged Exec mode)
debug mpls ldp targeted-neighbors	**debug tag-switching tdp directed-neighbors**	Displays information about the target neighbor mechanism. (Privileged Exec mode)
debug mpls ldp peer state-machine	**debug tag-switching tdp peer state-machine**	Displays information about state transitions for LDP sessions. (Privileged Exec mode)
debug mpls ldp messages	**debug tag-switching tdp pies sent**	Displays information about LDP messages sent to or received from LDP peers. (Privileged Exec mode)
debug mpls ldp session io	**debug tag-switching tdp pies received**	Displays the contents of LDP messages sent to and received from LDP peers. (Privileged Exec mode)
debug mpls ldp session state-machine	**debug tag-switching tdp session state-machine**	Displays information about state transitions for LDP sessions. (Privileged Exec mode)
debug mpls ldp transport connections	**debug tag-switching tdp transport connections**	Displays information about the TCP connections used to support LDP sessions. (Privileged Exec mode)
debug mpls ldp transport events	**debug tag-switching tdp transport events**	Displays information about events related to the LDP peer discovery mechanism. (Privileged Exec mode)
debug mpls lfib cef	**debug tag-switching tfib cef**	Displays detailed information about label rewrites being created, resolved, and deactivated as CEF routes are added, changed, or removed. (Privileged Exec mode)
debug mpls lfib enc	**debug tag-switching tfib enc**	Displays detailed information about label encapsulations while label rewrites are created or updated and placed into the label forwarding information base (LFIB). (Privileged Exec mode)

Table A-1   *MPLS Commands (Continued)*

MPLS Command	Tag-Switching Command	Description
debug mpls lfib lsp	**debug tag-switching tfib tsp**	Displays detailed information about label rewrites being created and deleted as TSP tunnels are added or removed. (Privileged Exec mode)
debug mpls lfib state	**debug tag-switching tfib state**	Traces what happens when label switching is enabled or disabled. (Privileged Exec mode)
debug mpls lfib struct	**debug tag-switching tfib struct**	Traces the allocation and freeing of LFIB-related data structures, such as the LFIB itself, label rewrites, and label-info data. (Privileged Exec mode)
debug mpls packets	**debug tag-switching packets**	Displays labeled packets switched by the host router. (Privileged Exec mode)

Table A-2 displays various MPLS Virtual Private Network commands, which are used to configure MPLS VPNs on label-switched routers.

Table A-2   *MPLS VPN Commands*

MPLS VPN Command	Description
address-family	Enters the address family submode for configuring routing protocols such as BGP, RIP, and static routing. (Router mode)
address-family ipv4 [unicast]	Configures sessions that carry standard IPv4 address prefixes. (Router mode)
address-family ipv4 [unicast] vrf vrf_name	Specifies the name of a VPN routing/forwarding instance (VRF) to associate with submode commands. (Router mode)
address-family vpnv4[unicast]	Configures sessions that carry customer VPN-IPv4 prefixes, each of which has been made globally unique by the addition of an 8-byte route distinguisher. (Router mode)
clear ip route vrf	Removes routes from the VRF routing table. (Exec mode)
exit-address-family	Exits the address family submode. (Address-Family mode)
import map	Configures an import route map for a VRF. (VRF mode)
ip route vrf	Establishes static routes for a VRF. (Global mode)
ip vrf	Configures a VRF routing table. (Global mode)
ip vrf forwarding	Associates a VRF with an interface or subinterface. (Interface mode)
neighbor activate	Enables the exchange of information with a neighboring BGP router. (Address-Family mode)

continues

Table A-2 *MPLS VPN Commands (Continued)*

MPLS VPN Command	Description
rd	Creates routing and forwarding tables for a VRF. (VRF mode)
route-target	Creates a route-target extended community for a VRF. (VRF mode)
show ip bgp vpnv4	Displays VPN address information from the BGP table. (Exec mode)
show ip cef vrf	Displays the CEF forwarding table associated with a VRF. (Exec mode)
show ip protocols vrf	Displays the routing protocol information associated with a VRF. (Exec mode)
show ip route vrf	Displays the IP routing table associated with a VRF. (Exec mode)
show ip vrf	Displays the set of defined VRFs and associated interfaces. (Exec mode)
show tag-switching forwarding vrf	Displays label forwarding entries and information for advertised VRF routes associated with a particular VRF or IP prefix. (Exec mode)
debug ip bgp	Displays information related to processing BGPs. (Exec mode)

Table A-3 displays various MPLS traffic engineering commands, which are used to configure MPLS TE on label-switched routers.

Table A-3 *MPLS Traffic Engineering Commands*

MPLS Traffic Engineering Command	Description
append-after	Inserts a path entry after a specific index number. (IP-Explicit-Path mode)
index	Inserts or modifies a path entry at a specific index. (IP-Explicit-Path mode)
ip explicit-path	Enters the subcommand mode for IP explicit paths to create or modify named paths. (Global mode)
list	Shows all or part of the explicit path or paths. (IP-Explicit-Path mode)
metric-style narrow	Configures a router to generate and accept old-style TLVs. (Router mode)
metric-style transition	Configures a router to generate and accept both old-style and new-style TLVs. (Router mode)

Table A-3 *MPLS Traffic Engineering Commands (Continued)*

MPLS Traffic Engineering Command	Description
metric-style wide	Configures a router to generate and accept only new-style TLVs. (Router mode)
mpls traffic-eng	Turns on the flooding of MPLS traffic engineering link information into the indicated IS-IS level. (Router mode)
mpls traffic-eng area	Turns on MPLS traffic engineering for the indicated IS-IS level. (Router mode)
mpls traffic-eng administrative-weight	Overrides a link's IGP administrative weight (cost). (Interface mode)
mpls traffic-eng attribute-flags	Sets the user-specified attribute flags for the interface. (Interface mode)
mpls traffic-eng flooding thresholds	Sets a link's reserved bandwidth thresholds. (Interface mode)
mpls traffic-eng link timers bandwidth-hold	Sets the length of time that bandwidth is "held" for an RSVP Path message while waiting for the corresponding RSVP Resv message to come back. (Global mode)
mpls traffic-eng link timers periodic-flooding	Sets the length of the interval used for periodic flooding. (Global mode)
mpls traffic-eng logging lsp	Logs certain traffic engineering label-switched path (LSP) events. (Router mode)
mpls traffic-eng logging tunnel	Logs certain traffic engineering tunnel events. (Router mode)
mpls traffic-eng reoptimize	Forces immediate reoptimization of all traffic engineering tunnels. (Exec mode)
mpls traffic-eng reoptimize events	Turns on automatic reoptimization of MPLS traffic engineering when certain events occur, such as when an interface becomes operational. (Router mode)
mpls traffic-eng reoptimize timers frequency	Controls the frequency at which tunnels with established LSPs are checked for better LSPs. (Global mode)
mpls traffic-eng router-id	Specifies that the traffic engineering router identifier for the node is the IP address associated with the given interface. (Router mode)
mpls traffic-eng signaling advertise implicit-null	Uses MPLS encoding for the implicit-null label in signaling messages sent to neighbors that match the specified access list. (Global mode)
mpls traffic-eng tunnels	Enables MPLS traffic engineering tunnel signaling on a device. (Global mode)

continues

Table A-3 *MPLS Traffic Engineering Commands (Continued)*

MPLS Traffic Engineering Command	Description
mpls traffic-eng tunnels	Enables MPLS traffic engineering tunnel signaling on an interface. (Interface mode)
next-address	Specifies the next IP address in the explicit path. (IP-Explicit-Path mode)
tunnel mpls traffic-eng affinity	Configures tunnel affinity (the properties the tunnel requires in its links) for an MPLS traffic-engineered tunnel. (Interface mode)
tunnel mpls traffic-eng auto-bw	Configures a tunnel for automatic bandwidth adjustment and to control the manner in which the bandwidth for a tunnel is adjusted. (Interface mode)
tunnel mpls traffic-eng autoroute announce	Instructs the IGP to use the tunnel in its SPF/next-hop calculation (if the tunnel is up). (Interface mode)
tunnel mpls traffic-eng autoroute metric	Specifies the MPLS traffic engineering tunnel metric used by an IGP autoroute metric. (Interface mode)
tunnel mpls traffic-eng bandwidth	Configures bandwidth required for an MPLS traffic engineering tunnel. (Interface mode)
tunnel mpls traffic-eng path-option	Configures a traffic engineering path option. (Interface mode)
tunnel mpls traffic-eng priority	Configures the setup and reservation priority for a traffic-engineered tunnel. (Interface mode)
tunnel mode mpls traffic-eng	Sets the mode of a tunnel to MPLS for traffic engineering. (Interface mode)
show ip explicit-paths	Displays the IP explicit paths. An IP explicit path is a list of IP addresses, each representing a node or link in the explicit path. (Exec mode)
show ip ospf database opaque-area	Displays lists of information related to traffic engineering opaque link-state advertisements (LSAs), also known as Type-10 opaque link area link states. (Exec mode)
show ip ospf mpls traffic-eng	Displays information about the links available on the local router for traffic engineering. (Exec mode)
show ip rsvp host	Displays RSVP terminal point information for receivers or senders. (Exec mode)
show isis database verbose	Displays information about the IS-IS database. (Exec mode)
show isis mpls traffic-eng adjacency-log	Displays a log of 20 entries of MPLS traffic engineering IS-IS adjacency changes. (Exec mode)

Table A-3   *MPLS Traffic Engineering Commands (Continued)*

MPLS Traffic Engineering Command	Description
show isis mpls traffic-eng advertisements	Displays the last flooded record from MPLS traffic engineering. (Exec mode)
show isis mpls traffic-eng tunnel	Displays information about tunnels considered in IS-IS next-hop calculation. (Exec mode)
show mpls traffic-eng autoroute	Displays tunnels that are announced to IGP, including interface, destination, and bandwidth. (Exec mode)
show mpls traffic-eng link-management admission-control	Displays which tunnels have been admitted locally, and their parameters (such as priority, bandwidth, incoming and outgoing interface, and state). (Exec mode)
show mpls traffic-eng link-management advertisements	Displays local link information currently being flooded by MPLS traffic engineering link management into the global traffic engineering topology. (Exec mode)
show mpls traffic-eng link-management bandwidth-allocation	Displays current local link information. (Exec mode)
show mpls traffic-eng link-management igp-neighbors	Displays IGP neighbors. (Exec mode)
show mpls traffic-eng link-management interfaces	Shows per-interface resource and configuration information. (Exec mode)
show mpls traffic-eng link-management summary	Displays a summary of the link management information. (Exec mode)
show mpls traffic-eng topology	Displays the MPLS traffic engineering global topology as currently known at this node. (Exec mode)
show mpls traffic-eng topology path	Displays the properties of the best available path to a specified destination that satisfies certain constraints. (Exec mode)
show mpls traffic-eng tunnel	Displays information about traffic engineering tunnels. (Exec mode)
show mpls traffic-eng tunnel summary	Displays summary information about traffic engineering tunnels. (Exec mode)
debug ip ospf mpls traffic-eng advertisements	Displays information about traffic engineering advertisements in OSPF LSA messages. (Exec mode)

continues

Table A-3   *MPLS Traffic Engineering Commands (Continued)*

MPLS Traffic Engineering Command	Description
debug isis mpls traffic-eng advertisements	Displays information about traffic engineering advertisements in ISIS LSA messages. (Exec mode)
debug isis mpls traffic-eng events	Displays information about traffic engineering-related ISIS events. (Exec mode)
debug mpls traffic-eng areas	Displays information about traffic engineering area configuration change events. (Exec mode)
debug mpls traffic-eng autoroute	Displays information about automatic routing over traffic engineering tunnels. (Exec mode)
debug mpls traffic-eng link-management admission-control	Displays information about traffic engineering LSP admission control on traffic engineering interfaces. (Exec mode)
debug mpls traffic-eng link-management advertisements	Displays information about resource advertisements for traffic engineering interfaces. (Exec mode)
debug mpls traffic-eng link-management bandwidth-allocation	Displays detailed information about bandwidth allocation for traffic engineering LSPs. (Exec mode)
debug mpls traffic-eng link-management errors	Displays information about errors encountered during any traffic engineering link management procedure. (Exec mode)
debug mpls traffic-eng link-management events	Displays information about traffic engineering link management system events. (Exec mode)
debug mpls traffic-eng link-management igp-neighbors	Displays information about changes to the link management database of IGP neighbors. (Exec mode)
debug mpls traffic-eng link-management links	Displays information about traffic engineering link management interface events. (Exec mode)
debug mpls traffic-eng link-management preemption	Displays information about traffic engineering LSP preemption. (Exec mode)
debug mpls traffic-eng link-management routing	Displays information about traffic engineering link management routing resolutions that can be performed to help RSVP interpret explicit route objects. (Exec mode)
debug mpls traffic-eng load-balancing	Displays information about unequal-cost load balancing over traffic engineering tunnels. (Exec mode)
debug mpls traffic-eng path	Displays information about traffic engineering path calculation. (Exec mode)

Table A-3   *MPLS Traffic Engineering Commands (Continued)*

MPLS Traffic Engineering Command	Description
debug mpls traffic-eng topology change	Displays information about traffic engineering topology change events. (Exec mode)
debug mpls traffic-eng topology lsa	Displays information about traffic engineering topology LSA events. (Exec mode)
debug mpls traffic-eng tunnels errors	Displays information about errors encountered during any traffic engineering tunnel management procedure. (Exec mode)
debug mpls traffic-eng tunnels events	Displays information about traffic engineering tunnel management system events. (Exec mode)
debug mpls traffic-eng tunnels labels	Displays information about MPLS label management for traffic engineering tunnels. (Exec mode)
debug mpls traffic-eng tunnels reoptimize	Displays information about traffic engineering tunnel reoptimizations. (Exec mode)
debug mpls traffic-eng tunnels signalling	Displays information about traffic engineering tunnel signaling operations. (Exec mode)
debug mpls traffic-eng tunnels state	Displays information about state maintenance for traffic engineering tunnels. (Exec mode)
debug mpls traffic-eng tunnels timers	Displays information about traffic engineering tunnel timer management. (Exec mode)

Table A-4 displays various MPLS quality of service commands, which are used to configure MPLS QoS on label-switched routers.

Table A-4   *MPLS Modular QoS CLI (MQC) Commands*

MPLS QoS Command	Description
access-list rate-limit	Configures an access list for use with committed access rate (CAR) policies. (Global mode)
bandwidth	Specifies a minimum bandwidth guarantee to a traffic class. A minimum bandwidth guarantee can be specified in kilobits per second or by a percentage of the overall available bandwidth. (Policy map class submode)
class	Specifies the name of the class whose policy you want to create, to change, or to specify the default class before its policy is configured. (Policy map mode)
class-map	Creates a class map to be used for matching packets to the class whose name you specify. (Global mode)

continues

Table A-4 *MPLS Modular QoS CLI (MQC) Commands (Continued)*

MPLS QoS Command	Description
default	Sets a command to its default value. (Policy map class submode)
fair-queue	Specifies the number of queues to be reserved for the class. (Policy map class submode)
match access-group	Configures the match criteria for a class map based on the specified access-control list (ACL) number. (Class-map mode)
match any	Configures the match criteria for a class map to be successful match criteria for all packets. (Class-map mode)
match class-map	Uses a traffic class as a classification policy. (Class-map mode)
match cos	Matches a packet based on a Layer 2 IEEE 802.1Q/ISL class of service marking. (Class-map mode)
match destination-address mac	Uses the destination MAC address as a match criterion in class-map configuration mode. (Class-map mode)
match input-interface	Configures a class map to use the specified input interface as a match criterion. (Class-map mode)
match ip dscp	Identifies a specific IP differentiated service code point (DSCP) value as a match criterion. (Class-map mode)
match ip precedence	Identifies IP precedence values as the match criteria. (Class-map mode)
match ip rtp	Configures a class map to use the Real-Time Protocol (RTP) protocol port as the match criteria. (Class-map mode)
match mpls experimental	Configures a class map to use the specified value of the EXP field as a match criterion. (Class-map mode)
match not	Specifies the single match criterion value to use as an unsuccessful match criterion in class-map configuration mode. (Class-map mode)
match protocol	Configures the match criteria for a class map based on the specified protocol. (Class-map mode)
match qos-group	Identifies a specific QoS group value as a match criterion. (Class-map mode)
match source-address mac	Uses the source MAC address as a match criterion in class map configuration mode. (Class-map mode)
police	Specifies a maximum bandwidth usage by a traffic class through the use of a token bucket algorithm. This command is used to police and apply various actions on input traffic. (Policy map class submode)
policy-map	Creates or modifies a policy map that can be attached to one or more interfaces to specify a service policy. (Global mode)

Table A-4   *MPLS Modular QoS CLI (MQC) Commands (Continued)*

MPLS QoS Command	Description
priority	Specifies the guaranteed allowed bandwidth (in kbps or percentage) for priority traffic. The optional **bytes** argument controls the size of the burst allowed to pass through the system without being considered in excess of the configured kbps rate. (Policy map class submode)
queue-limit	Specifies the maximum number of packets queued for a traffic class (in the absence of the **random-detect** command). (Policy map class submode)
random-detect	Enables a weighted random early detection (WRED) drop policy for a traffic class that has a bandwidth guarantee. (Policy map class submode)
rate-limit	Configures CAR and DCAR policies. (Interface mode)
service-policy	Attaches a policy map to an input interface, output interface, or virtual circuit to be used as the service policy for that interface. (Global mode)
random-detect	Enables a WRED drop policy for a traffic class that has a bandwidth guarantee. (Policy map class submode)
set atm-clp	Sets the ATM cell loss priority bit. (Policy map class submode)
set cos	Specifies a CoS value or values to associate with the outgoing packet. The number is in the range 0 to 7. (Policy map class submode)
set ip dscp	Specifies the IP DSCP of packets within a traffic class. The IP DSCP value can be any value between 0 and 63. (Policy map class submode)
set ip precedence	Specifies the IP precedence of packets within a traffic class. The IP precedence value can be any value between 0 and 7. (Policy map class submode)
set mpls experimental	Configures a policy to set the MPLS experimental field within the modular QoS CLI. (Policy map class submode)
show policy	Displays the configuration of all classes comprising the specified service policy map or all classes for all existing policy maps. (Global mode)
show policy-map class	Displays the configuration of the specified class of the specified policy map. (Global mode)
show policy-map interface	Displays the configuration of all classes configured for all service policies on the specified interface. (Global mode)

Table A-5 displays various MPLS Netflow commands, which are used to configure MPLS Netflow on label-switched routers.

Table A-5   *MPLS Netflow Commands*

MPLS Netflow Command	Description
ip flow-aggregation cache	Enters aggregation cache configuration mode and enables an aggregation cache scheme (as destination-prefix, prefix, protocol-port, or source-prefix). (Global mode)
mpls netflow egress	Enables MPLS egress Netflow accounting on an interface. (Interface mode)
show mpls forwarding-table	Displays the contents of the MPLS Label Forwarding Information Base (LFIB). (Exec mode)
show mpls interfaces	Displays the interfaces that have MPLS egress Netflow accounting enabled. (Exec mode)
show ip cache flow	Displays a summary of Netflow switching statistics. (Exec mode)
show ip cache flow aggregation	Displays the contents of the aggregation cache. (Exec mode)
debug mpls netflow	Displays debug messages for MPLS egress Netflow accounting. (Exec mode)

MPLS Equipment Design Specifications

The selection of edge and core LSR equipment depends on the design and capacity planning of the service provider core network. The tables in this appendix provide equipment specifications that help the MPLS network designer select equipment based on the service type, access, and redundancy options incorporated in the design.

Table B-1   *MPLS ATM-Edge Equipment Specifications*

Equipment	Type of Services	Access Lines	Processor Redundancy	Comments
3600	IP only	Relatively small numbers of async, modem, serial/Frame Relay, 10-Mbps Ethernet, ISDN BRI and PRI, HSSI, E1/T1 serial, Fast Ethernet, OC-3/STM-1 ATM, voice interfaces, and others	None	A small number of Label Virtual Circuits (LVCs) supported on ATM cards leads to limitations on MPLS network size. Not recommended for provider ATM MPLS networks.
4700	IP only	Relatively small numbers of serial/Frame Relay, 10-Mbps Ethernet, ISDN BRI, E1/T1 serial, Fast Ethernet, E3, T3 or OC-3/STM-1 ATM, and others	None	A small number of LVCs supported on ATM cards leads to limitations on MPLS network size. Not recommended for provider ATM MPLS networks.
7200	IP only	Serial/Frame Relay up to E1/T1, 10-Mbps Ethernet and Fast Ethernet, ISDN BRI, HSSI, high-speed serial, E3, T3 or OC-3/STM-1 ATM, packet-over-SONET/SDH and others	None	Minimum recommended for provider networks

continues

Table B-1   *MPLS ATM-Edge Equipment Specifications (Continued)*

Equipment	Type of Services	Access Lines	Processor Redundancy	Comments
7505 7507 7513	IP only	Serial/Frame Relay or ISDN up to E1/T1, 10-Mbps Ethernet, Fast Ethernet, and Gigabit Ethernet, HSSI, high-speed serial, ATM, packet-over-SONET/SDH, and others	Warm-standby processor	The 7500 series routers are the platform of choice for ATM Edge LSRs used to enable MPLS VPNs.
12008 12012	IP only	Packet over SONET (POS) and ATM at OC-3 to OC-48 rates, and Gigabit Ethernet **Note:** The highest ATM bandwidth density supported by the 12000 series port cards is $1 \times$ OC-12 per slot. Because all traffic in an ATM Edge LSR must go through an ATM interface into the ATM MPLS network, this relatively low ATM bandwidth density of the 12000 limits its capacity as an ATM Edge LSR.	Warm-standby processor redundancy	Suitable for high-speed peering between providers.
Catalyst 5500 with Route Switch Modules	IP+ATM	10-Mbps Ethernet and Fast Ethernet, E3, T3, OC-3/STM-1 and OC-12/STM-4 ATM, and others	None	The Catalyst 5500 is primarily a LAN switch, but it also has limited Edge LSR capability. The Catalyst 5500 may be connected only to an ATM MPLS network by tunneling.
6400	IP+ATM	ATM at E3/T3 to STM-4 rates. Also Ethernet and Fast Ethernet	Warm-standby processor redundancy	The 6400 provides ATM Edge LSR MPLS support.
MGX 8850	IP+ATM	High numbers of 56/64 kbps Frame Relay, T1/E1 Frame Relay, channelized, and ATM, and higher-speed Frame Relay, serial, and channelized T3	Full warm-to-hot standby	The MGX 8850 has hot-standby 1:N redundancy capability for customer access lines, hot-standby control for PVCs, and hot-standby trunks.

Table B-1   *MPLS ATM-Edge Equipment Specifications (Continued)*

Equipment	Type of Services	Access Lines	Processor Redundancy	Comments
BPX 8650	IP+ATM	High numbers of 56/64 kbps Frame Relay, T1/E1 Frame Relay, channelized, and ATM, ATM at E3/T3 to STM-4 rates, and others	Excellent redundancy in general, but there is a single point of failure for Edge LSR function.	See BPX 8680.
BPX 8680	IP+ATM	High numbers of 56/64 kbps Frame Relay, T1/E1 ATM, Frame Relay, and channelized. Also ATM at E3/T3 to STM-4 rates and others. Extra 6400, 7200, or 7500 routers (or label switch controller packages) might be required to act as Edge LSRs. E3/T3 or faster ATM access lines are used. If IP service is to be supported for large numbers of ATM links at T3/E3 rates and above, it is more cost-effective to use separate standalone routers.	Full warm-to-hot standby with FCS limitations	BXM trunk cards must be used. BXM cards are required. MPLS is not supported on BNI cards, except if the BNI cards are used as feeder trunks. BCC cards must be BCC3-64 or later. BCC4 cards are strongly recommended. The BPX 8680 can include up to 16 MGX 8850 shelves, with n:1 redundancy. Full redundancy for the combined device relies on redundancy for the label switch controller for the BPX 8600 shelf.

Table B-2   *MPLS ATM-LSR Specifications*

Equipment	Type and Number of ATM Trunks	Number of Connections Supported	VC Merge	Processor Redundancy	Comments
MGX 8850 with PXM1	4 × OC-3/STM1	8,000 to 16,000 full-duplex connection legs are supported on the PXM card of the MGX 8850. If both legs of all connections are on the PXM card, 8,000 connections are supported.	No	Full warm-to-hot standby	The MGX 8850 is intended primarily to be an Edge LSR, but it also has limited ATM LSR capability.

continues

Table B-2   *MPLS ATM-LSR Specifications (Continued)*

Equipment	Type and Number of ATM Trunks	Number of Connections Supported	VC Merge	Processor Redundancy	Comments
LS1010	32 × T1/E1 with Inverse Multiplexing over ATM (IMA) 32 × T3/E3 32 × OC-3/STM-1 8 × OC-12/STM-4	64,000	Yes	None	The LS1010 does not require a label switch controller to function as an ATM LSR.
6400	16 × T3/E3 16 × OC-3/ATM-1 8 × OC-12/STM-4	64,000	Yes	Warm-standby processor redundancy	
BPX 8650	144 × T3/E3 96 × OC-3/STM-1 24 × OC-12/STM-4	192,000	Rel 9.3	Some redundancy features at FCS. Full redundancy is possible later.	All MPLS interfaces must be on BXM cards. BCC cards must be BCC3-64 or later. BCC4 cards are strongly recommended. The BPX 8650 supports hot-standby trunks and switching fabrics. Full redundancy relies on redundancy for the label switch controller for the BPX 8600 shelf.
8540 MSR	64 × T1/E1 with IMA 64 × T3/E3 64 × OC-3/STM-1 32 × OC-12/STM-4 8 × OC-48/STM-16	256,000	Yes	Warm-standby processor redundancy	

Table B-2   *MPLS ATM-LSR Specifications (Continued)*

Equipment	Type and Number of ATM Trunks	Number of Connections Supported	VC Merge	Processor Redundancy	Comments
MGX 8800 with PXM-45 card(s)	192 × T3/E3 144 × OC-3/STM-1 48 × OC-12/STM-4 12 × OC-48/STM-16	384,000	Yes	Full warm-to-hot standby	

Table B-3   *MPLS ATM-Edge LSR LVC Capacity*

Device	Interface Hardware	Number of Active LVCs Supported	Notes
3600	NM-1A ATM network modules	1024	
4700	NP-1A ATM network processor module	1023	
7200 7500	PA-A1 or standard ATM port adapter	2048	
Catalyst 5500 7200 7500	PA-A3 ATM port adapter	4096	
6400	Node Route Processor (NRP)	2048	Capacity is reduced by one LVC for each active PVC that terminates on the NRP.
MGX 8850 IP+ATM switch	Route Processor Module (RPM)	4096	Capacity is reduced by one LVC for each active PVC that terminates on the RPM. In addition, the PXM is limited to 16,000 LVCs.
12000 series routers	4 × OC-3 ATM line card	2047	The 2047 active VCs are shared between all four ports. Network capacity is reduced by one destination prefix for every second and subsequent route chosen for each destination according to equal-cost multipath routing if the extra routes are on the same card.
12000 series routers	1 × OC-12 ATM line card	2047	

Table B-4   *MPLS ATM-LSR LVC Capacity with VC Merge*

Device	Interface Hardware	Number of Active LVCs Supported	Number of Active Merging LVCs Supported
LS1010	Any ATM port hardware	4096 per OC-3 port 16,000 per OC-12 port 16,000 per OC-48 port	64,000 per switch
6400	Any ATM port hardware	4096 per OC-3 port 16,000 per OC-12 port 16,000 per OC-48 port	256,000 per switch
8540 MSR	Any ATM port adapters	4096 per OC-3 port 16,000 per OC-12 port 16,000 per OC-48 port	256,000 per switch
BPX 8650 or 8680	BXM-E cards	32,000 per BXM, shared among up to 12 interfaces	32,000 per BXM, with a maximum of 16,000 per port on OC-3 BXM cards and 2 × OC-12 BXM cards. T3/E3 BXM cards and 1 × OC-12 BXM cards have a limit of 32,000 per port.
MGX 8800 with PXM-45	AXSM cards	128,000 per AXSM, shared among up to 16 interfaces	128,000 per AXSM

Table B-5   *MPLS CoS Features Supported on Packet Interfaces*

MPLS CoS Packet Feature	Cisco 7500 Series	Cisco 7200 Series	Cisco 4x00 Series	Cisco 36x0 Series	Cisco 2600 Series
Per-interface WRED	X	X	X	X	Untested
Per-interface, per-flow WFQ	X	X	X	X	Untested
Per-interface, per-class WFQ	X	X	X	X	Untested

Table B-6   *MPLS CoS Features Supported on ATM Interfaces*

MPLS CoS ATM Forum PVCs Feature	Cisco 7500 Series	Cisco 7200 Series	Cisco 4x00 Series	Cisco 36x0 Series	Cisco 2600 Series
Per-VC WRED	X[1]	X[1]	—	—	—
Per-VC WRED and per-VC, per-class WFQ	—	X[1]	—	—	—

Table B-6   *MPLS CoS Features Supported on ATM Interfaces (Continued)*

MPLS CoS ATM Forum PVCs Feature	Cisco 7500 Series	Cisco 7200 Series	Cisco 4x00 Series	Cisco 36x0 Series	Cisco 2600 Series
MPLS CoS Multi-VC or LBR Feature					
Per-interface WRED	X^2	X^2	—	—	—
Per-interface, per-class WFQ	X^2	X^2	—	—	—

[1]This feature is available only on the PA-A3.

[2]This feature is available only on the PA-A1.

Table B-7   *MPLS CoS Features Supported on ATM Switches*

MPLS CoS ATM Forum PVCs Feature	BPX 8650 Series	MGX 8800 Series	LightStream 1010 ATM Switch[1]	Catalyst 8540 MSR[1]
MPLS CoS ATM Forum PVCs	X	X	X	X
MPLS CoS Multi-VC or LBR-per-class WFQ	X	—	—	—

[1]This can be used for the core only.

MPLS Glossary

This MPLS glossary provides a list of the various MPLS-related terminology used in this book. Some of the definitions have several meanings when used in a different internetworking context. For information on abbreviations and acronyms not covered in this glossary, refer to the Internetworking Terms and Acronyms page at www.cisco.com/cpress/cc/td/doc/cisintwk/ita/index.htm.

A

AAL. ATM adaptation layer. The AAL accepts data from different applications and presents it to the ATM layer in the form of 48-byte ATM payload segments. AALs differ on the basis of the source-destination timing used, whether they use CBR or VBR, and whether they are used for connection-oriented or connectionless mode data transfer. At present, the four types of AAL recommended by the ITU-T are AAL1, AAL2, AAL3/4, and AAL5.

ABR. Available bit rate. The QoS class defined by the ATM Forum for ATM networks. ABR is used for connections that do not require timing relationships between source and destination. ABR provides no guarantees in terms of cell loss or delay, providing only best-effort service.

ADM. Add drop multiplexer. Digital multiplexing equipment that provides interfaces between different signals in a network.

admission control. The set of actions taken by a network to admit or deny a recognized single aggregated flow. Such a set of actions can be resource- and/or policy-based.

AF. Assured Forwarding. A Differentiated Services classification for packets that also specifies the drop precedence of each packet.

affinity. An MPLS traffic engineering tunnel's requirements on the attributes of the links it will cross. The tunnel's affinity bits and affinity mask bits must match the attribute bits of the various links carrying the tunnel.

APS. Automatic protection switching. A switching mechanism that routes traffic from working lines to protect them from component failure or fiber cut. APS was standardized in SONET Phase II.

ATM. Asynchronous Transfer Mode. An international standard for cell relay in which multiple service types (such as voice, video, or data) are conveyed in fixed-length (53-byte) cells. Fixed-length cells allow cell processing to occur in hardware, thereby reducing transit delays. ATM is designed to take advantage of high-speed transmission technologies such as SONET.

ATM edge LSR. An ATM router that is connected to the ATM-LSR cloud through LC-ATM interfaces. The ATM edge LSR adds labels to unlabeled packets and strips labels from labeled packets.

ATM-LSR. A label switch router with a number of LC-ATM interfaces. The router forwards the cells among these interfaces using labels carried in the VPI/VCI field of the ATM cell header.

B

BA. Behavior Aggregate. A collection of packets that have the same DSCP value in them and that are crossing a network element in a particular direction.

BGP. Border Gateway Protocol. An interdomain routing protocol that exchanges reachability information with other BGP systems. It is defined in RFC 1163.

C

call admission precedence. If necessary, an MPLS traffic engineering tunnel with a higher priority preempts an MPLS traffic engineering tunnel with a lower priority. Tunnels that are harder to route are expected to have a higher priority and to be able to preempt tunnels that are easier to route. The assumption is that lower-priority tunnels will be able to find another path.

CAR. Committed access rate. This is used for policing and traffic conditioning and in providing PHB for AF classes at the edge and in the core of a DS domain.

CBR. Constant bit rate. A QoS class defined by the ATM Forum for ATM networks. CBR is used for connections that depend on precise clocking to ensure undistorted delivery. CBR can be used to emulate TDM circuits.

CBWFQ. Class-based weighted fair queuing. Allows you to define traffic classes that are based on certain match criteria, such as access control lists, input interface names, protocols, and quality of service labels.

CE router. Customer edge router. The CE router is a CPE router that is part of a customer network and that interfaces to a provider edge (PE) router. CE routers are not aware of associated VPNs.

CEF. Cisco Express Forwarding. An advanced Layer 3 IP switching technology. CEF optimizes network performance and scalability for networks with large and dynamic traffic patterns.

classification. The assignment of a recognized single aggregated flow to an IP precedence and/or 802.1p priority.

CLEC. Competitive local exchange carrier. A local service provider, formerly a telephone company, that competes against incumbent local exchange carriers.

CO. Central office. A common carrier switching center housing equipment that terminates users' lines.

congestion avoidance. A set of actions taken by the network in order to avoid circumstances in which aggregated flows no longer receive their associated service levels. Such actions could include implicit or explicit feedback to the traffic source to reduce their current transmit rate.

constraint-based routing. Procedures and protocols that determine a route across a backbone. They take into account resource requirements and resource availability instead of simply using the shortest path.

COPS. Common Open Policy Service. An open architecture for implementing QoS policy on network elements using QoS policy manager application software.

CoS. Class of service. A feature that provides scalable differentiated types of service across an MPLS network.

CPE. Customer premises equipment.

CR-LDP. Constraint-Based Routing Label Distribution Protocol. A set of extensions to LDP that enable constraint-based routing and QoS reservation in an MPLS network.

CSPF. Constraint shortest path first. An extension of the shortest path first (SPF) algorithm in which only the links that meet certain specified constraints are considered for inclusion in the shortest-path tree.

D

dark fiber. An inactive optical fiber. Typically when fiber is laid, some initially remains dark, or in reserve, for future use. Active fiber is called lit fiber.

DiffServ. Differentiated services. A quality of service architecture that utilizes the Type of Service bits in the IP header to classify packets.

DLCI. Data-link connection identifier. A label used in Frame Relay networks to identify Frame Relay circuits.

DSCP. Differentiated services code point. The first 6 bits in the Type of Service field in the IP header. Used to identify up to 64 classes of service.

DWDM. Dense wavelength division multiplexing. Optical transmission of multiple signals over closely spaced wavelengths in the 1550 nm region. Wavelength spacings are usually 100 GHz or 200 GHz, which corresponds to 0.8 nm or 1.6 nm.

E

EDFA. Erbium-doped fiber amplifier. Optical fibers doped with the rare-earth element erbium, which can amplify light in the 1550 nm region when pumped by an external light source.

Edge LSR. Edge Label Switch Router. A label switch router (LSR) that applies a label to a packet at ingress or removes the label at egress.

EF. Expedited forwarding. Packet markings that guarantee minimal delay and low loss.

ERO. Explicit route object. An object carried in an LSP setup protocol such as RSVP or LDP to specify the sequence of hops that an explicitly routed LSP must traverse.

F

FDM. Frequency-division multiplexing. Consists of separate channels that are assigned to individual frequencies across the frequency bandwidth on a common transmission facility. ADSL technology, for example, has a frequency range of 30 kHz to 1.1 MHz that can be divided into two nonoverlapping areas used for upstream and downstream transmission.

FEC. Forwarding Equivalence Class. A set of Layer 3 packets that are forwarded in the same manner over the same path, with the same forwarding treatment.

flow. A traffic load entering the backbone at one point (point of presence [POP]) and leaving it from another that must be traffic-engineered across the backbone. The traffic load is carried across one or more LSP tunnels running from the entry POP to the exit POP.

frame merge. Label merging, when it is applied to operation over frame-based media, so that the potential problem of cell interleave is not an issue.

FRTS. Frame Relay traffic shaping. A mechanism used to shape traffic over Frame Relay networks by using parameters such as the committed information rate (CIR), forward and backward explicit congestion notification (FECN/BECN), and the discard eligibility (DE) bit.

FTN. FEC-to-NHLFE map.

G - H - I

GTS. Generic traffic shaping. GTS provides a mechanism to control the traffic flow on a particular interface. It reduces outbound traffic flow to avoid congestion by constraining specified traffic to a particular bit rate (also known as the token bucket approach) while queuing bursts of the specified traffic.

headend. The upstream, transmit end of a tunnel.

IGP. Interior Gateway Protocol. An Internet protocol used to exchange routing information within an autonomous system. Examples of common IGPs include OSPF, IS-IS, and RIP.

ILEC. Incumbent local exchange carrier. Term used to describe the primary existing carriers, formerly known as Regional Bell Operating Companies (RBOCs). Distinguished from new competitive carriers coming out of the deregulation of the telecommunications industry.

ILM. Incoming Label Map.

IntServ. Integrated Services. An overall quality of service architecture developed by the IETF. The RSVP signaling protocol is an IntServ protocol.

IP explicit path. A list of IP addresses, each representing a node or link in the explicit path.

IP Precedence. A 3-bit value in a ToS byte used for assigning precedence to IP packets.

IS-IS. Intermediate System-to-Intermediate System. An OSI link-state hierarchical routing protocol in which intermediate systems (routers) exchange routing information based on a single metric to determine network topology.

IXC. Interexchange carrier. All long-distance carriers who operate across multiple local access and transport areas are called interexchange carriers, in contrast to a local exchange carrier (LEC).

L

label. A short, fixed-length, physically contiguous identifier that is used to identify a FEC, usually of local significance.

label imposition. The action of putting the first label on a packet.

label merging. The replacement of multiple incoming labels for a particular FEC with a single outgoing label.

label stack. An ordered set of labels.

label swap. The basic forwarding operation, consisting of looking up an incoming label to determine the outgoing label, encapsulation, port, and other data-handling information.

label swapping. A forwarding paradigm allowing streamlined forwarding of data by using labels to identify classes of data packets, which are treated indistinguishably when forwarding.

label switch. A node that forwards units of data (packets or cells) on the basis of labels.

label switched hop. The hop between two MPLS nodes, on which forwarding is done using labels.

label-switched path. The path through one or more LSRs at one level of the hierarchy, followed by packets in a particular FEC. A label-switched path can be selected dynamically, based on normal routing mechanisms, or it can be configured manually.

Layer 2. The data link layer. The swapping of short fixed-length labels occurs at Layer 2 regardless of whether the label being examined is an ATM VPI/VCI, a Frame Relay DLCI, or an MPLS label.

Layer 3. The network layer at which IP and its associated routing protocols operate.

LCAC. Link-level (per-hop) call admission control.

LC-ATM interface. Label-controlled ATM interface. An interface on a router or switch that uses label distribution procedures to negotiate label VCs.

LDP. Label distribution protocol. The protocol used to distribute label bindings between LSRs as defined by the IETF.

LEC. Local exchange carrier. A telephone company that provides customer access to the worldwide public-switched network through one of its central offices.

LER. Label edge router. A router that performs label imposition.

LFIB. Label forwarding information base. The data structure used by label switching to hold information about incoming and outgoing labels, interfaces, and the associated FECs.

LIB. Label Information Base. A database used by an LSR to store labels learned from other LSRs, as well as labels assigned by the local LSR.

LLQ. Low latency queuing. Enforces strict priority queuing for class-based weighted fair queuing (CBWFQ). Strict priority queuing allows delay-sensitive data such as voice to be dequeued and sent first (before packets in other queues are dequeued), giving delay-sensitive data preferential treatment over other traffic.

loop detection. A method of dealing with loops in which loops may be set up and data transmitted over the loop. However, the loop is later detected and eliminated.

loop prevention. A method of dealing with loops in which data is never transmitted over a loop.

LSA. Link-state advertisement. A flooded packet used by OSPF that contains information about neighbors and path costs. In IS-IS, receiving routers use LSAs to maintain their routing tables.

LSP. Label-switched path. LSP tunnels are configured connections between two routers in which label switching techniques are used for packet forwarding.

LSP tunnel. Label-switched path tunnel. A configured connection between two routers in which label switching is used to carry the packets.

LSR. Label-switching router. An MPLS node that can forward native Layer 3 packets. The LSR forwards a packet based on the value of a label attached to the packet.

LVC. Label switch controlled virtual circuit. LVCs are ATM virtual circuits that are set up through ATM LSR label distribution procedures.

M

merge point. A node at which label merging is done.

MPLS. Multiprotocol Label Switching. A set of IETF standards designed to allow packet flows to be switched on the basis of labels instead of the full destination address. MPLS is based on the concept of routing at the edge and switching in the core.

MPLS domain. A contiguous set of nodes that operate MPLS routing and forwarding and that are also in one routing or administrative domain.

MPLS edge node. An MPLS node that connects an MPLS domain with a node that is outside of the domain because it does not run MPLS and/or because it is in a different domain. Note that if an LSR has a neighboring host that is not running MPLS, that LSR is an MPLS edge node.

MPLS egress node. An MPLS edge node that handles traffic as it leaves an MPLS domain.

MPLS ingress node. An MPLS edge node that handles traffic as it enters an MPLS domain.

MPLS label. A label that is carried in a packet header and that represents the packet's FEC.

MPLS node. A node that is running MPLS. An MPLS node is aware of MPLS control protocols, operates one or more L3 routing protocols, and can forward packets based on labels. An MPLS node may optionally be able to forward native L3 packets.

MQC. Modular QoS CLI. MQS refers to the modular implementation of QoS on a network using the IOS command-line interface.

N

NHLFE. Next Hop Label Forwarding Entry.

NHRP. Next Hop Resolution Protocol. A protocol used to enable cut-through paths to be established between logical IP subnets on an ATM network.

NLRI. Network Layer Reachability Information. BGP sends routing update messages containing NLRI to describe a route and how to get there. In this context, an NLRI is a prefix. A BGP update message carries one or more NLRI prefixes and the attributes of a route for the NLRI prefixes. The route attributes include a BGP next-hop gateway address, community values, and other information.

O - P

OADM. Optical add drop multiplexer. Optical multiplexing equipment that provides interfaces between different signals in a network.

OTDR. Optical Time Domain Reflectometer. An instrument used in design and diagnostics that locates faults or infers attenuation in optical networks.

PE router. Provider edge router. The PE LSR is part of a service provider's network. PE routers are connected to a customer edge (CE) router. All VPN processing occurs in the PE router.

PHB. Per-Hop Behavior. Refers to the packet scheduling, queuing, policing, or shaping behavior of a node on any given packet belonging to a BA.

PNNI. Private Network-Network Interface. An ATM routing protocol used between ATM switches.

policing. The set of actions taken by a network to monitor and control traffic in order to protect network resources such as bandwidth against unauthorized or malicious use.

POS. Packet over SONET. A technology in which IP packets are mapped into SONET frames with intervening use of an ATM layer.

P-router. Provider core router. The P-router is an LSR that does not terminate customer VPNs. It could be an ATM LSR or a packet-based LSR.

PVC. Permanent virtual circuit. A virtual circuit that is provisioned permanently for a Layer 2 technology such as ATM or Frame Relay.

Q - R

QoS. Quality of service. A measure of performance for a transmission system that reflects its transmission quality and service availability.

QoS policy. The binding of traffic recognition and registration profiles to specific network behaviors—including, though not limited to, admittance or denial of identified traffic getting anything better than best-effort QoS. It also includes simple prioritization or specific bandwidth reservation for identified or aggregated flows.

RD. Route distinguisher. An 8-byte value that is concatenated with an IPv4 prefix to create a unique VPN IPv4 prefix. The route distinguisher is used by MBGP/MPLS VPNs to ensure uniqueness of address prefixes among VPNs when multiple VPNs use the same address space.

RED. Random early detection. A congestion avoidance mechanism that utilizes TCP's congestion control mechanism. By randomly dropping packets prior to periods of high congestion, RED tells the packet source to decrease its transmission rate. Assuming that the packet source is using TCP, it decreases its transmission rate until all the packets reach their destination, indicating that the congestion is cleared.

reoptimization. Reevaluation of the most suitable path for a tunnel to use, given the specified constraints.

route target. An extended community that identifies a group of routers and, in each router of that group, a subset of forwarding tables maintained by the router that may be populated with a BGP route carrying that extended community.

RSVP. Resource Reservation Protocol. A protocol for reserving network resources to provide quality of service guarantees to application flows.

S

scheduling. A set of mechanisms within the network that physically allocate and schedule network resources to an individual flow or aggregated flow.

SDH. Synchronous Digital Hierarchy. A European standard that defines a rate and format standards for the transmission of optical signals over fiber using ATM and SONET.

signaling. The means to signal a QoS requirement on individual devices or as part of aggregated flow from end to end (enterprise-wide), either in-band (for example, IP precedence) or out-of-band (for example, RSVP).

SONET. Synchronous Optical Network. An interface standard developed by Bellcore and widely used by the telecommunications industry for high-speed synchronous transport over optical fiber.

SVC. Switched virtual circuit. A virtual circuit that is dynamically established on demand and that is torn down when transmission is complete. SVCs are used in situations where data transmission is sporadic. Called a switched virtual connection in ATM terminology.

switched path. Synonymous with label-switched path.

T

tail-end. The downstream, receive end of a tunnel.

T-carrier. A generic designator for any of several digitally multiplexed telecommunications carrier systems. The two most common are T1, which transmits DS-1 formatted data at 1.544 Mbps, and T3, which transmits DS-3 formatted data at 44.736 Mbps.

TDM. Time-division multiplexing. A technique in which information from multiple channels is allocated bandwidth on a single transmission medium based on assigned time slots. SONET is a TDM technology.

TDP. Tag Distribution Protocol. Cisco's prestandard protocol used to distribute label bindings to LSRs.

TFIB. Tag Forwarding Information Base. The data structure used by tag switching to hold information about incoming and outgoing tags, interfaces, and the associated FECs.

traffic engineering. The techniques and processes used to cause routed traffic to travel through the network on a path other than the one that could have been selected if standard routing methods had been applied.

traffic engineering tunnel. A label-switched tunnel that is used for traffic engineering. Such a tunnel is set up through means other than normal Layer 3 routing. It is used to direct traffic over a path different from the one that Layer 3 routing could cause the tunnel to take.

traffic profile. A set of traffic parameters defining a traffic flow that is both quantitative (for example, bandwidth, delay, jitter) and qualitative (such as packet loss) in nature. In IntServ parlance, this translates as the flowspec. In ATM/Frame Relay, this translates as the Traffic Management traffic descriptor.

transponder. In a DWDM system, a module that receives an input signal and converts that signal to a wavelength to be optically multiplexed with other wavelengths.

TSR. Tag switching router. A prestandard MPLS node that can forward native Layer 3 packets. The TSR forwards a packet based on the value of a tag attached to the packet.

tunneling. An architecture that provides the services necessary to implement any standard point-to-point data encapsulation scheme.

U - V

UBR. Unspecified bit rate. A QoS class defined by the ATM Forum for ATM networks. UBR allows any amount of data up to a specified maximum to be sent across the network, but there are no guarantees in terms of cell loss rate and delay.

VBR. Variable bit rate. A QoS class defined by the ATM Forum for ATM networks. VBR is subdivided into a real-time (RT) class and a non-real-time (NRT) class. VBR-RT is used for connections in which there is a fixed timing relationship between samples. VBR-NRT is used for connections in which there is no fixed timing relationship between samples but that still need a guaranteed QoS.

virtual circuit. A circuit used by a connection-oriented Layer 2 technology such as ATM or Frame Relay, requiring the maintenance of state information in Layer 2 switches.

virtual circuit (VC) merge. Label merging in which the MPLS label is carried in the ATM VCI field (or a combined VPI/VCI field) to allow multiple VCs to merge into a single VC.

virtual path (VP) merge. Label merging in which the MPLS label is carried in the ATM VPI field to allow multiple VPs to be merged into a single VP. In this case, two cells would have the same VCI value only if they originated from the same node. This allows cells from different sources to be distinguished via the VCI.

VPN. Virtual Private Network. A secure closed user group Layer 3 network that shares resources on one or more Layer 2 networks. A VPN contains geographically dispersed sites that can communicate securely over a shared backbone.

vpnv4. Used as a keyword in commands to indicate VPN-IPv4 prefixes. These prefixes are customer VPN addresses, each of which has been made unique by the addition of an 8-byte route distinguisher.

VRF. VPN routing/forwarding instance. A VRF consists of an IP routing table, a derived forwarding table, a set of interfaces that use the forwarding table, and a set of rules and routing protocols that determine what goes into the forwarding table. In general, a VRF includes the routing information that defines a customer VPN site that is attached to a PE router.

W

WFQ. Weighted fair queuing. WFQ queues traffic according to traffic class definition, guaranteeing each queue some portion of the total available bandwidth. WFQ goes further to apportion available bandwidth on the basis of individual information flows according to message parameters.

WRED. Weighted random early detection. WRED combines the capabilities of the RED algorithm with IP Precedence. This combination provides for preferential traffic handling for higher-priority packets. WRED can also be configured to ignore IP precedence when making drop decisions so that nonweighted RED behavior is achieved

References

This appendix contains a list of the references used to write this book. You might find them helpful for furthering your research on MPLS topics.

Published References

L. Andersson *et al., LDP Specification,* Internet draft draft-ietf-mpls-ldp-05, June 1999.

D. Awduche, *MPLS and Traffic Engineering in IP Networks,* IEEE Communications, Vol. 37, Dec. 1999.

D. Awduche, A. Hannan, and X. Xiao, *Applicability Statement for Extensions to RSVP for LSP-Tunnels,* IETF Internet draft, work in progress, July 1999.

D. Awduche *et al., Extensions to RSVP for LSP Tunnels,* Internet draft draft-ietf-mpls-rsvp-lsp-tunnel-03, Sept. 1999.

D. Awduche *et al., Extensions to RSVP for Traffic Engineering,* IETF Internet draft, work in progress, Feb. 1999.

D. Awduche *et al., Requirements for Traffic Engineering Over MPLS,* RFC 2702, Sept. 1999.

L. Berger, D. H. Gan, and G. Swallow, *RSVP Refresh Reduction Extensions,* draft-berger-rsvp-refresh-reduct, work in progress.

S. Blake *et al., An Architecture for Differentiated Service,* RFC 2475, Dec. 1998.

R. Braden *et al., Resource ReSerVation Protocol (RSVP), Version 1 Functional specification,* RFC 2205, Sept. 1997.

N. Brownlee, C. Mills, and G. Ruth, *Traffic Flow Measurement: Architecture,* Internet RFC 2063, Jan. 1997.

R. Callon *et al., A Framework for Multiprotocol Label Switching,* Internet draft draft-ietf-mpls-framework-05, Sept. 1999.

T. Chen and T. Oh, *Reliable Services in MPLS, IEEE Communications,* Vol. 37, Dec. 1999.

B. Davie, P. Doolan, and Y. Rekhter, *Switching in IP Networks,* Morgan Kaufmann, 1998.

B. Davie and Y. Rekhter, *MPLS Technology and Applications,* Morgan Kaufmann, 2000.

D. Estrin, Y. Rekhter, and S. Hotz, *A Unified Approach to Inter-Domain Routing,* RFC 1322.

A. Ghanwani *et al., Traffic Engineering Standards in IP Networks Using MPLS, IEEE Communications,* Vol. 37, Dec. 1999.

R. Guerin, A. Orda, and D. Williams, *QoS Routing Mechanisms and OSPF Extensions,* GLOBECOM '97, 3-8 Nov., 1997.

J. Guichard and I. Pepelnjak, *MPLS and VPN Architectures,* Cisco Press, 2000.

S. Halabi, *Internet Routing Architectures,* Cisco Press, 2000.

B. Jamoussi, Ed., *Constraint-Based LSP Setup Using LDP,* Internet draft draft-ietf-mpls-cr-ldp-02, Aug. 1999.

D. Katz and D. Yeung, *Traffic engineering extensions to OSPF,* draft-katz-yeung-ospf-traffic, work in progress.

Le faucheur *et al., MPLS Support for Differentiated Services,* work in progress, draft-ietf-mpls-diff-ext-08.txt, Feb. 2001.

T. Li, *MPLS and the Evolving Internet Architecture, IEEE Communications,* Vol. 37, Dec 1999.

T. Li, G. Swallow, and D. Awduche, *IGP Requirements for Traffic Engineering with MPLS,* IETF Internet draft, work in progress, Feb. 1999.

A. Mankin *et al., Resource Reservation Protocol (RSVP)—Version 1 Applicability Statement: Some Guidelines on Deployment,* RFC 2208, Sept. 1997.

D. Mills, *Exterior Gateway Protocol Formal Specification,* RFC 904.

J. Moy, *OSPF—Anatomy of an Internet Routing Protocol,* Addison-Wesley, 1998.

Y. Ohba, *Issues on Loop Prevention in MPLS Networks, IEEE Communications,* Vol. 37, Dec. 1999.

Y. Rehkter and T. Li, *A Border Gateway Protocol 4 (BGP-4),* RFC 1771.

E. Rosen *et al., Multiprotocol Label Switching Architecture,* RFC 3031, Jan. 2001.

N. Shen and H. Smit, *Calculating IGP Routes over Traffic Engineering Tunnels,* IETF Internet draft, work in progress, June 1999.

H. Smit and T. Li, *IS-IS Extensions for Traffic Engineering,* draft-ietf-isis-traffic, work in progress.

G. Swallow, *MPLS Advantages for Traffic Engineering, IEEE Communications,* Vol. 37, Dec. 1999.

A. Viswanathan *et al.*, *Evolution of Multiprotocol Label Switching, IEEE Communications*, Vol. 36, May 1998.

J. Wroclawski, *The Use of RSVP with IETF Integrated Services*, RFC 2210, Sept. 1997.

Reference URLs

1   www.cisco.com/warp/public/121/mpls_cos_atm.html

2   www.cisco.com/warp/public/cc/so/neso/vvda/ipatm/tagsp_wi.htm

3   www.cisco.com/univercd/cc/td/doc/product/software/ios121/121newft/121t/121t5/mct1214t.htm

4   www.cisco.com/warp/public/cc/pd/iosw/ioft/iofwft/prodlit/difse_wp.htm

5   www.cisco.com/univercd/cc/td/doc/product/software/ios120/120newft/120limit/120st/120st14/aband wth.htm

6   www.cisco.com/univercd/cc/td/doc/product/software/ios120/120newft/120limit/120st/120st14/ ldp_14st.htm

7   www.cisco.com/univercd/cc/td/doc/product/software/ios121/121newft/121t/121t5/egress.htm

8   www.cisco.com/univercd/cc/td/doc/product/software/ios120/120newft/120limit/120s/120s5/ mpls_te.htm

9   www.cisco.com/warp/public/cc/pd/iosw/prodlit/1306_pp.htm

10   www.cisco.com/warp/public/cc/pd/olpl/metro/on15327/prodlit/ipto_wp.htm

11   www.cisco.com/univercd/cc/td/doc/product/software/ios121/121newft/121t/121t3/rtr_13t.htm

12   www.cisco.com/univercd/cc/td/doc/product/software/ios121/121cgcr/switch_c/xcprt4/ xcdtagov.htm

13   www.cisco.com/univercd/cc/td/doc/product/wanbu/mgx8850/rpm/rpm14/rpmch7.htm

14   www.cisco.com/univercd/cc/td/doc/product/wanbu/bpx8600/mpls/9_3_1/mpls03.htm

15   www.cisco.com/univercd/cc/td/doc/product/software/ios120/120newft/120limit/120xe/120xe5/ mqc/mcli.htm#79359

16   www.cisco.com/warp/public/cc/pd/hb/vp5000/prodlit/iplsc_wp.htm

17   www.cisco.com/univercd/cc/td/doc/product/software/ios120/120newft/120t/120t5/vpn.htm#xtocid23 4850

INDEX

D

K-L

R

S

V

CCIE Professional Development

Cisco LAN Switching

Kennedy Clark, CCIE; Kevin Hamilton, CCIE

1-57870-094-9 • AVAILABLE NOW

This volume provides an in-depth analysis of Cisco LAN switching technologies, architectures, and deployments, including unique coverage of Catalyst network design essentials. Network designs and configuration examples are incorporated throughout to demonstrate the principles and enable easy translation of the material into practice in production networks.

Advanced IP Network Design

Alvaro Retana, CCIE; Don Slice, CCIE; and Russ White, CCIE

1-57870-097-3 • AVAILABLE NOW

Network engineers and managers can use these case studies, which highlight various network design goals, to explore issues including protocol choice, network stability, and growth. This book also includes theoretical discussion on advanced design topics.

Large-Scale IP Network Solutions

Khalid Raza, CCIE; and Mark Turner

1-57870-084-1 • AVAILABLE NOW

Network engineers can find solutions as their IP networks grow in size and complexity. Examine all the major IP protocols in-depth and learn about scalability, migration planning, network management, and security for large-scale networks.

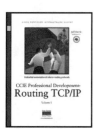

Routing TCP/IP, Volume I

Jeff Doyle, CCIE

1-57870-041-8 • AVAILABLE NOW

This book takes the reader from a basic understanding of routers and routing protocols through a detailed examination of each of the IP interior routing protocols. Learn techniques for designing networks that maximize the efficiency of the protocol being used. Exercises and review questions provide core study for the CCIE Routing and Switching exam.

Cisco Press

www.ciscopress.com

Cisco Career Certifications

Cisco CCNA Exam #640-507 Certification Guide
Wendell Odom, CCIE

0-7357-0971-8 • AVAILABLE NOW

Although it's only the first step in Cisco Career Certification, the Cisco Certified Network Associate (CCNA) exam is a difficult test. Your first attempt at becoming Cisco certified requires a lot of study and confidence in your networking knowledge. When you're ready to test your skills, complete your knowledge of the exam topics, and prepare for exam day, you need the preparation tools found in *Cisco CCNA Exam #640-507 Certification Guide* from Cisco Press.

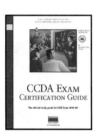

CCDA Exam Certification Guide
Anthony Bruno, CCIE & Jacqueline Kim

0-7357-0074-5 • AVAILABLE NOW

CCDA Exam Certification Guide is a comprehensive study tool for DCN Exam #640-441. Written by a CCIE and a CCDA, and reviewed by Cisco technical experts, *CCDA Exam Certification Guide* will help you understand and master the exam objectives. In this solid review on the design areas of the DCN exam, you'll learn to design a network that meets a customer's requirements for perfomance, security, capacity, and scalability.

Interconnecting Cisco Network Devices
Edited by Steve McQuerry

1-57870-111-2 • AVAILABLE NOW

Based on the Cisco course taught worldwide, *Interconnecting Cisco Network Devices* teaches you how to configure Cisco switches and routers in multi-protocol internetworks. ICND is the primary course recommended by Cisco Systems for CCNA #640-507 preparation. If you are pursuing CCNA certification, this book is an excellent starting point for your study.

Designing Cisco Networks
Edited by Diane Teare

1-57870-105-8 • AVAILABLE NOW

Based on the Cisco Systems instructor-led and self-study course available worldwide, *Designing Cisco Networks* will help you understand how to analyze and solve existing network problems while building a framework that supports the functionality, performance, and scalability required from any given environment. Self-assessment through exercises and chapter-ending tests starts you down the path for attaining your CCDA certification.

Cisco Press   **www.ciscopress.com**

Cisco Press Solutions

Enhanced IP Services for Cisco Networks
Donald C. Lee, CCIE

1-57870-106-6 • AVAILABLE NOW

This is a guide to improving your network's capabilities by understanding the new enabling and advanced Cisco IOS services that build more scalable, intelligent, and secure networks. Learn the technical details necessary to deploy Quality of Service, VPN technologies, IPsec, the IOS firewall and IOS Intrusion Detection. These services will allow you to extend the network to new frontiers securely, protect your network from attacks, and increase the sophistication of network services.

Developing IP Multicast Networks, Volume I
Beau Williamson, CCIE

1-57870-077-9 • AVAILABLE NOW

This book provides a solid foundation of IP multicast concepts and explains how to design and deploy the networks that will support appplications such as audio and video conferencing, distance-learning, and data replication. Includes an in-depth discussion of the PIM protocol used in Cisco routers and detailed coverage of the rules that control the creation and maintenance of Cisco mroute state entries.

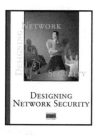

Designing Network Security
Merike Kaeo

1-57870-043-4 • AVAILABLE NOW

Designing Network Security is a practical guide designed to help you understand the fundamentals of securing your corporate infrastructure. This book takes a comprehensive look at underlying security technologies, the process of creating a security policy, and the practical requirements necessary to implement a corporate security policy.

Cisco Press   **www.ciscopress.com**

Hey, you've got enough worries.

Don't let IT training be one of them.

Get on the fast track to IT training at InformIT,
your total Information Technology training network.

  | **www.informit.com** |

■ Hundreds of timely articles on dozens of topics ■ Discounts on IT books
from all our publishing partners, including Cisco Press ■ Free, unabridged books
from the InformIT Free Library ■ "Expert Q&A"—our live, online chat
with IT experts ■ Faster, easier certification and training from our Web- or
classroom-based training programs ■ Current IT news ■ Software downloads
■ Career-enhancing resources

InformIT is a registered trademark of Pearson. Copyright ©2001 by Pearson.

CISCO SYSTEMS

Cisco Press

c i s c o p r e s s . c o m

Committed to being your long-term learning resource while you grow as a Cisco Networking Professional

Help Cisco Press **stay connected** to the issues and challenges you face on a daily basis by registering your product and filling out our brief survey. Complete and mail this form, or better yet ...

Register online and enter to win a FREE book!

Jump to **www.ciscopress.com/register** and register your product online. Each complete entry will be eligible for our monthly drawing to win a FREE book of the winner's choice from the Cisco Press library.

May we contact you via e-mail with information about **new releases, special promotions**, and **customer benefits**?

❏ Yes   ❏ No

E-mail address _____

Name _____

Address _____

City _____ State/Province _____

Country_____ Zip/Post code _____

Where did you buy this product?

❏ Bookstore   ❏ Computer store/Electronics store   ❏ Direct from Cisco Systems
❏ Online retailer   ❏ Direct from Cisco Press   ❏ Office supply store
❏ Mail order   ❏ Class/Seminar   ❏ Discount store
❏ Other_____

When did you buy this product?   _____ Month   _____ Year

What price did you pay for this product?

❏ Full retail price   ❏ Discounted price   ❏ Gift

Was this purchase reimbursed as a company expense?

❏ Yes   ❏ No

How did you learn about this product?

❏ Friend   ❏ Store personnel   ❏ In-store ad   ❏ cisco.com
❏ Cisco Press catalog   ❏ Postcard in the mail   ❏ Saw it on the shelf   ❏ ciscopress.com
❏ Other catalog   ❏ Magazine ad   ❏ Article or review
❏ School   ❏ Professional organization   ❏ Used other products
❏ Other_____

What will this product be used for?

❏ Business use   ❏ School/Education
❏ Certification training   ❏ Professional development/Career growth
❏ Other_____

How many years have you been employed in a computer-related industry?

❏ less than 2 years   ❏ 2–5 years   ❏ more than 5 years

Have you purchased a Cisco Press product before?

❏ Yes   ❏ No

CISCO SYSTEMS

Cisco Press

ciscopress.com

How many computer technology books do you own?
❏ 1   ❏ 2–7   ❏ more than 7

Which best describes your job function? (check all that apply)
❏ Corporate Management   ❏ Systems Engineering   ❏ IS Management   ❏ Cisco Networking
❏ Network Design   ❏ Network Support   ❏ Webmaster   Academy Program
❏ Marketing/Sales   ❏ Consultant   ❏ Student   Instuctor
❏ Professor/Teacher   ❏ Other

Do you hold any computer certifications? (check all that apply)
❏ MCSE   ❏ CCNA   ❏ CCDA
❏ CCNP   ❏ CCDP   ❏ CCIE   ❏ Other _____

Are you currently pursuing a certification? (check all that apply)
❏ MCSE   ❏ CCNA   ❏ CCDA
❏ CCNP   ❏ CCDP   ❏ CCIE   ❏ Other _____

On what topics would you like to see more coverage?

_____

_____

Do you have any additional comments or suggestions?

_____

_____

Thank you for completing this survey and registration. Please fold here, seal, and mail to Cisco Press.

Advanced MPLS Design and Implementation (1-58705-020-X)

Indianapolis, IN 46278-8046
P.O. Box #781046
Customer Registration—CP0500227
Cisco Press

ciscopress.com
Indianapolis, IN 46290
201 West 103rd Street
Cisco Press

Place
Stamp
Here